4 the
conju... ...od.
He ...ngel of
...gh ...but really is a
wolf in sheep clothing

The Facts about "Drug Abuse"

The Drug Abuse Council

THE FREE PRESS
A Division of Macmillan Publishing Co., Inc.
NEW YORK

Collier Macmillan Publishers
LONDON

The Free Press
A Division of Macmillan Publishing Co., Inc.
866 Third Avenue, New York, N.Y. 10022

Collier Macmillan Canada, Ltd.

Library of Congress Catalog Card Number: 79-54668

Printed in the United States of America

printing number

3 4 5 6 7 8 9 10

Library of Congress Cataloging in Publication Data

Drug Abuse Council, Washington, D.C.
  The facts about "drug abuse".

  Includes bibliographical references.
    1. Drug abuse—United States—Addresses, essays, lectures.   2. Narcotics, Control of—United States —Addresses, essays, lectures.   I. Title.
HV5825.D772   1980   362.2'93'0973   79-54668
ISBN 0-02-907720-6

Contents

Foreword

In 1970, at the peak of the drug scare, the trustees of the Ford Foundation decided that piecemeal measures were not enough. As a first step in a major program the Foundation asked Patricia M. Wald, now a United States Circuit Judge in the District of Columbia, and Peter B. Hutt, a Washington lawyer, to undertake a survey in depth of drug abuse and to suggest what private foundations might contribute to understanding, if not solution, of the problem. In their report to the Foundation published in 1972 —*Dealing with Drug Abuse*—Judge Wald and Mr. Hutt said:

> It is of fundamental importance that man has and will inevitably continue to have potentially dangerous drugs at his disposal, which he may either use properly or abuse, and that neither the availability of these drugs nor the temptation to abuse them can be eliminated. Therefore, the fundamental objective of a modern drug-abuse program must be to help the public learn to understand these drugs and how to cope with their use in the context of everyday life. An approach emphasizing suppression of all drugs or repression of all drug users will only contribute to national problems.
>
> There is an urgent need for effective nongovernmental leadership toward a more reasoned approach to drug abuse in this country. A void exists that we believe can be filled by the creation of a new Drug Abuse Council. In our best judgment, the Council could successfully exert this leadership and could have a substantial and beneficial impact on drug abuse in this country.

According to McGeorge Bundy, then President of the Ford Foundation,

> The second important step was to join with three other foundations that have shared our concern with drug abuse—the Carnegie Corporation, the Commonwealth Fund, and the Henry J. Kaiser Family Foundation—in financing one of the principal recommendations of the report, namely, the establishment of an independent national Drug Abuse Council.

(The Equitable Life Assurance Society joined the foundations in contributing to the expenses of the Council.)

The Council was organized in January 1972, but only after it had been determined that a widely representative board of directors and a highly competent staff could be assembled for about five years of active service. The last formal meeting of the board was held in June 1978, and since then the President of the Council, Dr. Thomas E. Bryant, and the staff have been engaged in the preparation of this Final Report.

The Report demonstrates that widespread misuse or abuse of dangerous drugs—not just heroin, marijuana, and cocaine, but alcohol and caffeine, and a great variety of stimulants and tranquilizers, some prescribed, some sold over the counter—is not an evil that can be extirpated by legislation or other means. Yet it is believed that an informed society, aware of the complexities of the issues and evidence, will be better able to cope constructively with the use of drugs. This belief underlies this Final Report.

It is not the function of a foreword to anticipate the findings and conclusions of a massive study. It would, however, be gross neglect not to acknowledge in this foreword the exceptional contributions of the directors, the officers and staff and consultants of the Council, and the foundations and many others who have enabled the Council to apply knowledge and reason to the understanding and treatment of a major national problem. These include:

Judge Wald and Mr. Hutt, the Co-chairmen, and James V. DeLong, the extraordinarily able Executive Director of the Ford Foundation survey staff, who produced *Dealing with Drug Abuse*—the seminal study that led to the creation of the Council.

The directors of the Council for regular attendance at meetings, for the information and wisdom and wit that enriched the deliberations of the board, and especially Dr. Bryant for the personal and professional qualities that underpinned his indispensable leadership.

And, of course, the Ford Foundation, the Carnegie Corporation, the Commonwealth Fund, the Henry J. Kaiser Family Foundation, and the Equitable Life Assurance Society, for the financial support essential to a major private enterprise.

And the Council here records special gratitude to the senior officers and responsible staff of the Ford Foundation for six years of unfailing interest and support.

BETHUEL M. WEBSTER
Chairman

Board of Directors of the Drug Abuse Council

Acknowledgments

The individuals cited on the title page of each of the staff report chapters were a major source of assistance to the authors in the preparation of those chapters. In addition, the authors collectively wish to acknowledge their special gratitude to Jean R. Johnson for her unstinting efforts in the preparation of this book, to Margo C. Backas and Paul Danaceau for their assistance in editing, and to Norman E. Zinberg, Rayburn Hesse, Sibyl Cline Halper, Carl Akins, David E. Smith, Robert Newman, James M. Duke, and Mary Ann Orlando who reviewed the manuscripts in their several drafts. Also deserving of grateful mention are the efforts of Marie P. Thompson, Jane Silver, William P. Vasquez, and William J. Haney.

The Contributors

Thomas E. Bryant holds both a medical and a law degree from Emory University in Atlanta. Since 1971, he has served as President of the Drug Abuse Council. During 1977 and 1978 he shared those responsibilities with his service as Chairman of the President's Commission on Mental Health. Prior to the Drug Abuse Council, Dr. Bryant headed the Health Affairs Office of the Office of Economic Opportunity. He is a member of the Institute of Medicine of the National Academy of Sciences and has served as a member of the President's Committee on Mental Retardation, the American Medical Association's Committee on Health Care for the Poor, the Health Task Force of HEW, and the American Bar Association's Commission on Mental Disabilities and as Chairman of the Interagency Committee on Emergency Food and Medical Service. Dr. Bryant is currently Chairman of the Public Committee for Mental Health.

Erik J. Meyers is a graduate of the Fordham School of Law and Georgetown University's School of Foreign Service. Since 1974 he has been legal counsel and a policy analyst for the Drug Abuse Council. He is a member of the New York and District of Columbia Bar Associations and has served as legal advisor to the Public Committee for Mental Health and the National Association for City Drug Coordination.

Peter B. Goldberg, a graduate of the State University of New York at Albany, has been a senior policy analyst for the Drug Abuse Council since 1971. One of the original staff authors of *Dealing with Drug Abuse*, Mr. Goldberg has pursued postgraduate work in urban planning at George Washington University. He helped to organize the National Association for City Drug Coordination and is Chairman of its National Advisory Committee and a member of the Editorial Board of *Urban Concerns* magazine. He is currently Special Assistant to the Director of the National Institute on Alcohol Abuse and Alcoholism.

John R. Pekkanen, a Nieman Fellow at Harvard University in 1970–71 and a Drug Abuse Council Fellow in 1974–75, has written several nonfiction works on drug, health, and criminal justice topics. Among his recent works are *The Best Doctors in the U.S.* (Seaview Books), *Victims* (Dial Press), and *The American Connection* (Follet Publishing Co.). Mr. Pekkanen has written numerous articles for *Life* magazine, *Human Behavior*, *The New Republic*, *Atlantic Monthly*, *Town and Country*, and is a former bureau chief for *Life* magazine. He is presently a freelance writer in Washington, D.C.

David C. Lewis is a graduate of Brown University and the Harvard Medical School. He has been a Senior Fellow at the Harvard Laboratory of Community Psychiatry and a Sloan Foundation Fellow at Harvard Medical School. He has served as Chairman of the Mayor's Coordinating Council on Drug Abuse of the City of Boston since 1972 as well as serving on the National League of Cities Task Force on Drug Abuse, National Institute on Drug Abuse's Research Review Committee and the National Association for City Drug Coordination (founding chairperson). Dr. Lewis is currently Associate Professor of Medicine and Donald G. Miller Distinguished Scholar in Alcoholism Studies at Brown University, Director of Alcoholism and Drug Abuse in the Brown University Program in Medicine, Director of the Alcoholism and Substance Abuse Division at Roger Williams General Hospital in Providence, Rhode Island, and former Medical Director of the Washingtonian Center for Addictions in Boston. He has authored numerous articles on alcohol and drug abuse issues in professional journals.

John C. Sessler is a graduate of Rutgers University and the University of Southern California and holds a doctorate in physics from Georgetown University. He has been a senior program analyst for evaluation and survey projects for the Drug Abuse Council from 1972 to 1978. Prior to his work at the Council, Dr. Sessler worked for the Center for Naval Analysis. He has authored several technical articles on a variety of scientific topics, co-authored several Drug Abuse Council publications, and contributed a chapter to *The Evaluation of Social Programs* (Sage Publications). He is currently Evaluation Coordinator for the Public Health Service of the Department of Health and Human Services.

Robert R. Carr is presently Executive Director of The Fund for Constitutional Government. He has thirteen years experience in Washington a Congressional aide, public policy analyst, political organizer, and write

Employed since 1973 as the Senior Program Officer at the Drug Abuse Council, he was involved in drug law reform through testimony before state legislatures, television and radio appearances, and the publication of several articles in popular journals. In 1978, he was appointed to the drug use/misuse task panel of the President's Commission on Mental Health.

Final Report Of The Drug Abuse Council

IN 1972 *Dealing with Drug Abuse: A Report to the Ford Foundation*[1] concluded that the national drug policies at that time were not effective and were not likely to eliminate or even greatly affect "drug abuse." That report, describing the complex nature of psychoactive drug use and misuse, identified flaws in programs and laws which had been designed to reduce the harm to individuals and society of the indiscriminate, nonmedical use of psychoactive drugs. Public policy was found to be unrealistic and unresponsive to cultural, social, psychological, and economic factors underlying the widespread use of drugs.

The report to the Ford Foundation was issued at the end of a decade of increasing drug use and increasing concern about such use. Drugs seemed to be everywhere; a generation of young Americans had been urged to "turn on, tune in, and drop out" with a wide variety of mood-altering drugs. The United States was described as a nation of "pill poppers." Deeply held public fears were heightened as city after city reported heroin addiction of epidemic proportions. From suburban neighborhoods, long considered secure and stable, came reports of heroin experimentation by high school students from middle- and upper-income families. Thousands of American soldiers in Vietnam were said to be addicted to heroin. New words and phrases—"pot," "downers," "uppers," drug "trips"—became part of the popular vocabulary.

In 1972 it was estimated that between three- and six-hundred thousand Americans—the vast majority of whom were said to be inner-city blacks and Hispanics—were addicted to heroin. Nearly 25 million Americans were reported to have tried marijuana and 10 million were said to use it regularly. Millions of others regularly used stimulants, depressants, hallucinogens, and tranquilizers for non-medical purposes. However, al-

1

cohol and nicotine continued to be the most widely used and misused drugs.

Illicit drugs—marijuana, heroin, and cocaine in particular—were singled out for attention, yet the misuse of legally available drugs was often ignored. While various methods or approaches for "solving the drug problem" were presented, confusion prevailed. Drug issues, particularly that of the relationship between drug use and crime, were constantly publicized and politicized. Many Americans thought the increase in street crime during the late 1960s resulted largely from illicit drug use and therefore responded enthusiastically to calls for a war on drugs to keep illicit drugs and their users apart. Heroin was labelled "Public Enemy Number One." New "get tough" laws were proposed, and many were enacted. Hundreds of millions of dollars were appropriated for programs to stiffen law enforcement, improve public education, and expand treatment efforts.

At the height of public concern in 1972, *Dealing with Drug Abuse* urged caution and restraint. It called for a climate of reason which would permit identification of the real risks of drug misuse and rejection of policies and programs based on misinformation and sensationalism. It pointed out that drug use and drug problems were not new but have persisted throughout history, not only in the United States but in many other countries, cultures, and societies as well. It noted that knowledge about the causes of drug misuse was inadequate, as was knowledge about its prevention and treatment. Moreover, the report revealed much of what was then accepted as fact to be erroneous, out of date, or misleading.

The authors of *Dealing with Drug Abuse*, the sponsoring private organizations which funded the Drug Abuse Council, and, subsequently, the council's board of directors perceived a pressing need for independent analyses of public drug policies and programs. They felt that lawmakers and public officials, particularly in the federal government, were reacting to drug-related problems from a limited, crisis-oriented perspective when a longer-range view was necessary, and that the effectiveness of law enforcement and treatment strategies was often overstated by public officials, which led to unrealistic expectations of rapid and sweeping solutions. Thus these individuals and groups agreed to sponsor an independent organization capable of providing the public with a less emotional, more apolitical perspective. As a result the Drug Abuse Council was established in early 1972.

As of this writing, the Drug Abuse Council has been in existence for nearly seven years. During this time the council has, through staff-directed projects, research grants, and contracts, assessed many aspects of the use and misuse of psychoactive drugs.[2] This work has been undertaken with the unhampered view and resources of a national, independent, nonprofit, nongovernmental organization.

The council has had resources sufficient to examine drug-related issues in depth and over time. It began by analyzing the assumptions underlying public perceptions and policies. It examined the accepted knowledge of the interaction of chemical substances with the human body and mind. It studied various aspects of contemporary society to identify socioeconomic and cultural factors relating to drug use and misuse. The council has reviewed and assessed laws, programs, and projects—federal, state, and local; governmental and private—which have been adopted in response to psychoactive drug use and misuse.

In pursuit of its efforts to learn more about drug use and misuse, the council gathered information from public officials, scientists, historians, and law enforcement and treatment program personnel. It canvassed widely and deeply the experiences and views of current and former drug users, of minority groups and individuals, and of other informed or concerned persons.

The council has periodically published its findings on many aspects of drugs and has sought to bring about changes in policies and programs it considers unsound. Through these activities, it has sought to provide leadership in the private sector.

When operations began in 1972, a five-year period of activity was planned. In the fifth year, the board of directors decided to continue some of the council's functions for an additional two years. Now, as this seven-year period comes to an end, we feel a responsibility to share our major observations, findings, and suggestions for the future in the form of a final report.

This final report consists of two major sections: first, the report of the directors of the Drug Abuse Council; and second, six chapters on various drug policy topics prepared by the council's staff and consultants. While not every judgment or suggestion advanced in these staff report chapters is specifically endorsed by the council's board of directors, they do form the analytic base from which the board drew its observations, conclusions, and recommendations.

The Report of the Directors

As this report developed, it became increasingly clear that the most valuable document we could provide would be one addressed to the concerned citizen, not just to the professional in the drug field. We stepped back from the day-to-day concerns of those who work in research, treatment, prevention, and law enforcement to begin to address the broader philosophical, social, moral, legal, and pragmatic issues influencing national drug policies and the expenditure of public funds. Thus readers of this report will find few recommendations about the particulars of program efforts in treatment, prevention, or enforcement. We do not mean by this to suggest that there are no improvements that can be made in program operations; there are in fact many. We have, however, chosen to focus our discussion instead on the public policies and attitudes from which these program efforts stem. We believe that substantial benefits can come only as a result of a significant rethinking of our approach to drugs, not from tinkering with the mechanisms of our public program response.

This report is a conscious effort to stimulate public interest in drug policy issues and to promote greater public understanding of them. By indicating the costs and benefits of past and present efforts, we can begin to formulate and accept principles with which more reasonable and effective alternative approaches to drug misuse can be constructed. We have no blueprint for a step-by-step solution to the nation's problems with drugs; in our opinion it would be a mistake for anyone to think such a plan could be devised, given present knowledge. It would, however, be equally erroneous to think that nothing can be done to improve the current situation.

Since the creation of the Drug Abuse Council in 1972, what is often termed "the American drug scene" has changed in several ways. As a general observation, more Americans appear to be using more psychoactive substances. Drug use and misuse have become among the most compelling realities of contemporary existence. Among legally available drugs, alcohol has increased in the number of its users, particularly among younger people. Among illicit drugs, marijuana has steadily increased in use, as has cocaine more recently. Although recent research has provided evidence of substantial numbers of occasional, nonaddicted heroin users, federal officials report that heroin addiction has declined over the past two to three years.

Greater changes can be observed in the nation's response to drug use and misuse in terms of changes in laws and publicly supported programs. In some respects, the situation has improved. Given the magnitude of federal expenditures on drug treatment programs and law enforcement efforts—estimated to be nearly $6 billion since 1971—some improvements should be demonstrable. For example, the passage of the Drug Abuse Office and Treatment Act of 1972 has led to the creation of a nationwide network of drug treatment programs, chiefly for heroin dependence. As a result, treatment for those dependent on heroin is now more readily available. The federal National Institute on Drug Abuse reports that between 1971 and 1978 hundreds of thousands of individuals have received treatment in about two thousand federally funded clinics throughout the country. However, many more have not voluntarily sought treatment.

Another area of improvement over the past few years is in basic research, work which has broadened understanding of the addictive process and the biochemistry of the brain and central nervous system. More questions remain unanswered than have been answered, but recent progress is encouraging.

Perhaps the most significant change may be the decline in the emotional fervor that once dominated public discussion of drugs. Public concern is still intense; nonetheless, there is wider public acknowledgment that simple, quick solutions to our drug problems will not be forthcoming. As a result, public expectations are more moderate—a development that may encourage more realistic law enforcement and control objectives.

While we consider these to be changes for the better, the basic situation remains: Despite progress in a number of areas, more Americans use and misuse more psychoactive drugs than ever. Since in our considered judgment this situation will prevail at least through the next few years, it is necessary for us as a nation to plan carefully and thoughtfully how to handle it most responsibly. This planning requires a basic rethinking of national goals, policies, and strategies regarding the use and misuse of psychoactive drugs. The underlying social dynamics and problems that lead to drug misuse are so exceedingly complex as to as yet elude totally satisfactory solutions; the rational course, then, is to begin with what has been learned from history, particularly from the experience of the past several years.

The council has several general observations that we regard as of central importance to this process of rethinking, but before submitting them, we emphasize again that we have no step-by-step blueprint for solving the nation's drug problems. We can, however, indicate where past experience and current analysis should direct us, and we can begin to strive toward more consistent, coherent, and responsible approaches to drug use and misuse in the future. The following observations are, in our view, central to this process.

1. Psychoactive substances have been available for use since the beginning of recorded time and will predictably remain so. Man will undoubtedly continue to use such substances for a variety of reasons: to relax, to escape, to enjoy, to worship, to delude, to destroy. At given times in history certain drugs have had greater appeal or easier availability and have consequently been used more widely, but the essential point is that *some psychoactive drugs are almost always readily available* to enable people to achieve what they wish or need for alteration of mood or mind. As we search for more effective policies and programs, this certainty of drug availability should be at the forefront of our thinking.

2. *While the use of psychoactive drugs is pervasive, misuse is much less frequent.* A failure to distinguish between the misuse and the use of drugs creates the impression that all use is misuse or "drug abuse." This is particularly true in the case of illicit drugs. For example, while millions of Americans of high-school and college age have experimented with various drugs and many use some of them regularly, clearly the majority exercises personal restraint or obeys social controls in drug-taking behavior. To

state this in another way, the number of young Americans who are in serious personal difficulty because of the misuse of drugs is relatively small. However, the frequent depiction of the minority who do misuse drugs, especially illicit ones, as typical conveys the mistaken impression that misuse is pervasive if not inevitable.

3. While not enough is known about why certain individuals misuse drugs, it is known that *there is a definite correlation between pervasive societal ills—such as poverty, unemployment, and racial discrimination—and drug misuse.* When such conditions predominate—as they do in the inner-city areas of many large American cities—the manifestations of widespread drug misuse and trafficking in illicit drugs can be seen in their most pernicious forms. So long as these adverse social conditions persist, widespread drug misuse can be expected. Drug misuse resulting from such societal conditions aggravates other urban problems, and makes restoring the vitality of our inner cities more difficult to achieve.

4. *Attempts to control the availability of drugs often present a conflict between the desires of individuals and the aspirations of society.* When harm to both the individual and society is clearly demonstrable, the conflict may be resolved. When harm to either is less clearly demonstrable, it is less easily resolved. This may lead to dissension of considerable magnitude, involving sensitive questions of individual rights and the limits of governmental powers. To state it plainly, the price of an effective strategy for eliminating drug misuse would be perceived by many Americans as too high in terms of the invasion of privacy and the abrogation of individual freedoms. National drug policies must reflect careful balancing of these concerns in order to enjoy substantial public support.

5. Drug-related laws and policies center too often on the drugs themselves and not often enough on the problems of the people misusing them. This leads to *preoccupation with and elaboration of the adverse aspects of certain drugs,* as if they themselves were somehow culpable. Such thinking can reinforce a focus on eliminating or legalizing the availability of certain drugs as "solutions" to related problems. Drug policies should instead be primarily focused on people and their problems.

6. Too many Americans have *unrealistic expectations about what drug laws and programs can accomplish.* All too often, these laws and programs are expected to eliminate drug problems. More disturbing, drug laws and programs have been expected to contribute substantially to other social objectives as well, such as reducing crime, increasing employment, or restoring family cohesion. Such expectations place overwhelming and unfair burdens on laws, programs, and those administering them, and make failure and public frustration commonplace. Our drug policies and laws need to be more realistically stated to command public support.

7. Finally, we Americans should resist the temptation to blame our drug problems on others. We have done this too often in the past. *Our*

drug problems are peculiar to our own national experience. They derive from our history and cultural traditions, our mistakes and prejudices, our societal ills and flaws—not those of Turks, Mexicans, Burmese, or Colombians. Certainly, many aspects of drug problems are international in scope, and much can be gained by multinational research and education efforts. At times we must seek the cooperation of other peoples and other countries in order to try to curtail the flow of illicit drugs into this country. However, the chances for success in these cooperative efforts would be enhanced, in our view, if they were undertaken with an acceptance that the most fundamental aspect of American drug problems is the magnitude of demand for drugs and that the problems leading people to misuse drugs will not vanish even if the supply of one or two drugs is eliminated.

It is against the backdrop of these general observations that the council submits its conclusions and recommendations. We repeat, they will not dispose of our drug problems. However, if applied they would, in our view, mitigate much of the harm that comes from present policies and approaches—harm that in the minds of many is damaging in a free society.

As we observed above, Americans tend to overlook the capacity for misuse of licit drugs and overestimate the misuse of illicit drugs. As a consequence, we pursue widely divergent courses, depending upon the legal status of a particular psychoactive substance.

For example, some drugs, such as caffeine, are freely available in a wide variety of forms. Use is frequently promoted and misuse largely unacknowledged. Other drugs, such as nicotine and alcohol, are considered potentially more harmful, but their use is largely controlled by social attitudes and their misuse, though discouraged, is not prohibited. Actions taken under the influence of such drugs that have a potential for injury to others—drunken driving, for instance—are subject to criminal sanctions, although misuse itself is not.

Still other drugs, such as barbiturates, amphetamines, and tranquilizers, have generally recognized legitimate medical uses, yet they also have significant potential for harm if misused. There is growing public awareness of this potential harm, and the availability of these drugs is more carefully controlled, as, for example, by prescription of licensed physicians. Criminal sanctions are employed to discourage diversion from legitimate channels.

Then there are some drugs, such as heroin and marijuana, which are considered to be harmful to individuals and society and without legitimate medical uses. National policy toward these drugs over the past seven years has been a two-pronged effort to control the supply or availability and reduce the demand. Thus, laws are designed to eliminate the availability of these drugs by prohibiting their use, production, or distribution, and criminal sanctions are employed to enforce them. On the demand side, assistance—primarily treatment for heroin addiction through publicly funded clinics—is offered and sometimes mandated for those using these drugs.

Public drug policies are in essence a reflection of prevailing attitudes about psychoactive drugs, and current attitudes are, conversely, strongly influenced by past and present policy. In this manner current policies reflect assumptions and events more than a half century old, despite the fact that many of those assumptions were erroneous or founded in demogoguery. Unfortunately, in the view of the council, drug policies and prevailing public attitudes continue to represent misunderstanding and wishful thinking more than sober analysis. For example, it is still widely believed that by prohibiting the use of a particular drug through the criminal law, that drug can be eliminated from society. Despite sobering experiences to the contrary, it is still hoped that more resources for law enforcement and treatment or more stringent laws will end problems with drugs.

Individuals use and misuse all kinds of licit and illicit drugs for a wide variety of reasons, some with greater potential for harm to themselves and society than others. For example, some drug use is clearly experimental or inquisitive; individuals want to know what a drug will do to them, how it will make them feel and act. Other drug use is recreational; individuals use drugs to relax, to enhance enjoyment of a social situation. Still other drug use is demonstrably harmful and antisocial; individuals use drugs in ways harmful to themselves or society.

As it is now constituted, however, national drug policy does not reflect an adequate appreciation of these very real differences in drug-using behavior—yet at the same time most Americans in their day-to-day experience are at least generally aware of such differences. For example, most are aware of the difference between social drinking and alcoholism. They perceive the difference between taking an occasional tranquilizer and taking tranquilizers compulsively, between taking prescribed narcotics to relieve pain and being addicted to them. Many Americans have begun to recognize the difference between smoking an occasional marijuana cigarette and being constantly "high" on marijuana. *To command informed public support, public policies must recognize these differences in the patterns and circumstances of drug use.*

Public policy regarding heroin can probably never be the same as policy respecting marijuana or alcohol. These drugs differ pharmacologically, and people generally use them for different reasons and in different situations. However, the principles upon which the control mechanisms of public drug policies are based can and should be consistent. As the public begins to appreciate the differences in drug use patterns and behavior, some changes in attitudes and policy approaches are occurring.

For example, many states have lessened the severity of their laws regarding marijuana possession. The use and misuse of sedatives and tranquilizers are under scrutiny. Responsible national organizations such as the National League of Cities and the U.S. Conference of Mayors have publicly called for new approaches to heroin addition. Others have urged caution in our response to the observed increase in cocaine use, lest an ill-advised response make matters worse.

The federal government's attitude about drugs also has been affected. The Ford administration's 1975 *White Paper on Drug Abuse*, which expressed the federal strategy, differed dramatically in tone from the "war on drugs" approach of the early 1970s. Although the *White Paper* had little immediate impact, it opened the door for substantial future changes. The Carter administration's appeal for the "decriminalization" of marijuana has provided additional evidence that change is possible.

Because the country does appear to be in a relatively calm mood regarding drugs and a process of rethinking is evident, it is a good time to look to the future. Given the council's belief that in the future there will in all probability be more, not less, use and misuse of psychoactive drugs, it is essential to consider ways in which society may face this situation.

Suggestions for the Future.   To state it plainly, the challenge facing America regarding drugs is to determine how best to live with the inevitable availability of psychoactive drugs while mitigating the harmful aspects of their misuse. A case can be made that we are, in fact, learning to do just that.

For example, the latest national survey indicates that two-thirds of American adults regularly use alcohol and some 13 million adult and youthful drinkers are said to be problem drinkers. Currently, federal efforts are increasingly focused on determining the underlying causes of alcohol misuse in the hope of developing more effective preventive and treatment measures. However, despite very deep concerns, there are no serious proposals for a return to Prohibition. The lessons of that experience were well learned—the criminal justice system could not and should not be society's chief agent for controlling alcohol abuse. Instead, attention is now directed at more effective public education and health measures. The public seems to wish to reduce the dangers and risks associated with the misuse of alcohol and yet continue to enjoy the perceived benefits derived from responsible use. While no one argues that we have been successful in eliminating the enormous social costs of alcoholism and alcohol-related problems, current policies are largely regarded as both reasonable and responsible.

Similarly, a case can be made that, with nearly 50 million Americans having tried marijuana and 16 million of these reporting current use, the public (on the basis of opinion polls) believes that marijuana use will not decrease markedly over the next few years and that society must adapt to this use in a more reasonable, responsible manner. While this usage, too, is seen by many as a disturbing development, appreciable numbers think that responsible adaptation is possible. To date, eleven state legislatures have removed the threat of criminal arrest and imprisonment for the possession or use of small amounts of marijuana. This development reflects an understanding that severe criminal sanctions against the use of small amounts of marijuana are neither appropriate nor effective. The harm to society associated with the use of small amounts of marijuana is not seen as sufficient to justify the use of criminal sanctions in attempts to control it.

Another case in point is the great increase in public awareness during the past ten to fifteen years of the potential harm of excessive cigarette smoking. Increased awareness has led to new approaches in education and to ordinances and laws imposing civil fines for smoking in designated "no smoking" areas. Yet there have been no serious proposals to jail those who smoke. Since smoking is perceived as at worst a public health problem, not a criminal activity, more effective public education and health measures are seen as the most appropriate policy response.

These changes are encouraging. Perhaps they offer directions for changes in public policy regarding the use of other psychoactive drugs. In developing such new approaches to the use and misuse of these drugs, the nation must first set realistic, consistent goals. *In this regard, the primary goal the council urges is that society seek to minimize the harm and dysfunction that can accompany the misuse of any psychoactive substance, whether that drug is currently classified as licit or illicit.*

To accept this goal entails accepting factors which up to now have not enjoyed wide acceptance—e.g., the continued use of illicit drugs by many Americans. It also entails accepting that not all illicit drug use is necessarily harmful. Further, it indicates that seeking to minimize harm from drug misuse is not synonymous with seeking to eliminate drug use.

If our goal is to minimize harm and dysfunction, then the target of national efforts should logically be the harm and dysfunction which come from indiscriminate drug use. *Such a target calls primarily for education, public health, treatment, and rehabilitation measures.* Such measures could be more effective in reducing the misuse of drugs if other drug policies themselves were more reasonable, consistent, and realistic. The experience of decades makes it clear that only in reducing the misuse of drugs is there real hope for effectively reducing drug problems. This is *not* to say that society should sanction the unbridled use of psychoactive drugs. To the contrary, public policy should make clear society's strong disapproval of the misuse of such drugs. This disapproval will be more persuasive if it is expressed in terms of concern for individual health and well-being.

This is also not to say that the nation should immediately abandon all domestic and international law enforcement efforts aimed at reducing the availability of illicit drugs. Though by no means are all drug law enforcement and control efforts effective, it would be highly inaccurate to say that they have produced no benefits. While many of these benefits (e.g., reduction in the availability of particular drugs) have proved temporary in the past, even such temporary gains are welcome developments. To the extent that law enforcement efforts curtail the supply of illicit drugs in a responsible manner, they should be continued.

The problems with drug law enforcement are complicated. Americans have historically overemphasized drug law enforcement and control measures and, at least until recently, underemphasized policies aimed at reducing the misuse of drugs. In so doing we have paid enormous costs in both dollars and other, less quantifiable ways, such as increased burdens on the criminal justice system, corruption, and decreased respect for law and those enforcing it. All too often these law enforcement efforts have continued blindly and repetitiously without a careful assessment and balancing of their costs and benefits.

Perhaps the greatest costs have been those attendant to criminalizing users of illicit drugs. For example, to brand as criminals hundreds of thousands of American youths otherwise leading normal lives, by virtue of their experimental or recreational marijuana use, presents a fundamental problem in a society founded on principles of justice and respect for law. It leads directly to suspicion of and disrespect for the law. Similarly, to persist in depicting addiction to opiate drugs as leading inexorably to violent criminal behavior fosters further disrespect for law. As is well documented, many opiate addicts do engage in certain kinds of criminal behavior, particularly "crimes against property" in order to raise funds to support their drug habits; but addiction itself, whether to narcotics, alcohol, or nicotine, is essentially a psychological and physiological phenomenon. There are social, cultural, and economic factors which demonstrably influence this phenomenon or are intimately related to it, but addiction is a "crime" only because we have traditionally labeled it as such.

At this stage in our history, there is a clear need to redress the long-standing imbalance between publicly funded efforts to reduce misuse and efforts to reduce supply. The primary focus of public policy should be on the former. We submit that such a redressing would encourage more realistic expectations—even public acceptance—of what law enforcement strategies and agencies can accomplish in reducing drug availability.

The most important aspect of such a change in emphasis would be that public policy would reflect contemporary and foreseeable realities in a straightforward manner.

By placing the major emphasis on reducing the misuse of drugs, society will be confronted with the necessity of improving program effectiveness in that regard; the record of the past is not exemplary. There is an urgent need to expand the base of knowledge concerning educational, preventive, and treatment methodologies and techniques. This means a far greater investment in basic and applied research and evaluation. In addition to increasing the research investment, it will be necessary to develop a national research strategy which can provide direction and coordination to these efforts. Since it is unlikely that answers will be instantly forthcoming, this strategy should be applied for the next several years and assure continuity of the research effort. Public officials must also be more willing to change policies if necessary in response to expanded knowledge. Only by taking these steps can there be a realistic expectation of attracting the calibre of research scientists that could make a difference.

While we think such an expanded research effort will produce more understanding and better guidance for educational, preventive, and treatment approaches, certain steps can be taken now, based on available knowledge and experience, to make the publicly funded response to drugs more reasonable and more effective.

At the federal administrative level, for instance, there should be much closer coordination between domestic and international drug law enforcement efforts and agencies on the one hand and prevention and treatment strategies and agencies on the other. Effective coordination can occur only at the highest levels of the executive branch of government, whether by a special-purpose, cabinet-level committee or by a special staff in the executive office, because the important drug program functions are lodged in several departments and agencies throughout the executive branch.

Such a high-level coordinating body or staff could meet two essential criteria for greater effectiveness in national drug policy development and implementation: First, it could develop a cohesive policy, and, second, it could advise the President and provide accountability to Congress, and thereby to the public.

This concept is, of course, not new. The 1972 Drug Abuse Office and Treatment Act created the White House Special Action Office on Drug Abuse Prevention which was succeeded in 1976 by the Office for Drug Abuse Prevention. This latter office ceased to function in 1978, to be succeeded—at least in some of its functions—by a Special Assistant to the President for drug issues, a small staff within the White House's Domestic Policy Staff, and a Federal Strategy Council composed of public officials and private citizens. However, while it thus appears that a coordinating mechanism does now exist at the highest level of the executive branch, it is our impression that this mechanism is not currently achieving its major objectives, namely, the development and implementation of a cohesive national drug policy and closer coordination of law enforcement and treatment agencies.

In addition to the more effective coordination mechanism that we recommend, other improvements in the performances of drug agencies are possible. This is as true for treatment and prevention programs as it is for law enforcement agencies, particularly as they relate to heroin addiction. Again, however, we stress that for such improvements to make a lasting impact they must be preceded by substantial changes in public policy.

In drug treatment activities at present, improvements are both possible and needed. Some improvements can come by applying the new knowledge gained in recent years; others can come by seeking more aggressively to increase that knowledge. At the same time there is a need to acknowledge the limitations of drug treatment, imposed by social and economic conditions well beyond the influence of drug treatment programs.

One development that has begun to affect drug treatment during recent years is change in the concept of heroin addiction. There is convincing evidence that more individuals use heroin than are addicted to it. Since most heroin treatment has been founded on the principle that to use heroin is to be addicted to it, the existence of large numbers of nonaddicted heroin users has substantial implications. It is also known that the typical heroin addict, once thought to use heroin to the exclusion of all other drugs, is more likely to use many drugs, some in concert with heroin, others when heroin is unavailable. One implication of this is that when heroin is unavailable today's heroin addicts are as likely to turn to other drugs as they are to treatment.

The past eight to ten years have seen substantial progress in the treatment of heroin addiction. Various treatment approaches have evolved, the most widely publicized of which has been the use of the synthetic opiate methadone as a "maintenance" drug for individuals addicted to heroin. There are currently seventy-eight thousand individuals enrolled in methadone maintenance programs throughout the country, the majority of which are publicly funded.

During this same period there has been a corresponding increase in the number of individuals enrolled in what are most often termed "drug-free" treatment programs, i.e., those based on the principle of abstinence from drug use and using psychological and behavior modification techniques to achieve this goal. There are currently an estimated 132,000 individuals receiving treatment in this type of program.

There now exists a nationwide network of treatment programs and facilities none of which existed prior to 1972. This network was initiated primarily by federal grants and contracts through state drug abuse coordinating agencies to local governmental or nonprofit programs. As a result, federal officials are frequently quoted as saying that any heroin addict who wants treatment can receive it. While this statement may be theoretically accurate, there are two major caveats. First, the accomplishments of treatment efforts are limited by lack of funding, societal conditions (e.g., the general employment picture), and the difficulties of providing "successful" treatment under any circumstances. Second, for every heroin addict who is in treatment on any given day, there are an estimated three who are not. They have neither volunteered nor been referred by the criminal justice system.

While there has been dramatic progress in making treatment more available, serious problems remain. Perhaps the most frustrating of these problems is the fact that no one—including the council—appears able at this time to provide definitive, persuasive answers about the comparative effectiveness of the various treatment approaches. The basic problem with ascertaining treatment effectiveness is that there is no public or professional consensus about what treatment should accomplish or what constitutes "successful" treatment. Different approaches—e.g. abstinence, methadone maintenance, and detoxification—are needed to respond to the broad diversity of people in trouble from the misuse of drugs. Treatment success should be gauged by the improved function of the individual in society as measured by personal stability, employment, and related criteria. Treatment for drug dependence need not have as its primary goal abstinence from all drug use for its own sake. To the extent that abstinence is attainable for certain individuals, it should be a goal; for others, such a goal may be unrealistic, premature, or even self-defeating. Treatment goals should reflect the complex nature of drug dependence, which varies from person to person.

Successful treatment for drug dependence may foster such a degree of stability in an individual that he or she is able to be gainfully employed; employment may in turn become a major reinforcing factor in the success of treatment. It is, however, unrealistic to expect too much regarding employment from treatment and rehabilitation efforts since the individuals in treatment often have little or no work experience and few skills to offer in a job market characterized by fluctuating economic conditions. Successful treatment may also result in such stability that the individual no longer engages in criminal activities to support a costly drug habit. In each case, the goal of drug treatment should be the degree of stability necessary to lead to later developments, not those developments themselves. While some may brand such differences as only matters of semantics, we believe they are of crucial importance to the search for realistic goals in the treatment of drug dependence.

Further problems with treatment become evident when attention is focused on the quality of different programs. There are not enough programs which offer the wide range of assistance needed by those dependent on drugs who seek rehabilitation. Numerous factors have contributed to this situation, not the least of which is the rapid proliferation of programs which occurred in the early 1970s. Many weak programs were funded then and are still in existence. The nature and quality of the clinical process in many programs have also been adversely affected by the increased number of treatment clients coming to them by referral from the criminal justice system. This development has led some drug treatment programs away from a properly therapeutic function into an increasingly custodial role with their patients.

Health and drug treatment providers should not have to become society's agents for the control of social deviance or criminal activity. The primary responsibility of treatment systems should be treatment. If modification of drug-taking behavior, even of life styles, is a component of treatment then it should be presented as such. *Treatment for drug dependence should be available chiefly because people need help, not as a behavior or crime control measure.* Conversely, efforts to curtail drug-related crime should be presented as such and not mislabeled as therapeutic approaches to drug dependency.

For now, pending the outcome of further study and evaluation as well as research developments, there is a clear need to integrate the treatment of heroin addiction more closely with the general health care system. Drug treatment is now too isolated; the cross-fertilization of new ideas and trends from other disciplines which should be occurring is not observable. For drug treatment to retain its vitality in the immediate future, it cannot remain entirely apart from the mainstream of traditional physical and mental health care, nor on the other hand can it be totally absorbed by that system.

Our final suggestion on treatment is that we should immediately enter into a more active phase of research and experimentation with heroin, particularly regarding the potential of using the drug itself in the treatment of heroin addiction. We do not know enough about the treatment of heroin addiction or about what types of treatment are effective to be able to close our minds to alternative approaches. Through experience we have learned much about the use of methadone in treatment; we need to learn more about the potential of similar use of heroin. Several highly qualified research scientists have designed a variety of research protocols which call for the use of heroin at some stage in the addiction treatment process. Under present law, these projects could be funded; we are convinced that the most promising of them should be.

This research should emphasize local and state options and flexibility. What may prove efficacious in one setting may not in others, and what may prove effective for one individual may be inappropriate for another. While we have much to learn from the experience of other countries, particularly England, heroin addiction in America presents unique problems requiring creative approaches. Thus, our call for research and experimentation into the use of heroin in treatment should not be misconstrued as an endorsement of the concept of heroin maintenance (i.e., the provision of heroin to registered addicts). We have serious reservations as to whether such an approach would prove beneficial in this country. On the other hand, we submit that we do need direct experience with the use of heroin in treatment settings; otherwise, we will not be able to learn what we should know before making decisions regarding fundamental policy changes.

Just as we think treatment program efforts and policies can be improved, we feel that drug law enforcement can also be improved. The basic problem with law enforcement efforts lies with the drug laws themselves. As long as these laws separate drugs into licit and illicit categories, there will be a necessity for such agencies as the Drug Enforcement Administration, with its primary mission of controlling the availability of illicit drugs. The elimination of the availability of these drugs is in our view unachievable; still, as long as the laws remain in effect, they should be responsibly enforced.

Earlier we indicated our belief that national drug policy ought to be based on the *way* in which a drug is used rather than on the properties of specific drugs. This enlightened approach is generally characteristic of our public policies with respect to alcohol, tranquilizers, and a host of other potentially abusable drugs. Society accepts responsible use of these drugs, while seeking to prevent their misuse and, if necessary, punishing both those who jeopardize the safety of others by irresponsible usage behavior and those who illegally manufacture or sell such drugs. However, our laws regarding illicit drugs such as marijuana, cocaine, and heroin do not distinguish responsible from irresponsible use; thus, under the law, any use of these drugs constitutes misuse or "drug abuse." Drug law enforcement is consequently directed, at least theoretically, against all users and suppliers of illicit drugs. This is where problems with drug law enforcement begin. It is not, however, where they end.

Many proponents of a national policy of total prohibition of illicit drug use are beginning to acknowledge the impossibility of achieving such a goal. Revised goals, such as containment rather than elimination of availability, are now being advanced. Infrequently acknowledged, however, even with the more cautious goals, are the attendant costs of attempted prohibition, such as criminalizing and stigmatizing hundreds of thousands of users and using questionable practices in developing cases against them.

Nor are we convinced of the supposed benefits of many current drug law enforcement efforts. It is commonplace to assume that laws and law enforcement efforts decrease the number of people who would otherwise use these contraband substances. However, there are reasons to doubt this assumption. Exhaustive study has revealed little deterrent impact from the so-called "get tough" drug laws of New York State. This study showed little change in the incidence and prevalence of heroin or other illicit drug use as a result of the new law. Similarly, in Oregon, where annual surveys have been conducted to assess the impact of that state's enactment of marijuana "decriminalization," no appreciable increase in use has been observed over time or in comparison to other jurisdictions where marijuana penalties have remained stringent. In fact, other surveys indicate that the primary reason people have chosen either not to begin use or to discontinue it is simple lack of interest; the existence of criminal sanctions against use ranks quite low as a reason given for not using marijuana. While such examples do not offer sufficient evidence from which to draw firm conclusions, they do raise important questions requiring careful examination.

The most important recommendation the Drug Abuse Council can make in the area of drug law enforcement has little to do with specific law enforcement approaches. *We propose a major research effort to analyze the actual effects of drug laws and drug law enforcement on personal decisions to use or not use illicit drugs.* A well-designed national study, similar to that of New York drug laws undertaken in 1974 by the Bar Association of the City of New York, could furnish much useful guidance in this sensitive area.

In addition to encouraging us to recommend such general policy research, our years of examination of the issues involved in the widespread use of marijuana in contemporary society have convinced us, beyond a doubt, that the use of criminal law and criminal procedures to deter marijuana use results in more harm to society than is warranted by present knowledge regarding its potential harm with moderate use. This conviction should not be misconstrued as giving marijuana a clean bill of health. Much about this drug remains unknown. Research should continue, particularly multi-year studies which seek to examine the consequences of marijuana use by humans over long periods of time. Enough is now known to warrant considerable caution with its use, particularly heavy use; use by pregnant women and by adolescents should be avoided. *However, we also believe that legislative efforts to decriminalize at federal and state levels the possession of small amounts of marijuana for personal use should continue. States should be encouraged to try different legislative models, the effects of which could be assessed over time, in an effort to learn which works most effectively to minimize potential harm from the indiscriminate use of marijuana.*

The above observations and suggestions about drug treatment and law enforcement lead us to the conclusion that, by adhering to an unrealistic goal of total abstinence from the use of illicit drugs, opportunities to encourage responsible drug-using behavior are missed. Individual decisions about drug use invoke value judgments seldom made in isolation; peer pressure and social, economic, and cultural variables must all be taken into consideration as we seek to minimize harm and prevent misuse.

Public education efforts should attempt to place the use and misuse of psychoactive drugs in accurate perspective for all members of society, not just younger members. In order to be helpful in minimizing the harm of drug misuse, information must be credible, coherent, and verifiable. It must be believable when placed in the context of life experiences. For example, it strikes us as inconsistent to issue calls for total abstinence from some drugs while "happy hours" with two drinks for the price of one are promoted for another. Such inconsistencies are readily apparent to the youth of our country and engender skepticism on their part as to the wisdom of official drug policies—and of the older generation in general.

Many of our suggestions and observations have been directed toward policymakers in the public sector, those elected and appointed public officials who make national drug policy through their actions and decisions at federal, state, and local levels. It is no less true today than it was seven years ago when the Drug Abuse Council was created that the views of these officials tend to be crisis-oriented and short-range. While public officials have a duty to lead as well as to administer, there are limitations to their ability to go much beyond prevailing public attitudes in matters as volatile as drug issues. The private sector, on the other hand, can and should play a critical, responsible role in developing longer-range views and policies and improved public attitudes.

The Drug Abuse Council has been one such effort in the private sector. Other alternatives either already exist or could be created. Any such entity will require the exertion of private-sector leadership and the investment of resources sufficient to undertake independent research and legislative, budgetary, and policy analyses. Much basic examination and reexamination has occurred and does not require repeating. With modest annual expenditures, an organization within the private sector could help keep the American public informed and provide leadership for the development of broad public support for sensible drug policies and programs. *It is our conviction that the private sector needs to continue to take an active role in both developing and assessing public drug policies and programs.*

A Final Thought and Suggestion.   The goal of the council was stated in its 1972 Annual Report. The chairman said,

> The Directors of the Drug Abuse Council, widely representative in personal and professional exposure and involvement, are determined not to look to exhortations or crash programs for illusory solutions or cures. Instead, because the Council was initiated and is supported as a private independent agency, unencumbered by shibboleths or taboos or political or bureaucratic pressures, the Directors have been free—and have exercised their freedom—to begin to learn, and to publish what they have learned, about drug abuse and treatment in a drug using society.

Since 1972 the many publications of the council—and of persons and agencies supported by the council—have reported what we have learned about drugs, about their use, misuse, and our response to them. In the concluding paragraphs of one of the last and most significant studies initiated and supported by the council, *The Nation's Toughest Drug Law: Evaluating the New York Experience*,[3] it is stated that,

> First, the use of heroin and other opiates is but one element of a larger problem. The misuse of all dangerous drugs—alcohol, cocaine, opiates, and other mood-changing drugs, some prescribed and some sold over the counter—all together constitutes "the drug problem." Problems with so many components do not yield to one-dimensional solutions. As no single drug treatment method is suitable for all users, so there is not likely to be a single legal approach that is suitable for all offenders.
>
> Second, whether or not illicit drug use is for the most part a medical concern as some contend, it is incontrovertibly deeply rooted in broader social "maladies." Narcotics use in particular is intimately associated with, and part of, a wider complex of problems that includes family break-up, unemployment, poor income and education, feeble institutional structures, and loss of hope.
>
> The final observation is a corollary of the second: it is implausible that social problems as basic as these can be effectively solved by the criminal law.

If this statement is accurate—and we are convinced that it is—it reinforces our considered judgment that drug misuse is primarily a social, medical, and public health problem, a problem that will not yield to single or simplistic solutions or approaches. And it reinforces our judgment that solutions or approaches that might be useful in one place or with some individuals would not necessarily be so in another setting or with other people.

Recognizing that deeply felt attitudes and established policies reflect fears and judgments that will yield slowly, if ever, to facts and conditions described in the council's publications, we recommend that serious consideration be given to the use of individual state or local option as a means of attempting solutions appropriate in one place but not in others. Local option could encourage greater flexibility and ingenuity rather than reliance upon an unrealistic, rigid homogeneity in national drug policy. We need to respond to the diversity of people who use and misuse drugs, base all our policies on a consistent set of principles seeking to discourage misuse, and keep our seemingly innate drug-using behavior within reasonable limits through means which do not themselves cause more harm than they prevent.

1 The Federal Government's Response to Illicit Drugs, 1969–1978

Peter Goldberg

Note on Acronyms

ACRONYMS ARE USED throughout this chapter for a number of federal agencies. Among those most often referred to are:

ADAMHA	Alcohol, Drug Abuse, and Mental Health Administration
BNDD	Bureau of Narcotics and Dangerous Drugs
DEA	Drug Enforcement Administration
FBN	Federal Bureau of Narcotics
NIDA	National Institute on Drug Abuse
NIMH	National Institute of Mental Health
ODALE	Office of Drug Abuse Law Enforcement
ODAP	Office of Drug Abuse Policy
OMB	Office of Management and Budget
SAODAP	Special Action Office for Drug Abuse Prevention

Introduction

Throughout the twentieth century the government of the United States has engaged, in one form or another, in efforts to prevent its citizens from using certain designated psychoactive drugs. The use of nonapproved drugs has been defined as illegal, and billions of taxpayer dollars

The author acknowledges with gratitude the contributions of Alan S. Garber.

have been spent and millions of man-hours devoted to curtailing the availability of such drugs. Yet in spite of these efforts there are now as many users and abusers of illicit drugs as ever before. Similarly, the misuse of legally available drugs has dramatically increased.

Data on the use of illicit drugs do not conclusively demonstrate that the federal government's antidrug efforts have failed, but they do provide compelling reasons to undertake a thorough reappraisal of federal policies and programs. Evaluations made by both federal government study groups and private organizations[1] have resulted in changes—particularly in preventive and treatment approaches—but federal drug policies have remained fundamentally the same for decades.

This chapter will concentrate on the response of the federal government to the issues of illicit drug use and misuse from 1969 to the present. It was during this period that our country experienced an unprecedented growth in the governmental response to the use of illicit drugs. This period also roughly coincides with the years during which the Drug Abuse Council has been studying drug issues and policy.

To understand the U.S. government's response to illicit drugs in the 1970s it is necessary to know something of the history. Our nation's current drug policies and programs are the result of over seventy years of development. Detailed analyses such as those provided by David Musto[2] and Rufus King[3] offer insight into this process. It is clear from these analyses that the government's response to public fear of certain drugs and drug users has primarily consisted of law enforcement or quasi-enforcement strategies intended to prohibit both new and continued use of nonapproved substances. The belief that some drugs are so innately harmful that the citizens of this country should and could be prevented from using them has been the basic tenet of American drug policy for the past seven decades.

Historical Review

Several major pieces of drug legislation and presidential initiatives have shaped public policy in the drug field. The first pertinent legislation in this area passed by Congress was the District of Columbia Pharmacy Act in 1906.[4] Although this act applied only to the District of Columbia, it set a precedent for Congress to deal with drug issues. This act permitted a physician to prescribe narcotics to addicts, but only when "necessary for the cure" of addiction; the prescription of narcotic drugs to nonaddicted persons was limited to the treatment of injury or disease. The intent of the act was to prevent the further spread of addictive drug use. It first raised the difficult philosophical question of government regulation of physician prescribing practices with respect to addictive drugs, an issue still actively debated.

The Harrison Narcotic Act,[5] passed in late 1914, marked the official entry of the government into the area of narcotics control. This act simplified recordkeeping on the dispensation of certain narcotic drugs, and required that standard forms be filed and maintained for two years on the sales of narcotic drugs. Revenue agents could inspect these records at will. However, physicians were allowed to dispense drugs without keeping records if in actual attendance on their patients. Numerous patent medicines containing small amounts of morphine, cocaine, opium, and heroin were still permitted to be sold by mail order or in general stores.

Through regulations issued by the Treasury Department pursuant to the Harrison Narcotic Act, the federal government hampered the treatment of heroin and morphine addiction to such a degree that by the early 1920s those clinics in the country which regularly provided opiates to registered addicts (so-called "maintenance clinics") were closed, and few private physicians dared to provide these drugs to addicts.[6] This effectively ended the medical profession's active involvement in the treatment of drug addiction until the 1960s. From the 1920s on, the federal government was for all practical purposes in charge of attempts to control illicit drug use. Although there were, at the time, serious questions raised about the constitutionality of using federal police powers to restrict, and eventually prohibit, the use of certain drugs, the popular belief was that the use of these drugs must be eliminated even when occurring in the context of medical treatment for addiction.

In 1929 Congress passed the Porter Act,[7] ostensibly addressing the treatment needs of convicted addicts. The Porter Act called for the building of two narcotics "farms" in which those convicted of the "crime" of drug addiction would be housed in order to receive compulsory treatment. The underlying assumption of the act seemed to be that treatment—enforced abstinence—required isolation and a controlled environment. Although the Porter Act became law in January 1929, the first farm did not open until 1935 in Lexington, Kentucky. A second farm opened in 1938 in Fort Worth, Texas. The treatment rendered at these farms was not successful, with most addicts returning to addiction after discharge.[8] In reality the farms were little more than specialized prisons. In fact, Musto reports that "not until the late 1960s were the bars removed from the Lexington facility and the cells turned into rooms."[9]

In 1930 the first federal agency specifically devoted to the control of illicit drugs, the Federal Bureau of Narcotics (FBN), was established. Because the federal regulation of narcotic drugs was based on the taxing power of Congress, the FBN was made part of the Treasury Department and was concerned only with enforcement issues. The FBN was responsible, at least initially, for enforcing the Harrison Narcotic Act and controlling only what were then thought of as the most dangerous drugs—cocaine and the opiates. The FBN's policies were predicated on the belief that "the most effective way of gaining public compliance with a law regulating a dangerous drug was a policy of high fines and severe mandatory prison sentences for first convictions."[10]

The FBN did not initially support a federal antimarijuana effort. However, newspaper accounts of serious crimes attributed to marijuana users and the drug's "Mexican purveyors" triggered a series of events that culminated in the passage of the Marihuana Tax Act of 1937.[11] The FBN changed its policies after this act was passed, vigorously enforcing the federal laws prohibiting marijuana.[12]

Passage of the Marihuana Tax Act in effect imposed a total prohibition on marijuana use. Marijuana was described in congressional hearings as impairing the ability to think rationally, dangerous to the mind and body, and leading to insanity. It was further claimed that marijuana led to the commission of violent crimes, spread drug use to school children, and resulted in impotence in the habitual user. It was not until the early 1970s that many of these views began to be modified. To this day, however, their effects on public attitudes and policies linger.

During the late 1940s and early 1950s there were reports that rates of heroin addiction had risen, particularly in inner-city minority communities. This period coincided with the beginning of the so-called "McCarthy era," a time when public fear of nonconforming behavior was high and tolerance of it low. Drugs were linked to communism. As David Musto has written, "The Federal Bureau of Narcotics linked Red China's attempts to get hard cash, as well as to destroy Western society, to the clandestine sale of large amounts of heroin to drug pushers in the United States."[13] In addition, a theory that addicts began with marijuana use and moved inexorably to the use of heroin (or morphine or cocaine)—the "progression" or "stepping-stone" theory—was widely believed.

In this atmosphere, the Boggs Act[14] was passed in late 1951. The Boggs Act increased penalties for all drug law violators and for the first time made penalties for violation of the marijuana laws the same as those for narcotic drugs. This act also introduced, at the federal level, the concept of minimum mandatory jail sentences for drug law offenders.

The Boggs Act—and later amendments which further increased penalties[15]—reflected an undeviating reliance on law enforcement activities and harsh penalties to deal with the perceived "drug menace." The Boggs Act—and the later Narcotic Control Act of 1956—passed after only cursory hearings, which did not delve into either the causes or the nature of the use of illicit drugs. The widespread fear of communism and intolerance of nonconforming views and behavior at the time made it politically feasible—even desirable—to advocate reliance on the criminal justice system to control and punish narcotics users. The need for treatment was ignored. Most Americans directly affected by these laws were politically impotent, disliked, and distrusted because of prevailing racial and ethnic prejudices.

The first notice of change in official attitudes came in 1963 with President Kennedy's appointment of an Advisory Commission on Narcotic and Drug Abuse (the Prettyman Commission) to review the nation's drug problems and the government's response to them. The Prettyman Commission report[16] challenged many of the assumptions which had long dominated official thinking in the drug area. It recommended a decreased use of minimum mandatory sentences, an increase in appropriations for research, and the transfer of the FBN to the Department of Health, Education, and Welfare. It also recommended that the final judgment on the legitimate medical use of narcotics be given back to the medical profession.

The Prettyman Commission noted the fragmentation of federal activities in the drug field and recommended that "the President appoint a Special Assistant for Narcotic and Drug Abuse from the White House staff to provide continuous advice and assistance in launching a coordinated attack."[17] Although the commission made many recommendations, few were implemented at that time.

One recommendation of the commission which did receive attention was that a civil commitment system be established "to provide an alternative method of handling the federally convicted offender who is a confirmed narcotic or marijuana abuser." Such a system was instituted by the Narcotic Addict Rehabilitation Act of 1966 (NARA).[18] Although NARA ostensibly considered drug addiction a "medical problem," addicts committed under NARA programs were basically perceived as prisoners.

By the mid-1960s, illicit drug use had become a highly visible and emotional issue throughout the United States. It was widely believed that illicit drug use was increasing rapidly and for the first time reaching into the suburbs and affecting white middle-class youth. News reports often tended toward sensationalism in presenting stories on LSD and hallucinogenic drug use on college campuses. Anti–Vietnam War protestors became identified with marijuana use. The use of illicit drugs was, in general, identified as an antisocial gesture and was associated in the public's mind with mental illness and rising rates of street crime.

In February 1968 President Johnson established "a new and powerful Bureau of Narcotics and Dangerous Drugs (BNDD)" within the Justice Department.[19] Johnson had seen that the federal enforcement of narcotics laws was fragmented. The Federal Bureau of Narcotics in the Treasury Department had some responsibilities, while the Bureau of Drug Abuse Control (BDAC)—an agency created only three years earlier in 1965 in the Department of Health, Education, and Welfare—had been assigned certain regulatory functions having to do with nonnarcotic drugs. In an attempt to unify the federal response, the FBN and BDAC were abolished and the new BNDD was given full authority to enforce all U.S. narcotics laws, from worldwide operations to work with state and local law enforcement officials. In addition, BNDD was directed to "conduct an extensive campaign of research and a nationwide public education program on drug abuse and its tragic effects." In fact, in President Johnson's message to Congress proposing Reorganization Plan No. 1, the only mention of any federal effort in research, treatment, or education was in the context of the Justice Department's BNDD. The emphasis was again on law enforcement and the relationship between drugs and crime.

Understanding the Growth of the Governmental Response to Illicit Drugs

During Richard Nixon's presidential terms, the issue of "drug abuse" was given a higher priority and greater visibility than at any other time in our country's history. In January 1969 the annual federal budget for drug treatment, education, research, and law enforcement was $81.4 million; five years later it was $760 million—nearly a tenfold increase. A series of major legislative, organizational, and programmatic changes accompanied these dramatic budget increases. The reasons for this enormous increase in the federal response can be traced to three unforeseen circumstances of need and opportunity.

The Need to Reduce Rates of Urban Street Crime. Rising street crime was a key issue in the 1968 presidential campaign. The urban riots of the mid-1960s and the rising crime-rate figures issued by the FBI provided fuel for much of the campaign rhetoric about the growing "lawlessness" and "violence" of America. "Law and order" emerged as the dominant domestic theme of the 1968 Republican presidential campaign.[20]

Campaign promises to "get tough" with urban street crime are historically easier to make than to fulfill. The jurisdiction and power of the federal government to prevent burglaries and armed robberies—among the most common types of urban street crime—are limited. Except in the District of Columbia, such violations are usually matters for state, not federal, action. Even if Congress had extended the legal authority of the federal law enforcement agencies, these agencies (FBI, IRS, BNDD) did not have the manpower to address urban street crime effectively.

In spite of the passage of "tough" legislation such as preventive detention, harsh prison sentences, and "no-knock" warrantless searches, crime rates continued to rise, as reported by the FBI, jeopardizing the administration's promised law and order. Even in the District of Columbia, where the federal government could exercise some control, the crime rate increased during the first year of the Nixon presidency.

Clearly, from a political perspective the Nixon administration needed to show progress in some area of crime control before the 1972 election. This was one element underlying the growth since 1969 of the federal government's efforts to control the use of illicit drugs.

The Public's Increasing Concern About Heroin Addiction.   The association of illicit drug use with street crime and violence developed over a long period of time. By the late 1960s, the relationship between heroin "addiction"* and street crime was generally accepted as fact, despite the absence of any careful research and documentation.[22] Heroin had become inextricably linked in the public's mind with the urban crisis; and as public anxiety about crime grew, so too did the fear of heroin and heroin addicts.

The public's fear of heroin was intensified by reports of increased use of narcotics among American soldiers stationed in Vietnam. The thought of "soldier-junkies," trained in guerilla warfare, returning to the streets of urban America heightened public concern and led to further demands for government action. "Drug abuse" (particularly heroin addiction) rapidly became a major public concern, as reflected in the opinion polls of that time, adding another argument for an expanded government effort.

But neither the need for an effective crime reduction program nor the growing public concern about heroin explain by themselves the increased federal response: a third element was crucial. In all likelihood the government's efforts to prevent "drug abuse" would have expanded without this third element, but it is doubtful that the expansion would have been anywhere near the same magnitude.

The Emergence of New Approaches to the Problem of Heroin Addiction.   Three new avenues of response to the problems of heroin addiction and heroin-related crime emerged. Although distinct from one another, these three approaches in time became interrelated in subsequent government programs. The opportunities they presented led—some say misled—federal policymakers to believe that they could respond to the problems of heroin addiction more successfully than previously.

First, the legislative basis for federal drug law enforcement efforts changed. Federal regulations and controls on drugs before 1970 were based primarily on the power to levy taxes and prohibit traffic in smuggled goods. Thus virtually all federal drug law enforcement programs were administered by the Treasury Department—until the creation of the Bureau of Narcotics and Dangerous Drugs in the Justice Department by executive

---

*In the late 1960s no distinction was made between heroin use and heroin addiction—all use of heroin was believed addictive. More recent studies indicate that this is not necessarily accurate.[21]

order in 1968; simultaneously the Treasury Department's Federal Bureau of Narcotics was abolished. This transfer of jurisdiction was given a statutory basis in 1970 with the passage of the Comprehensive Drug Abuse Prevention and Control Act.[23]

This act addressed a broad range of drug program efforts, providing increased support for drug treatment, rehabilitation, and education as well as enforcement. The enforcement provisions of this legislation (Title II of the act) were part of a larger attempt to reduce criminal activity through improved federal law enforcement. Congress and the Nixon administration sought through this legislation to recodify the existing drug laws into one comprehensive law. Most narcotics law enforcement powers were given to the Justice Department, thus allowing the Attorney General to exercise control over all dangerous drugs (e.g., amphetamines and barbiturates) and narcotics. This was the first federal law making it illegal to traffic in or possess certain drugs which did not refer to the taxing authority. Instead, the justification for federal—as opposed to state—enforcement was shifted to the power of Congress to regulate interstate commerce. The concept of the "interstate commerce" powers of Congress had greatly expanded in the decades prior to this new drug legislation. Supreme Court rulings on the "New Deal" legislation of the 1930s and 1940s and on the civil rights cases of the 1960s had clearly broadened the scope of activities that Congress could regulate under its constitutional authority to regulate "interstate commerce."

This shift in the constitutional basis of drug law enforcement allowed the federal government to become more directly involved in suppressing one presumed major cause of urban street crime about which there was great public fear. It offered some hope that expanded and intensified efforts to combat trafficking in illicit drugs could succeed where past efforts had failed.

A second new avenue of response centered around bilateral agreements to reduce the international flow of illicit drugs—particularly heroin—into the United States. For more than sixty years, beginning with the Hague International Opium Convention of 1912, the United States has negotiated bilateral and multilateral international agreements to keep illicit opiates out of the country. Since opium, of which heroin is a derivative, is not grown anywhere in the United States, all the heroin used by addicts in this country comes from foreign sources; hence the concept that if opium is not cultivated elsewhere, heroin will not be available for use here. Since, however, it is virtually impossible to prevent the growth of the opium poppy everywhere, a second line of defense has been to disrupt international trafficking in opium, its chemical conversion into heroin in foreign laboratories, and its subsequent shipment into the United States.

In January 1969, up to 80 percent of the heroin used in the United States was believed to be of Turkish origin. The major processing country for converting Turkish opium into heroin for shipment to American East Coast port cities was reputed to be France. The operations in these two countries were frequently blamed for the rising rates of heroin addiction reported in the United States in the late 1960s.

The Nixon administration sought greater international cooperation to keep illicit drugs from entering the United States.[24] In early 1971, just as public concern about heroin was reaching its peak, separate agreements were reached with France and Turkey enlisting their formal assistance in keeping heroin out of the United States. The French government agreed to take steps to close down the clandestine laboratories operating principally around Marseilles and to prevent the traffic of opium into, and heroin out of, France. The agreement with Turkey—the culmination of five years of negotiations—amounted to a total ban on poppy cultivation in Turkey in return for American financial aid for crop substitution programs and income compensation for Turkish farmers.

It was anticipated that these two agreements would significantly reduce the flow of heroin to the United States, and that the resulting shortage would reduce the levels of heroin addiction and heroin-related crime. They were touted as major victories on the international front of the new "war on drug abuse." The federal government sought to capitalize on these agreements by negotiating agreements with other potential "source" and "processing" countries. The hoped-for success of these efforts to control international supplies thus emerged as the second new avenue of the government's heroin control effort.

The third new avenue of response was the use of methadone to treat heroin addiction. Methadone is a synthetic analgesic developed by the Germans during World War II as a substitute for morphine. After the war and throughout the 1950s, methadone was used in the United States as a detoxifying agent for heroin addicts. In 1964 Drs. Vincent P. Dole and Marie E. Nyswander of the Rockefeller Institute in New York City found that they were able to maintain six heroin addicts on a stable dosage-level of methadone without their craving heroin. Dole and Nyswander soon began an expanded program of methadone maintenance to both demonstrate methadone's potential and evaluate the program's impact. In 1966 they reported the initial results of their work: Among the most widely publicized of their results was that criminal activity among the enrolled addicts had been "virtually eliminated."[25] Public and government interest in the concept of methadone maintenance grew, and by the late 1960s methadone programs were in operation in many urban centers, providing addicts with an alternative to the more traditional forms of treatment which emphasized abstinence, and which had not proved successful for large numbers of addicts.

While methadone maintenance programs are generally considered "treatment," particularly by their staffs and clients, the idea of using methadone treatment as part of the larger national effort to reduce urban street crime had begun to take hold by late 1969. The proposition put forth was that if an addict's dependence on heroin was broken (by substituting legally prescribed methadone), the crime rate would be reduced, because—so the theory went—addicts committed a large proportion of the street crime in order to feed their illicit habits. A 1970 Domestic Council Summary Option Paper on Drugs stated, "The Federal government has only one economical and effective technique for reducing crime in the streets—methadone maintenance."[26]

Methadone thus offered an important new form of treatment to heroin addicts as well as a possibility of reducing urban street crime. Which aspect was considered more important is difficult to determine. In any event, the emergence of methadone treatment was a crucial part of the developing "solution" to the problems of heroin addiction and heroin-related crime.

Thus in the late 1960s and early 1970s several new and potentially significant approaches developed. Many believed that if effectively applied in concert they could substantially reduce the rate of heroin addiction and associated problems, particularly the crimes committed to raise money to support heroin addiction. These developments, coinciding as they did with the political commitment to reduce urban street crime and respond to the growing public concern about heroin addiction, had much to do with the enormous growth of the federal response to illicit drugs which began in 1969.

The Federal Response, 1969–1971

In January 1969 the federal goverment's response to illicit drugs as measured in dollars spent was small; $86 million was spent in fiscal year 1969 (FY 69), and only a modest increase to $101.9 million was requested for FY 70.[27]

The principal federal agencies involved in the drug field during this period were the National Institute of Mental Health (NIMH) in the Department of Health, Education, and Welfare; the Bureau of Narcotics and Dangerous Drugs in the Justice Department; and the Customs Bureau of the Treasury Department. These three agencies accounted for the bulk of the federal drug effort in four operational areas: treatment and rehabilitation; education, prevention, and training; research; and law enforcement. NIMH was the major federal sponsor of all non–law-enforcement programs, while BNDD and Customs each held some responsibility for the federal drug law enforcement effort. The emergence of BNDD created an intense bureaucratic rivalry with Customs regarding jurisdictional responsibilities for drug law enforcement programs. Although this dispute was supposed to have been settled in 1969 when BNDD was authorized to conduct overseas operations and Customs was restricted to border searches, it has surfaced frequently in subsequent years; even now the situation seems merely a temporary truce. (See Staff Paper 2, "Drug Law Enforcement Efforts," below.)

The FY 71 budget was the first to be completely developed by the Nixon administration, and in it the federal drug budget more than doubled to a total of $212.5 million. The major increases in the FY 71 budget were for treatment and rehabilitation and education, prevention, and training. While the drug law enforcement budget rose by more than 50 percent, it was for the first time surpassed in absolute numbers by expenditures for treatment and rehabilitation, which by this time were assuming added dimensions as part of the crime reduction effort (see Figure 1.1).

Since the use of illicit drugs was of growing public concern and government interest, federal budget makers were clearly more receptive to agency budget requests for new drug programs, and by FY 71 there were fifteen separate federal agencies involved in some kind of drug-related effort. For some, such as the Office of Education, the Veterans Administration, and the Department of Transportation, FY 71 marked the first year they had undertaken specific drug activities. For others, such as the Department of Housing and Urban Development and the Office of Eco-

FIGURE 1-1.   **Federal Drug Budget by Function: Comparison of Fiscal Years 1970 and 1971**

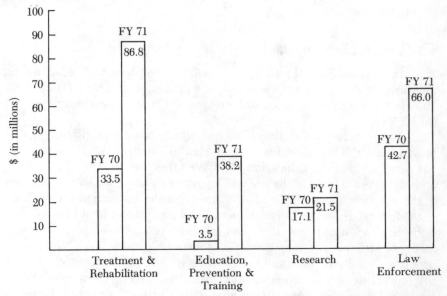

Source: Peter Goldberg and James V. DeLong, "Federal Expenditures on Drug Abuse Control," in *Dealing with Drug Abuse: A Report to the Ford Foundation*, pp. 303–304.

nomic Opportunity, drug-related expenditures, which until then had
been minimal, rose dramatically. This expansion of the federal drug budget was accompanied by greater problems of interagency coordination.
Although federal response to the use of illicit drugs was growing, it generally lacked cohesion and overall purpose (other than a commitment to
"solve the drug problem"). This lack of coordination led Hutt and Wald
to comment in 1972, "Federal activities in the drug abuse field tend to be
ad hoc reactions to current crises rather than well-considered, long-term
programs."[28]

The proposed FY 72 budget, announced in February 1971, projected a drug budget of $265 million—an increase of just over $50 million.
This proposal envisioned federal expenditures of $96 million for law en-
forcement, $101 million for treatment and rehabilitation, $24 million for
research, and $44 million for education, prevention, and training. By this
time there were sixteen separate federal agencies involved in the drug effort, with little coordination between them. The resulting bureaucratic
nightmare was graphically depicted in a government report covering all
federal drug efforts except law enforcement (Figure 1.2).

In early 1971, the National Commission on Marihuana and Drug
Abuse began work on the first of two consecutive one-year studies it was
to undertake. The appointment of this federal study commission, the
scope of its work, and the schedule for the completion of its two reports

FIGURE 1-2.

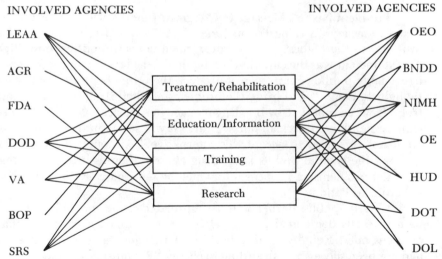

INVOLVED AGENCIES   INVOLVED AGENCIES

LEAA   OEO

AGR   BNDD

              Treatment/Rehabilitation

FDA   NIMH

            Education/Information

DOD   OE

                Training

VA   HUD

               Research

BOP   DOT

SRS   DOL

Source: Chart taken from Strategy Council on Drug Abuse, *Federal Strategy for Drug Abuse
and Drug Traffic Prevention, 1973* (Washington, D.C.: U.S. Government Printing Office,
1973), p. 76.

had been delineated in the Comprehensive Drug Abuse Prevention and Control Act of 1970. (The Senate and the House of Representatives each appointed two members to the thirteen-member commission; President Nixon selected the remaining nine.) Congress had stipulated that the commission first complete a comprehensive study of marijuana-related issues by March 1972 (discussed more fully in Staff Paper 5, "Marijuana and Cocaine," below). In the commission's second year, Congress directed it to complete a more general examination and analysis of the nature, causes, and significance of the "drug abuse" problem in the United States, and further directed it to present recommendations for legislative and administrative actions consistent with the commission's findings and conclusions.

However, on June 17, 1971, long before the scheduled completion of the commission's second report, President Nixon sent to Congress a special message on drug abuse in which he requested a supplemental budget of $155 million and a reorganization of responsibilities regarding drug treatment, education, prevention, research, and, most notably, coordination. Citing the immediacy of the drug problem and the need for a more effective response, Nixon simultaneously issued an executive order establishing the position of Special Consultant to the President for Narcotics and Dangerous Drugs in order to "institute to the extent legally possible" the legislation which he proposed to Congress. It was at this point that the fundamental restructuring of the federal government's response to illicit drugs began.

President Nixon's Message to Congress, June 17, 1971.[29]   President Nixon's message to Congress on June 17, 1971 raised the issue of illicit drug use to the highest level of government concern and responsibility. This statement was the culminating step in the declaration of a strong and irrevocable public commitment to reduce the crime heroin addicts were thought to commit and bring the problems of illicit drug use under control. "If we cannot destroy the drug menace in America," Nixon informed Congress and the American public, "then it will surely in time destroy us. I am not prepared to accept this alternative." Although the President spoke of the general problems of "drug abuse," there is little doubt that the chief problems and concerns to which he referred were those relating to heroin addiction.

Clearly, public alarm about heroin-related crime and addicted Vietnam veterans demanded a more effective governmental response than previous ones. Equally clear was the fact that increased funding alone had not been successful. According to Nixon: "We must now candidly recognize that the deliberate procedures embodied in present efforts to control drug abuse are not sufficient in themselves. The problem has assumed the dimensions of a national emergency."

Forceful measures were required, so the thinking went, if the twin problems of heroin addiction and urban crime were to be curtailed. Speed was essential to the Nixon administration because of the political aspects of illicit drug use. Predictably, the policies and programs it advocated were consistent with enforcement and quasi-enforcement approaches which had characterized past federal efforts. The government's response to the use of illicit drugs in 1971 sprang from the same assumptions about their innate harmfulness and arrived at fundamentally the same conclusions as had been espoused for more than sixty years. The changes proposed were those of technique, size, and scope only.

The president acknowledged the problems of undirected growth in the government's response.

> We must recognize that piecemeal efforts, even where individually successful, cannot have a major impact on the drug abuse problem unless and until they are forged together into a broader and more integrated program involving all levels of government and private effort. We need a coordinated effort if we are to move effectively against drug abuse.

A two-sided approach was developed to coordinate the federal drug effort. On the "supply" side were all federal drug law enforcement efforts to halt the illegal production, distribution, and use of prohibited substances. On the "demand" side were all federally sponsored efforts at treatment and rehabilitation and education, prevention, training, and research. Each approach was envisioned as separate and independent of the other, although they shared the same goals of eliminating illicit drug use and drug-related crime in America.

To control "demand" the Nixon administration proposed a dramatic reorganization which would temporarily centralize responsibility for all federally sponsored efforts in drug treatment, rehabilitation, education, prevention, training, and research in a new White House Agency, the Special Action Office for Drug Abuse Prevention (SAODAP). The director of SAODAP was to be immediately accountable to the President. From an organizational standpoint it made sense to coordinate the many federal agencies involved. To have ignored the management problems displayed in Figure 1.2 above would have led to further chaos and undercut the potential of any federal response. However, this does not explain why such coordinative responsibilities were lodged in the White House under presidential supervision. Other federal programs also involved a number of federal agencies, yet coordination could usually be achieved through more regular bureaucratic measures such as cabinet- or sub–cabinet-level working agreements. What made the drug issue different?

One explanation lies in the deteriorating relationship at that time between the White House staff and various federal agencies. Particularly with respect to the funding of methadone maintenance programs, the

White House felt that there was considerable bureaucratic "foot-drag-ging."[30] Administration officials had become persuaded of the benefits of methadone maintenance as a way to reduce "heroin and criminal recidi-vism," but they had been unsuccessful in gaining the full support and cooperation of NIMH, the agency which normally would have funded and overseen these programs. NIMH officials were cautious of govern-ment "sanctioning one addiction [to methadone] in order to reduce the burden on society of heroin addiction," and continued to resist White House pressures to fund a greater number of methadone programs.[31] The administration contended that NIMH opposed the programs because to endorse the concept of methadone maintenance would have been tanta-mount to admitting the failure of the psychiatric profession to successfully treat heroin addiction.[32]

While mention of methadone is made only once in President Nixon's message to Congress, the proposed creation of SAODAP and the accompa-nying redelegation of authority would help circumvent NIMH and in-crease federal support for methadone. The administration sought thus to bypass—since it could not cajole—a reluctant bureaucracy. The presi-dent's designation of Dr. Jerome Jaffe—a prominent supporter of the use of methadone in treatment—as his Special Consultant for Narcotics and Dangerous Drugs until SAODAP could be legally constituted by Congress left no doubt as to the administration's intention. Indeed, when Dr. Jaffe assumed leadership responsibilities in mid-1971, there were 135 federally funded drug treatment programs; eighteen months later, with a signifi-cantly increased drug treatment budget, the number had nearly tripled to 394.[33] Treatment for heroin addiction was emphasized in this program ex-pansion and the rate of growth of methadone treatment programs was ac-celerated.

A second explanation for centralizing drug-policy–making responsi-bilities in the White House is that the administration anticipated a suc-cessful campaign against illicit drug use and drug-related crime and wanted to take political credit for it. If the needs were great, so were the opportunities. The president's message to Congress exuded confidence in spite of the crisis rhetoric in which it was couched; the message sought to portray illicit drugs as the villain in a domestic war which could only be won by forceful presidential leadership, as the following excerpt suggests.

> Narcotics addiction is a problem which afflicts both the body and the soul of America. It is a problem which baffles many Americans. In our his-tory we have faced great difficulties again and again, wars and depressions and divisions among our people have tested our will as a people—and we have prevailed.
>
> The threat of narcotics among our people is one which properly frightens many Americans. It comes quietly into homes and destroys chil-dren, it moves into neighborhoods and breaks the fiber of community which

makes neighbors. . . . And we are not without the will to deal with this matter. We have the moral resources to do the job. Now we need the authority and the funds to match our moral resources. I am confident that we will prevail in this struggle as we have in many others. But time is critical. Every day we lose compounds the tragedy which drugs inflict on individual Americans. The final issue is not whether we will conquer drug abuse, but how soon.

The message drew upon traditional perceptions and fears of illicit drugs and illicit drug users in order to rally public support for a renewed crusade against a social evil. The rhetoric was consistent with the tenor of the times. Leading a war against illicit drugs was certain to enhance any politician's popularity. And, although the public pronouncements tended towards the dramatic, the reorganization and expansion called for, particularly regarding federal efforts in drug treatment and prevention, were clearly warranted.

The president's message leaves no doubt that the administration thought a war against illicit drugs could be won. The president proposed only a three-to-five-year life for SAODAP because it was to be "an emergency response to a national problem which we intend to bring under control." This "war" was going to be swift, requiring immediate and decisive action and sufficient financing. SAODAP's role was to give the White House direct involvement, visibility, and credit.

Development of the Expanded Federal Response

Having made a public commitment to respond forcefully to the problems of illicit drug use, the administration commenced a period of whirlwind activity. Each of the three new avenues of response—methadone treatment, international negotiations, and domestic drug law enforcement programs—were vigorously pursued in an attempt to launch a comprehensive attack on the perceived problems. Funding was increased commensurately. In his message to Congress the president had requested a supplemental budget of $155 million to bolster the new drug programs. When passed by Congress, this supplemental appropriation raised the FY 72 drug budget to $418 million—four times what it had been only two years earlier.

Treatment. When he took office in 1971, President Nixon's new drug advisor, Dr. Jerome Jaffe, turned first to the problems of the Vietnam soldier and veteran, among whom rates of addiction were reported to be extraordinarily high. The drug treatment programs of the Veterans Administration (VA) were expanded; many new centers opened, enabling the VA to attract more addicted veterans into treatment. And to stem the reported flow of drug-addicted soldiers returning to the United States, the

Defense Department initiated a massive urinalysis detection program to screen all Vietnam servicemen for illicit drug use before they left Southeast Asia; any heroin- or opiate-using soldiers testing positive were to be detained for treatment and rehabilitation. President Nixon informed Congress, "We will be requesting legislation to permit the military services to retain for treatment any individual due for discharge who is a narcotic addict. All of our servicemen must be accorded the right to rehabilitation."[34] In all, nearly $50 million of the president's supplemental budget was applied to expanding the drug treatment and rehabilitation capabilities of the Defense Department and Veterans Administration.

The SAODAP staff also immediately assumed responsibility for directing the expansion of drug treatment programs throughout the United States. Although NIMH received an additional $51 million for treatment and rehabilitation as a result of the supplemental budget, raising its total treatment and rehabilitation budget to $100 million, control of the expenditure of these funds was largely shifted from NIMH to SAODAP and the White House staff. With respct to program expansion, the emphasis was placed on heroin addiction treatment and "there was a massive expansion of methadone maintenance programs throughout the country."[35]

The first new goal of treatment was to enable any addict who wished it to obtain it without delay. This meant eliminating the waiting lists for entry at many programs, and expanding treatment in communities where it was needed but not yet available. When Dr. Jaffe assumed responsibilities in June 1971, federally funded treatment programs were located in 54 cities; only eighteen months later the number of cities involved had quadrupled to 214.[36] The speed and size of this expansion was dramatic by any account. The earliest available federal estimate places the number of clients in federally funded treatment programs at just over twenty thousand in October 1971; by December 1972 the figure was over sixty thousand.[37]

The only recognized approaches for heroin addiction other than the expanding methadone treatment were abstinence oriented and usually took place in a residential community setting. While popular and sometimes effective treatment approaches for small numbers of addicts, these abstinence programs had not and—according to federal policy makers— could not have a significant impact on urban crime. Methadone thus became a new hope, in spite of the objections of the Food and Drug Administration about insufficient research or the opposition from minority communities about the underlying philosophy of using one addictive drug to treat another.[38] In December 1972, the Food and Drug Administration published new regulations which loosened federal controls over methadone, changing its status from that of an investigational new drug to a new drug requiring ongoing, long-term study.[39] By October 1973, nearly eighty thousand persons were enrolled in methadone maintenance programs.[40] Some of these programs were federally funded; all operated with federal government approval.

From the government's perspective, methadone treatment programs had certain advantages over therapeutic community programs. Methadone allowed greater numbers of people to be treated in fewer programs, thus making rapid program expansion easier. For a large number of heroin addicts unable to successfully remain drug-free, the expansion of methadone programs offered an invaluable alternative to heroin addiction. Moreover, the cost per client of methadone maintenance was substantially less than the cost in a therapeutic community. And although methadone treatment could not meet the public's demand for drug abstinence, it could satisfy the even more popular demand for a reduction in heroin-related crime. Finally, methadone programs staffed with medical doctors and operated in more traditional medical clinical style could be more easily understood by the public. The encounter sessions and heavy psychological orientation of the therapeutic community were often misunderstood, even though the drug-free orientation was commended. Thus, the expansion of heroin treatment programs—particularly using methadone treatment—became SAODAP's first objective.

International Activities. In his June 1971 message to Congress, President Nixon had proposed an all-out global war on international drug trafficking. To dramatize his intentions, Nixon called together the U.S. ambassadors to Turkey, France, Mexico, Luxembourg, Thailand, the Republic of Vietnam, and the United Nations to discuss ways to encourage greater cooperation from other nations in the effort to control the illegal growing and trafficking of opium worldwide. "I sought to make it . . . clear," he told Congress of this meeting, "that I consider the heroin addiction of American citizens an international problem of grave concern to this Nation, and I instructed our Ambassadors to make this clear to their host governments. We want good relations with other countries, but we cannot buy good relations at the expense of temporizing on this problem."[41]

Two weeks later President Nixon formally announced that the Government of Turkey had agreed to impose a total ban on opium poppy cultivation following the 1972 harvest. In return the United States pledged $35.7 million in aid over a five-year period to compensate Turkey for the projected financial loss on legitimate sales of opium, and to help Turkish farmers develop substitute crops offering new sources of income. The agreement was hailed as a "most significant breakthrough" even though the ban was not to take effect until a year after its announcement.[42] The Turkish agreement was intended to help launch a concentrated American effort to halt all illicit opium production throughout the world. During the following twelve months, however, that effort far surpassed any tangible results.

In September 1971 President Nixon established a new Cabinet Committee on International Narcotics Control, to oversee the further development of U.S. international drug control efforts. The Cabinet Committee, chaired by the Secretary of State, directed the U.S. embassies in fifty-nine countries to prepare Narcotics Control Action Plans to be used as a basis for negotiating bilateral agreements with foreign countries in furtherance of U.S. international drug control programs. Apparently, however, it was decided that other countries were not to be offered the same type of broad-based economic assistance which had been extended to Turkey. Rather, the Narcotics Control Action Plans were to be more limited in scope, essentially offering law enforcement assistance to improve the "intelligence capability and law enforcement capacity of the host."[43] Furthermore, whereas Turkey had been offered the "carrot," other nations were threatened with the "stick" of, among other things, termination of economic and military assistance.[44] This change in strategy suggests that the administration was aware, even before the Turkish ban took effect, of the severe limitations of this approach. There simply were too many countries where opium could be grown and converted to heroin for sale in the lucrative U.S. market.[45] It would have been difficult to negotiate similar agreements with *all* other potential "source" countries, and even if diplomatically possible the cost would have been prohibitive. Moreover, because of the remoteness of many areas from their governments, not every country could successfully impose an opium ban even if it agreed to try. Gradually, therefore, international interdiction efforts replaced prevention of opium cultivation as the major objective of the U.S. international drug control effort.

Thus, despite active presidential involvement, no dramatic bilateral agreements other than that with Turkey and the aforementioned one with France were produced to show success on the international front.

In addition to bilateral efforts, efforts were also made to strengthen the enforcement provisions of the 1961 Single Convention on Narcotic Drugs, the governing international agreement on illicit drug control. In 1971 the United States submitted proposed amendments to the Single Convention which were largely directed toward improving controls on illicit opium cultivation in source countries. These amendments were formally agreed upon at a plenipotentiary conference in 1972 and submitted to the signatory countries for their ratification. The Nixon administration apparently regarded the amendments as a bold new approach in international narcotics control, despite the ineffectiveness of the basic treaty.[46]

In return for strengthening the 1961 Single Convention, the opium-growing countries pressured the United States to support a second international agreement which would for the first time place multinational controls on synthetic, "psychotropic" drugs such as hallucinogens, amphetamines, barbiturates, and tranquilizers. This treaty, also drafted in 1971, became known as the Psychotropic Convention.[47] The opium-producing countries viewed its ratification as a demonstration of the industrialized nations' seriousness about controlling the spread of nonnarcotic drug misuse. American support of the Psychotropic Convention thus became a necessary quid pro quo for support from the opium-producing nations on strengthening the Single Convention.

President Nixon sent the Psychotropic Convention to the Senate for approval on June 29, 1971. The proposed treaty met strong opposition because it threatened to limit domestic flexibility in regulating various psychoactive drugs. It was argued that the treaty would further remove the medical and scientific professions from decision-making responsibilities in U.S. domestic drug policy. To date neither the Psychotropic Convention nor the changes in domestic law that it would have required have been passed.

Domestic Drug Law Enforcement. Until 1970 BNDD and its principal predecessor, the Federal Bureau of Narcotics, were often accused of concentrating too much law enforcement effort on users and street dealers in order to inflate the number of arrests made. In 1970 BNDD claimed this policy had been reversed, with efforts being redirected to the higher levels of the illicit drug distribution structure. BNDD director John Ingersoll explained the anticipated result of this change to a House Appropriations subcommittee in March 1970.

> The shift in emphasis of federal narcotic and dangerous drug law enforcement from the addict, abuser, and small-time street peddler to the important illicit traffickers and illegal supply sources will undoubtedly result in fewer total arrests. But those made should have a greater impact on the supply of narcotics and drugs available for distribution to the consumers in this country than a larger number of less significant arrests.[48]

However, in 1971 the administration sought to increase the number of arrests by getting BNDD to move once again against street-level dealers.[49] The administration apparently believed that this would suggest a more active and successful "offensive" in its "war" on illicit drugs and drug users. BNDD resisted the change, contending that such efforts should be carried out by state and local agencies, and it continued to go after the higher levels of the drug distribution systems. Like NIMH, BNDD was not immediately responsive to the administration's wishes. And so once again the White House created a new agency under direct White House control. In January 1972 the Office of Drug Abuse Law Enforcement (ODALE) was created by executive order within the Justice

Department.[50] ODALE was made "responsible for the development and implementation of a concentrated program throughout the federal government for the enforcement of federal laws relating to the prevention of drug abuse and for cooperation with state and local governments in the enforcement of their drug abuse laws."[51] The director of ODALE was also made a special consultant to the president for drug-abuse law enforcement, thus becoming the nation's chief drug law enforcement spokesman.

Within a month after its establishment, ODALE had selected thirty-three target cities and had deployed strike forces consisting of federal investigators and agents, assistant U.S. attorneys, and state and local police officers. These strike forces concentrated on the lower and middle levels of the domestic heroin distribution systems, and, according to one observer, were instructed to "make arrests by any lawful means possible, even if it meant bypassing the normal channels."[52] By combining the specialized enforcement authorities and powers of various federal agencies— e.g., the Internal Revenue Service, Customs, BNDD, the Immigration and Naturalization Service, the Alcohol, Tobacco, and Firearms Agency, etc.—ODALE was in a unique position to "bypass normal channels." The strike forces were sufficiently funded to be able to make extensive use of undercover agents and "buy money" to purchase drugs and pay informants; investigative grand juries were empaneled; and ODALE was empowered to use court-authorized wiretaps and "no-knock" warrants in making arrests. As expected, the number of arrests rose quickly and the increased figures were publicized. Rapidly and dramatically, ODALE became a prominent, highly visible part of the administration's "war on drugs."

The Congressional Response: Passage of the Drug Abuse Office and Treatment Act of 1972

Congress responded to President Nixon's challenge for quick and decisive action by passing the Drug Abuse Office and Treatment Act of 1972 (P.L. 92–255), just nine months after his June 1971 message and a year in advance of the scheduled completion of the second report of the National Commission on Marihuana and Drug Abuse.[53] This new legislation reorganized a major part of the federal drug effort, effected important changes in the roles of state and local government in the planning and funding of drug treatment services, and expanded the overall size of the federal drug effort by voting higher budget authorizations. Compared with most major legislation, action on this bill was quick and thorough: Two Senate committees and one House committee held hearings on the proposed legislation; after the Senate and House passed differing versions, a Conference Committee ironed out the differences, and then both bodies passed the compromise legislation by unanimous votes.

The final wording of the Drug Abuse Office and Treatment Act showed Congress and the president to be in general agreement on the best organizational arrangements for effectively coordinating the federal drug effort. The basic "supply" and "demand" approach was adopted, and SAODAP was established to coordinate and oversee the development of federal drug-abuse prevention activities,* the "demand" side of the equation. Congress acceded to the president's request that SAODAP be made a part of the executive office of the president. Since at this time the question of the limits of executive authority was uppermost in the minds of many legislators, this was generally interpreted as a strong affirmation of congressional intent to deal decisively with the drug issue. Congress agreed with the president that SAODAP need be only a temporary agency, and established June 30, 1975 as the date by which SAODAP would be replaced by a new National Institute on Drug Abuse, operating within the traditional channels of the Department of Health, Education, and Welfare.

SAODAP's primary responsibilities were to reorganize and direct the federal programs in drug treatment, rehabilitation, education, prevention, training, and research. Moreover, SAODAP would be responsible for coordinating these "demand" efforts with the federal drug law enforcement programs, though the agency would have no authority over the latter. SAODAP's position was a difficult one: Congress and the president expected it to coordinate, "from outside and above," the activities of fourteen agencies that until then had existed in relative autonomy; to attain its goal in a short period of time; and to coordinate these activities in a field where there was considerable disagreement as to the most effective means of dealing with the problems.

To help the new agency accomplish these formidable tasks, Congress included in the legislation several provisions designed to insure a coordinated federal drug effort.[54] First, it established SAODAP as a kind of mini–Office of Management and Budget, though limited to the drug-abuse prevention programs of the various federal agencies. SAODAP was empowered to reprogram an agency's drug-abuse prevention funds if necessary to insure greater conformity with the overall policies and priorities it would set. Second, Congress established a special fund of $40 million for SAODAP for each of three fiscal years "to provide additional incentives to Federal departments and agencies to develop more effective drug-abuse prevention functions and to give the Director [of SAODAP] the flexibility to encourage, and respond quickly and efficiently to, the development of promising programs and approaches." Although Congress stipulated that at least 90 percent of these funds had to be spent by federal

---

* The legislation used the term "drug abuse prevention" to refer to all non–law-enforcement drug efforts including treatment and rehabilitation; education, prevention, and training; and research.

agencies other than SAODAP, they had to be spent according to SAODAP directives. Third, SAODAP received the power of "management oversight review." This power, although never actually exercised, gave it the authority to assume the drug-abuse prevention functions of an uncooperative federal agency for up to thirty days. The explicit legislative granting of such power is very rare; the potential authority is usually enough to persuade any recalcitrants of the advantages of cooperation.

Although the purpose of this reorganization was to streamline, coordinate, and make more efficient the federal response, it also effectively muted opposition. In fact, when he signed the legislation enacting SAODAP, President Nixon warned that "heads will roll" if the agency directors did not cooperate with the new office.[55] The president named Dr. Jaffe to direct SAODAP and expand the work he had already begun under executive order. When SAODAP formally began in March 1972, policy and programmatic decisions had essentially been made; it was simply a matter of carrying them out. What reservations there were within and without government were largely ignored or overridden. Recommendations such as those put forth by the National Commission on Marihuana and Drug Abuse in 1972 and 1973 were quickly rejected because they were inconsistent with the policies and programs the administration had already chosen to pursue.

In sum, up to and through the 1972 presidential elections the Nixon administration sought to be (1) *responsive* to the public concern about heroin addiction and heroin-related crime, (2) *effective*, in contrast to the lack of success which had characterized past drug efforts, and (3) *quick*, so that "progress" could be claimed at the earliest possible moment. Most of the bureaucratic restraints which might have impeded the Nixon administration's "war on drugs" had been overcome, so its potential to "solve the drug problem" could be tested.

Deemphasis of the Drug Issue and Emergence of the National Institute on Drug Abuse (NIDA)

Eighteen months after the enactment of the Drug Abuse Office and Treatment Act, and only ten months after his reelection, President Nixon signaled a change in direction by announcing in September 1973, "We have turned the corner on drug addiction in the United States."[56] Although caveats followed this declaration, the announcement was an important milestone in the history of the government's response to illicit drugs. In addition to being a statement of "victory," the president's message also implied disengagement from the war.

In the days and weeks following this announcement, administration officials offered evidence in support of the President's statement.[57] This "evidence" included claims of an apparent shortage of heroin on the East

Coast, an increase in the street price of the drug, an increase in the number of drug seizures and arrests, the expansion of drug treatment availability and utilization, a reported decline in the incidence of new heroin use, and heroin-related crime being down. Not everyone agreed: Some challenged the accuracy of the statistics, others challenged their interpretation. Still other accepted the evidence, but cautioned that the downward trend might only be temporary.

In retrospect, it is clear that the "turn the corner" speech was based on more than statistics. Other factors were also at work, and a brief review of certain events which occurred between June 1971 and September 1973 will help to explain the turnabout.

First, the 1972 presidential election had passed. Though it is difficult to assess what part this may have played in the administration's response to the drug issue, there is little doubt that it had some importance. Illicit drugs were a major political issue, and anyone running for national elective office was expected to address it.

Second, the armies of addicted Vietnam soldiers never materialized. The severity of the problem had been overestimated; among those soldiers who did use opium or heroin in Vietnam, subsequent research showed that relatively few were either dysfunctional or addicted users after their return to the United States.[58]

Third, public interest in the drug issued waned. There were a host of possible explanations for this: The problems had been overdramatized and public fears exaggerated, the rate of urban crime had leveled off, other domestic issues had taken precedence, the media had run out of things to say, or it was simply part of the natural ebb and flow of public interest. Whatever the reasons, there is little question that the public's attention had become diverted elsewhere.

Fourth, the new avenues of response to the use of illicit drugs, which had been pursued with varying degrees of success, had in their combined effect failed to measure up to original expectations, and it seemed unlikely that any further improvement would result from an expanded or intensified effort in these areas.

For example, federal law enforcement efforts against street-level drug activities had backfired. ODALE was not always well received by local law enforcement agencies, and its ability to have a significant impact on street-level drug activities was seriously questioned.[59] In April 1973, ODALE agents were involved in two criticized "no-knock" entries into homes in Collinsville, Illinois. The events in Collinsville precipitated a thorough review of the agency and a reevaluation of the need for unique enforcement authorities against drug dealers and users. In effect, ODALE had gone too far in "bypassing the normal channels." Instead of becoming a positive symbol of how to win a war on drugs, ODALE became the focal point of criticisms about the excesses of that war. On June 30, 1973,

ODALE was abolished in yet another drug-law–enforcement agency re-organization.[60] The position of special consultant to the president for drug-abuse law enforcement matters was also abolished, and Congress subsequently repealed the no-knock and preventive detention sections of the federal statutes. Federal law enforcement strategy reverted to a concentration on the upper levels of drug distribution systems.

The Turkish opium ban did contribute to a shortage of heroin in 1973, principally in the eastern United States. But because the government had been unable to negotiate any other significant bilateral agreements, it became clear that the Turkish ban would have only a temporary effect. The period immediately after the Turkish ban took effect was the high point in terms of any practical significance which it could have had. The demand for heroin and the consequent profits to be realized were bound to generate new supplies and supply routes—it was only a matter of time. Bilateral agreements thus failed to provide any lasting "solution."

Drug treatment programs, methadone programs in particular, had been expanded to a point where everyone voluntarily seeking treatment could get it. Overall, the quality of the treatment offered in methadone as well as drug-free programs improved. Program personnel gained experience and with it increasing expertise. Increased funding assured greater program stability. However, treatment supply exceeded treatment demand; in this crucial respect the administration's goal had been reached: Unless more people were to enter treatment, the maximum short-term impact of this approach had also probably been reached.

The administration, through SAODAP, had also achieved a more coordinated federal effort on the "demand" side. Much overlapping, duplication, and inefficiency had been eliminated. Within the framework of its policies and programs, the federal response was functioning much more smoothly.

And the budget was sufficient; the total FY 74 drug budget was $760 million. Lack of funds no longer limited the potential of the federal drug response; at the same time there was no indication that increasing the budget further would measurably improve the situation.

There seemed little need to any longer maintain a strong White House identification with the drug issue. Within the framework of the policies and programs the administration had chosen to pursue the situation was probably as good as it would get in the foreseeable future. Politically, this may have suggested to the federal government that the issue could be returned to a more "normal" status within the bureaucracy and be dealt with like most other urban and social problems.

Whether or not the president's assessment of the situation in his "turn the corner" speech was correct, it triggered a turn in government activity in the drug field. The more extraordinary measures of the previ-

ous years could no longer be justified. On the contrary, it became necessary for government budget- and policymakers to make major changes in
the federal drug effort in order to prove that a victory had been won.[61]
Even before the president's pronouncement, drug law enforcement programs had been moved away from active White House involvement to a
newly formed Drug Enforcement Administration within the Department
of Justice. Federal efforts against street-level drug dealers and users were
quietly abandoned. International efforts to curtail illicit drug cultivation
and trafficking continued, but were less publicized. SAODAP remained
in existence until June 30, 1975, but it lost its influence after the "turn the
corner" speech. The trend in budget requests was also reversed: The overall treatment and rehabilitation budget for FY 75 (proposed in January
1974) was $33 million less than in the previous fiscal year, marking the
first drug budget cutback in the Nixon administration.[62] Furthermore, the
administration sought increasingly to shift drug programming responsibilities to the states, under the aegis of its "new federalism" policies.

The combined effect of these actions was significantly to reduce the
visibility and controversy of the federal drug effort. This was beneficial in
the sense that the drug issue was temporarily freed from the political rhetoric that had bound it. But the loss of momentum was unfortunate to the
extent that the government's opportunity to shape a more comprehensive
approach to drug problems in America was not decisively acted upon.

One of the most important and lasting byproducts of this chain of
events was the creation of a new agency, the National Institute on Drug
Abuse (NIDA) within HEW. This was created by a departmental reorganization announced by the Secretary of Health, Education, and Welfare on September 23, 1973. The announcement occurred more than a
year in advance of the congressional requirement in the Drug Abuse Office and Treatment Act of 1972 for the creation of such an agency no later
than December 30, 1974.[63]

Organizationally, NIDA was made a fourth-level agency in HEW.
As Figure 1.3 illustrates, the director of NIDA is one of three agency directors reporting to the administrator of the Alcohol, Drug Abuse, and
Mental Health Administration (ADAMHA). The administrator of
ADAMHA is, in turn, one of six Public Health Service officials reporting
to the assistant secretary for health, who in turn is one of many assistant
secretaries reporting to the secretary of HEW.

Despite this organizational arrangement, NIDA was charged with
providing "leadership, policies and goals for the Federal effort in the prevention, control and treatment of narcotic addiction and drug abuse, and
the rehabilitation of affected individuals." Clearly, NIDA was intended
to succeed SAODAP as the lead agency on the "demand" side of the federal drug effort.

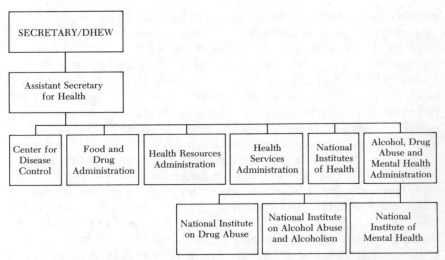

Source: Peter Goldberg and Carl Akins, "Issues in Organizing for Drug Abuse Prevention," in *Governmental Response to Drugs: Fiscal and Organizational* (Washington, D.C.: Drug Abuse Council, 1974), p. 27.

FIGURE 1-3.   NIDA Position within the HEW Hierarchy

But NIDA was not and could not be a substitute for SAODAP. SAODAP was designed to be a policy and coordinating office, with minimal direct program responsibilities. NIDA was given the bulk of drug treatment program responsibilities but very limited coordinating powers. Much of SAODAP's authority was contained in P.L. 92–255, and most of those powers were not transferable to NIDA without congressional approval. Even if the powers were to be transferred, the decisions and directions taken by NIDA, buried as it was within HEW, would obviously have attracted less attention and carried less weight than when the very same actions were announced by a White House office.

Although the earlier-than-anticipated emergence of NIDA and diminution of SAODAP made many of those involved with drug treatment and prevention anxious about the future, some found solace in the fact that the drug treatment and prevention effort had been removed from the immediate control of NIMH. Under the HEW reorganization NIDA was established as separate and equal to NIMH. Similarly, responsibility in the alcoholism field had been removed from NIMH and given to another new separate and equal agency, the National Institute on Alcohol Abuse and Alcoholism. The effect of removing NIMH control from these fields was to allow each to more fully develop its own approaches. Inasmuch as drug problems in many respects lie outside traditional mental health concerns, the creation of NIDA independent of NIMH was applauded by many people in the drug treatment and prevention fields.

The Arguments for and against the Continuation of SAODAP

Even though NIDA was in full operation by mid-1974, SAODAP continued to function until its expiration date of June 30, 1975, though with greatly reduced staff levels and diminished bureaucratic status. It was maintained to exercise those coordinating functions which could not legally be transferred to NIDA. Moreover, it provided the drug treatment and prevention fields with a symbolic organizational parity with drug law enforcement concerns, a role which NIDA could not fulfill.

By early 1975, questions were being raised about the implications of SAODAP's impending demise. The future direction and scope of the federal drug effort seemed uncertain. Gerald Ford had succeeded Richard Nixon as president, and Ford's views and commitment regarding the drug field were largely unknown.

In March 1975, Senator William Hathaway, chairman of the Senate Subcommittee on Alcoholism and Narcotics, introduced legislation amending the Drug Abuse Office and Treatment Act of 1972. The proposed legislation called for a modified version of SAODAP, to be called the Office of Drug Abuse Prevention Policy (ODAPP), which would continue certain policymaking and coordinating functions of the predecessor agency. The expiration of SAODAP along with other provisions of P.L. 92–255—including funding authorizations for future federal treatment, prevention, and research efforts—gave Congress its first opportunity to review both the 1972 legislation and the status of the federal response.[64]

This congressional review prompted President Ford to direct the Domestic Council to undertake its own assessment in order to define more clearly the administration's drug policies and prepare the administration's response to any congressional action.[65] These congressional and executive office assessments reconsidered the tone and approach of the government's response to illicit drug use in a distinctively less politicized way than had marked the crisis atmosphere during the Nixon administration.

Both Congress and the administration sought to back away from the warlike rhetoric of the Nixon administration. The emphasis on "victories" and "solutions" was replaced by more cautious statements about "goals" and "objectives." Congress amended its Declaration of National Policy by adopting more temperate wording. The Domestic Council Report to the president was even more straightforward with respect to its assessment of goals:

> We should stop raising unrealistic expectations of total elimination of drug abuse from our society. At the same time, we should in no way signal tacit acceptance of drug abuse or a lessened commitment to continue aggressive efforts aimed at eliminating it entirely. The sobering fact is that some members of any society will seek escape from the stresses of life

through drug use. Prevention, education, treatment, and rehabilitation will curtail their number, but will not eliminate drug use entirely. As long as there is demand, criminal drug traffickers will make some supply available, provided that the potential profits outweigh the risks of detection and punishment. Vigorous supply reduction efforts will reduce, but not eliminate, supply. And reduction in the supply of one drug may only cause abuse-prone individuals to turn to another substance.

All of this indicates that, regrettably, we will probably always have a drug problem of some proportion. Therefore we must be prepared to continue our efforts and our commitment indefinitely, in order to contain the problem at a minimal level, and in order to minimize the adverse social costs of drug abuse.[66]

This acknowledgment of the persistence of drug problems and the impossibility of achieving a quick victory had no direct effect on the operational aspects of the various drug programming efforts; it only sought to adjust public expectations of them.

Congress and the Ford administration relieved some of the anxieties felt in the drug treatment field after the "turn the corner" speech by halting the one-year budget cutback which had been initiated with that speech. Although questions were raised about the adequacy of the administration's budget proposal, many agencies and individuals were pleased simply by this temporizing action.

More serious difficulties between Congress and the president arose over whether some modified version of SAODAP should be continued. Many in Congress argued for such an agency; President Ford and his administration were opposed to it. The proponents of a successor agency to SAODAP contended that White House coordination of the drug effort was still necessary.[67] They held that without some successor to SAODAP the earlier organizational difficulties could easily reappear, maintaining that the logic which dictated congressional approval of SAODAP in 1972 extended to the proposed Office of Drug Abuse Prevention Policy in 1975. Congressional proponents further argued that NIDA, as a fourth-level HEW agency, would never be able to exercise any real control over the "demand" side of the federal drug effort. They pointed out that 51 percent of all federal expenditures for drug prevention programs were made by agencies other than NIDA, and thus concluded that "for NIDA to coordinate and lead the Federal drug abuse prevention effort, both from a structural and from a fiscal perspective, would be difficult at best and, more likely, actually impossible."[68]

President Ford and the Domestic Council Task Force agreed on the need for continued coordination, but they differed with the proponents of ODAPP on the way to achieve it. Rather than have a special White House agency just to coordinate the "demand" side of the federal drug effort, President Ford opted for "strong Cabinet management" of the program.

In April 1976 he created the Cabinet Committee for Drug Abuse Prevention (CCDAP), chaired by the Secretary of HEW, which included the Secretaries of Defense and Labor and the administrator of the Veterans Administration. CCDAP was given responsibility for the oversight and coordination of all federal activities involving drug prevention, treatment, and rehabilitation, integrating the efforts of all the cabinet departments and agencies involved. Moreover, CCDAP was expected to "give HEW, ADAMHA, and NIDA the organizational strength and authority to provide the interdepartmental and interagency coordination needed to maintain the progress which has been made in drug abuse treatment and prevention."[69]

ODAPP's sponsors sought to extend its projected responsibilities of review, formulation, and coordination of drug policies and priorities to *all* drug policies and programs, including drug law enforcement programs and international negotiations. This was to be the major difference between ODAPP and SAODAP, whose authority had been confined to drug treatment, rehabilitation, education, prevention, and research. This proposed extension of authority for ODAPP gained support for several reasons: First, it sought to reconceptualize the federal drug effort by bridging the gap between the enforcement and treatment approaches. ODAPP was envisioned as the forum in government by which the long-standing philosophical conflicts between the medical and law enforcement communities could be faced and, ideally, reconciled.[70] At the very least, ODAPP was being designed to insure a more comprehensive review of the drug programs and policies of the various federal agencies.

Second, this extension of ODAPP's authority was proposed at a time when the balance between drug law enforcement and drug treatment and prevention programs was once again shifting in favor of law enforcement.[71] The drug law enforcement budget was rising while drug treatment and prevention funds remained level; and, bureaucratically, DEA was a higher level agency within the Justice Department than was NIDA in HEW. ODAPP was supported partly in the hope that it could keep a balance between these two principal agencies and their respective approaches to the drug problem.

Third, support for ODAPP stemmed from the congressional desire to have one single administration official with overall responsibility for national drug policy who would be accountable to Congress. At the time Congress was considering ODAPP, officials of the Office of Management and Budget (OMB) were refusing to testify before Congress on drug policy issues, and the directors of the various drug agencies (NIDA and DEA in particular) spoke only for their own programs and policies. The unresolved areas, as well as the overall concerns, of national policy could easily be unintentionally overlooked in this situation. ODAPP was designed to rectify this.[72]

President Ford and the Domestic Council Task Force also recognized the need to coordinate treatment and enforcement approaches. In its report the Domestic Council stated, "Strong coordinative mechanisms are necessary to ensure that the efforts of these [Federal] departments and agencies are integrated into an effective overall program, and that the approach adopted in each is consistent with the President's priorities."[73] However, the administration maintained that such coordination could be attained without a White House agency. Instead, it chose to formalize the division of the drug functions developed during the Nixon administration. Thus the government's response split the effort into three separate areas, each with a "lead agency."[74] The Drug Enforcement Administration was designated as the "lead agency" for drug law enforcement, the State Department for international activities, and NIDA for prevention and treatment. To strengthen interagency coordination within each functional area, President Ford convened three separate cabinet committees, each with oversight and coordination responsibilities within one area.

Going a step further in acknowledging some need for "program oversight and limited interagency coordination at the Executive Office level,"[75] President Ford and the Domestic Council accordingly made several more recommendations.[76] Foremost among them was the recommendation that the Strategy Council on Drug Abuse* be revitalized to provide overall policy guidance and that a small staff at OMB be maintained to assist the Strategy Council and executive office in formulating drug policy. However, these recommendations fell considerably short of a White House Office for drug abuse.

The argument that Congress needed one person or office to be accountable to it for total federal drug policy was rejected by the administration. "The best places to get such information and to seek accountability for progress," said President Ford, "are the departments and agencies which have direct responsibility and program authority."[77]

In point of fact, the arguments raised both for and against ODAPP were illusory. There were other ways to satisfy the needs cited by the proponents of ODAPP, and the creation of ODAPP would not have guaranteed the advantages envisioned anyway. For example, the Ford administration could have coordinated its response to the drug problems of America without an ODAPP, just as it could have allowed the partitions between the medical and legal approaches to continue despite ODAPP's presence.

The ODAPP concept was strongly supported by the majority of individuals, associations, and private organizations working in the drug treatment, rehabilitation, education, prevention, and research fields. All had felt seriously threatened by the funding cutbacks of the Nixon administra-

---

* The Strategy Council, mandated in 1972 by P.L. 92–255, consists of government officials and private citizens appointed by the president.

tion's last budget, and the elimination of SAODAP had added to the uncertainty about future federal commitment. Accordingly, these associations and organizations, many of which had developed during the years of budget expansion, vigorously lobbied Congress to support the small White House agency for drugs as a sign of their support for the drug field. Congressional spokesmen took note of the symbolic importance of ODAPP, explaining that "there is a clear danger that elimination of that office [SAODAP or ODAPP] would have enormous symbolic significance to this field. There is no way in which this move [the elimination of SAODAP], coupled with recent proposals to cut funds, can appear to be anything but a drastic retrenchment in Federal priorities."[78]

The Ford administration's opposition to ODAPP was also symbolic, but not in relation to the drug field. President Ford had committed himself to a reduction of executive office power and a restoration of the powers of the various cabinet departments and federal agencies. He wished to reverse the concentration of power in the White House which had characterized the Nixon administration—a trend to which SAODAP was both a symbolic and a real contributor. To the Ford administration, the negative symbolism of a new White House drug office—even a small one—overrode any positive symbolism it might have conveyed to the drug field.

In March 1976, eight months after SAODAP had expired, Congress passed legislation creating in the White House the Office of Drug Abuse Policy (ODAP, a slight shortening of the originally proposed name).[79] Compared to SAODAP, ODAP was organizationally small and its legislatively granted powers limited, but its coordinating responsibilities extended to law enforcement and international negotiations, thus giving it broader scope than its predecessor.

President Ford signed the legislation creating ODAP only because sections of the same bill contained the necessary funding authorizations to continue federal efforts in drug treatment and prevention. The president remained steadfastly opposed to ODAP in principle, and in signing the legislation he said:

> I have voiced strong opposition to the reestablishment of a special office for drug abuse in the White House. I believe that such an office would be duplicative and unnecessary and that it would detract from strong Cabinet management of the Federal drug abuse program. Therefore, while I am signing this bill because of the need for Federal funds for drug abuse prevention and treatment, I do not intend to seek appropriations for the new Office of Drug Abuse Policy created by the bill.[80]

This impasse continued throughout Ford's presidency; ODAP had been legally constituted but remained a "paper" agency with neither staff nor funds. Instead, President Ford continued his plan for supervision of government response to illicit drug use through three cabinet committees, one each for law enforcement, international narcotics control, and treatment and prevention.

Government Response under Presidents Ford and Carter

Drug problems and issues faded from the limelight during the Ford administration, a change generally viewed as salutary when compared to the tumultuous years preceding it. Funding levels in all areas remained reasonably stable, as did program operations. Although whatever gains had resulted from the Turkish opium ban were reversed by the new availability of Mexican heroin, no new "wars" were proclaimed. Utilization of existing treatment capacity did increase throughout the country and funding was increased to treat several thousand more people. The Drug Enforcement Administration continued to confiscate large amounts of illicit drugs, but the overall impact on illicit trafficking was marginal.

Guided by the Domestic Council's "White Paper on Drug Abuse," the Ford administration accepted the verdict that the "drug problem" could not be eliminated. Instead of trying to rally public support to end "drug abuse," the administration started seeking to develop greater public tolerance of this ineradicable phenomenon.

Although the style was different and the goals less ambitious, the Ford administration's response to illicit drugs was largely predicated on the same assumptions about the innate harmfulness of illicit drugs that have guided the government's response to drugs throughout the twentieth century. The administration's response continued to rest upon law enforcement or quasi-enforcement strategies fundamentally intended to prohibit new or continued use of nonapproved psychoactive substances. Though these assumptions were not challenged, the limits of any attempt to "solve" the problems of illicit drug use were at last openly acknowledged—a significant change from previous administrations.

In his one major public statement on the use of illicit drugs, President Ford devoted less than three paragraphs to treatment and prevention issues. The remainder of his six-page message to Congress[81] addressed the drug-crime nexus, law enforcement efforts, proposals for mandatory minimum sentences for traffickers and bail denial, the activities of Customs, use of the Internal Revenue Service to go after traffickers, international control and cooperation, and the like. Support for programs in treatment and prevention was derived, as with enforcement, from the longstanding fears and assumptions about illicit drugs, their users, and their effects on society.

When Jimmy Carter became president some observers of the drug field expected swift and significant policy and programmatic changes to result, in part because of Carter's close association with Dr. Peter Bourne, a highly regarded drug program expert. In March 1977, under some pressure from Congress, President Carter activated ODAP, naming Dr. Bourne as its director. It was believed that ODAP might devise a more unified and coordinated government response to illicit drugs, melding the goals and concerns of the treatment, prevention, and enforcement communities.

No sooner had ODAP been activated, however, than President Carter announced his intention of abolishing the office. This announcement was made as part of the Reorganization Plan No. 1 of 1977, in which President Carter sought to streamline and reduce the White House staff. As a result, ODAP expired in April 1978, after completing a series of drug policy studies spanning the treatment, prevention, and enforcement fields.[82] ODAP's legal functions were transferred to the president. Dr. Bourne remained as special assistant to the president in part to "advise the President on drug policy and assist in the coordination of interagency efforts," until his resignation in July 1978. Several ODAP staff members were transferred to the Domestic Policy Staff, where they continue to provide some overall review of drug policy issues. The results of this reorganization resemble the plan of strong cabinet management with "some" executive coordination advocated by the Ford administration.

Shortly after announcing his reorganization plan, President Carter presented Congress with his first major message on drug issues.[83] His primary concern was the fragmentation and lack of coordination among drug programs and agencies. (This organizational problem has persisted in spite of all the attention it has received.) President Carter stressed the continuing need for international cooperation, and directed the individual agencies involved to give the drug issues a high priority. Like Presidents Nixon and Ford before him, Carter stressed international law enforcement efforts to eradicate the illicit cultivation of drugs and interrupt international trafficking networks. And like his predecessors, he urged Congress to ratify the Psychotropic Convention.

With respect to law enforcement, President Carter announced support for programs which would promise "swift and severe punishment" to traffickers in drugs. These programs include the investigation of links between organized crime and drug trafficking, revocation of passports and freezing assets of known major traffickers, support of legislation raising the dollar value of property seized from and forfeited by a drug violator through administrative action, study of possible denial of bail or any release prior to trial for certain major drug-traffic offenders, and the possible emendation of the Tax Reform Act to allow for easier investigation of major traffickers (if this would not infringe on the privacy of citizens). For the most part, these proposals are conceptually indistinguishable from those made by Presidents Nixon and Ford; all sought to enact measures that would deter major drug traffickers in the hope of reducing the availability of illicit drugs at the street level.

As for drug treatment, President Carter called upon NIDA to include more programs for abusers of barbiturates, amphetamines, and combinations of drugs (including alcohol). He supported expansion of rehabilitation and job-training programs for former heroin addicts. President Carter also expressed the need for better coordination of federally sponsored research efforts on a variety of drugs, including opiates, alcohol, and tobacco. He expressed the hope that this would save money and "lead to greater scientific understanding of addiction problems."

In recent years the barbiturates have been recognized as a major drug problem (this problem has resulted in part from their widespread licit medical use). The special attention that President Carter directed to be given to these and other sedative-hypnotic drugs will cover the whole gamut of federal drug response: Prescribing practices of physicians will be reviewed, more intensive efforts will be made to prosecute physicians who deliberately overprescribe, DEA will investigate street marketing activities and audit companies lawfully manufacturing the drugs, and HEW will study the question whether barbiturates should remain on the market. In focusing such specific attention on barbiturate abuse, President Carter took a significant step toward extending the federal government's response to drugs beyond a traditional concern with such illicit drugs as heroin, cocaine, and marijuana.

And in what amounted to his most significant policy break with Presidents Nixon and Ford, Carter endorsed the decriminalization of possession of small amounts of marijuana for personal use, noting that "penalties against possession of a drug should not be more damaging to an individual than the use of the drug itself."

Nevertheless, the overall thrust of President Carter's first major statement on drug issues does not suggest any fundamental changes in the specifics of government response. The tone does suggest a less emotional approach than that of the early 1970s; the inclusion of licit drugs which can be dangerously misused suggests a broader understanding of the concept of "drug abuse"; and the adoption of a marijuana decriminalization position suggests that fundamental changes in government response could occur *after* current policies and programs are clearly, repeatedly shown not to work. But in a broader context President Carter's drug statement further reflects the tortuously slow process by which public opinion and public policy change.

Some Concluding Thoughts

The overriding observation which emerges from a review of the federal government's history of response to illicit drugs is that its drug policy changes slowly if at all. Federal drug *programs* have changed considerably in the past decade, but *policy* remains essentially unchanged. Faith remains strong in the power of criminal sanctions to deter illicit drug use and the effectiveness of law enforcement efforts to eliminate that use which does occur.

Two deeply rooted premises have guided federal response: One is that there are certain drugs which people *should* be prohibited from using under any circumstances. The second is that the government *can* then prevent their use. The first premise is philosophical in nature, the second pragmatic.

The philosophical question of the justification of prohibition can always be argued at great length; there is no single "answer" as such. With respect to the pragmatic issue, the belief that government can prevent illicit drug use, there is more concrete evidence to analyze. The experience of the 1970s clearly shows that even with an extensive, generally efficient, and popularly supported federal effort, it is impossible to prohibit the presence of nonapproved drugs in American society. It is difficult to conceive how that effort might have been expanded or intensified to be more successful while still respecting the traditional values of a free society.

Federal policymakers are by now generally cognizant of the limits of current federal drug policy. Why then do they continue to pursue the same fundamental policies? Because the public demands it; to relax the prohibitionary goal is tantamount to being "soft on drugs" (a most pejorative term that has been used in ugly ways to cast aspersions on those who question the wisdom of prohibition). In a democratic society, policymakers cannot stray too far from what the public wants or they will simply be replaced. Federal drug policy will not change substantially until there is public support to do so.

But federal drug officials have not conveyed to the public an understanding of the limits to their potential accomplishments; it is far easier politically to highlight occasionally successful programs and to emphasize long-range goals or aspirations. Policymakers also seem reluctant to engage the public in a discussion of the philosophy of drug prohibition. One reason for this difficulty is that for many years the federal government fueled the popular demand for drug prohibition. Yet those who are familiar with drug policy recognize now that the designation of certain drugs as illicit and as targets for prohibition has roots in racism, hysteria, and sensationalism. It is also now apparent, based on current knowledge about drugs and their effects, that prohibition has been based on much misinformation and misunderstanding.

In the context of these general observations, the following concluding thoughts are offered:

1. The most important contribution which federal drug agencies can now make to future drug policy is to provide the American public

with opportunities to carefully and sensibly reexamine the wisdom of drug prohibition. Even though they are now more than five years old, the two reports of the National Commission on Marihuana and Drug Abuse would still make an excellent starting point for this reappraisal process.

2. Until the drug issue becomes less vulnerable to sensationalism, there is no way to guarantee that excesses in the federal drug effort, such as those of the early 1970s, can be prevented. Federal drug policies and programs ought to be the product of careful, thoughtful consideration. Impulsive, hastily conceived programs such as ODALE can do great damage to our society.

3. The federal drug effort needs greater coordination; the treatment, enforcement, and international components cannot be left to go their own ways. Coordination without "teeth" has been more superficial than substantive.

4. From a policy, bureaucratic, and budgetary perspective, criminal justice and drug law enforcement agencies have been too dominant in our national response to the abuse of psychoactive drugs. This dominance has not served society well; rather than bringing out the best in us, it has led us to rely too heavily on our meaner, more punitive instincts.

APPENDIX A: A Budget Perspective

Overview of Fiscal Years 1970–1978.   It is impossible to account exactly for all funds expended on the federal government's response to illicit drugs. The figures presented in this report are, however, sufficiently accurate to be used for an overall fiscal analysis and review of significant trends and priorities. Table 1.1 presents the federal drug budget by function for fiscal years 1970–1978.

From July 1969 through September 1978, the federal government spent approximately $5.7 billion on its drug-related efforts. Of this total, $2.4 billion was spent on treatment and rehabilitation, $2.3 billion on law enforcement, and the remainder ($.95 billion) was spent on education, prevention, and training ($.4 billion), research ($.4 billion), and planning ($.15 billion).

The effect which the "war on drug abuse" had on the budget is clearly demonstrable beginning with FY 72 (which began July 1, 1971, two weeks after President Nixon's special message to Congress). (See Figure 1.4.) The most rapid expansion of the federal drug budget occurred during FY 72 and FY 73. After FY 74 and Nixon's "turn the corner" speech, the rate of budget expansion slowed considerably. (In fact, if adjusted for inflation, the buying power of the federal drug effort was lower in FY 78 than it had been since FY 72.) Still, although the annual rate of growth of the federal drug budget slowed, the absolute size at which its annual total more-or-less leveled off was much higher than ever before. The average annual federal drug expenditure for the years 1974–78 was over $800 million; for 1973–78—a six-and-one-quarter-year period—it totaled $5 billion.

Perhaps the most useful index of federal priorities in the drug area is a comparison of the treatment and rehabilitation budget with the law enforcement budget. Figure 1.4 displays the rapid growth of the treatment and rehabilitation bud-

TABLE 1.1   Federal Government Drug Budget by Function, FY 70–78

	Treatment and Rehabilitation[a]	Education, Prevention, and Training	Research	Planning	Total for Drug Abuse Prevention	Law Enforcement	Total
FY 70	33.5[b]	8.5	17.1		59.1	42.8	101.9
71	86.8	38.2	21.5		146.5	65.9	212.4
72	196.1	50.4	42.2		288.7	125.8	414.5
73	350.3	45.7	64.3	23.9	484.2	200.0	684.2
74	329.4	58.6	52.1	21.7	461.8	292.1	753.9
75	309.9	65.6	48.3	23.0	446.8	320.8	767.6
76	321.9	55.6	46.4	28.5	452.4	370.8	823.2
TQ[c]	80.5	13.9	11.6	7.1	113.1	92.7	205.8
77	367.6	47.1	43.8	25.3	483.8	381.5	865.3
78	366.0	48.2	43.8	25.5	483.5	400.6	884.1
TOTAL	2,442.0	431.8	391.1	155.0	3,419.9	2,293.0	5,712.9

[a]Beginning with FY 73, treatment and rehabilitation estimates include estimates for SRS (later HCFA) funds expended through Medicaid/Medicare and other assistance programs of that agency. FY 78 HCFA funds are estimated at FY 77 level. Budget Authority is used wherever and whenever possible.

[b]In millions of dollars.

[c]Transition Quarter between administrations computed as 25 percent of FY 76 totals.

SOURCES: FY 70, 71, 72 figures from *Dealing with Drug Abuse;* FY 73 figures from *Governmental Response to Drug Abuse: Fiscal and Organizational;* FY 74, 75, 76, 77, 78 figures from charts prepared for ODAP.

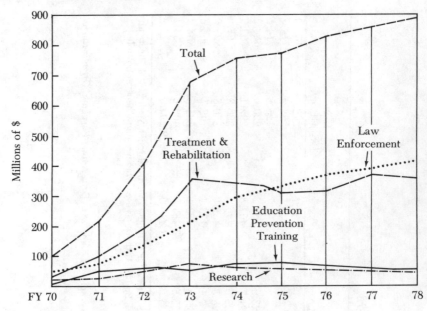

Source: See Table 1-1.

FIGURE 1-4.   Federal Government Drug Budget by Function, FY 1970-78

get between FY 71 and FY 73; however, since FY 73 it has alternately declined and increased, ending up at nearly the same level as in FY 73 ($366 million in FY 78 compared to $350 million in FY 73). The drug law enforcement budget, on the other hand, has risen steadily, doubling in size from $200 to $400 million in the same time period.

If we look at these items in a slightly different way—as a percentage of the total federal drug expenditure for each year—we find a rapid expansion of the treatment and rehabilitation strategy between FY 71 and FY 73 and detectable slippage since FY 73 (Figure 1.5). In contrast, the percentage of the total drug effort allocated to law enforcement rose from a low of 29 percent in FY 73 to 45 percent, its highest level, in FY 78.

This apparent reversal in strategy in the period FY 71-73—with treatment more heavily funded than enforcement—is explainable insofar as one accepts the thesis that drug treatment programs—in particular, methadone treatment programs—derived at least part of their government support from concern more with reducing criminal recidivism that with reducing heroin recidivism. If so, then recent government response to illicit drug use has remained rather consistently dominated by an enforcement approach, as indeed it has since the early 1900s. Moreover, insofar as drug treatment has been funded because of its crime reduction potential, it may have been in part ill-defined as "treatment" in a traditional health context. The pursuit of this avenue of response—crime reduction through treatment—may offer a reasonable explanation for the brief reversal during FY 71-73 in the traditional balance between treatment and enforcement approaches. If so, this adds greater credence to the contention that the underlying assumptions

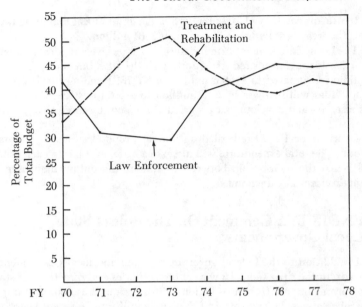

Source: See Table 1-1.

FIGURE 1-5. **Comparison of Federal Drug Budget for Drug Law Enforcement and Treatment and Rehabilitation, FY 1970–78**

and strategies of the government's response to illicit drugs has changed very little in the 1970s.

The FY 79 Budget Request. President Carter released his proposed FY 79 budget on January 20, 1978. Inasmuch as this budget request is the first one fully prepared by the Carter administration it is logical to turn to it for any signs of impending changes in the government response to drugs. The currently available budget documents suggest that it will remain essentially unchanged. However, a complete analysis is precluded because neither OMB nor ODAP has compiled drug-related expenditures on an agency-by-agency basis as they previously did every year since 1971. Without that compilation it is not possible to add in agency expenditures for third-party reimbursement, nor is it possible to estimate accurately either the non-line-item expenditures of federal agencies or how block grants will be used.

Thus at this time it is not possible to include the FY 79 figures in our tables and figures. This absence of an overall analysis of the drug budget by either OMB or ODAP could allow a return to a situation where agency drug budgets dictate overall federal drug policy rather than the other way around.

In the absence of an overall analysis of the federal drug budget, the budget proposals for NIDA and DEA—the two principal federal drug agencies—may serve as a useful surrogate. NIDA's budget will increase to $275.2 million in FY 79, a $13.1 million increase over FY 78. The greater part of this increase—$11.8 million—is earmarked for research, in response to the preliminary recommendations of the president's Commission on Mental Health. NIDA will continue to support a treatment capacity of 102,000, with a maximum local matching rate of 40 percent; the treatment budget will remain at $161 million.

The Drug Enforcement Administration will receive a modest budgetary increase if President Carter's request is approved; the DEA budget for FY 79 will be $193 million, compared to $188.5 million in FY 78. Funding for direct enforcement activities will increase by $4.2 million to a total of $137.2 million, while DEA's research and development program will be cut by more than half to $2.3 million.

Overall, the FY 79 federal drug budget proposal seems to maintain the status quo. The total expenditure will increase a little, as it has in each of the past several years; the relationship between treatment and enforcement approaches will remain essentially unchanged.

APPENDIX B: A Comment On The Role of State and Local Governments*

In addition to the federal government, state and local governments have been active in the drug field. However, the activities and directions of state and local governments vary from jurisdiction to jurisdiction, thus making it impossible to generalize about these efforts as if they were uniform. In recent years, organizations such as the National Association of State Drug Abuse Program Coordinators, the National League of Cities, and U.S. Conference of Mayors have attempted to catalog expenditures at the state and local level and offer some general analysis of policy decisions and program directions. The Drug Abuse Council cannot add substantively to that information.

One important issue, however, deserves comment, that of the intergovernmental system for planning and programming established by the Drug Abuse Office and Treatment Act of 1972 (P.L. 92–255). The system, perhaps inadvertently, has resulted in a nearly total absence of any sustained, systematic large-city government participation in the state or federal policy making and program planning processes. It is an inexplicable situation, since the nation's most severe drug problems are concentrated in its large central cities.

The conditions of heroin addiction and crime which initially prompted an expanded federal response to illicit drug use in the early 1970s were concentrated in the larger cities of this country. In fact, the increased federal response was required partly because the scope and extent of the problems associated with addictive drug use had far transcended the ability of city governments to respond effectively. Also, state governments—whose legislatures were frequently dominated by rural and suburban interests—were often reluctant to become extensively involved in what they felt was essentially a central-city problem. Before the passage of the Drug Abuse Office and Treatment Act of 1972, only New York, California, and Illinois had undertaken major efforts in drug treatment and prevention.

Nevertheless, when the federal government began its large-scale expansion of the drug effort, the states lobbied for and succeeded in obtaining the major role in that effort. The role of local government was ignored; large cities—where the

* The material for this appendix is largely drawn from a paper by Peter Goldberg, "The Role of the City in Responding to the Problems of Drug Abuse," in *Rehabilitation Aspects of Drug Dependence*, ed. Arnold Schecter (Cleveland: CRC Press, 1977).

social costs of illicit drug use are the most severe—were left out of the formal policymaking and funding process. This imbalance between city and state responsibilities can be traced to the congressional authorization of annual formula (block) grants to states, detailed in Section 409 of the Drug Abuse Office and Treatment Act. In return for the block grants, Congress required each state to establish a drug abuse coordinating agency and annually prepare a drug abuse plan to meet treatment and prevention needs. Thus Congress, in effect, required even nonurban states such as North Dakota, Vermont, and Montana—states having comparatively small drug problems—to plan a drug abuse response effort, while cities such as Newark, Detroit, New Orleans, Boston, and Los Angeles were ignored in the legislation.

The resulting problems were first of all political. Large-city concerns and needs tend to be underrepresented at the state level of government, where rural and suburban interests are disproportionately powerful. Moreover, blacks and other minority populations have added yet another political concern, most clearly articulated in a resolution passed by the National Black Caucus of Local Elected Officials in June 1974.

> Whereas, unfortunately, the problems of drug abuse have disproportionately affected large numbers of Black and Spanish-speaking Americans, these minority populations tend to be most underrepresented at the state level where drug abuse policies are being increasingly formulated, thus creating a large discrepancy between those most afflicted by the problems and those establishing the policies and procedures to solve the problems.

In addition to these political concerns, the drug problems themselves in rural and suburban areas are often quite different from those in the central city. While heroin may be the major drug of abuse (alcohol excepted) in the large cities, other parts of a state are usually concerned with other drugs. And while treatment may be the most pressing need in dealing with heroin addiction in the central city, the emphasis desired or demanded by the rest of the state may be for education and prevention programs. Although the larger cities may want increased funding for methadone programs, other areas of the state where heroin is not a problem may be unsympathetic to this use of one addictive drug to treat another. In the final analysis, different units of government are bound to have different needs, priorities, and philosophies, all justified from their own perspectives.

The imbalance between state and large-city determinations of problems and priorities has become further aggravated as the principal federal drug treatment and prevention agency, NIDA, has sought to become more reliant on state plans in determining federal funding decisions. In fact, NIDA has recently announced its intention to fund virtually all of its treatment and prevention efforts through statewide services contracts with state governments by 1979. It is argued that this will be administratively efficient; but this increasing substitution of state decision making for federal does not augur well for the large cities, where drug and drug-related problems are most severe.

In some instances a strong state role has worked well; this is most often true in states where there are no large urban centers. But in many other instances, potentially serious problems between state and large-city governments have impeded the effective flow of funds and delivery of services. City organizations such as the National League of Cities and the U.S. Conference of Mayors have repeatedly expressed their dissatisfaction with the lack of state responsiveness to large-city needs in the drug area. Representatives of a number of large-city governments have also voiced strong and specific complaints about this. There is clearly a need to make some adjustments in the state planning process so that plans more adequately and appropriately allow for large-city needs and participation. Such adjustments can be made without dismantling the state planning system.

NIDA and the cities need to communicate more directly on drug issues and learn more from one another. To an unfortunate extent federal drug policies are formulated without discussion or collaboration with local elected officials from areas where drug and drug-related problems are particularly severe. This situation must be remedied if our drug policies and programs are to work more efficiently. NIDA needs to develop mechanisms by which it can more aggressively and systematically seek large-city government input in its deliberations, and, conversely, cities need to develop a better understanding of why NIDA does what it does. The concept of an Office of Urban Services within the NIDA bureaucracy to facilitate these crucial interactions would seem to have merit.

Finally, NIDA should seriously consider initiating a program to fund city coordinating agencies with responsibility for developing city-wide drug abuse plans in a number of cities with the highest concentrations of drug-related problems. These plans should provide for interaction with the state government. Cleveland needs such an agency and plan far more than does the state of Idaho, Atlanta more than Vermont.

A federal system that funds only state drug abuse plans and agencies is either focusing solely on administrative ease or operating in ignorance of the actual problems. Plans should not proliferate uncontrollably across the country, but if the federal government is to require planning it should at least make certain that there will be direct participation from those areas most afflicted and concerned. An additional benefit of funding city agencies would be that it would give local elected officials a dependable and developed local source of advice and assistance on drug issues and problems.

2 Drug-Law Enforcement Efforts

John R. Pekkanen

WHEN THE CITY of San Francisco passed an ordinance in 1875 banning the smoking of opium in "opium dens," it marked the first time a law prohibiting the use of narcotics was enacted in this country. Since then cities, states, and the federal government have enacted a great number of drug laws. Some have been stringent, others more lenient. Some were passed during politically volatile periods when "get tough" approaches were thought to be the answer; others were passed during calmer times when more moderate approaches were sought.

To understand why we embarked on a course of prohibition for particular drugs is a difficult and elusive undertaking, too affected by deeply rooted attitudes and prejudices to allow for completely dispassionate inquiry. Drug laws from their inception were a special breed. In effect, the passage of these prohibitory laws created crimes by definition; drug activities derived their criminal label more from prevailing attitudes and prejudices than from actual threats to persons or property. These were laws by which people could and did express social disapproval, and were not in the tradition of laws enacted to protect us from those who steal, murder, or commit fraud. They were the means by which right and wrong were distinguished according to popular but arbitrary national values and mores.

In many instances, a proposed drug law would begin as an attempt to control the use of a certain substance, such as opium, cocaine, or mari-

The author acknowledges with gratitude the contributions of James Weissman and Paul Danaceau.

juana. The rhetoric surrounding the proposed antidrug law would usually call for the preservation of predominant social and moral values, and it would be offered as a means of restoring those "lost" values. Frequently such a law would be directed at an outcast or minority segment of society identified with the use of the drug.[1] Supporters of the law would offer it as a solution to a wide range of social, moral, racial, political, and economic problems—from unemployment and crime in the streets to preserving the white race.

Early in the consideration of the Harrison Narcotic Act (the first major federal antinarcotics act[2]), there was some discussion about the hazards of legislating morality, but these cautions were soon put aside. In essence, the Harrison Narcotic Act was a tax law enacted to achieve a moral end, similar in that regard to the Volstead Act prohibiting alcohol. Since then, drug laws and the enforcement policies which flow from them have never been seriously challenged.

In his study of alcohol prohibition, *Symbolic Crusade: Status Politics and the American Temperance Movement*,[3] Joseph Gusfield examines the components of criminal law and separates them into "instrumental" and "symbolic" aspects. Applied to antidrug laws, the "instrumental" aspect is what the law states as its intention—i.e., the prevention of the use and availability of certain drugs. The "symbolic" aspect may have an importance as great as or greater than that of the instrumental*: In the case of antidrug laws, part of the symbolic function has been to define users of particular drugs as abnormal and to designate their behavior as criminal. When this labelling process was attempted with alcohol prohibition as well, it failed because the number of alcohol users in the country was so large and diverse that no one group could be singled out and designated as "abnormal" exclusively because of drinking alcohol.

However, the use of certain drugs, such as opium, heroin, and—until the 1970s—marijuana was most often primarily confined to subgroups and minorities, whose separation and isolation were more easily accomplished. This fact partly explains why only congressional approval was needed to ban narcotics and marijuana, while alcohol prohibition required a constitutional amendment, and why when antidrug laws have appeared to be unsuccessful their total repeal has never been seriously considered, although repeal was possible with alcohol prohibition.

In the material that follows, the law enforcement approach to the control of certain drugs will be discussed from five perspectives: the development of the laws themselves; how the agencies charged with enforcing drug control laws have gone about their task; the relationship between

---

*These two functions of the law were best exemplified by the report of the National Commission on Marihuana and Drug Abuse, which called for the retention of laws against simple marijuana possession but not enforcement of those laws. The law by itself would discourage use, it was argued, and not enforcing it would avoid stigmatizing those who did use the drug.

drug use and crime; a case study of the impact of the nation's "toughest" drug control law, the New York State Drug Law Amendments of 1973; and the impact of drug law enforcement on illicit drug-using behavior.

Drug Control Laws and Policies

Efforts to control certain drugs have come in cycles, focusing on specific drugs during specific periods.[4] Generally, the demand for tough drug control has been most vociferous during periods of economic or political turmoil in the United States. The antiopium crusade began during the depression of the 1870s; the anticocaine crusade came during a period of racial turmoil in the South.[5] Federal sanctions against selected drugs toughened considerably betwen 1915 and 1920, during the first "Red Scare"; the prohibition of alcohol was of course also effected during this period. Later, during the depression of the 1930s, the entry of many Mexicans and Mexican-Americans into the labor market in the Southwest appears to have been a major cause of the antimarijuana crusade and attendant laws. The creation of the Federal Bureau of Narcotics (FBN) in 1930 established the preeminence of law enforcement in the drug field, a fact which has not changed over the years. The FBN's initial major drug targets were heroin and marijuana; this policy lasted for more than thirty-five years.[6]

In the 1940s drug control activities remained relatively stable. There were no new demands for harsh laws or policies. States adopted legislation comparable to the Harrison Act, the major federal drug law, and this tightened the nation's drug prohibition policy. There were also outbreaks of concern over the misuse of legitimately produced drugs—amphetamines and barbiturates were the most widely abused—but these drugs escaped the full force of the antidrug effort. By 1950, however, the atmosphere had changed, and many voices demanded new, tougher antidrug laws.[7]

Between 1947 and 1950, an apparent increase in illicit drug use was reported among blacks and Puerto Ricans in many northern cities. This caused alarm, creating support for passage of a new, more stringent drug law in 1951. Commonly called the Boggs Act after its sponsor, the late Representative Hale Boggs, it enacted the harshest penalties for drug law violations to date.[8] Historian David Musto notes in *The American Disease*, "Hale Boggs's bill, which contained mandatory sentences, was passed in 1951 at the beginning of the McCarthy era and fears of Societ aggression, the 'betrayal' of China to the Communists, and suspicion of domestic groups and persons who seemed to threaten overthrow of the government."[9] In 1956 an even more severe federal narcotics bill was enacted which empowered a jury to impose the death penalty on anyone over the age of eighteen selling heroin to anyone under the age of eighteen.[10] Several states also enacted extremely harsh laws during this period, imposing heavy penalties for both sellers and users.

This "tough" approach was eventually moderated; the mid-1960s marked the beginning of a more comprehensive approach to drug law enforcement. New criminal laws regulated "dangerous drugs"—i.e., legally produced hallucinogens, stimulants, and depressants. These laws were more moderate in tone and substance, and marked a belated attempt at more uniform policy at the federal level for the control of legitimate and illegitimately produced drugs. The previous concern had been exclusively with a very few illicit drugs like heroin, cocaine, and marijuana.

The present era in drug law enforcement, an outgrowth of the 1960s, was inaugurated during the Nixon administration which organized an intensified, coordinated federal antidrug program. This was the heralded "war on drug abuse."[11] The Comprehensive Drug Abuse Prevention and Control Act of 1970 replaced the former crazy-quilt of criminal drug law statutes which had been gradually patched together since the beginning of the century.[12] Through the Controlled Substances Act portion of the legislation, psychoactive drugs were placed into five schedules according to their presumed potential hazards. The federal drug bureaucracy, which had gradually grown since the 1920s, was restructured and further expanded.

As important as these steps were in modernizing the American approach to drug control and in moderating the Draconian criminal penalties of the 1950s, the new era did not break significantly with the past in any fundamental way. The law enforcement approach to drug use remained fixed and, except for a relatively brief period, continued to receive the bulk of federal dollars expended in the drug field. Popular notions about drugs were not significantly altered, nor were traditional responses seriously questioned. The beliefs in the almost mystical power of illicit drugs over people may have become more sophisticated, but they did not change radically. Users of opiate drugs, instead of being viewed merely as criminals, were now charitably viewed as "sick" criminals. But they were still viewed as criminals, and still are.

Perhaps one of the most important ideas to remain unchanged was the belief in a direct link between illicit drugs and crime. This presumed link, which had been the basis for the harsh drug laws of the past, remained a permanent fixture. The nature of this assumed relationship—as is discussed in later sections of this chapter—has undergone some changes, but the basic belief in a causal link has not.

Whatever the causes and motives behind the nation's drug laws, the inescapable conclusion from the more than one hundred years of experience since the first prohibitory law was enacted is that they have not stopped or even diminished the use of illicit drugs. For example, in 1924 the U.S. Public Health Service estimated the opiate addict population at two hundred fifteen thousand[13]; although imprecise, this figure is considered to be the most reliable of that period. In 1976 the National Institute on Drug Abuse (NIDA) estimated the heroin addict population at five hundred thousand; other recent studies indicate that the figure for all types of heroin users may be two to four million.[14] Allowing for population increases, there are more heroin users today than there were a half century ago. The same appears to hold true for users of other illicit drugs.

Because of such findings, our drug laws and policies are more openly questioned today than at any point in the past. On one hand there are those who argue that government has no right at all to intervene in the private lives of individuals. This view holds that drug use is essentially a private act, and that therefore government ought not intervene unless drug-taking leads to socially disruptive or criminal behavior. A more pragmatic aspect of this position is the feeling that laws and policies can do little to diminish the supply of illicit substances because of the enormous profitability involved and the consequent development of highly organized "black market" distribution networks. It is argued that the government's resources could be better used in attempting to change the conditions that contribute to illicit drug use—i.e., poverty, unemployment, and other social problems—than to continue self-defeating efforts to eliminate the supply and use of particular drugs.

On the other hand, there are those who feel the government's anti-drug effort is doing about as well as can be expected in cutting back the supply of illicit drugs, short of abridging everyone's civil liberties. They argue that if law enforcement programs did not attempt to diminish supply and frighten some individuals from using drugs, our drug problems might be far greater than they are. Then there are those who argue we are not doing nearly enough, that more severe and repressive approaches and policies are needed if we are to combat and eradicate the "enemy, drug abuse." In its extreme form, this latter view holds that no price is too great to pay in order to achieve this end.

However, much of the debate over drug control laws has failed to focus sufficiently on the difficulties involved in enforcing them. Passing a drug law is only one part of a control effort; enforcing it is quite another. It is important to understand that even when operating at maximum effectiveness, there are serious limits to what law enforcement agencies can achieve.

One of the primary problems that American drug law enforcement must face is that the drug laws and drug policies have been consistently oversold by public officials. Burglary laws are not expected to eliminate burglary, and penalties for armed robbery are not expected to eliminate that crime; yet drug laws are expected to eliminate illicit drug sale and use. A standard has been set for drug laws that was never set for other laws. More has frequently been promised than could possibly be delivered. Consequently, as long as illicit drug use has persisted, the policies against it have been regarded by some as abject failures. What is needed in any discussion of drug control policies is a realistic notion of what they can and cannot achieve, and what their costs and benefits are. Only when we understand this will the long cycle of overreaction to the use of particular drugs subside.

Law Enforcement Activities

Basically, there are two strategies by which law enforcement seeks to discourage illicit drug use: The first seeks to disrupt and discourage use by enforcing domestic laws against drug use and internal trafficking; the second seeks to prevent supplies of illicit drugs from entering the country, either by preventing their cultivation abroad or by intercepting shipments to the United States. The latter strategy is largely the work of federal agents, although state and local agencies may occasionally participate. The efforts to control illicit drug use within the United States are conducted by federal, state, and local agents. Occasionally these different levels of government join forces and work together; all too frequently, however, they act independently, jealously guarding their "turf" (i.e., their resources and sources of information) from one another.

At the federal level the Drug Enforcement Administration (DEA), at present the chief drug enforcement agency, has over four thousand employees, of whom over two thousand are agents.[15] (While this number may sound impressively large, it merely approximates the size of the New York City Transit Authority Police, a force that patrols the subways and buses in that city). Several other federal agencies play various roles in the enforcement of federal drug laws: Among these are the Customs Service, which attempts to screen incoming persons and freight for illicit drugs; the Internal Revenue Service, which pursues tax law violations of illicit drug traffickers; the Law Enforcement Assistance Administration, which provides research and funding support for state and local drug enforcement; and the U.S. Coast Guard, which patrols coastlines and harbor areas for illicit drug trafficking.[16]

At the state and local level there is a substantially larger number of personnel actively engaged in drug enforcement—the police; but an exact count is not available, since regular patrolmen generally enforce drug laws along with their other duties. Special narcotics units have been established in virtually every major-city police department as well as in many state police departments; most major cities also give some drug law enforcement training to their uniformed patrolmen.

The strategies for controlling both drug use and supplies incorporate a number of variables. The analyses that follow attempt to summarize each strategy and identify some of their costs and benefits.

Controlling Drug Use. Drug enforcement is unlike most other types of police enforcement activities, where generally a crime is committed and reported and the police investigate, gathering evidence and making their case. The victim is central to this process; he or she initiates the police investigation; it is often the testimony of the victim during the trial that convicts the offender.

In drug cases, police usually do not have victims on whom to rely. Not only are there no complainants, but everyone involved conspires to conceal the crime from the police. As a result most illicit drug offenses go entirely undetected; the percentage of violations which result in arrest are extremely low.[17]

Of those drug violations which do result in arrest, more than 75 percent are "spontaneous" arrests involving no prior police investigation.[18] These drug arrests are often incidental to an another investigation. For example, if the driver of an automobile is stopped for a traffic violation and the arresting officer sees marijuana or suspects its presence and finds evidence of a drug law offense, a drug arrest may follow. Such arrests are not due to any overall drug enforcement strategy, but are rather the result of normal, day-to-day police enforcement activities. This helps explain why the overwhelming number of drug arrests are for simple possession, with a majority of these involving marijuana.

Arrests for simple illicit drug possession have little if any impact on the overall availability of illicit drugs because they largely fail to affect drug distribution. The major distributors of illicit drugs conduct their drug transactions in secret, and, as in other activities involving drugs, there are no complainants. Major drug dealers have developed very sophisticated methods of concealment, including drop systems and other subterfuges. Even well-known dealers are usually able to avoid creating probable cause for arrest. Because of this secrecy and the absence of complainants, the fundamental problem police face in making arrests for drug trafficking is proving that something illegal took place. While this can be difficult enough in cases of simple possession, it is extremely difficult with drug trafficking, particularly in developing the so-called "high-level" cases. While many who use illicit drugs participate to some degree in drug distribution (whether for profit or not), those who import and deal in large quantities of particular illicit drugs are not easy to identify, apprehend, or successfully prosecute.

Undercover Investigations. Narcotics officers at the federal, state, and local levels often work undercover, and may become participants in aspects of the offense in order to gather sufficient evidence to prove a crime has been committed. This work is hazardous, time-consuming, and, as one former Deputy Attorney General told Congress, "a dirty, miserable business."[19] The most serious practical shortcoming of undercover operations is that, despite the publicity such operations receive when successful, they result in the arrest of only a miniscule proportion of those engaged in major drug trafficking. Moreover, each undercover operation is so time-consuming, and the number of policemen with the temperament and skill for this work so limited, that the percentage of major arrests would not increase substantially even if every undercover operation were successful.

These problems of investigation are as true at federal as at state and local levels. In fact, one of the persistent criticisms of the federal drug enforcement effort is that the overwhelming majority of arrests are of relatively low-level dealers. A 1975 analysis by the Government Accounting Office of 1974 Drug Enforcement Administration (DEA) arrests revealed that only 604 (3.6 percent) of the total 16,796 arrests were Class I violators, and of these only 63 were convicted.[20] (Class I violators are major international drug traffickers, drug laboratory operators, or wholesalers.)[21] In addition, GAO found only 5 percent of the arrests to be Class II violators, a lesser but still significant category of offenders. However, following congressional hearings and considerable public criticism, DEA appears to have made a major effort to pursue more Class I and II offenders even at the expense of overall arrest figures. DEA statistics for 1976 show only 6,143 total drug arrests, but of these 15 percent were for Class I and 11.9 percent for Class II offenses. Still, nearly three-quarters of the arrests were Class III and IV arrests, a statistic that indicates that major drug trafficking arrests continue to be elusive in spite of increased efforts.[22]

An important consequence of undercover operations is that with arrest and trial of the suspect the undercover officer's cover is "blown" and his usefulness in that line of work in that region is usually ended. This is a serious problem, because good undercover officers are few and far between. Undercover operations also pose a number of legal problems; for example, defense attorneys often argue, sometimes successfully, that the undercover officer is guilty of "entrapment" by having enticed the defendant into committing the crime in question.

Another hazard here is the potential for police corruption. The possibility of corruption through payoffs is always present, because the sums of money involved in illicit drug traffic are enormous—generally estimated to involve several billions of dollars nationally per year—and because the salaries of policemen are generally rather low. Additionally, substantial amounts of "buy" money are provided by law enforcement agencies for this work; in fiscal year 1976, for example, the DEA budget called for $9 million for "buy" money to be used in procuring information and allowing agents to "buy into" drug transactions in the gathering of evidence.[23] All major-city and state narcotics enforcement agencies have substantial amounts of this "buy" money. With these great sums of money the possibilities for corruption can be great. Temptation can be abetted by the fact that the undercover agent is operating in a lawless environment where one's normal sense of right and wrong can become distorted.* In New York City the corruption of narcotics investigators reached serious proportions.[24] After the Knapp Commission revelations, the New York City Police Department instituted a procedure whereby any undercover officer on the Street Crime Unit is required to obtain specific approval by a superior officer to make a drug arrest, and, furthermore, that arrest must be witnessed by the superior officer. This rather cumbersome policy is still in effect today.

Not all forms of corruption involve money, however. As mentioned above, there can also be a corruption of attitude caused by a police officer's constant exposure to the mores of the underworld. In *Buy and Bust* Mark Moore writes, "They [undercover agents] will know more about the violation and the violators they attack than police usually do, and will sometimes have personal interests at stake in the arrests. This invites them to exercise their authority in accordance with their intimate knowledge rather than what the law requires."[25] For example, in some cases undercover police might protect certain dealers who have acted as informants and select others for arrest. Such choices are made not on the basis of law but upon past collaboration or even friendship. Close relationships bred by undercover work can influence a police officer to change his views on the law, what it means, and his requirements to uphold it.[26]

Intelligence Gathering. Many critics have argued that if drug enforcement agencies were to gather and organize intelligence in a more systematic way, more could be done to successfully investigate major drug traffickers. Such intelligence presumably would give more detailed information about the methods drug traffickers employ and accordingly provide a better overall picture of trafficking operations. However, the assumption that better intelligence would lead to more successful enforcement here is open to question. Nevertheless, this debate does highlight another basic problem: That drug enforcement agents traditionally have been hostile toward intelligence functions performed by special units within their own agencies. As Moore notes, "No investigator would be happy to admit [to an intelligence analyst] that he had not mined the files of his organization for every nugget of relevant information."[27] One result is that different agents with different items of information, which if systematically collected and analyzed might provide greater information about drug transactions and networks, often do not share it. Thus the efforts of intelligence units within the DEA and other drug enforcement agencies are often thwarted.

Lack of Coordination. Although many state and local police agencies rely on federal help to train and establish their narcotics units, there is a notable absence of uniformity and coordination between the various levels of law enforcement agencies. As a police chief in one large American city has remarked,

> It's always been a problem over the years to sort out the roles of federal, state and local agencies. My obligations to the citizens of my city are not the same as the Bureau of Narcotics and Dangerous Drugs [now the DEA], for example. They take a systems approach, then make a management by objectives analysis, they can target people and work on them. In the metropolitan police departments, such as this one, we're at the low rung of the law enforcement ladder, and we can't do that. We have to be responsive to the citizen who calls in with just a meager amount of information but expects and is entitled to action on it.[28]

Overlapping jurisdictions, as well as the different emphases given to different drugs and to various aspects of enforcement models, have created conflict. As a result, some local police believe federal drug enforcement should confine itself to interstate and international trafficking and should not involve itself in "local" investigations.

✗ While the basic assumption has been that local police will enforce laws against small-time street dealers and users, state police will enforce laws against the larger dealers, and the federal government will concentrate on the major traffickers and wholesalers, this has not always been the case. The federal government investigates cases throughout the country, sometimes informing state or local police agencies and sometimes not doing so; its cases do not necessarily involve truly major interstate or international violations. Because of these overlaps, the three levels of drug enforcement remain to this day uncoordinated, competitive, and at times conflicting. This continuing lack of coordination, coupled with the other pitfalls of domestic drug enforcement, have at times led to an acute sense of frustration on the part of police, policymakers, and the public. As a consequence, excessive measures periodically find support. One recent, well-known example of this process of frustration and overreaction involved the now defunct Office of Drug Abuse Law Enforcement.

ODALE: A Case History. The Office of Drug Abuse Law Enforcement (ODALE) was established in early 1972 by executive order of President Nixon and charged with the mission of waging an even tougher "war" on illicit drug users and dealers than had been attempted in the past.[29] The brief history of this short-lived agency illustrates the excesses to which a "war on drugs" philosophy can lead. It also highlights the difficult position of drug law enforcement in attempting to enforce the law justly without overstepping constitutional safeguards.

ODALE was criticized from its inception for being an "election-year stunt" while being simultaneously lauded as a bold attempt to fight drug traffickers. ODALE was ostensibly controlled by the Justice Department but actually operated by direction of the White House. Its initial creation was something of a curiosity in that the federal government already had two competing agencies, the Bureau of Narcotics and Dangerous Drugs (BNDD) and the Customs Bureau, in the forefront of its drug control effort. ODALE's potential for engendering yet more bureaucratic rivalry was soon realized; within the space of a few months, the agency had eclipsed the other traditional federal drug enforcement efforts in influence.[30]

ODALE was staffed by employees from a number of federal agencies, including BNDD, Customs, the Internal Revenue Service (IRS), and the Bureau of Alcohol, Tobacco, and Firearms. The agents from these departments were deployed into "strike forces" which were authorized to use "no-knock" search warrants, court-authorized wiretaps, and other search privileges when "incidental to arrest." Furthermore, ODALE could forward the names of suspected drug traffickers to a special committee in IRS which could then initiate special audits or investigations of them.[31]

ODALE received most of its funds from the Law Enforcement Assistance Administration (LEAA), which is empowered by Congress to fund state and local law enforcement units. While it was not within the authority of LEAA to directly fund ODALE, a federal agency, this barrier was skirted by having LEAA make grants to local police departments participating in drug raids with ODALE agents. This funding process also allowed ODALE to circumvent budget appropriation proceedings in Congress. These steps, while apparently within the letter of the law, were not in its spirit, but they went largely unchallenged in the name of fighting "drug abuse."[32]

One of ODALE's first acts was to establish the "heroin hotline," a toll-free number which people could call if they knew or suspected someone of dealing in illicit drugs. Although the "hotline" received abundant publicity its accomplishments in aiding drug enforcement were minimal at most. Only a few months after it was installed, "hotline" callers were told by a recording to call another number; the "hotline" was out of business.[33]

The excesses this new agency fostered came vividly to light on the night of April 23, 1973 in Collinsville, Illinois, when ODALE agents broke into the house of Mr. and Mrs. Herbert J. Giglotto, asleep at the time, routed them out of bed, roughed them up, and accused them of drug dealing. But the ODALE agents had made a mistake and come to the wrong house. They made a second mistaken raid in another home that very night. These events led to the suspension of the involved agents. Eventually they were brought to trial on criminal charges, but were acquitted.[34]

The adverse publicity generated by the Collinsville raids crippled ODALE's effectiveness and power. But the creation of that agency and the extraordinary powers given to it demonstrate how the impulse to combat the use of particular drugs and the uncritical attitude accompanying that impulse can lead to an overzealous approach which can seriously erode constitutional safeguards. The excesses of ODALE were almost predictable, as in past instances when the climate for stamping out illicit drug use was equally extreme.

A number of questions surround ODALE even after its bureaucratic demise. Was it created solely to combat illicit drug use? Why was such a unique agency with unique powers believed to be needed? The answers to these questions are not and may never be clear, because of different interpretations of what ODALE was or attempted to be. What does seem to be clear, however, is that ODALE represented one more attempt to allay public fears by striking hard at illicit drug use with tough enforcement. What is also clear is that in spite of the hoopla surrounding its inception, ODALE's arrest statistics reveal that virtually every individual arrested by the agency was a minor, street-level dealer of little or no consequence.[35]

Controlling Drug Supplies. In addition to efforts to control the numbers of users and distributors of illicit drugs through the criminal justice process, the federal government also has sought to reduce the quantity of illicit drugs available for use. There are two ways American law enforcement agencies have sought to control the supply of illicit drugs: intercepting them as they come into the country, and destroying them at their source in other countries.

Interdiction. Many of the illicit drugs used in this country are produced in foreign nations. One exception is marijuana, which is grown both within and without the United States, although the bulk of it is produced in foreign countries; other exceptions are synthetic psychoactive drugs produced in laboratories (rather than refined from a harvested plant)—e.g., amphetamines, barbiturates, and some hallucinogens. Cocaine and heroin, officially considered to be the major illicit drugs of abuse in the United States, originate in other countries. An obvious—some might say simplistic—drug control strategy is to try to prevent these illicit substances from reaching this country. Upon closer examination, this strategy proves to be an awesome task.

Anyone who has ever passed through American Customs at the Canadian or Mexican borders or our sea- or airports realizes that there is rarely any thorough inspection. The vast numbers who daily cross into and out of American jurisdiction make thorough inspection of every traveler a practical impossibility. In addition, American borders have traditionally been open; constitutional safeguards define the manner and circumstances of searches. Successful seizures of illicit drugs therefore depend more on intelligence information than on the luck of random searches. This intelligence information is usually supplied by American drug agents in foreign countries, who attempt to identify drug traffickers to later be either arrested at the border or kept under surveillance and arrested within the United States. *

However, even with good intelligence information, preventing illicit drugs from entering this country is a difficult, indeed nearly impossible task.[36] When the estimated amount of illicit drugs consumed in this nation is compared with amount seized at our borders or other ports of entry, it is clear that only a very small percentage of the drugs being smuggled into the country are confiscated.

It is estimated, for example, that from twelve to twenty thousand pounds of high-purity heroin are smuggled into this country each year[37]; but in fiscal year 1974 only 115 pounds of high-purity heroin was seized at all U.S. borders and ports. This means that, combining this with the amount of heroin seized internally by the authorities in domestic operations, only 670 pounds of heroin were confiscated that year.[38] By fiscal year 1976, after intensive effort, domestic seizures had increased to a total of 1,124 pounds of heroin, still far short of the total incoming amount. The publicity accorded these seizures, however, often has conveyed the impression that law enforcement agencies are making major inroads against illicit drug smuggling. To a large extent this publicity has been generated by the agency involved in the seizure, for both political and bureaucratic reasons.

Perhaps the most widely used technique for embellishing the importance of a seizure of illicit drugs is to state the "street value" of the seized drug.[39] A seizure of fifteen pounds of heroin, therefore, might not be merely a fifteen-pound seizure, but a seizure of "thirty million dollars' worth of drugs." The "street value" figure is elastic and sometimes exaggerated; it often reflects the most optimistic price a dealer might possibly ask for his drugs. This is analogous to estimating the value of rustled cattle by the price they would bring as steaks at the best restaurants. What is omitted in these claims of the "street value" of drugs seized is the fact that between $5 and $11 billion worth of illicit drugs is sold in this country each year.[40] Thus, $30 million or even $300 million, while significant, is still but a tiny fraction of the total, and has little if any impact on the total amount of illicit sales. However, when seizures drop, enforcement agencies frequently also use the decline to indicate the success of their efforts.

---

*Additionally, international interdiction also has included investigations by U.S. agents abroad in cooperation with foreign governments, and the arrests of drug traffickers in certain countries. However, U.S. agents are now prohibited by law from participating in the arrest of individuals in foreign countries.

By this self-serving logic, the drug law enforcement agencies nearly always can appear to be successful.

Although drug seizure data have often been misused by competing drug agencies to enhance their public images, seizures can have a disruptive effect and present an economic risk to drug traffickers. In addition, limited amounts of these drugs are of course kept out of the illicit market.

Historically, border interdiction has been a major source of rivalry among the federal agencies charged with controlling illicit drugs—specifically, between the Customs Bureau and the Justice Department's drug agencies, from the Federal Bureau of Narcotics to the Bureau of Narcotics and Dangerous Drugs to the present Drug Enforcement Administration.[41] Government reorganizations, as well as a number of other attempts to reconcile these disputes—such as specifying which international areas each agency should be responsible for—have not completely succeeded in quieting this rivalry, although DEA's incorporation of some of the drug enforcement duties of Customs has certainly allayed it.

These jurisdictional disputes have appeared at many critical points in the federal drug enforcement effort. For example, when drug agents in a foreign country obtain information regarding a significant drug-smuggling attempt, this information would ideally be relayed to the U.S., in order to effect an arrest on U.S. territory; here, however, the federal drug law enforcement process often broke down. In some cases Customs would insist that the drugs be intercepted at the border, to make certain they did not enter the country, while FBN, BNDD, or DEA would insist that the smuggler be allowed through the border, whence he might lead to "higher ups" in the smuggling operation. In point of fact, however, many times the true reason for these differences was the desire of each agency to make the drug seizure and arrest itself. The competing agencies eventually began circumventing one another, refusing to reveal what they were doing or whom they were investigating. Sometimes one agency would deliberately interrupt the investigation of another with a premature arrest. In one celebrated instance, two agencies, unknown to one another, were involved in the same investigation; in a showdown shooting erupted, with agents from two federal agencies of the United States government mistakenly shooting at each other.[42] How often disruptions of this kind occurred is difficult to estimate, but it is clear that the rivalry was a serious impediment to effective federal drug control and an embarrassment to the government generally.

Another problem with border interdiction is simply that our borders with both Mexico and Canada are so easily accessible; trying to make them less accessible in order to seize more drugs would not only erode freedom of entrance and egress, but probably would not work anyway. As noted, the major border drug seizures generally result from intelligence information supplied to border agents. Few illicit drugs are uncovered in random searches, as Operation Intercept—an attempt to cut off drug supplies at the Mexican border—amply demonstrated in September 1969. That effort affords another illustration of the ineffectiveness of extreme measures taken in the name of fighting illicit drugs.

Operation Intercept: A Case History.   The Mexican border has traditionally been a major trafficking point, both because large quantities of illicit drugs are produced in Mexico and because the 1,945-mile border is mostly unguarded. In addition to bridge and river crossings, it is believed that 200 aircraft carrying illicit drugs daily fly illegally from Mexico into the United States.[43]

In September 1969 President Nixon ordered "the country's largest peacetime search and seizure operation by civil authorities" along the United States–Mexico border.[44] Two thousand Customs and border patrol agents began systematically searching all cars and persons coming from Mexico into the United States. There were delays of several hours in what is normally a very quick crossing process over the border. Individuals who appeared suspicious or argumentative were often stripped and bodily searched. The tourism traffic between the two countries was seriously interrupted. And although more than five million people passed over this border during the three weeks Operation Intercept was in full gear, virtually no heroin or any other illicit drug was confiscated. In defense of the project, the government later explained that its primary intention was not to interdict drugs at the border, but rather to pressure Mexico into eradicating its crops of marijuana and opium.[45] While it may have had this effect eventually, the project had little direct impact on illicit drug trafficking.

Elimination of the Supply.   The most recent major American supply reduction strategy is "eradication at the source." This policy was created in part because of the lack of success in controlling supply through traditional domestic enforcement and international interdiction and in part because advanced technology seemed to make it more feasible than before. In brief, the objective is to eliminate the crops which furnish illicit drugs to the American market.

Bolivia, Peru, and Columbia are the major U.S. sources of cocaine, while opium (the raw material for heroin) is grown in many countries throughout the world, including Thailand, Cambodia, Vietnam, Mexico, Turkey, India, and Iran. Marijuana is grown throughout Mexico and Central and South America in addition to the United States. However, heroin is the major drug priority of the federal government, and the most advanced "eradication at the source" program underway now is against the opium poppy. Although substantial amounts of cocaine—from fifteen to one hundred tons annually—regularly flow into the United States, cocaine remains a lower priority.[46] No major cocaine eradication program has been attempted, because of the hardy nature of the coca plant (from which cocaine is derived) and because these plants are grown near drinking water supplies and closely intermingled with food crops, making eradication programs extremely difficult if not impossible to accomplish in safety. Marijuana, despite official disclaimers of interest, results in the greatest annual seizures[47] and is the object of current American-supported eradication efforts in Mexico.[48]

The key to any eradication program's success is the cooperation of the foreign government in whose country the drug is grown and the ability of that government to effect an eradication policy in its rural areas. Basically, the theory of eradication rests on the simple premise that if opium poppies or marijuana plants are eliminated in sufficient numbers the drugs they produce will also be largely eliminated. To this end, the United States now actively participates in eradication programs for both of these illicit drugs.

Opium poppies are grown in many regions of the world; no special climate or soil conditions are needed. The main requirement is cheap, abundant manual labor to do the painstaking work of harvesting. It is estimated that only sixty to one hundred tons of raw opium are required each year to supply the entire illicit U.S. market with heroin, an amount which could be produced from only ten square miles of opium poppies.[49] (One hundred tons of opium yields approximately ten tons of pure heroin[50]; the raw opium, which is extracted directly from the opium poppy, is converted into a morphine base and then into heroin by a relatively simple cooking and chemical-bonding process.)

There are two other significant factors which work against the success of the eradication strategy. First, the opium poppy has a long tradition in many cultures where it is grown; it is used for fodder, fuel, oil, and as a pain-killing agent. In many regions of the world indigenous families have been growing opium poppies for centuries. Second, opium poppies are a valuable cash crop in those regions. Even when sold legally, the poppy crops support many farmers and their families. There are few substitute crops that will earn more per unit of land.[51]

Although the United States has encouraged worldwide prohibition of illicit opium cultivation through bilateral and multilateral agreements for more than sixty years, these efforts have largely failed. One of the reasons for this is that our prohibition of heroin has inflated the price of the drug, thereby making it even more profitable to cultivate opium poppies illegally.

In 1971 this country launched a major effort to restrict the cultivation of foreign opium when it reached an agreement with Turkey to ban the cultivation of opium poppies there. In return, the United States agreed to reimburse the Turkish government $35 million for lost revenues.

(Ultimately, only part of this amount was actually paid to Turkey.)[52] Although the United States selected Turkey as the site for trying its new policy because Turkish opium was believed to account for 80 percent of the illicit heroin used in the U.S., there was no way to verify this estimate, since it is nearly impossible to trace heroin back to its original source.[53] It is in fact uncertain that Turkish opium poppies did supply 80 percent of American heroin, since it is also believed that Turkey grew only about 8 percent of the world's opium poppies.[54] In addition, the existence of other opium-growing areas and the profitability of the American heroin trade would make the long-term impact of such a ban questionable; other countries growing larger amounts of opium had controls as lax as Turkey's, and much of the opium from these countries also found its way into the black market. It has also been suggested that Turkey was selected because, as a NATO ally, it was more susceptible to U.S. leverage than many other countries.

Whatever the reasons for choosing Turkey, the results of the opium ban not only failed to stop the flow of heroin into this country but seriously strained relations between the two countries until Turkey unilaterally rescinded the ban in 1975.[55] In place of the opium-growing ban, the Turkish government at this time initiated a centralized poppy-harvesting method called the "poppy straw process": This process requires that the opium poppies be harvested whole rather than lanced, meaning that the raw opium is brought to secure, central locations before the extraction process is carried out, and forbids farmers to lance the poppy pods themselves. This change has reduced if not eliminated the export of illicit Turkish opium. This stoppage of Turkish opium, however, led to a substantial increase in illicit heroin from Mexican sources. As one study noted,

> Although the opium ban in Turkey, together with a major enforcement effort in France which broke up a ring of French and French-Corsican chemists and traffickers in 1973, did put a temporary crimp in the supply of heroin in the U.S., Mexican opium growers and traffickers rapidly took over the market. By 1975 the U.S. government was declaring that over 80 percent of the heroin available in the U.S. came from Mexico, instead of Turkey.[56]

As the illicit Turkish opium supply dwindled and the price of heroin rose in response, the economics of heroin trafficking thus became even more favorable, and new suppliers were attracted to it. For example, in opium-producing countries an investment of $250 now buys one ounce of 90 percent pure heroin; when cut with forty dollars' worth of quinine, thereby converting the original ounce of heroin into one kilo of 2½ percent purity (an average level for American heroin), the value becomes $15 per gram, or a total of $15,000 for the original investment of $290.[57] These economics keep the international heroin market flourishing and make significant and lasting eradication extremely difficult to accomplish.

Mexican heroin—noted for its brown color, a result of the refining process which has no effect on the quality of the heroin—quickly filled the vacuum created by the Turkish poppy ban. In fact, heroin is a great economic boon to regions in northern Mexico; that mountainous and largely inaccessible region produces some twenty tons of heroin a year. As noted in one report on the Mexican heroin trade,

> Assuming, however, that only the 10 tons of heroin (from the tri-state area) reached the border where it would sell in 1975 at $45,000 a kilo (border value), the value of that crop alone would be $450 million. The heroin crop alone is thus Mexico's most valuable commodity. Sugar, shrimp, coffee and cotton, the next four most valuable commodities, do not total $450 million together.[58]

In response to this new influx of heroin, the United States and Mexico agreed in 1973 to attempt another type of eradication strategy. Essentially, the United States agreed to provide technical assistance and equipment for a herbicide-spraying program to eradicate illicit Mexican drug-producing crops. Although marijuana was included, the opium poppy was the primary target of the eradication program from the American point of view. This program remains the United States' most ambitious eradication effort.[59]

During the early phases of the program less than ten thousand opium poppy fields per year were destroyed manually. These ten thousand fields represented approximately three to four thousand acres. In November 1975 aerial spraying began, and by 1976 the total number of fields reportedly destroyed had risen to twenty thousand. In 1977, some forty-seven thousand poppy fields, representing an estimated fourteen thousand acres, were destroyed. This increase was primarily due to the change from manual to aerial herbicide spraying.[60]

The spraying program is conducted year-round and affects large sections of Mexico, including nearly half of the western coast. At the present time the herbicide paraquat is used to eradicate marijuana—a major goal of the Mexican government—and the chemical "2,4-D," is used on opium poppies. The program is assisted by the U.S. government in a number of ways. A State Department official recently described the Mexican eradication effort to a congressional committee thus:

> The principal forms of State Department–administered support to the Mexican drug effort have included the furnishing of aircraft and telecommunications equipment, together with the requisite training to enable the Mexicans to use them in modern applications to drug detection, poppy eradication, and enforcement work. Our technical assistance together with

certain commodities, is also helping them to establish and administer a network of forward bases in the important eradication areas and to improve intelligence collection, retrieval, and analysis. Training and salary supplements are provided to aid the [Mexican] Federal Judicial Police to develop and hold a cadre of qualified narcotics agents.[61]

The United States provided Mexico with approximately $50 million in assistance funds for marijuana and opium poppy control from 1973 to 1977. Proposed assistance for 1978 was estimated to be about $13.3 million. Most of these funds are used to purchase aircraft and support services for the aerial eradication program. Aircraft supplied by the United States includes more than forty helicopters and thirty-five fixed-wing aircraft. In addition, some twenty to twenty-five DEA agents are assigned full time with the Mexican eradication effort to provide technical assistance.[62]

As an enforcement strategy, eradication at the source may have some advantages over other reduction and control strategies. First, there is less potential for domestic police corruption. Second, as compared to interdiction and undercover efforts it is a relatively inexpensive way of preventing illicit drugs from entering the United States.

However, the criteria for determining the success of such an operation are uncertain. For instance, it is not known what quantity of illicit drugs were smuggled into this country from Mexico either before the program or now. However, the State Department and the Drug Enforcement Administration report that Mexican brown heroin, which formerly accounted for 80 to 85 percent of the heroin available in this country, has dropped to 60 to 65 percent of the total. Also, the retail and wholesale prices of heroin have reportedly increased as much as 50 to 75 percent along the U.S.–Mexican border, and increases of as much as 150 percent have been noted.[63] However, a rise in heroin prices is not in itself a totally accurate indication of the effects of a control strategy on heroin use. In fact, higher heroin prices may be, at best, a mixed blessing.

Eradication policies, when they successfully interrupt illicit drug production, as the Mexican opium poppy program has apparently done, may reduce the American heroin supply for a time, perhaps two or three years. In 1977, heroin-related deaths dropped approximately 40 percent in this country, a possible indication that the eradication program was having a beneficial effect.[64] It was also reported by enforcement officials that American heroin supplies in 1978 were at their lowest level in several years; however, they admit they have little hard evidence on which to base that estimate. Moreover, as will be discussed later, reducing the heroin supply may lead to other social problems.

There are a number of possible side-effects to such an eradication program which must also be considered. For example, Mexican marijuana sprayed with paraquat has reached the United States; samples seized near the border after the eradication program began showed that 21 percent were contaminated with significant levels of paraquat.[65] It has been indicated that paraquat may pose a significant health danger to those who ingest it. The Secretary of the Department of Health, Education, and Welfare announced a National Institute on Drug Abuse study in March 1978.

> The report's preliminary findings suggest that if an individual smokes three to five heavily contaminated marihuana cigarettes each day for several months, irreversible lung damage will result. The report cautions, however, that there could be a risk of lung damage for individuals who use marihuana less often or in smaller amounts. Although these results are preliminary, the report concludes that Paraquat contamination may pose a serious risk to marihuana smokers.[66]

Although one might argue that anyone who uses an illegal substance like marijuana must bear the consequences and the risks, the fact remains that as many as forty-five million Americans have tried marijuana and approximately eleven million are regular users. The preponderance of medical evidence to date shows that marijuana is a relatively harmless intoxicant when used moderately. Therefore, it seems ironic that an official program may itself produce a serious health risk for the individual smoker, when the ostensible reason for prohibition in the first place was to protect users from harming themselves.

The eradication strategy has another shortcoming as well: Experience has shown that as one opium supply system is diminished, another develops to take its place, at even more attractive profits due to the rise in heroin prices caused by the temporary shortage. Shortly after the Mexican eradication program began, for example, white heroin from the "Golden Triangle" in Southeast Asia began to enter the country. Drug enforcement officials suspect that many Turkish nationals are involved in this Southeast Asian traffic, which suggests that the Turkish opium ban may have been more effective with the crop than with the traffickers.

There is a larger problem, however, which holds the greatest potential danger. If the country designated for crop eradication efforts—in this case Mexico—is not part of a vigorous ongoing program, then its illicit opium production will probably be revived after the eradication efforts slow or stop. And it may revive at a time when other areas of the world are also producing large amounts of illicit heroin for the U.S. market. Then, rather than facing illicit heroin smuggling from only one major area, this country could be faced with two or more major supply sources. This possibility remains a strong one, because the eradication program depends upon the internal policies and politics of foreign governments, any one of which for any reason could end existing agreements and permit the former state of affairs to reappear.

Drugs and Crime

The persistent belief that illicit drug use is inextricably linked to crime has traditionally been advanced as a reason for laws and policies against particular drugs. A 1972 survey by the National Commission on Marihuana and Drug Abuse found that 58 percent of adults believed that marijuana users often commit crimes they would not have committed had they not used marijuana. In that same survey, more than 90 percent of those interviewed believed that, in the commission's words, "Heroin users often commit crimes to get the money to buy more heroin."[67]

Crimes that relate to illicit drugs can generally be placed into four categories.[68] Two of these are not germane to this discussion; these are crimes among individuals involved in the illicit-drug distribution system—e.g., drug or money thefts by one drug dealer from another—and the crimes of simply using, possessing, or selling the drug itself, activities which are criminal by definition, since they are illegal.

Generally, the perceived drug and crime relationship which most concerns the public falls into two basic categories. The first category involves the pharmacological effect of a drug on the user. Historically, the presumed pharmacological connection between illicit drug use and assaultive crime has been the impetus behind antidrug laws. However, the evidence to date shows that alcohol and secobarbital—both legally produced psychoactive substances—are the drugs most likely to be involved with subsequent assaultive behavior. There is no substantial evidence to link the use of any other drug, licit or illicit, with assaultive crime.[69] Some stimulant drugs, such as the amphetamines, have reportedly led to aggressive behavior in some individuals, but there is insufficient evidence to show a causal link between their use and assaultive crime.

The second category consists of revenue-producing crimes like burglary, shoplifting, and larceny. More recently, the use of heroin has been linked to crimes of this sort. The assumption is that the use of heroin invariably results in addiction; that heroin addicts require ever-increasing amounts of the drug; and that, due to the high cost of the drug on the American market, they must commit various crimes to support their use. As pointed out by the press and electronic media, the stereotypic portrait of the heroin user is of a dishevelled, trembling individual without motivation or legitimate source of income. However, while there is evidence to suggest that many heroin users may commit property crimes to support use,[70] nobody really knows how much crime is actually committed to obtain money to support heroin habits. Police and court records do not contain this information, and estimates—which are not particularly reliable—vary, calling it anywhere from 10 to 50 percent of all revenue-producing crimes, depending upon the type of offense and the location.[71]

A survey by the Law Enforcement Assistance Administration of ten thousand inmates of correctional facilities concluded that 13 percent of the inmates had used heroin at the time of their arrest. The same survey estimated between 13 and 60 percent of incarcerated criminals to have been heroin users.[72] Although this kind of data suggests links between heroin use and crime, nothing was established in that survey to demonstrate that these individuals began to commit crimes because of their heroin use, nor does the study indicate whether the correctional population surveyed was typical of all those arrested, or of all committing crimes. It may indicate a tendency to jail heroin users in disproportionate numbers.

The studies which indicate that after the onset of opiate addiction individuals generally increase their criminal activity come closest to demonstrating a causal link between drug use and crime.[73] These studies suggest that although an individual may have been a criminal before he used heroin, his heavy use led to an increase in criminal activity to meet the new income need. On its face, this implies a connection between heroin use and crime. However, there is an across-the-board increase in crime among men between ages eighteen and twenty-five, irrespective of drug use.[74] Thus, any data suggesting increased crime because of heroin use would have to correct for the general increase in crime for this age bracket.

The evidence relating to a heroin-crime link could best be described as showing that regular, heavy opiate use in the United States probably means a higher rate of revenue-producing crime by the addict. Because of its broad political appeal, however, this connection has been repeatedly overstated and even misrepresented to support tough enforcement policies. For example, Governor Rockefeller of New York told the legislature, by way of introducing a "get tough" drug law, that addicts were "robbing, mugging, murdering day in and day out for their money to fix their habit."[75] The state estimated that drug addicts committed a total of $6.5 billion per year in crime. If that were in fact the case, it would have meant that these addicts were committing on the order of 44 million robberies, muggings, and murders each year in New York to support their habit, 400 times more than all of the reported crimes in New York, well beyond any conceivable total of reported and unreported crimes in that state.[76]

Other data indicate that such figures had little factual basis. The Federal Bureau of Investigation's 1971 Uniform Crime Index reported a total of $1.3 billion in theft in 1970 for the entire nation. Thus, New York State's claim of $6.5 billion in crime losses for New York alone exceeded the national figure by five times.[77] Another study, an economic analysis by the Hudson Institute of New York of the extent of heroin use nationwide, estimated that in 1970 there were 250,000 addicts who were responsible for a maximum of $1.7 billion in crime.[78]

The New York figures disseminated by Governor Rockefeller's office were misleading in another important respect. In New York City, which is generally acknowledged to have more illicit drug use than any other American city, only a small percentage of the 110,000 reported crimes in 1973 (the year of the "tougher" New York drug law's passage) were attributed by police to heroin users. The New York Police Department estimated only 4.4 percent of those arrested for felonies against a person—which would include robbery, muggings, and murder—could be classified as heroin users, and only a small percentage of those users could be classified as addicts.[79]

In a 1974 study by the Crime Analysis Unit of the New York City Police Department it was found that among arrested criminal heroin users and nonusers, the rates of property crime were about the same, suggesting that there is little difference in patterns of property crime between them. However, the percentage of nonusers who committed serious crimes against a person was substantially higher than for heroin users.[80] A Hudson Institute study reported even lower figures for assaultive property crimes among heroin users in New York City. It reported that less than 2 percent supported their heroin use by either robbery or muggings.[81]

These studies call into question the more dramatic statements about the extent of crime committed by those who use illicit drugs, particularly heroin. It does seem that property crimes are committed by some unknown proportion of regular heavy heroin users not as a result of the drug itself but of the high cost of obtaining it in America's black market. Little hard statistical evidence exists to show a cause-and-effect relationship between the use of any drug and criminal behavior.

The Impact of Demand and Price.   One goal of drug enforcement is to cut back the supply of heroin and thereby raise the street price, which in theory will drive heroin addicts into treatment. This concept has proved to be more unpredictable and complex than simple cause-and-effect scenarios generally concede. There are studies which demonstrate that such law enforcement policies may be a double-edged sword, at least in the short run.

A study of heroin prices in Detroit indicates that as heroin prices rise because of diminished supply there is a consequent increase in property crime. The study, performed by the Public Research Institute of the Center for Naval Analyses noted,

> The relationship between drug addiction and criminality is complex and, because of the lack of data, hard to supply. This study has shown that the level of property crime in Detroit is in part affected by the price of heroin. When the price rises, crime rises. When the price falls, crime falls. This finding supports the general hypothesis that criminal heroin users as a class

try to maintain their level of consumption in the face of price increases, and that they rely partly on property crime for the additional funds. The level of personal crime is little affected by the price of heroin.[82]

The Detroit study also found that the areas hardest hit by the crime increases were the poor neighborhoods. It said, "We have preliminary evidence that poor people are victimized by addict criminals; thus, law enforcement policies that tend to raise the price of heroin hurt this income class."[83] The impact of many national policy shifts is often felt most acutely in neighborhoods with the least political power; this phenomenon is particularly profound with drug policies.

The reason why diminished heroin availability may lead to more crime relates to the economics of the illicit heroin market, which lies at the raw edge of laissez-faire capitalism. It rests on the fundamental economic principle of supply and demand: When the supply is less, the price is more. It should be kept in mind, however, that supply is but one factor governing the price of heroin; the purity of the drug and experience of the dealer, as well as other factors, also affect its price. Supply of the drug remains, however, one of the strongest single influences on price. A 1971 East Coast dock strike, for example, is believed responsible for a temporary heroin shortage and a consequent rise in street-level prices. After settlement of the strike, supplies increased and prices dropped, from a high in New York of sixty-two dollars per gram (for a two-gram purchase at 10 percent purity) to fifty dollars, all over a period of three months.[84]

The predicted crime increase is of course based on the idea that if it costs more for a heroin user to support his use and he has no other income sources than crime, he will need to commit more crimes to support use at the same level. Also, because many users support themselves by selling small quantities of drugs there is the possibility that they could turn to other forms of crime besides dealing.

The American experience in Vietnam in attempting to eradicate use of a drug without fully considering the possible consequences is also instructive. When the army clamped down on marijuana use the demand for a drug among soldiers who had used it did not decrease; when they could not get marijuana, they turned in large numbers to another easily purchased and more easily concealed drug—heroin. It was a classic example of attempting to control supply without addressing demand.[85*]

Despite these occurrences the notion persists that use of illicit drugs can be brought under control with enforcement policies, and that bringing it under control will in great measure solve the crime problem. In part, this notion persists because of the common stereotype of the heroin user as an unscrupulous individual willing to commit any crime for his

---

* The Vietnam drug experience also underscores other important points about illicit drug use, i.e., the setting and the availability. The setting in Vietnam, at once boring and very dangerous, created a situation which encouraged many individuals to use drugs there. Also, the fact that drug supplies were so plentiful contributed to their widespread use.

next fix. Like all stereotypes, it does not encompass the diversity of the individuals who use drugs compulsively. Many illicit drug users and opiate addicts hold steady, legitimate jobs. Not all heroin users are, as previously assumed, heroin "addicts." Some, perhaps many, enjoy the euphoric effects of heroin but do not have a compulsive need for it.[86] Many, perhaps most, of these would not consider stealing in order to buy their drugs. These occasional heroin users, sometimes called "chippers," may, if mathematical projections are correct, outnumber compulsive heroin users by as much as six to one.[87] The very notion that they can exist is frequently met with skepticism because it is contrary to the well-entrenched belief that to use heroin is to be addicted to it.

Because heroin users are a diverse group with no uniform patterns of drug use and widely different ways of earning money, one cannot simply multiply estimated users by a single monetary figure to arrive at an accurate estimate of the amount of crime they commit. It is interesting, however, to speculate on what might happen to the crime rate if no heroin were available in this country. The Nixon administration, which like other administrations before it adopted the conventional assumption of a direct link between heroin and crime in many of its public utterances, did not find such a link in a private study it commissioned. While stating publicly that American drug-related crime amounted to $18 *billion* a year, a 1971 White House Domestic Council decision paper circulated within the Executive Office noted, "Even if all drug abuse were eradicated, there might not be a dramatic drop in crime statistics on a national level, since much crime is not related to drug abuse."[88]

The difficulty of threading through all of the data on drugs and crime and arriving at any certainties will persist, as will the unpredictability of the effects of various enforcement policies. Despite these uncertainties, however, the drug-crime issue often invokes emotional responses having little to do with the facts. It is therefore likely that the presumed drug-crime link will continue to inspire "get tough" approaches to drug law enforcement in the future.

The New York Drug Law

During the early 1970s, a period when the country was greatly concerned about illicit drugs, New York State embarked on the strictest "get tough" enforcement approach to illicit drugs in the country. It is difficult to discern with precision how much of the zeal for the new law came from an angry and frustrated citizenry and how much came from the state's leaders, or how much they coincided. In any case, the new law received wide national publicity and was passed amid bold promises that it would squarely address the drug problem in that state.

There was general agreement that the practice of the 1960s of diverting low-level drug users into treatment and meting out harsher penalties for higher-level traffickers had largely failed. New York had heavily committed its resources to "civil commitment" during the 1960s, a program described at the time as a model for other states to adopt. However, 1972 overdose deaths in New York were six times greater than they had been in 1960; the tougher new laws were regarded by many as a solution.

The new legislation, which went into effect on September 1, 1973, had two principal objectives. First, it sought to frighten illicit drug users out of using and drug dealers out of trafficking. Second, it aimed to reduce crimes commonly associated with drug addiction, i.e., burglaries, robberies, and theft; it was believed that potential illicit drug users would be frightened off by the law and that hardened criminals would be given long prison sentences, thus reducing the crime rate.[89]

The new law was aimed primarily at heroin trafficking, in particular at the lower-level "street" dealers. The law divided heroin dealers into three groups, placed them in the highest felony category in the state, and required minimum periods of imprisonment plus mandatory lifetime parole supervision for each group. The groups were:

I.   The highest level dealers. Those who sell *one ounce* or more, or possess more than two ounces. These dealers were subjected to the most severe penalty: a prison sentence of indefinite length, but with a minimum of between fifteen and twenty-five years and a lifetime maximum.

II. The middle level dealers. Those who sell *one-eighth of an ounce* or more, or possess one or two ounces. These offenders were subjected to prison sentences of indefinite length, with a minimum term of between six and eight-and-one-third years, and a lifetime maximum.

III. Street level dealers, also referred to as "sharer-pushers." Those who sell *less than one-eighth* of an ounce or possess up to an ounce with the intent to sell. These dealers were made liable to prison sentences of indefinite length, with a minimum term of between one year and eight-and-one-third years, and a lifetime maximum.[90]

The mandatory minimum prison sentences were made a major provision of the New York law, even though such sentences had previously been abandoned in federal and state drug laws. Restrictions on plea bargaining were another controversial aspect of this law; a person indicted on a low-level felony charge was not permitted to plead guilty to a misdemeanor, a provision which eventually led to court congestion and a slowdown of the judicial process as well as precluding any cooperation of suspects with police seeking information on higher-level dealers and suppliers.

New York State became in effect a laboratory in which the effectiveness of a "get tough" drug law could be examined. By comparing the drug-related statistics for New York before and after the new law went into effect, and by examining similar statistics from neighboring states whose laws had not changed, comparisons could be drawn and evidence could be weighed. A study commissioned by the Association of the Bar of the City of New York to find out the effects of the law concluded that neither heroin use nor the crime commonly associated with it declined in New York State as a result of the tough new legislation. With respect to heroin use, the study found the following:

- Heroin use [in New York City] was as widespread in mid-1976 as it had been when the 1973 revision took effect, and ample supplies of the drug were available.
- The pattern of stable heroin use in New York City between 1973 and mid-1976 was not appreciably different from the average pattern in other East Coast cities.
- The new law may have temporarily deterred heroin use [in New York City and other New York State jurisdictions].
- There is no evidence of a sustained reduction in heroin use after 1973 [in New York State as a whole or in upstate New York].
- Most evidence suggests that the illegal use of drugs other than narcotics in New York City was more widespread in 1976 than in 1973, and that in this respect New York was not unique among East Coast cities.[91]

With respect to crime, the study found:

- Serious property crime of the kind often associated with heroin users increased sharply [in New York State] between 1973 and 1975. The rise in New York State was similar to increases in nearby states.
- There was a sharp rise in non-drug felony crimes between 1973 and 1975 [in New York City]. However, the rise was apparently unconnected with illegal narcotics use: non-drug felony crimes known to have been committed by narcotics users remained stable during that period.
- The available evidence suggests that the recidivist sentencing [predicate felony] provisions of the 1973 law did not significantly deter prior felony offenders from committing additional crimes [in New York City].[92]

In addition, the study found little enthusiasm for the 1973 law within the criminal justice system.

> Many judges and prosecutors felt that the mandatory sentencing provisions reduced the possibility of individual treatment of offenders, and, therefore, the quality of justice. Some were troubled because the penalties imposed on low-level drug traffickers were more severe than those applicable to crimes that most citizens consider heinous. . . . New York City prosecutors tended to believe that the 1973 law was forcing them to scatter their limited resources on what they considered relatively minor offenses. (Note: The Class III (lowest level) felony accounted for 41% of all drug indictments in New York City and 61% of the trial workload.) . . . As for the police, the New York City Police Department believed that a policy of all-out street level enforcement would be only marginally productive and would hopelessly inundate the courts.[93]

Because of the large volume of street-level drug activity in New York City, the New York City Police Department had the opportunity to make large numbers of street-level arrests under the new drug law. It did not elect to do so, for the reason that past efforts had been perceived as ineffective. As the study recorded,

> In 1969, the Department had implemented a policy similar to the one implied by the new law. Large numbers of low-level drug arrests had been encouraged, and the number of felony drug arrests had risen from 7,199 in 1967 to 26,379 in 1970. In 1971, however, Police Commissioner Patrick Murphy abandoned this policy because (a) only a small percentage of the arrests were resulting in prison or jail sentences and (b) the mass arrest policy did not appear to be having a significant impact on the drug traffic. In the Department's view, the mass arrest policy was also creating serious workload problems for the courts. Immediately after the change in policy, arrests fell sharply; in 1973, there were only a little more than one-third as many as two years earlier. . . . According to Donald Cawley, New York City Police Commissioner when the 1973 law became effective, the Department decided not to change its enforcement policies in response to the 1973 legislation. The Department continued to focus its enforcement activities on the middle and upper levels of drug distribution rather than upon street-level drug activity.[94]

The study concluded, "The key lesson to be drawn from the experience with the 1973 drug law is that passing a new law is not enough. What criminal statutes say matters a great deal, but the efficiency, morale, and capacity of the criminal justice system is even more of a factor in determining whether the law is effectively implemented."[95] In addition, the study noted that implementation of the new law, which included the hiring of new narcotics case judges, prosecutors, defense attorneys, and support staff, cost the state of New York $32 million.

What the study of the New York law indicates is that there are serious limits to what any law can control. It is apparent now that the rhetoric which helped create a climate for the new law—i.e., statements which attributed exaggerated amounts of crime to drug addicts—was also in part responsible for the failure of the law to live up to expectations. This is not to suggest that law enforcement approaches to illicit drug use should be abandoned because they fail in what they attempt to do. Rather, it means that our expectations should be realistic, because our ability to deal with these complex problems is limited. In New York, administrative problems, court congestion, the doubts which many judges and prosecutors had about the new law, and the difficulties of policing illicit drugs under any circumstances all joined together to reduce the law's effectiveness. The conclusion is that this law changed very little in New York.

The Impact of Drug Law Enforcement on Drug-Using Behavior

An interesting contrast to the New York "get tough" law is the Oregon law of 1973 which "decriminalized" the possession of a small quantity of marijuana. The state took this action following the recommendations of the National Commission on Marihuana and Drug Abuse. The new Oregon law—and those in other states which subsequently enacted similar legislation—eliminated the possibility of imprisonment for simple possession of an ounce or less of marijuana. A civil fine, similar to a traffic citation, was substituted for the former criminal penalties. There were to be no criminal arrests for such offenses nor would there be court arraignment.

Critics of the new law predicted an explosion of both experimental and regular marijuana use in Oregon. This prediction was rooted in the persistent belief that it is primarily the law that restrains people from using illicit drugs—the same view which in part prompted the tough New York law.

However, annual surveys conducted in Oregon during the four years following enactment of the new law have shown little change at all in marijuana use patterns.[96] Marijuana users have increased gradually in number, but this is true across the nation. Regular users have remained relatively constant, a pattern that is also typical of other state and national trends.

Since Oregon passed its law, only ten other states have adopted the reduced penalty for possession of small amounts of marijuana, despite the preponderance of available evidence that marijuana is not a major health hazard when used moderately and that criminal laws apparently do not deter millions from using it.

The New York law was aimed primarily at heroin, and did little, if anything, to change use patterns there. The Oregon law was aimed at marijuana, and it too did little, if anything, to change use patterns. What both these experiences suggest is just how little the criminal law influences an individual's decision to use a particular drug, illegal or not. Similarly, the prohibition of alcohol in the early part of this century did little to prevent millions of Americans from consuming it.

These recent legislative developments underscore another point. Generally, the public and its policymakers have focused narrowly on eliminating the consumption of one or two drugs in particular, without giving much thought as to the effect of this restricted concentration. These policies seem to be based upon the theory that once marijuana or heroin or cocaine is eliminated then the problems of drug abuse in the United States will be solved.

In 1971 the Institute for Defense Analyses (IDA), an organization established by the Joint Chiefs of Staff to develop independent information and analysis, examined aspects of illicit drug use in this country. The IDA study concluded that heroin addicts are probably willing to switch to amphetamines, barbiturates, and other drugs should heroin become prohibitively expensive or unavailable.[97] Through studies of the urinalysis screening program of inmates of the Washington, D.C. jails, the Institute found that before the East Coast dock strike of 1971 nearly 20 percent of the inmates tested positive for opiates. During the strike, however, this percentage dropped to zero while that for barbiturate and amphetamine use rose from its former 3 or 4 percent level to nearly 20 percent.[98] While it is not conclusive, the study did underscore the fact that we have very little hard data on the habits, preferences, alternatives, and attitudes of heroin users. Models, analyses, and other information offer a limited glimpse of these factors, and then for only a limited time frame.

This study and other more recent ones[99] have suggested that the usage patterns for heroin may be more flexible than is generally believed, and therefore less vulnerable to strategies that focus on the elimination of supply. Although better domestic enforcement, border control, and foreign eradication efforts might tighten the heroin market to some extent, any long-range improvement as regards drug-related problems remains uncertain. Despite this, and the limited ability of the criminal justice system to alter human behavior, when laws fail to discourage an activity that the majority in a society deems undesirable the natural impulse is to toughen them to attain the desired effect.

Concluding Thoughts

Since federal antinarcotics laws have been in force in this country for more than sixty years—and local ordinances for more than a century—it seems appropriate to ask what such laws can or have accomplished. If we were expecting our drug laws to eradicate illicit drug use, then the local, state, and federal antidrug effort must be judged an abject failure. Tough laws have not been a solution to the drug abuse crisis. If, however, one was hoping for a containment policy, then enforcement efforts might be judged a partial success, because only a relatively small number of people use heroin, the drug with which we seem most concerned today. This conclusion, of course, is impossible to prove. Moreover, mere containment of heroin use was never the stated goal of our drug control efforts.

The best way to judge the value of our present drug control policies is to weigh their benefits and costs. This may give us some clues with which to better analyze our current policies and reach a clearer understanding of their worth. In making this assessment, it is natural that drug law enforcement be examined more critically than other approaches, such as treatment or education. Drug enforcement has received the majority of the available time, money, technology, and hope and faith for the past seven decades. It is not unreasonable to say that law enforcement efforts have been given the greatest possible opportunity to respond to illicit drugs, and that those efforts ought to be evaluated in light of their performance.

What then are the costs of drug law enforcement? Several can be identified: money outlays for enforcement; such side effects as the stigma of arrest, the risk of impure drugs and associated health hazards, the creation of a black market, a potential rise in non-drug crime rates, and the risk of police corruption; the alienation of many segments of society; selective enforcement patterns; diversion of scarce resources; erosion of the rule of law; invasion of privacy; reduction of personal freedom; hostility between police and the community; and potential police perjury and official deception. These are some costs generally ascribed to the current prohibitionist policy approach to particular drugs.

The benefits are less specific and less provable. We can point to the arrest of individuals who traffic in illicit drugs as a benefit, at least in the small percentage of cases where arrest is followed by conviction and punishment. But we cannot point to drug enforcement generally and argue that it has had a dramatically successful impact in prohibiting these activities. One benefit often cited is the channeling into treatment by means of criminal justice diversion of illicit drug users who might otherwise not have entered; however, this process may have a negative impact in deterring voluntary applicants from seeking help (see Staff Paper 3, "Heroin Treatment", below). Law enforcement efforts may also have had an impact in containing the spread of illicit drug use, but this position is debatable in light of the steady increase in illicit drug use during years when strong penalties have been on the books and substantial efforts were made to enforce those laws. While drug law enforcement efforts undoubtedly do harass some low-level operatives in the illicit drug market and make them afraid to deal openly on the street, this may be a marginal benefit, in that it makes it likely that users will only become more cautious and harder to detect. While ease of availability does appear to have some influence on the numbers who will use a particular drug, making availability harder does not eliminate the demand for a particular drug or psychoactive substances generally.

The key question remains: Is the current system of drug control worthwhile? An abundance of data has been collected—some of it presented in this chapter—but it is consistently contradictory, imprecise, of questionable reliability, and laden with the values we impute to it. Nevertheless, we would conclude that the costs are greater than the benefits derived. Part of the difficulty with criminal law as a control measure lies in the fact that it has been consistently oversold as a cure for illicit drug use. A serious consequence of this is that drug law enforcement has rarely been viewed dispassionately; rather, it has been the object of either heated attack or staunch defense, and rarely the object of thoughtful analysis.

Our current drug control policies exact a heavy toll in social costs, while data showing a solid return on the investment are difficult to find. This imbalance has been known for some time, but the knowledge of it has not materially changed our drug control policies and laws. The basic policy established a century ago continues today, and there are no immediate prospects of the government, federal or state, seriously reconsidering its heavy reliance on the criminal justice system to deal with illicit drugs.

3 Heroin Treatment: Development, Status, Outlook

David C. Lewis and John Sessler

THE GROWTH OF heroin treatment over the last decade has been truly remarkable. There are presently an estimated two hundred and forty thousand drug treatment "slots" in the United States.[1] Approximately 60 percent of these are for heroin users, the remainder for users of other drugs; of the heroin treatment "slots," there are approximately eighty-four thousand nationwide for methadone maintenance.[2] Nearly 85 percent of all those treated receive drug treatment services on an outpatient basis, 8 percent are in residential programs, and the remainder are in hospital, prison, or day-care settings.[3] Over $ .5 billion will have been spent on drug treatment and rehabilitation during 1978. Of this amount $196 million will come from the federal government's National Institute on Drug Abuse, while the remainder will come from other federal agencies as well as from state and local governments and private sources.[4]

Heroin treatment has achieved the status of a major American industry during the 1970s. It is, however, an industry unlike any other, and its unique development, problems, and benefits are examined in the following sections of this chapter.

Early History

The first identifiable population of opiate addicts in the United States were wounded Civil War veterans who used morphine to relieve

The authors acknowledge with gratitude the contributions of Peter G. Bourne, Robert Newman, and Norman E. Zinberg.

the chronic pain of war injuries.[5] Their use of morphine, at least initially, had a legitimate medical purpose. Even if the addictive qualities of morphine had been fully recognized and appreciated at the time, addiction to it would probably have been preferable to the alternative of extreme physical pain.

By the end of the nineteenth century, morphine came to be used more widely.[6] In addition to its continued use for the relief of chronic pain among disabled veterans, morphine was used by other groups as well, particularly middle-aged white females in rural areas. Increasingly, morphine was used to relieve not only severe or chronic pain but minor discomfort and general irritability. In fact, there came to be large-scale marketing of opiate-containing tonics which purportedly relieved a wide range of maladies. Morphine use during this period was accepted as legitimate, even when it became excessive and the individual became addicted.

As opiates became used more frequently as "medicine," concern about the potential for opiate addiction increased and "cures" were promoted. Most of these cures were in the form of patent medicines which individuals administered to themselves. However, many of the cures actually contained opiates. In fact, when heroin was introduced around 1900, it was promoted for the treatment, among other things, of morphine addiction.[7]

Formal treatment at this time was viewed solely in a medical context. Physicians saw physical withdrawal from the addictive drug as being the entire problem. There was little appreciation of the psychological or social aspects of addiction.[8] Although elaborate physiological explanations were propounded by physicians to explain opiate addiction, little attention was given to the possible causes of addiction or to methods of preventing readdiction after withdrawal. While Freud and others began to address the psychological etiology of addiction, their views did not achieve wide attention or acceptance during this period.[9]

In the early 1900s addiction to heroin and morphine was thought to be increasing, and was found to exist within urban populations. An association between addiction and crime was asserted. A new kind of drug addict—in the public's view, a less benign kind—was thought to be emerging. This change in attitude led to growing public pressure for government action to control addiction, which culminated in the passage of the Harrison Narcotic Act in 1914.

The Harrison Act was a crucial watershed for national drug policy, as it set the course for government action and public attitudes for the next fifty years.[10] Although it was not seen as such at the time, it in effect defined addiction as primarily a law enforcement rather than a public health problem. Although initially the act seemed to promote a medical definition of addiction by making opiates available only through a physician's prescription and discontinuing sale in the open market, the ultimate authority over physician-prescribing practices was put in the hands of federal Treasury Department agents.

Abruptly cut off from previously available and inexpensive heroin and morphine supplies, opiate addicts in the tens of thousands turned to physicians for help. A Treasury Department survey in 1918, four years after the Harrison Narcotic Act took effect, showed more than seventy thousand addicts "under treatment."[11] However, because of the narrow conceptualization of opiate addiction along purely physiological lines, "treatment" meant continuing the provision of narcotic drugs and little else.

Many physicians were reluctant to accept the increasingly unpopular task of treating addicts. Accordingly, a number of cities established morphine maintenance clinics to dispense opiates for limited periods of time as a public health measure. Between 1918 and 1920, forty-four of these drug maintenance centers were opened.[12] While it has been stated that they were a failure and the federal government subsequently moved to close them for that reason, in fact these treatment programs were probably reasonably successful in what they set out to achieve—namely, to undercut the illegal, "black market" supply system, alleviate the burden on physicians in private practice, and generally minimize on a short term basis the dysfunction of the addict. However, what the clinics could not achieve was long-term abstinence. Although the Public Health Service and other medical authorities claimed that any withdrawal method would result in getting the addict off drugs,[13] addicts in fact would usually resume using drugs if available soon after withdrawal. Therefore one major problem the clinics encountered was that they were unable to address the longer-term problems characteristic of narcotic addiction; in spite of the claims of many "experts," there was no medically proven treatment for narcotic addiction.

The very existence of the clinics was diametrically opposed to what lawmakers, law enforcement officials, and many doctors saw as the solution to the problem, i.e., total abstinence. It was commonly believed that the clinics were merely another supply source for those desiring drugs for comfort or pleasure.

A 1919 survey conducted by the Revenue Bureau of the U.S. Treasury Department solicited the views of leading American physicians and scientists on the current state of narcotic addiction treatment and the wisdom of ambulatory programs.[14] The results showed that medical opinion was mostly opposed to the ambulatory treatment of addicts. Subsequently, the Narcotic Division of the Revenue Bureau, having received formal support from the American Medical Association in its opposition to ambulatory maintenance programs, moved to close the maintenance clinics. That decision was not as mindless as some have suggested; rather it was based on a series of specific, well-documented considerations that are understandable within the context of the attitudes and beliefs of that time. As a result, in 1919 the federal government began closing the clinics, and by 1925 the last one was gone.[15]

The passage of the Harrison Narcotic Act and the subsequent closing of the maintenance clinics reflected both a complete usurpation by the Treasury Department of all policy-making authority over narcotic drugs and a total abdication by the medical profession of any role in shaping drug policies. Once the maintenance clinics were closed, law enforcement officials moved to consolidate their authority in this area by vigorously prosecuting any physician personally prescribing narcotic drugs for a suspected addict. Between 1914 and 1938, around twenty-five thousand were arrested, and more than five thousand actually went to jail, merely for prescribing narcotics to suspected addicts.[16] No physician dared treat an acknowledged addict; a degree of trepidation was engendered that would influence the attitude of the medical profession toward narcotics for generations. Within a few short years, any possible view of opiate addiction as a disease or at least as a primarily medical matter had been eliminated.

In the decade of the 1920s there was essentially no source of drug treatment in America. Yet addiction to narcotics persisted even though this truly hard-line approach was being pursued. By the early 1930s there was growing concern in the U.S. Public Health Service about the country's considerable addict population, particularly in the federal prison system. The obvious need for some kind of action led to the institution of two federal narcotic treatment facilities by the Public Health Service at Lexington, Kentucky (1935) and Fort Worth, Texas (1938).[17]

The underlying philosophy of the Lexington and Fort Worth programs was that the key to successful treatment was complete detoxification in prolonged isolation from the environment where addiction occurred. Thus, physical isolation from access to drugs and withdrawal under medical supervision formed the basis of their program. This approach to treatment in the Lexington and Fort Worth programs stood in marked contrast to the earlier community-based morphine maintenance clinics.

The limitations of the Public Health Service hospital program were recognized early. Patients experienced severe problems in readjusting psychologically and socially upon returning home to their communities, and recidivism was high.

The facilities at Lexington and Fort Worth remained the sole sources of help for opiate dependents for twenty years. While it has been easy in the light of subsequent developments to fault these programs, the clinical experience gained and the research conducted there formed the basis of opiate addiction studies upon which many subsequent advances in the field were built.

A major development in the evolution of drug treatment programs came in 1952 with the opening of a treatment facility for juvenile opiate addicts at Riverside Hospital in New York City.[18] Although hospital-based and in some respects similar to the Lexington and Fort Worth programs, the Riverside Hospital program was different in one important way: It was near enough to the patients' homes so that staff could help them readjust to the community and work with them after withdrawal was complete and they were no longer institutionalized. Thus the Riverside Hospital program became the first community-based program in the United States in thirty years.

Recent Program and Policy Developments

Therapeutic Communities. In 1959 a new heroin treatment concept appeared, that of the drug-free therapeutic community. The forerunner of this movement was the Synanon program in Los Angeles, California,[19] the first organized effort by addicts themselves to solve their problems through self-help techniques. The Synanon program was premised on the belief that only a former addict could break through the shell of denial and pathological lying of the addict. The Synanon leaders prided themselves on their rejection of the traditional medical approach to addiction. Instead, they concentrated on the psychological factors contributing to readdiction, and tried to restructure the addict's character so that a return to drugs would be unimaginable. The Synanon program espoused the view that those who entered the program must from that time forward be drug-free and reliant only on the discipline and support of their peers. In some respects, Synanon resembled Alcoholics Anonymous, but was was strikingly different in its demand for total immersion into a thoroughly disciplined lifestyle involving indefinite residence in the Synanon facility.

The Synanon approach to the treatment of heroin addiction came to be commonly referred to as the "therapeutic community" approach. By the late 1960s, therapeutic communities were in operation in many urban areas throughout the country.[20] Although there were wide variations in their philosophies and styles of operation, most therapeutic communities viewed heroin addiction as the result of psychological problems. Consequently, they relied upon intensive therapeutic techniques in a residential setting to restructure the client's character and personality so that he or she would assume a normal drug-free lifestyle. Most therapeutic communities held to a rather rigid structure of daily schedules and used a complex system of punishment and reward. Often these programs were run by former heroin addicts, many of whom held a deep mistrust of the traditional medical and mental health professions. Financially, many of these early therapeutic communities were independent from government support.

The therapeutic-community concept has continued to develop in several ways beyond its original Synanon form, so that present-day therapeutic communities differ appreciably from their predecessors. Among more recent changes has been a greater acceptance of government funding, to the point where many therapeutic-community programs could not exist without government financial support. Similarly, the earlier total rejection of medical and psychiatric professionals in favor of an ex-addict staff composed of nonprofessional peers of the clients has been tempered over the years; many therapeutic communities have moved to involve professional staff along with their paraprofessional and ex-addict counselors and staff. However, the focus of the therapeutic community movement continues to be on confronting the character and developmental faults of the treatment client in an effort to "remake" the individual's personality in an intensive, supportive residential setting.[21]

Predictably, as therapeutic-community programs have advanced beyond infancy, they have become increasingly sophisticated in both their treatment delivery plans and their organization and administration. Administratively, greater emphasis has been placed on program accountability in the provision of treatment services and on the development of standards for their operation.[22] In addition, an important shift has occurred in operational philosophy toward an emphasis on preparing the client for reentry to the community rather than on a continued reliance on the protective environment of the program.

The therapeutic communities have also encountered a number of problems, the greatest of which is the lack of voluntary participation as clients by a large number of addicts. Even for those who do seek this type of treatment, retention in treatment continues to be a problem area. On the other hand, it does appear that for those who do remain in treatment, this approach can elicit significant changes in individual attitudes, personality, and drug-using behavior.[23]

There are a number of other issues that therapeutic communities will have to address. An increasing number of their clients are referred from the criminal justice system, a development at odds with the original concept of purely voluntary admission. Other issues are connected with the above-mentioned acceptance of greater professionalism, such as the degree to which traditional medical and social science professionals can be more involved in the therapeutic-community program and the consistency with which certain standards of behavior toward clients can be adopted by the staffs of therapeutic communities.

Today's therapeutic communities must also examine their ability to handle the growing numbers of potential treatment candidates whose primary drug is not heroin. Related to this issue is how a therapeutic program ought to react to problems of alcohol misuse following successful heroin addiction intervention. Lastly, given the traditional therapeutic community stance for total abstinence from all substances in the wide range of psychoactive drugs, they must also now respond to greater societal acceptance of reasonable, moderate use of alcohol and marijuana.

Heroin Treatment and the Criminal Justice System. It is a central fact that the physical and mental health aspects of heroin treatment in the United States have always been related to the criminal justice system, albeit at some times more closely than at others. The above discussion of the growth and development of the therapeutic-community concept, and subsequent discussions of methadone maintenance, detoxification, and other heroin treatment approaches to be presented below all point out the continued interrelationship of heroin treatment and law enforcement.

One approach to emerge in the 1960s was dubbed "civil commitment." It could be described as "nonpunitive incarceration of an addict for the purpose of rehabilitation."[24]

Although civil commitment as such was first instituted by California (1961) and New York State (1962),[25] the early thrust of this approach was the frequent use of civil commitment procedures to confine addicts at the Lexington and Fort Worth hospitals. These procedures allowed the courts to order drug treatment and rehabilitation in lieu of incarceration for convicted felons whose offenses were thought to be related to drug use. The rationale for this was that, while treatment is preferable to incarceration, a strong legal mechanism is needed to force heroin addicts into treatment, hold them there until it is completed, and help ensure their continued abstinence from drugs upon return to the community. A similar federal program, the Narcotic Addict Rehabilitation Act (NARA), was instituted in 1966.

As drug treatment capacity was expanded during the early 1970s to meet an observed increase in heroin use, many programs found their services underutilized. Fewer people than expected appeared voluntarily for treatment. In response to this problem, some of those who considered heroin addiction to be a major source of urban crime even advocated "quarantining" addicts, a move which would have substantially expanded the civil and criminal commitment programs; however, the constitutionally protected rights of the individual precluded any serious thought of implementing this. Other solutions were sought which would gain new clients for the existing treatment system. One way was the "diversion" of heroin addicts from the criminal justice system into treatment in lieu of criminal prosecution or sentencing.

The new diversion programs were similar in concept to the civil commitment programs, but they operated less formally. Drug-free programs became the primary recipients of "diverted" offenders. (The con-

cept of diverting heroin addicts from the criminal justice system to methadone programs, where clients would be maintained on a synthetic opiate,
was and is a sensitive issue.) Due to court-imposed restrictions, the drug-
free programs generally chosen were live-in facilities rather than outpatient abstinence programs. Thus, as heroin treatment availability of all
types expanded beyond voluntary demand, therapeutic communities
turned increasingly to referrals from the criminal justice system as a way
to keep their programs going.

In 1973 the federal government instituted a national diversion program for identified heroin users in the federal criminal justice system.
This program, named Treatment Alternatives to Street Crime (TASC),
provides referrals to federally supported, community-based treatment
programs and supervises the referred individuals's progress in treatment.

The TASC program has proven to be enormously popular, growing
from programs in threee cities in 1973 to over forty in 1978.[26] Moreover, it
has inspired state and local criminal justice agencies to create similar referral programs for criminal offenders or arrestees. These referrals have
been effective in filling up existing treatment "slots" with clients. However, the quasi-involuntary status of these clients has caused problems in
the philosophy and operation of treatment programs. The modification of
operating procedures toward an emphasis upon such things as urinalysis
checks and reporting and termination procedures illustrates a shift in program focus to accommodate not what is best for the client but what is best
for the courts. And the financial support from the National Institute on
Drug Abuse for drug treatment of criminal offenders has unfortunately
lessened both the financial and philosophical support for voluntary treatment.

Methadone.   The greatest impact in the last fifteen years on the
treatment of narcotic addiction has come with the use of the synthetic
opiate methadone for maintenance of heroin addicts. While methadone
had been used at the Public Health Service hospital in Lexington to aid in
the heroin withdrawal process since the late 1940s, it was not used as a
maintenance drug until the mid-1960s. The reason methadone was selected for testing as a maintenance drug was that, unlike heroin (whose
effects last three to five hours), methadone's effects last twenty-four
hours. Another difference is that methadone can be taken orally, whereas
heroin is injected intravenously.

In 1964, researchers Vincent Dole, an internist and biochemist, and
Marie Nyswander, a psychiatrist, described a difference between the behavior of chronic heroin addicts maintained on methadone at a consistent
dosage level and that of others maintained on heroin.[27] Those maintained
on methadone appeared more alert, energetic, and interested in constructive social activities. In contrast, apparently because of heroin's short dur-

ation of effect and the resultant need for frequent injections, the group maintained on that drug was difficult to "stabilize," became lethargic after a heroin injection, and underwent mild withdrawal as it wore off. Dole and Nyswander hypothesized that repeated heroin use induces biochemical changes in the body requiring subsequent indefinite therapy with an opiate, just as insulin is required to treat a biochemical deficit in diabetics. Since addicts could be "stabilized" on methadone, these researchers believed that this was the opiate that would leave the individual most functional.

The treatment program designed by Dole and Nyswander did more than simply provide a substitute drug to patients. Once patients were stabilized on a fixed daily dose of methadone, they were offered counseling, job training, and various other forms of intensive support to facilitate the development of a productive life away from heroin. The initial few hundred patients they treated did remarkably well, which result aroused considerable interest throughout the country. For the first time, a significant number of heroin addicts were being treated on an outpatient basis within their own communities, rather than being kept in protracted isolation.

By the late 1960s, therefore, three general approaches had emerged for the treatment of heroin addiction: drug-free therapeutic communities (residential), methadone maintenance (outpatient), and drug-free incarceration (including both prison programs and hospital programs).

Each type of program drew upon different concepts of addiction, and treatment objectives varied from program to program. Individual programs representing all of these categories appeared in most major American cities. In most instances, they operated independently of each other and in fact frequently competed for patients and public support. However, in some cities (e.g., Chicago, Atlanta, and Washington, D.C.) different types of programs were linked together under a single "umbrella" agency; this unifying-agency system was called the "multimodality" approach to treatment. Its strength was that it facilitated referral of clients to the treatment approaches best filling their individual needs. In several cities a central "intake" facility provided initial screening of prospective clients for all treatment modalities, and staff and client together chose the treatment program they felt gave the greatest chance for success.

However, there were deep philosophical and ideological divisions fragmenting the heroin treatment field. At times it seemed as if the search was for one "right" form of treatment. Those who thought of heroin addicts as criminals tended to view the most restrictive forms of treatment most favorably. Those who viewed addiction as a product of the societal conditions of the urban poor favored strengthening the social-rehabilitation components of treatment. A gulf which seemed particularly broad was that between supporters of methadone maintenance and those believing in the drug-free approach of therapeutic communities.

Even within specific treatment modalities there were wide divergences in program philosophy and program operation. Methadone program directors argued vigorously among themselves about appropriate admissions criteria, dosage levels, counseling techniques, and termination procedures. Therapeutic community directors argued with equal vigor among themselves about reward and punishment systems, duration of time in different phases of treatment, and involvement of medical professionals. These disagreements carried over into public forums, serving to confuse and divide the general public over the efficacy of various types of drug treatment programs. There was little acknowledgment at this time that there might be more than one type of heroin addict, more than one approach to treatment, or that the same person might benefit at one time from methadone maintenance treatment and at another from the therapeutic-community approach.

These debates during the late 1960s about treatment approaches to heroin addiction took place in the context of increasing heroin use and rising public concern. Pressure mounted for greater federal involvement in the drug field. But in contrast to drug law enforcement the drug treatment field was unable to present a unified position; federal support lagged. Heroin addicts were viewed more as criminals to be feared than as people in need of treatment and assistance. One would have hardly predicted the enormous expansion of drug treatment programs which soon occurred.

The two factors that prompted the unanticipated expansion of the national drug treatment effort in the 1970s were the development of a public health theory of heroin addiction and concern about returning heroin-addicted Vietnam War veterans. While both these factors soon receded in importance, the infrastructure of treatment programs created in response to them has remained generally intact.

Public Health Theory of Addiction.   The public health theory of heroin addiction emerged with the publication in 1969 of a paper entitled "The Spread of Heroin Abuse in a Community," which looked at the spread of heroin addiction within an English community.[28] The author, d'Alarcon, found that new heroin users tended to be introduced to the drug by those already addicted. He established a model that bore a close resemblance to that for the spread of infectious diseases in epidemics. His thesis suggested that traditional public health methods should be applied to the treatment of opiate addiction.

For those who endorsed d'Alarcon's theory, it was clearly unacceptable merely to treat small numbers, even if the quality of care was the best available; what seemed crucial was the involvement of as many heroin addicts as possible, even if treatment did not always measure up to desired standards. According to the public health theory, the more people involved the easier it would be to prevent the spread of heroin use and addiction. Theoretically, the client would also be less likely to become reinvolved with heroin when most of his peers were in treatment. In addition, according to adherents of the public health concept, the higher the percentage of addicts in treatment within a given community, the more the heroin market there would be undercut and the less lucrative it would become for traffickers.

This public health approach to treatment was an attractive concept for federal strategists concerned primarily about reducing heroin-related crime. It suggested that heroin treatment programs handling large numbers of addicts could reduce crime and prevent the continued spread of addiction as well as help rehabilitate heroin addicts. Moreover, the public health concept provided an alternative to civil commitment and incarceration, neither of which had proven to be satisfactory.

Returning Vietnam Veterans. Public support for drug treatment also grew out of fear over the large numbers of heroin-using returning Vietnam War veterans. These fears seemed to peak following a congressional report claiming heroin use to run as high as 100 percent in some units in Vietnam.[29] The prospect of addicted former soldiers trained in guerilla warfare left to roam the streets of urban America was alarming. Yet prison seemed a rather harsh, uncharitable response for those who had become addicted while in service to their country. Treatment of some kind, if it would work, seemed more desirable and humane.

Treatment thus rapidly became an important element in the overall national drug strategy, and federal funding increased substantially. However, federal support grew in rather haphazard ways; several separate federal agencies were funding different kinds of treatment programs, sometimes for different reasons.

The federal commitment to drug treatment entered a new era in June 1971 when the Special Action Office for Drug Abuse Prevention (SAODAP) was created by President Nixon's executive order. SAODAP was empowered to coordinate the federal drug treatment effort as it grew rapidly from $87 to $196 million in 1972.[30] Consistent with the public health theory of heroin addiction, federal strategists sought to provide treatment to every addict needing or wanting it. Large community-based programs were established across the country. Some individual urban programs enrolled more than ten thousand clients in both primary and satellite clinics. These large programs were most often "multimodality," offering a variety of programs to an entrant, who could then choose the one best suited to his or her needs. Transfer between programs was made relatively easy.

As previously stated, the primary goal of the new public health concept of heroin addiction was to get as large a percentage of the addict population into treatment as quickly as possible. However, therapeutic-community programs could handle only a small number of people at a time, and their cost per patient was high (from four to ten thousand per year).[31] Civil commitment could not do much better at involving large numbers; federal NARA and state civil commitment procedures were complicated, so the number of people under civil commitment was never very large. Of the available treatment approaches, methadone maintenance seemed the one best suited to the public health theory of heroin addiction.

Methadone maintenance.   The new, greater involvement of the federal government in heroin treatment had a distinct effect on the operating styles and characteristics of treatment programs. The new methadone maintenance programs were premised on the Dole-Nyswander pioneer program; in practice, however, they varied considerably from that original model and from each other. As the expanded system developed, a number of new maintenance programs emerged which only dispensed methadone and did not employ an intensive format of personal counseling, job training, and other rehabilitation efforts of the early Dole-Nyswander program. (As it turned out, the provision of counseling and ancillary social rehabilitation services proved to be a key variable in program design and practice.) In part these discrepancies were due to differing program philosophies, but the major factor was that funding for such program services in the new federal strategy was inadequate. Quantity received priority over quality.

The methadone maintenance programs were heavily regulated, due to concern over methadone's potential for diversion into the black market and the absence of complete safety and effectiveness data on methadone. Three federal agencies—the Drug Enforcement Administration, the Food and Drug Administration, and the National Institute on Drug Abuse—became involved in regulating methadone programs.

Guidelines specifying staffing requirements have led to improvements in the weakest programs, but these requirements for staffing are minimal. On the other hand, some professionals have contended that the considerable regulatory strictures that resulted have served to undermine methadone treatment's effectiveness by limiting program flexibility.[32] Rigid standards of program compliance have interfered with the delivery of high quality services in other programs. The argument against a high degree of standardization in treatment practices is that standards are often set which are inappropriate or written arbitrarily without sufficient program experience as a guide. The result has been a disruption of the delicate balance between the need for flexibility and creativity on the one hand and the need to protect treatment clients, the general public welfare, and public funds on the other.

Between June 1971 and June 1973 approximately one hundred thousand total treatment "slots" were created by federal funds in virtually every major urban center in the country. A commensurate dramatic increase in state funding also occurred; the governor of every state was required by federal law to designate one coordinating agency ("Single State Agency") for all drug treatment, rehabilitation, and prevention efforts within the state. Initially, funding by the federal government was almost entirely for the treatment of heroin addiction; however, many of the states even at this point concentrated more on non-opiate drug abuse and general drug abuse prevention and education.

Full utilization of treatment did not continue for long after this expansion was completed by late 1973. Among the heroin-using Vietnam War veterans, the need for drug treatment services turned out to be much lower than expected; very few of the returning soldiers continued to use heroin once back in the United States.[33] American heroin users and addicts who had not been in military service also appeared for treatment in smaller numbers than anticipated, and those who did generally remained in treatment for shorter periods of time than expected.

The fact that many Vietnam War veterans were able to give up heroin use on their own upon their return challenged the prevailing notion that heroin addiction caused irrevocable physiological craving for the drug. This experience had important implications for the use of methadone in treatment and eventually led to increased pressure on maintenance programs to detoxify clients from methadone rather than maintain stable dosage levels.

The inability of treatment programs to attract a high level of utilization also undermined the potential effectiveness of the public health addiction treatment concept. In a number of ways then, as the demand for heroin addiction treatment stabilized during the mid-1970s, treatment programs were assuming new goals and styles of operation.

Heroin Treatment and the General Health Care System

The expansion of drug treatment in the 1970s generally occurred apart from the mainstream of general health and mental health care delivery. Separate facilities were developed to provide treatment for heroin addicts. As a result, heroin treatment is now largely a stepchild in the federal health bureaucracy; there has been little effort to integrate it with other health care agencies and services.

Until 1971, the bulk of the federal heroin treatment effort had been administered by the National Institute of Mental Health (NIMH); the problem was generally viewed as a combined medical and psychiatric one requiring careful, individualized attention. However, the increase in public concern about heroin addiction during the late 1960s and early 1970s led to changes in public perceptions. Increasingly, heroin problems were seen as public health, social welfare, and criminal justice issues. When NIMH resisted this change, it ultimately lost its administrative role in the expanding federal drug treatment effort to the initiatives of the White House's Special Action Office for Drug Abuse Prevention. (SAODAP). Once the expansion process was complete, responsibility for maintenance of the system was returned to the Department of Health, Education, and Welfare (HEW) and its National Institute on Drug Abuse (NIDA), where it remains to this day.

There are a number of factors which have discouraged the incorporation of heroin treatment into the traditional health care system. There is the general reluctance of health care professionals to treat addicts and their related problems. There is also the absence of any system allowing for reimbursement with federal and private health dollars for services provided by nonprofessional, non–hospital-sponsored programs. Furthermore, contemporary heroin treatment programs simply do not resemble "treatment" in the conventional medical sense, but are focused more on social issues and the provision of rehabilitative social services.

As the number of drug treatment programs expanded during the early 1970s, the concept of treatment also grew. It is now common to refer to heroin treatment as "drug treatment *and* rehabilitation." Although both terms—"treatment" and "rehabilitation"—elude strict definition, "treatment" generally refers to the more narrowly defined medical functions of directly dealing with immediate physical and emotional ailments. "Rehabilitation" is a more encompassing term; it goes beyond the repair of immediately identifiable ailments, focusing instead on broader efforts at development or restoration of what society defines as a normal, acceptable life style.[34] Although there is some overlap between what constitutes treatment and what constitutes rehabilitation, it is clear that treatment can take place without rehabilitation—and often has done so.

The importance of rehabilitation as a component of treatment has clearly grown. One factor that might help explain this change is that heroin addiction in the 1970s has been more often associated with the inadequate conditions in which many of the urban poor live. Deteriorated economic and social conditions came to be seen as a major cause of heroin addiction among the urban poor, and heroin treatment programs were given increasing responsibility for helping their clients escape such conditions. This kind of social and economic rehabilitation became a very important component of drug treatment programs in the early 1970s and has remained so.

However, this development has made the absorption of heroin treatment into the traditional health and mental health care system even more

difficult, since critical components of the rehabilitative services provided—e.g., vocational training and legal counseling—would be unlikely
candidates for reimbursement under generally accepted notions of national health care schemes. To date, drug treatment programs have had only
limited success in securing "third-party" payments (i.e., Medicare, Medicaid, Blue Cross / Blue Shield) even for traditional treatment services. In
addition, community drug treatment needs are not ordinarily part of the
planning activities of the recently established nationwide network of
Health Systems Agencies (HSA), intended to plan for the nation's future
health care needs in a systematic fashion.

Some steps have been initiated to facilitate the adoption of drug
treatment into the overall health care network. An accreditation program
for drug treatment programs has been started through the Joint Commission on the Accreditation of Hospitals.[35] States now have licensing requirements for drug programs.[36] There is also much closer interaction
now between state drug agencies and state agencies for alcoholism and
mental health. Studies have been sponsored to examine possible accreditation systems for paraprofessional drug-treatment program workers.[37] Efforts are underway to insure more careful consideration of drug treatment
program needs within the HSA planning systems.[38] All these are encouraging signs of an awareness that drug treatment cannot continue to remain apart from the general health and mental health fields.

However, in spite of the vagaries involved in the old categorical
funding system for heroin treatment and the potential advantages in
greater coordination with traditional health care agencies, there are risks
in too complete an absorption. Drug treatment—particularly for heroin—is but a small portion of the totality of the nation's physical and
mental health care needs. Competing issues and needs might well reduce
the position of drug treatment in any reintegrated, total health care system. On the other hand, the advantages of lessening the stigma of drug
treatment and improving access to other elements of the health care system are substantial.

Current Status of Heroin Treatment

There are now four major heroin treatment types or modalities:
methadone and LAAM* maintenance programs (outpatient), detoxification programs (outpatient), drug-free programs (outpatient), and drug-
free therapeutic communities (residential). In addition, there are inpatient hospital programs for methadone maintenance and detoxification,
civil commitment programs, and drug-free programs in prisons. With the

*L-alpha acetyl methadol, a long-acting form of methadone.

amount of money spent on treatment exceeding the $.5 billion level in 1978, there is an ever-increasing need to evaluate and measure the effectiveness of these different programs and of heroin treatment generally.

However, there are major gaps in our knowledge which make it difficult to evaluate efficacy of treatment. For example, we do not have a thorough understanding of the natural history of opiate dependency in those who do not appear for treatment. We lack information on controlled and nonaddictive opiate use and on the spontaneous cessation of addictive use without treatment intervention.

An inherent problem in evaluating the effectiveness of treatment for an individual addict is that heroin dependency is mostly a *chronic* condition, whereas most treatment episodes and evaluations are short-term in nature. In fact, an addict who achieves a positive benefit from treatment will typically have had several treatment experiences. Therefore, the effectiveness of treatment for that individual cannot be evaluated solely on the basis of one treatment experience, but rather upon the ability of a number of treatment episodes to contribute to his or her eventual success. However, most evaluations of treatment do not follow the individual through several treatment episodes over the years, but rather describe the influence of a single treatment intervention. They do so for individuals having a broad variety of backgrounds and addiction histories.

In addition, the wide variation among treatment program objectives and practices, even within a single treatment modality, makes it extremely difficult to achieve accurate assessments of overall treatment capacity.

Studies of treatment program effectiveness are carried out in the face of continually changing client populations, major shifts in treatment approaches, and changes in social attitudes regarding psychoactive drug use and addiction. The longer-term evaluations of treatment outcomes are now assessing the impact of programs developed in the early 1970s, while current programs may have already changed in significant ways. Long-term consistent follow-up evaluation must of course follow the actual treatment experience by some considerable length of time, yet the results obtained would apply only to treatment as it existed when provided.

Other factors intrinsic to the complexity of drug use and addiction and independent of the kind of treatment provided influence the results of drug treatment. Older clients, for example, are generally less likely to relapse than younger users. The length of time in treatment, the number of previous treatment exposures, the motivation for entering drug treatment, and the socioeconomic status of particular clients all contribute to wide fluctuations in success rates from program to program and modality to modality.

Even less obvious are outside influences which may turn out to be the most important variables in drug treatment success. For example, changes in general economic conditions may play a vital role in the rehabilitation of a former, compulsive user and his assimilation into a productive lifestyle. But treatment evaluations do not take account of such factors, a situation which further qualifies and limits their relevance.

In reviewing the major treatment modalities a number of evaluative studies have been selected to illustrate the kinds of information we do have at hand. Due in large part to the various limitations described above, they have not provided a definitive answer to the public's question of what does and does not work.

Maintenance Programs: Methadone and LAAM. As noted earlier, the drug primarily used is the synthetic opiate methadone, which has similar pharmacological properties to heroin but a duration of effect of twenty-four hours in blocking narcotic withdrawal, as contrasted to heroin's three to four hours.[39] The longer duration of methadone allows the addict to be "stabilized" or maintained on a daily oral dose. LAAM (L-alpha acetyl methadol), a long-acting form of methadone, is now beginning to be used for maintenance purposes.[40] Unlike ordinary methadone, which has to be taken every twenty-four hours, LAAM has an effect lasting two to three days. Because LAAM only has to be administered three times per week, all of the drug can be administered at the clinic site, thereby eliminating any possibility of illicit diversion. LAAM has been tested thus far on several thousand addicts. For a number of reasons, not the least of which is that LAAM has fewer subjective effects than methadone,* methadone is still the preferred maintenance drug among clients; LAAM is unlikely to replace it on a wide scale. Its voluntary use will probably be limited to the select group of patients who prefer the absence of a subjective drug effect yet need a drug lasting two to three days or to programs that institute its use as a public health measure to eliminate the problems of diversion with "take-home" methadone.[41] Our maintenance treatment experience over a fifteen-year period has essentially centered on the use of one drug, methadone, and will probably continue to do so.

One early evaluation of methadone's effectiveness examined the Dole-Nyswander maintenance program in New York begun in 1964.[42] As of 1970, this evaluation showed remarkable program retention of clients, reduction in criminal activity, increases in productive activities (particularly employment), and cessation of illicit drug use. However, as later critics of this study pointed out, there were some significant limitations to the data which were not widely appreciated at the time.[43] Because of the relatively stable nature of this first group of maintenance patients, retention rates were unusually high. More recent federal statistics on methadone maintenance treatment show lower retention rates overall. Of the

---

* The client on methadone, while not experiencing a high (in fact, feeling quite the opposite), feels the effects of having taken a drug. This feeling is less pronounced with LAAM.

approximately 24,000 methadone treatment clients who for one reason or another left treatment in 1976, half had been enrolled for less than twenty weeks.[44] These more recent data reflect the varied capabilities, standards, and emphases of individual programs and the overall complexity of treating opiate addiction itself.

The crime reduction figures of the original Dole-Nyswander group were also misleadingly high at 90 percent. The evaluators had looked at the *rate* of criminal convictions as applied to total time in treatment, a process which overemphasized the long-term, noncriminal patients, since those convicted of crimes were discharged immediately.[45]

The results of this first evaluation of the methadone-maintenance heroin treatment modality, so impressive at the time, were a primary basis of the governmentally sponsored methadone treatment expansion in the early 1970s.

Later studies of patients who have been treated with methadone maintenance show somewhat contradictory results. Two optimistic assessments showed sharply diminished rates of drug misuse after treatment, compared with premethadone treatment levels.[46] But a number of other studies show significant rates of relapse to use of heroin and other drugs soon after termination of maintenance treatment.[47]

Researchers Dole and Joseph reported in 1977 the results of a study of a group selected from several thousand patients who entered the New York City methadone programs in 1972.[48] They compared the progress of a group which had dropped out of treatment with one remaining in treatment. Sixty-eight percent of the dropout out group had returned to some "street" narcotic use (although sometimes in small amounts), while only 7 percent of those who remained were still using illicit narcotics.[49] Alcoholism also emerged as a more serious problem after detoxification from maintenance than in the group remaining on maintenance. Altogether, 89 percent of the patients who had left maintenance treatment had either relapsed to narcotic use, used other drugs in a disabling way, become alcoholic, been arrested, or died. This figure should be compared with the 47 percent figure of those still in maintenance who experienced continuing problems with drug abuse, alcohol, or criminality.[50]

Another study, this one of the Santa Clara County methadone maintenance program in California (1975–77), showed a more positive outcome.[51] One quarter of the clients initially admitted to treatment five years previously had stayed in treatment, although not necessarily continuously. One-third of this group had been abstinent from heroin for a minimum of six months. However, a significant percentage of them (25 percent) were still using heroin regularly.[52] Half of those no longer in treatment were "successful" graduates of the maintenance program in that they were not incarcerated or using illegal narcotics.[53]

Effectiveness of maintenance treatment is also indicated by data on some 11,157 patients who remained in the New York City Methadone

Program. Correlating length in treatment with drug use and social rehabilitative parameters, this study by the former director of the New York program, Dr. Robert Newman, showed that gainful employment increased while arrests and heroin use decreased.[54]

These studies may simply be measuring the effectiveness of treatment per se compared to none at all. These data for methadone may just illustrate that heroin addicts can do well if engaged in some type of treatment. But the special feature of methadone maintenance is that it has involved the participation of a large number of addicts and has had relatively high retention rates compared to other treatment modalities.

Detoxification Programs. The second major approach to heroin treatment, detoxification, is designed to relieve withdrawal symptoms and to enable heroin dependents to be free, at least temporarily, of their addiction. The ordinary course of treatment in the United States lasts twenty-one days, although some large detoxification programs, such as that of New York City, prescribe a shorter period of seven to fourteen days.[55] The two primary goals of detoxification programs are to detoxify the heroin dependent—withdrawing him or her as rapidly as possible from dependence on the drug while mitigating the physical discomfort of the process—and outreach, i.e., involving the user in some form of treatment. Studies have found that these short detoxification programs can work reasonably well insofar as achieving the immediate goal of withdrawal is concerned. For the New York City detoxification program, 43 percent of over sixty thousand admissions completed the prescribed detoxification plan with an average stay of six days.[56] However, four recent studies of heroin detoxification show that only 2 to 7 percent of those receiving such treatment remain abstinent for substantial lengths of time.[57] In fact, one study found that on the average heroin use resumed within eight-and-one-half days after starting the brief twenty-one-day detoxification program cycle.[58]

Detoxification efforts are now viewed by many treatment experts as being of value in providing a first step in the involvement of compulsive heroin users in more comprehensive, longer-term forms of therapy, as well as in providing needed medical support during withdrawal. Programs have shown some success in inducing detoxified users into longer-term treatment. For example, the outpatient New York City detoxification program found that a small but significant 15 percent of its clients entered long-term treatment within the month following referral from the detoxification program.[59] In addition, whereas early detoxification efforts were primarily focused on getting the addict off heroin in the shortest possible time, the emphasis has now shifted to longer-duration detoxification. This shift has resulted from the clinical experience of methadone maintenance programs that rapid rates of detoxification from methadone are accompanied by early dropping out and a return to "street" heroin.[60]

There has also been more attention directed at providing the kinds of support during and immediately after detoxification that would help the client accomplish longer periods of abstinence. This has included increased attention to counseling and rehabilitative services and the testing of other pharmacological approaches. For example, several programs are now identifying addicts who show definite symptoms of depression during and immediately after detoxification, and are treating this group with antidepressant drugs. Another approach has been to find nonnarcotic aids to detoxification; one drug now being tested is *clonidine*, a drug which affects the neurotransmitters in the brain, but is not itself a narcotic.[61]

The introduction of *naltrexone* has also provided a new and different pharmacological support for heroin dependent patients. Naltrexone is a narcotic antagonist which, while not itself addicting, can completely block the effects of injected heroin; it can be taken orally on a daily or thrice-weekly basis. Unlike an earlier antagonist drug, *cyclazocine*, naltrexone has virtually no unpleasant side effects. Its safety and effectiveness are now undergoing clinical investigation[62]; approximately one thousand addicts have been treated with it. Thus far it appears that naltrexone is a safe and effective drug.

While the average heroin dependent who takes naltrexone does so for relatively short periods (a few weeks), a few stay on the drug for as long as a year; however, only a small number of heroin addicts have volunteered to take it, and for this reason it may have a relatively small impact on the total treatment effort. Preliminary studies of the drug's effectiveness show that it has provided significant support for heroin abstinence and is positively correlated with the achievement of social rehabilitative goals.[63] Whether the positive results are due to the antagonist drug itself or are simply an indication that the group electing to take it is more highly motivated, naltrexone is likely to remain an important but limited adjunct to treatment during the transition from detoxification to continued abstinence.

Outpatient Drug-free Programs. Another heroin treatment approach which emerged during the 1960s is outpatient abstinence. In marked contrast to the therapeutic communities and civil commitment programs, with their intensity, rigidity, and cost, outpatient abstinence programs seek to help drug-involved people through individual counseling, group therapy, employment assistance, job training, and other supportive services.

The statistics of this modality are difficult to interpret.[64] The federal treatment data show it to be a leading modality of treatment, but its impact on heroin treatment seems small. Where the outpatient drug-free modality is a component of a methadone maintenance program, it is frequently treating the heroin-addicted population. However, the free-standing outpatient drug-free programs are generally directed primarily not at heroin dependency but at other illicit drug use, including the misuse of prescription drugs.

As a heroin treatment modality, outpatient drug-free treatment is perhaps the most amorphous type. It can range from sporadic, follow-up counseling for clients detoxified from heroin or methadone to more intensive therapy groups of former addicts.

A study by Texas Christian University provides a limited amount of data on the effectiveness of outpatient drug-free treatment for heroin users.[65] Retention rates are low; in 1976 more than 50 percent of those discharged had been in treatment less than twelve weeks.[66] Despite the seeming lack of effectiveness of this modality, it continues to be used. One factor that may account for this high level of utilization in spite of its generally observed limitations is that funding for it is identical on a daily perpatient basis to that of the more intensively and extensively staffed and administered methadone maintenance programs. This funding situation coupled with the preference of criminal justice diversion programs for drug-free modalities over methadone has had the effect of channeling substantial numbers of clients through outpatient drug-free treatment programs.

Drug-Free Therapeutic Community Programs.   The focus of the therapeutic-community concept is on confronting the crucial faults in the personality and character of the former heroin addict within a residential group setting where the addicts' peers form the staff and support structure. It is in the nature of such programs that they are limited in size and, because of their residential character, more costly than outpatient programs. In spite of these limitations, since the therapeutic-community concept began in 1959 "TC" programs have grown greatly in number, involving thousands of heroin-dependent clients over the years. Evaluations of those programs have illustrated both their strengths and weaknesses.

One problem has been retention of clients. For example, during 1976 more than half of those leaving therapeutic-community programs had been in treatment less than eight weeks, according to data compiled by the National Institute on Drug Abuse.[67] As stated previously, drug treatment professionals generally feel that opiate addiction requires long-term involvement with treatment, and therefore tend to stress retention rates as a measure of a particular program's effectiveness. Thus, the difficulty of the therapeutic-community treatment modality in holding a majority of clients for a significant length of time is an important factor.

However, other studies have shown that those who do remain in the therapeutic-community program tend to do well. One large-scale study of former TC clients found 20 percent to be entirely drug abstinent and leading "constructive lives" four years after their initial entrance into treatment.[68] Another 25.3 percent were leading constructive lives but continuing to use some drugs—e.g., marijuana—or were in treatment at another program. Other studies have found similar indications of enhanced constructive behavior following a significant period in a therapeutic-community program.[69] However, as one experienced drug treatment research team has noted, "The subject probably enters treatment at precisely the point when he is most in trouble; later at any arbitrary follow-up point, he is statistically less likely to be using heroin or to be engaged in other episodic activity."[70] It should be pointed out that this statement, while referring to therapeutic communities, is likely to be true of all modalities for heroin treatment.

Other Approaches.   One suggestion for making treatment more acceptable to addicts who might not otherwise seek help has been the introduction of prescribed heroin into a treatment program. While a number of specific proposals of how this would be accomplished and evaluated have been made, no such study has yet been initiated. The idea has met with considerable controversy, possibly because critics have assumed that the proposals are for a long-term heroin maintenance system. In reality what has been proposed is that studies be conducted on the use of heroin in treatment, and that the heroin be used for only a limited time to assess whether short-term heroin maintenance can be followed by either transfer to methadone maintenance or detoxification, with abstinence treatment in an outpatient or residential setting to follow.

This brief review of the current status of the four major U.S. heroin treatment modalities has found certain differences in objectives and practices as well as in results. However, there are some recognizable similarities: All current forms of heroin treatment in the United States have abstinence from illicit drug use as their ultimate goal. Nearly all of the treatment types share an intermediate treatment objective, the reduction of criminal behavior by clients. They face common issues as well, such as the appropriate relationship between treatment programs and criminal justice agencies, accountability to funding sources, and confidentiality of patient treatment records.

What Are We Treating?

It is critical to an understanding of heroin treatment to examine exactly what it is that we are treating. While the answer may appear to be self-evident, a closer look reveals substantial disagreement and confusion within the field and among the general public as well.

The preceding discussion of the current status of heroin treatment demonstrates that a variety of results have been cited to illustrate the effectiveness or ineffectiveness of a particular program. This variety reflects in part considerable ambiguity concerning why we ought to provide treatment and what we expect from it. While one would think that consensus has been achieved regarding our motivations behind providing "drug abuse treatment," there are in fact several answers to the question, "What are we treating?" For the treatment system has embraced a number of diverse goals. Three of them—crime reduction, social rehabilitation, and abstinence—are examples of goals which have been taken for granted as being desirable, realistic, and achievable. What are the consequences of adopting such ambitious goals for the treatment effort?

Crime Reduction. The tremendous expansion in heroin addiction treatment efforts during the early 1970s would never have come about without the firm belief that heroin use was responsible for a large amount of crime. It is not surprising, therefore, that one of the prominent goals for many programs was reducing the criminal behavior of those using illicit opiates. Crime reduction is an example of a broadly supported social goal which readily became a treatment goal.

Making crime reduction a primary goal for heroin addiction treatment has had two major implications: One is a shift in emphasis from voluntary to involuntary treatment; the other, establishing as a consequence a close alliance with the criminal justice system as a source of client referrals. This shift sits well with those who advocate involuntary treatment, since they usually believe that it will serve the societal goal of reducing crime, but it creates basic problems. Where criminal justice system referrals comprise all or most of the client populations, "drug treatment" is often a misnomer. The primary motivation of the client referred by the criminal justice system is likely to be obtaining a lighter sentence, a dismissal of pending charges, or a punishment less severe than incarceration. The heavy influx of criminal justice referrals has also affected program operations by introducing more coercive procedures, which make them much less attractive to potential voluntary entrants.

This trend has affected not only the operating style of individual programs but the nature of entire treatment modalities as well. For example, as discussed earlier, drug-free programs have become increasingly dependent upon the criminal justice system as a source of clients. In 1976, one third of the heroin addicts admitted to residential drug-free programs were reported as involuntary, and one fifth of all heroin users admitted to drug-free outpatient programs were either involuntary or quasi-involuntary (e.g., civil commitment, the TASC program, or court referral).[71] This is an unfortunate development; the predominance of criminal justice clientele has shifted the program from the supportive group therapy approach to an increasingly custodial role. Thus, emphasizing crime reduction as a therapeutic goal has led to an overlap of values between treatment and criminal justice. This in turn has encouraged a trend toward involuntary approaches in heroin treatment. While involuntary treatment may be preferable to incarceration, it is not preferable to voluntary treatment.

It is not generally recognized that the differences between voluntary and involuntary treatment are of fundamental importance. Some argue that since many voluntary clients are "forced" into treatment because of some external pressures, there is really little difference between voluntary and involuntary treatment systems. This is not so; when a client is free to leave treatment without adverse legal consequences, he is more likely to recognize that treatment affords the opportunity for positive change, not because of a threat of adverse consequences, but because of his or her choosing to take a greater personal role in changing dysfunctional behavior. In other words, voluntary treatment challenges the concept that the opiate addict is a "helpless" victim, whereas involuntary treatment, by diminishing choice, perpetuates the status quo. And, possibly for this reason, involuntary treatment for addiction, while supported by some studies,[72] has been shown by others to be largely ineffectual.[73]

It seems certain that crime reduction goals have had and will have a potentially major influence on program operations. It is still questionable whether heroin treatment in fact significantly diminishes criminal activity.

The belief that drug treatment is an effective measure for reducing crime stems largely from the reported effectiveness of pilot methadone programs in reducing the criminal behavior of clients. For example, the initial results of five years of experience with the original Dole-Nyswander methadone maintenance program begun in 1970 showed that arrest rates dropped dramatically from pretreatment levels of 120 (arrests per patient years) to 5.5 during treatment.[74] However, as pointed out earlier, this study did not look at those who had dropped out of treatment or were otherwise discharged, who in fact showed rates similar to the pretreatment rate. In addition, those clients with the highest arrest rates prior to treatment were the least likely to remain in treatment. These limitations were largely unacknowledged at the time, as the public and policymakers alike saw only the impressive crime reduction statistics.

Overlooked in the push to provide heroin treatment as a means of reducing "street" crime was the fact that a large percentage of clients had criminal histories predating their initial use of illicit drugs. A 1976 review of drugs and crime sponsored by the National Institute on Drug Abuse cited ten separate studies showing that between 57 and 100 percent of clients admitted to a variety of treatment programs had been arrested prior to entering treatment.[75]

Subsequently, the Harvard Law School Center of Criminal Justice conducted a series of studies to determine the impact of heroin treatment on criminality.[76] This study reviewed criminal histories prior to the onset of heroin addiction, during addiction, and after treatment, reviewing aggregate arrest rates as well. The investigators distinguished between arrests for drug offenses and those for offenses against persons or property. They found that the level of criminal behavior as reflected by arrest rates did increase after addiction and decrease somewhat following treatment. However, the reduction observed in non–drug-related crime following treatment was not statistically significant; that is, it could have occurred by chance or through some factor other than the provision of treatment.

Other studies have indeed shown some correlation between the provision of heroin treatment and lowered crime rates. A study in Detroit conducted by the Public Research Institute analyzed crime rates and heroin-treatment enrollments for a four-year period. Results showed that property crimes decreased city-wide by 2.3 percent when treatment enrollments increased by 10 percent.[77] However, another study conducted in California found that arrests actually increased during treatment.[78] Given the difficulties with using arrest records as a reflection of actual criminal activity, most studies on the impact of drug treatment on criminality conclude that there is some reduction in crime among those in treatment compared to their earlier pretreatment behavior, but there are sometimes wide discrepancies from program to program. Such differences could be due to the studies themselves, the programs, the client population being treated, or some combination of these and other factors.

These studies do not address the question whether treatment's effect on criminal activity simply reflects the participation in any form of treatment of clients normally incapable of regulating their drug use or avoiding arrest. Nor do these evaluative studies answer whether the observed decline in criminal behavior could be due in part to the normal process of "maturing out" as regards crime and addiction, a phenomenon many observers have noted.[79] In short, while involvement in any type of heroin treatment appears to have some inhibitory effect on criminal activity as measured by arrests, these changes do not seem to be profound.

The more a program seeks specifically to reduce criminal behavior, the more the client is apt to view it as a branch of the criminal justice system, and voluntary entrance becomes less likely. For the program to maintain program funding, involuntary referrals become more likely. This cyclical situation reinforces the penal aspect of heroin treatment.

Social Rehabilitation. Treatment for heroin dependency is also viewed as a mechanism by which to produce social benefits other than crime reduction. Many inner city users come from broken families, live in substandard housing, experience inadequate education, and are unemployed. Whether these social conditions cause heroin addiction, or whether it is heroin addiction that prevents the individual from achieving a more productive lifestyle, it is believed that the addict can rehabilitate himself, and be free of the old environment, once free of heroin.

Treatment programs have become increasingly aware that specific social rehabilitation services are essential factors in successful treatment of many of their clients. Thus, treatment programs have now taken upon themselves the task of rectifying their clients' deficiencies in education, employment, and personal relationships, as well as treating addiction itself. Social rehabilitation is an example of a treatment program goal which is gradually, though grudgingly, gaining more support by the general public.

Employment is an example illustrative of the issues and problems involved in emphasizing social rehabilitative goals in heroin treatment. Employment is considered by many to be fundamental to the rehabilitative process; unemployment, after all, is high among heroin addicts. Periods of high unemployment affect unskilled, undereducated minority populations disproportionately, and for the past eight years, unemployment rates in general have been high. In the early 1970s, the federal government considered a subsidized program for employers who would hire former drug addicts.[80] However, before such a program could be enacted, the employment boom which had coincided with the Vietnam War leveled off, and jobs generally became more difficult to find. Nearly half the opiate addicts in treatment in 1976 had less than a high school education, and three quarters were unemployed at the time of entry into treatment.[81] Only 2 percent of all those in treatment in 1976 completed a "skills development" program while in treatment.[82]

Historically, outbreaks of "drug epidemics"—and outbreaks of public concern over drug use—have occurred during periods of job shortages and high labor surpluses, particularly at the bottom of the job-skill market. It has been hypothesized that such "drug epidemics" are the result of social class repression aimed at removing portions of the lower socioeconomic classes from the labor market by stigmatizing them as addicts and deviants.[83] This is compounded by the fact that more than half the clients entering treatment for opiates have criminal records.[84] This double stigmatization underscores the stereotypical portrait of heroin addicts as unmotivated and prone to steal, thus making potential employers extremely leery of hiring ex-addicts. The labor surplus and discriminatory hiring practices serve as disincentives to ex-addicts in seeking employment. These hurdles to finding jobs make recidivism to drugs and crime more likely, thus leading to a self-fulfilling prophecy which reinforces existing prejudices.

While many treatment programs consider vocational rehabilitation a priority, the proposed new federal methadone regulations suggest a near-total lack of federal concern with employment for drug treatment clients.[85] The new regulations provide only very general guidelines for referrals to community programs and a listing of employment and training services. There is no requirement for close coordination between programs and community organizations or for any kind of follow-up on the outcome of referrals. While recent interpretations of the 1973 federal statute forbidding discrimination against the handicapped include drug treatment clients and ex-addicts in their definition, increasing employer interest in hiring ex-addicts and otherwise lowering the barriers to employment have not been emphasized.[86] This situation persists despite the fact that several long-term studies have found employment to be one of the best predictors of success in treatment.[87] Although some of the large federal labor-training programs such as CETA (Comprehensive Employment and Training Act) accept treatment-program referrals, coordination has been weak and completion rates low. The few specific job development programs for former treatment patients that do exist have not been expanded much beyond the pilot stage.

In the private sector there have been some initiatives toward providing jobs for former addicts.[88] One effort in New York City, called the National Association on Drug Abuse Problems (NADAP), has organized the participation of industry and labor and placed some 800 recovered addicts in jobs in the New York City area over the past decade. Another innovative approach to developing employment for addicts was undertaken by the VERA Institute of Justice, also located in New York City. This program, the Wildcat Service Corporation, was later incorporated as a pilot program for job development by the federal government. While this project was geared toward skill development and training, it also demonstrated that, given a reasonable work environment with some support, former heroin addicts can be successful at work. During the first three years of the Wildcat experiment, over thirty-five hundred ex-addicts worked on public service projects; 69 percent continued working for six months or more or were hired into nonsubsidized jobs.[89]

The major drawback to supported-work programs is the difficulty in developing subsequent job opportunities following the supported-work experience. In the absence of long-term jobs, trainees remain in the supported jobs. For example, during the three-year period only 438 (12.5 percent) of the Wildcat graduates were able to move into nonsupported jobs.[90]

Obviously, training people for jobs which do not exist and trying to find employment for those not considered desirable employees handicap efforts to rehabilitate treatment clients. Treatment programs have been criticized for their failure to provide successful job programs; however, with unemployment rates in many areas exceeding 50 percent (especially in primarily black and Hispanic communities with large numbers of young unemployed), it would be truly extraordinary if addiction treatment programs could obtain employment for large numbers of clients. Unrealistic expectations of what can be accomplished in social rehabilitation—employment being but one example—inevitably foster feelings of failure and futility by the client, the program, and the public at large.

   Abstinence.   A goal to which nearly every American heroin treatment program gives special emphasis is abstinence from drugs. While some programs seek only abstinence from use of illegal opiates (e.g., heroin), most seek an end to all illicit drug use, and some try to limit the consumption of alcohol as well. Most programs view abstinence from all opiates, both illegal heroin and prescribed methadone, as a primary goal. Other psychoactive substances that are commonly regarded as "medicine" (prescription drugs and over-the-counter preparations) or are not considered to be drugs at all (nicotine and caffeine) do not ordinarily enter into the abstinence equation.

   Abstinence is often viewed as a preliminary step to achieving other treatment objectives such as crime reduction and social rehabilitative goals. However, though emphasis on abstinence certainly does not preclude working on these other treatment goals, seeking the elimination of all drug misuse may mean the treatment program is concerned more with the drug use of the client than with the problems at the root of the drug use. To put it another way, the focus may be on the use *per se* rather than on whether it is dysfunctional for the client. The degree to which abstinence is stressed as a program goal can have a marked effect on the nature of the treatment provided.

   For example, this concentration on abstinence, which may be a reflection more of society's cultural values than of concern for the client's personal benefit, has resulted in pressure against long-term methadone maintenance. This pressure exists in spite of data indicating that long-term maintenance may be the best treatment choice for a sizeable number of heroin addicts. Upon reflection, it is evident that stressing drug abstinence alone as an outcome of treatment may be much too narrow, simplistic, and difficult to achieve.

   Follow-up studies of abstinence success rates reveal one common theme, that long-term abstinence following treatment is difficult to achieve. Studies in New York and California have assessed abstinence at five and ten years after discharge following treatment. The New York City Program review showed that 32 percent of those discharged from treatment programs were not using opiates, while the California program found that 54 percent of the clients who had been discharged were still abstinent.[91]

   However, these studies of New York and California clients show very different results for the use of illicit opiates during methadone treatment. In the New York City program review, only 1 percent of those continuously in treatment showed regular illicit opiate use, with 6 percent showing intermittent use,[92] while in California a study reported the unusually high statistic that 25 percent of those in treatment were using heroin daily.[93]

Other follow-up studies of shorter duration on earlier programs show a startling range of results in terms of abstinence. One critique of follow-up studies reported abstinence rates following treatment being as high as 92 percent and as low as 6.6 percent.[94] Even studies that use a sample of clients from within the same institution show a remarkable range in the abstinence rates achieved through treatment. For instance, three studies of clients released from Lexington found abstinence rates of 25 percent, 13.5 percent, and 6.6 percent.[95]

The preponderance of evidence indicates that sustained abstinence is very difficult to achieve and usually requires a long period of treatment. Nearly two-thirds of all clients entering treatment for opiate addiction in 1976 had at least one prior treatment experience; 11 percent had been in treatment four or more times.[96] A twelve-year follow-up study assessing the outcome of 100 patients released from Lexington found that all but ten had become readdicted to heroin at least temporarily within the first two years.[97] Of the ten who did not, three had died within four years after discharge, two had turned to alcohol, and three had never been heavily addicted in the first place. "In other words, virtually all addicts who have been physically addicted and did not die, relapsed."[98]

The fact that the most encouraging results reported by all treatment modalities, including methadone, are for clients who remain in treatment shows that effective treatment for opiate dependency requires a long-term commitment on the part of society, the specific program staff, and the client. The overall efficacy of treatment cannot be judged on the basis of a brief episode of treatment or by the immediate achievement of abstinence. The experience of cigarette smokers is illuminating on this point: While many people quit on the first attempt, many more require two, three, or more attempts before they can sustain abstinence over a long term. Although backsliding is discouraging, the short periods of abstinence do provide a background from which to make future—perhaps more successful—attempts to control use.

Three goals of treatment have been reviewed to show the complexity and consequences of "what we are treating." One, crime reduction, is a societal wish that has become a treatment goal; the second, social rehabilitation, is a program goal that has gained gradual public acceptance; and the third, abstinence, is a goal shared by both the public and the treatment programs. It is evident that the more general and ambitious the goals of heroin treatment are, the less we can expect. It is also evident that when a treatment program places undue emphasis on the goals of public opinion, individualized care suffers. There is a need to clarify our treatment goals and make them more realistic and specific to each client's needs.

Conclusion

It is a mistake to view heroin treatment in monolithic terms. There are different kinds of heroin addicts, each with different problems and needs. There is no one treatment approach applicable in every situation; to the contrary, a multiplicity of approaches is indicated—some long term, others short term; some involving intensive therapy, others not; some emphasizing a drug-free orientation, others using chemotherapy. It is unwise to limit unnecessarily the availability of alternative treatment practices in a futile search to find a single "right" one. Instead, we ought to be encouraging a greater investigation of innovative approaches in heroin treatment and a broadening of treatment alternatives to attract as many troubled users as possible.

One of the most positive developments in the drug field over the past decade has been the growth of a nationwide drug treatment system capable of providing assistance to hundreds of thousands of dysfunctional drug users, users who previously had few alternatives. Drug treatment program workers provide this essential assistance under generally difficult and unattractive conditions. Under the best of circumstances it is hard to provide quality treatment, but under the circumstances characteristic of most programs—poor physical facilities and overworked staffs with limited training and little public appreciation of their efforts—these difficulties are compounded.

Despite the investments made in heroin treatment—particularly during this past decade—programs have not fulfilled public expectations, and government support has become tenuous. Yet the gap between program accomplishments and general public expectations is more attributable to unrealistic expectations than to any failure of the programs themselves. To the extent that treatment programs set unachieveable goals they diminish public comprehension of their role and genuine accomplishments, and thereby diminish public support.

Heroin treatment cannot eliminate crime. It cannot guarantee that all clients will not revert to misuse of drugs. Heroin treatment programs cannot take undereducated, unskilled, and often unstable addict-clients and change them all into educated, employed, and stable model citizens. When heroin treatment does result in an individual success story, the general retort is often "What about all the rest?" In this atmosphere it is difficult to appreciate either the limitations or the accomplishments of heroin treatment. Until the public can more readily accept heroin treatment for what it realistically is, rather than conceiving it as what many wish it to be, the future stability of treatment programs is likely to remain precarious. Furthermore, heroin treatment's increasing alliance with and reliance on the criminal justice system, coupled with a resistance against moving closer to the regular health care system, does not bode well for the future.

4 The Influence of Public Understanding and Attitudes on Drug Education and Prevention

Peter Goldberg and Erik J. Meyers

The Historical Context of Modern Drug Education and Prevention Programs

DURING THE LATE 1960s the American public became alarmed by increasing reports of illicit drug use. The use of widely known illicit drugs seemed to have spread beyond the confines of the inner cities and become more evident in all areas of the country, particularly among the young. In addition, a new wave of chemical compounds with sometimes frightening and unintelligible names appeared.

The immediate public reaction was almost universally negative: These illicit drugs, new or old, were inherently "bad," and all use ought to be prevented by every available means. The use of an illicit substance was automatically considered harmful. This societal reaction, however, seems to have been based more on subjective, emotionally held conceptions of what is socially and morally acceptable than on scientific knowledge. An overwhelming majority of adults associated any use of illicit drugs with a general disrespect for law, order, and societal mores.[1] One national survey taken in 1969 revealed that 42 percent of American parents would report their own children to the police if discovered using prohibited drugs.[2] Yet many youths, as part of a commitment to social, political, and economic change in American society, adopted illicit drug use as

The authors acknowledge with gratitude contributions of John Swisher, Rayburn Hesse, Robert R. Carr, John R. Pekkanen, and Norman Zinberg.

a concrete symbol of disaffection with generally prevailing national values.

Because of the increase in illicit drug use in the 1960s, government at all levels began to design and implement an increasing variety of programs calculated to keep people from using prohibited substances. The terms "drug education" and "prevention" were coined, becoming euphemisms for a campaign which sought to dissuade the young from using illegal drugs. Despite a lack of trained teachers and adequate educational materials, state legislatures passed laws mandating "drug education" courses in the schools; these drug education programs rapidly became a part of the standard public school curriculum.

When looking at the more recent progeny of early drug education programs, one must remember the turbulent social context in which they first appeared. It is this setting which has largely influenced the present goals, accomplishments, and problems of drug education and prevention.

This chapter is primarily devoted to examining the influence of public attitudes and understanding on drug education and prevention programs. That influence has been the critical factor in past and current program content and policy direction, and is likely to determine their future course as well. The first section of this chapter examines briefly the programs now in place and their recent historical development. The latter sections address what the authors perceive as critical topics in any discussion of drug education and prevention: first, the nature and extent of public knowledge and understanding of illicit drug use and misuse, and second, the real differences between drug use and misuse.

We have not set out to evaluate in any comprehensive fashion existing prevention efforts. Such evaluations already exist or are being prepared, generally with government funding.[3] Our discussion instead focuses on the assumptions underlying present efforts, examining the true determinants of our drug education and prevention policies—public attitudes and understanding.

School-Based Drug Education and Prevention

In the late 1960s and early 1970s it was common to refer to drug education and prevention as "drug abuse education" or "drug abuse prevention." Only in retrospect has it become apparent that the term "drug abuse" is an ambiguous and pejorative one. It is a term which has contributed to the underlying confusion within the drug field, among educators, and (even more broadly) among the general public as to when drug *use* becomes drug *misuse*. "Drug abuse" came to stand for *any* use of an illicit drug. It was a term not often used—in fact, it was generally avoided—in describing the misuse of licit drugs, such as prescription drugs, alcohol, or nicotine. The inability to define "drug abuse" in terms other than such polarities as licit versus illicit, medical versus nonmedical, or socially approved versus nonapproved suggests the value-laden nature of the term. It has also created difficult public-policy problems, particularly as regards the appropriate goal for drug education and prevention programs.

The basic confusion over the meaning of the term "drug abuse" is reflected in the lack of a widely accepted definition of "prevention." In their 1977 report on prevention, the Cabinet Committee on Drug Abuse Prevention, Treatment, and Rehabilitation acknowledged the ambivalence of the term and their difficulty in obtaining widespread agreement on what precisely one is seeking to prevent.[4] The term "prevention" is generally applied to activities seeking to persuade those likely to use potentially harmful psychoactive drugs to either abstain or moderate their use, depending upon the substance in question. However, prevention programs vary considerably in content: Some provide information on drugs, others on responsible decision making and values-clarification; other programs offer alternatives to drug use, such as organized sports, theater, and social work. However, by failing to differentiate the goal of preventing any drug use at all from that of preventing the harmful aspects of misuse, we are left with a confusing and ambiguous concept of prevention. Predictably, it has become difficult to separate the good programs from those that do not work.

Drug Education: The Development of Approaches.   The keystone of American drug prevention efforts has been school-based drug education. As with prevention generally, drug education programs are hard to characterize. Early education efforts tried to either frighten potential youthful drug users into abstinence by elaborating upon illicit drugs' potential for harm or produce abstinent behavior by providing information about various drugs in the belief that the "true facts" would deter use. These efforts were supplanted later by programs attempting to educate students regarding the process of making decisions about their values in areas of personal and social significance (including drug use). These ostensibly different programs were and often are still grouped together under the rubric of "drug education." However, as yet there is little agreement either among educators or the general public as to what topics or information ought to be taught and for what purposes.

As stated above, the underlying assumptions guiding early "educational" efforts were straightforward: Illegal drugs were by definition "bad" and dangerous and young people were ignorant of the dangers. It was also believed that an intensive educational campaign could significantly reduce the number of people who might otherwise use illicit drugs. Accordingly, the single criterion originally used to measure the success of drug education was the elimination of illicit use.

Among the earliest approaches to drug education were programs geared toward frightening potential and actual users from illicit drug use with often exaggerated reports on the harmful aspects. One critic of drug education describes a typical format for this kind of program in the following terms:

> The most prevalent but least effective theme in the drug education program is to "scare the hell out of them." Too often the program consists of one or more meetings at which a local physician, a law enforcement officer, and perhaps a former addict will endlessly catalogue the horrible outcome of drug usage. The physician will exaggerate the degree to which drugs can produce bodily damage. The law enforcement officer will gravely talk about the increasing flow of drugs into the community and will throw in a few anecdotes about young people he has seen ruined by drugs. Sometimes to show to his presumably horrified audience, the former addict, who is usually the star performer, will recount his sordid experiences as a drug user and will glowingly report the salutary effects of his reformation.[5]

This "horrors of addiction" approach to drug education failed. Reporting on the status of drug education efforts in *Dealing with Drug Abuse*, Wald and Abrams wrote of these early programs, "Virtually all experts now agree that such tactics have not proved effective. Indeed, in many cases, they have been counterproductive, causing disrespect, skepticism, and resistance to all advice on drugs."[6] Instead of frightening youth away from drugs, these early efforts made skeptics of many and often served to increase curiosity about illicit psychoactive substances. However, these observed negative results have not completely eliminated attempts to scare potential users.

A second prevalent form of early drug education programs was based on the simplistic premise that given the "facts" about illicit drugs a youthful audience would see their dangers and abstain from consumption. This factual approach to drug education assumed, first, that the facts about various drugs and drug-taking behaviors were undisputed; second, that such facts comported with society's goal of illicit drug abstinence; and, third, that, standing by themselves, they would be convincing and could be objectively provided. Although the more dramatic elements of the "horrors of addiction" approach were abandoned, abstinence was still considered the only acceptable program result and the emphasis was on teaching about the dangerous nature of illicit drugs.

Trouble cropped up almost immediately with this factual approach, as drug educators tried to fashion scientific arguments to prove that marijuana—the drug whose use increased most rapidly during the late 1960s and early 1970s—was a dangerous drug. Their inability to make a convincing case to students put school-based drug education in an embarrassing position. The dilemma of the factual approach was summarized in one report as follows:

> Most drug education programs are ambivalent. They profess an honest desire to tell the truth—but only up to a point. When known facts run

out or become controversial, as they almost certainly do when the subject [of marijuana] comes up, the approach reverts to imposed value judgments, half-truths, or presumptions that the law is right—devices easily seen through by the skeptical young.[7]

In short, conveying information on illicit drugs suffered from the predetermination that the drugs in themselves were "bad." Despite the hopes of educators and parents of school-age children, it proved to be difficult if not impossible to promote the desired abstinence from illicit drugs through the provision of varnished or even unvarnished scientific drug "facts."

The difficulty of providing information on drugs in an atmosphere free of social moral judgments was only one problem. More serious was that of the accuracy of the information conveyed; the demand for educational materials on drugs had developed so rapidly that one observer called the situation a "state of enthusiastic confusion," adding further, "The growth of drug education materials as a lucrative commercial market, nourished on community anxiety, had resulted in claim and counterclaim of effectiveness without any thought to testing or evaluation of efforts."[8] Essentially, no one was judging the accuracy of the information being produced.

The extent of the accuracy problems in drug education materials began to become apparent in 1972 when the National Coordinating Council on Drug Education (NCCDE) began a systematic review of drug education films. Of the 220 drug education films reviewed by NCCDE, one-third were rated so inaccurate or distorted as to be totally unacceptable and an additional 50 percent were judged to be unsuited for general audiences without a skilled instructor. Only 16 percent were rated both scientifically and conceptually acceptable by NCCDE.[9] More disturbing than the inaccuracies revealed was the realization of how much inaccurate information had been approved by the "experts" for student audiences and the general public.

The Refinement of Drug Education Approaches.   In the 1960s, when drug education was based on the belief that the "awful but true" facts would keep young people from using drugs, one could readily test students on their retention of drug information. Educational researchers were at first enthusiastic about conducting evaluations; their search was expected to show those methods leading to the greatest reduction in drug use. However, the results were not encouraging. As early as 1969, educators had become aware of the inadequacies of drug education programs. This was the most common reason given by school districts for not agreeing to participate in one large California study of drug education programs.[10] In the few evaluations that showed measurable gains in abstinent behavior as a result of drug education courses, the research methodology was eventually questioned and the positive results cast into doubt.[11]

These early drug education evaluations were of limited scientific quality. It was, however, consistently found that drug education programs did not substantially reduce either present or prospective drug use. In fact, even uninformed observers could readily see that illicit drug use was steadily increasing, with greater numbers of young people trying illicit substances. (Little attention, however, was given to their per capita consumption.) The early assurance with which drug education had been pursued began to weaken.

In March 1973, the National Commission on Marihuana and Drug Abuse recommended a comprehensive review and evaluation of the entire drug education effort.[12] First, the commission called for a moratorium on the production and distribution of new drug information materials until standards for accuracy could be developed and existing materials analyzed. The commission report declared, "No information at all is preferable to inaccurate, dogmatic information which destroys the credibility of the source."[13] The commission also recommended a moratorium on all drug education programs in the schools, "at least until programs already in operation have been evaluated and a coherent approach with realistic objectives has been developed."[14] Further, it recommended that the states repeal those laws mandating drug education courses in the public schools. Recognizing that the issues of drug education went far deeper than the provision of factual information, the commission saw the proposed moratorium as a breathing space during which goals, techniques, and program results could be assessed and revised.

A moratorium on the production of drug education and information materials was subsequently imposed by the federal government, but it was limited to federal agencies, recipients of grants, and contractors. After ten months of study and review, the moratorium was lifted and new federal guidelines were issued. In apparent recognition of the shortcomings of earlier drug education efforts, these guidelines sought to exclude messages that relied on a "fear element," inadvertently demonstrated how to use illegal drugs, or relied on stereotypes of authority figures to say "Don't use drugs."[15] Instead, the guidelines called for "messages that stress the complexity of the problem, the inconsistency of society regarding use of the range of psychoactive substances, the interaction of different variables on drug effects, and alternatives and positive role models for young people."[16] Essentially the guidelines continued to emphasize the development of materials which would reinforce and encourage drug-free behavior, albeit in a more reasonable and moderate fashion. The guidelines failed, however, to resolve the essential ambiguity involved in not differentiating any use of a drug from usage which can cause harm.

In the past several years since the issuance of the report of the National Commission on Marihuana and Drug Abuse, drug education has begun to focus less on abstinence from illicit drugs and more on the reasons why people choose to use them. Thus, emphasizing concepts seeking to enrich personal development and social growth, such as responsible decision making, values-clarification, "affective" education, and alternative activities has become popular. Although the goal of total student drug abstinence is now generally acknowledged to be unachieveable, it remains the impossible dream underlying these newer efforts. The reasoning behind this change in educational strategy may reflect a belief that, since abstinence was not achieved by providing the "facts" on illicit drugs, there must be something wrong with how the young arrive at their decisions.

However, a more moderate outlook on drug prevention has recently received greater official support. The 1977 prevention report of the Cabinet Committee on Drug Abuse Prevention, Treatment, and Rehabilitation openly acknowledged that many adolescents will continue to experiment with psychoactive drugs as part of the typical contemporary maturation process. In contrast to earlier, more dire, assessments, the report's authors characterized this fact as "not particularly distressing."[17] The emphasis on abstinence has also been changed; one of the report's recommendations was that education and prevention efforts be "primarily focused on moderating the effects of drug taking."[18]

In addition, the new federal prevention strategy report recommends that drug education and prevention efforts be broadened to apply to alcohol and tobacco products, since they are the first two psychoactive substances used by many people. For credible approaches to develop, the report contends, drug education and prevention programs cannot maintain the fiction that alcohol and tobacco, though legal, are not akin to other psychoactive substances. However, even with the inclusion of licit drugs in education and prevention efforts, it is generally difficult to think of them as attempting to provide information that will help people avoid the harmful consequences of any psychoactive substance. Given the current public climate, it is generally impossible to explicitly set the prevention of harm—rather than the prevention of use—as the primary goal of drug education.

Nevertheless, more complex and sophisticated concepts are beginning to influence the development of federal drug prevention policies.[19] These include such issues as the relative health dangers of different illicit substances, the relative health dangers between illicit substances and licit drugs such as alcohol and tobacco, and the relative health dangers associated with different levels of use of any drug, licit or illicit. Essentially these new concepts seek to move away from arbitrary distinctions among licit and illicit drugs and toward a more flexible response which would address, among other things, how a drug is used, how often, and in what kind of setting. In effect, the new goal—without ever being explicitly stated as such—is to educate to prevent harmful use. Assuming that these concepts become more widely adopted as guidelines at the program level, they can have a profound influence on future education efforts.

The Influence of Federal Policies on Local School Practices. The role of the federal government with respect to drug prevention has been generally limited to declarations of policy principles, support of research and demonstration programs, and provision of some training and technical assistance.[20] The actual practice of school-based drug education has remained under local control; the influence of recent federal pronouncements on local program efforts is uncertain.

In fact, it is possible to find indications of a wide gap between local school practice and federal policy pronouncements in the popular press.[21] For example, recent newspaper stories recorded the suspension and reprimand of a Maryland high school teacher for advising her students to avoid paraquat-contaminated marijuana if they smoked the drug. Another recent news article reported on Virginia school officials' encouragement of undercover police surveillance in the school to prevent student marijuana use. While such examples may not be typical, they nonetheless suggest some distance between new federal prevention policies and those local school districts where traditional views and public antidrug influences are strongest. Such examples also suggest that most public school educators remain trapped in the dilemma of having to choose between supporting the dominant public view demanding abstinence or being accused of undermining it by promoting "drug abuse" through free inquiry and decision making.

Another unresolved issue concerns how closely the educational system should relate to drug law enforcement efforts. Educators have traditionally been given the task of shaping human behavior to conform to the dominant moral view. But when normal educational techniques fail in this respect, how authoritarian should the school systems become?

The furthest extension of the enforcement approach in the schools probably came with the mandatory student urinalysis program tried in one New York City school and proposed in Montgomery County, Pennsylvania. (The Pennsylvania proposal was rejected as unlawful by court action.[22]) Similarly, police surveillance and searches on school property demonstrate the questionable roles the school system can assume when the demands on them to produce adolescent drug abstention become excessive.

Official school policy on student use or possession of illicit drugs has tended to reflect a strict approach. A 1972 survey found a large number of school systems that would suspend or dismiss a student for possession of marijuana, frequent failure in official school policy to distinguish between marijuana- and heroin-related offenses, and public schools with relative frequency referring students in drug possession cases to the police rather than to treatment programs.[23] The authors of the study concluded,

> The credibility of a school to educate students in any manner about the nonmedical use and misuse of drugs will be quickly challenged as hypo-

critical by a student body that itself often knows the difference between marijuana and heroin better than the school administrators seemingly do. In particular, the disruption of a student's education for the possession of marijuana is a punitive measure, not a rehabilitative or educational one. We question whether such a function is a proper one for the public school systems to assume.[24]

Evaluation of Drug Education Programs.   Despite the widespread support of prevention and education as means of limiting "drug abuse," evaluations of various drug education programs have not shown promising results. One reason may be simply that good drug education evaluations are not easily achieved; it is exceedingly difficult to isolate changes produced by a program from those caused by unrelated factors. This problem is compounded in any longitudinal study; yet such studies are particularly needed, because the purpose of drug education has been to affect the drug-using behavior of young people over an extended period of time. Nevertheless, among those evaluations which would generally be considered to meet scientific standards there is little empirical support for the pervasive notion that education can produce substantial changes in drug-using behavior.

The stated goal of traditional drug education is to discourage new or continued use of certain drugs, in particular those classified as illegal. There are, however, two intermediate purposes to these educational efforts: to increase knowledge about drugs and their effects and to improve attitudes toward drug use, the individual, and society. It was—and to some extent still is—expected that accomplishment of these intermediate goals would lead directly to the realization of the primary goal, reduced drug use. But the results of drug education evaluations which have attempted to measure both intermediate changes and desired ends fail to corroborate these expectations.

Still, increased knowledge—the traditional object of education—can be achieved. Adolescents and preadolescents frequently express interest in knowing more about drugs and their effects. While this interest is not too surprising in light of the widespread use of illicit drugs among American youth, it is somewhat surprising considering the long history of misinformation and "scare tactics" in formal drug education programs. In one national survey of high school students conducted during 1973–74, nearly 40 percent reported that their drug education courses did not teach them anything they did not already know, and nearly one-third of the students thought the information was used to "scare you."[25] Nevertheless, despite such criticisms there appears to be genuine interest in drug information both among youth and adults and thus a potentially valuable role for the school system to fill.

Some evaluations of drug education courses have shown significant knowledge gains for the students.[26] However, increased knowledge about drugs may result in an increase in actual or intended use rather than the desired decrease.[27] Most students know from observation and experience that drugs—licit and illicit—can be pleasurable, but also powerful and potentially harmful. Many of the young have a healthy respect for drug troubles and, short of abstinence, want to know how to prevent them. Students may want the educational system to do the job in the drug field that it is willing to do in others; that is, without condoning use at least offer information to help avoid the hazards of drug misuse. Accurate information not only increases an individual's knowledge, but by reducing the fear of the unknown enables him or her to discriminate lower-risk choices from the higher-risk ones. Thus, the result of knowledge development may be an acutal increase in less harmful types of illicit drug use coupled with a decrease in more harmful drug misuse.

Self-reported use and intentions to use must serve as the indicators of drug use and potential usage, since actual use is nearly impossible to determine. Two major experimental drug education programs showed only minimal reduction in drug use at best.[28] Other smaller research studies have shown similar results. The findings noted in a study of the Coronado school district program in California, one of the best evaluations of a highly regarded drug education program, provide perhaps the clearest indicators of the potential of drug education programs for reducing drug use. That evaluation concluded that the Coronado program effected only a *tendency* toward less drug use.[29] Furthermore, one of the few follow-up studies on the effects of any drug education program concluded, "In spite of a strengthening not to take or reducing of intentions to accept most drugs *immediately* after the lessons, there is *relatively* little change in *most* pupil's intentions to take any drugs in the longer term."[30]

Although it is impossible to prove that drug education cannot work, there is little empirical evidence to support the view that significant changes in drug-using behavior can be induced by it. The evidence on hand makes a reasonable case that drug education efforts are not likely to have a substantial impact on the frequency or variety of psychoactive substances used. Summarizing the research done on the effectiveness of drug education one comprehensive review stated, "There is an almost total lack of evidence indicating beneficial effects of drug education."[31]

In the final analysis, public satisfaction or dissatisfaction with the content and results of school-based drug education depends upon the public's understanding—or, as is too often the case, its lack of understanding—of the issues.

Public Knowledge and Attitudes

The Advance of Scientific Knowledge Versus Lack of Public Understanding. A notable result of the American government's concern with the drug field during the 1970s has been a greater knowledge and understanding of drugs and drug policies. Appreciably more is known now about illicit drugs than at the beginning of the decade. More is also known about who uses drugs and about the effectiveness of various treatment, prevention, and enforcement programs. Marijuana is a prime example of a drug that has received considerable research attention; even where questions remain—as with some possible health consequences of marijuana use—recent research studies have been invaluable in sorting out myths from realities. Yet another illustration of this increase in knowledge comes from the recent evaluation of the New York State "get tough" drug law, which provided important insights into the effects of criminal law on drug-using behavior. Such research reports and program experiences have advanced knowledge in nearly every aspect of drug use and misuse.

There is also, however, a growing realization of how much more there is to be learned. In many instances, what was thought to be known has turned out to be uncertain. Increasingly, among those who have been active in the drug field, the answers of earlier eras are being replaced with questions. Earlier generalizations about illicit drugs and their users are giving way to more complex theories.

Although research and evaluation have contributed to more informed discussion *within* the drug field, effective communication of these new, emerging concepts to the general public has been slow to develop. This failure to create widespread public understanding limits the benefits of any drug education or information program. It is not exaggerating to say that the future course of national drug policies will be determined by the ability of the drug field to convey the experiences, understanding, and knowledge developed in recent years.

Underlying the problem of effectively communicating a new set of concepts about illicit drugs and their users is the tenacity of traditional views. Public attitudes toward such drugs as marijuana, cocaine, and heroin evolved early and have remained fixed for many years; they have been reinforced by nearly every public and private institution. In 1973 the National Commission on Marihuana and Drug Abuse observed, "Society tended to view the problem exactly as the law defined it. . . ."[32] There was little room for alternative points of view. Those who voiced reservations about the effectiveness or desirability of strict antidrug laws were generally dismissed as loose-thinking "liberals". Those who openly used the prohibited substances were made into social outcasts.

The public's reaction to the threat of illicit drugs has exceeded factual, scientific bases of support. Yet concepts introduced in recent years which contradict the prevailing popular beliefs are at a competitive disadvantage. The newer ideas must, it seems, do more than make sense. Even overwhelmingly convincing evidence runs a difficult road in dislodging the familiar older assumptions. The experience of recent years suggests that the facts by themselves may not be sufficient to alter public perceptions and thus drug policy. Old drug myths apparently die remarkably hard.

Understandably, it is often difficult to separate myth from reality. In addition, many existing popular conceptions about illicit drugs, because simplistic, are more easily comprehended than more complex facts and theories. The complexity of the new concepts, coupled with the substantial disagreements within the field itself, creates a significant obstacle in the path of greater public understanding. Departing from the uniformity of the past, many differing views can find some support in research findings; sometimes the same research is used to "prove" opposite positions. Instead of black-and-white answers, the public is given several sets of facts and interpretations from which it is expected to select the best constructed line of reasoning.

The Current State of Public Knowledge

It is hard to generalize about the current state of public knowledge about illicit drugs. The preponderance of national polling data concerns attitudes rather than knowledge. Nevertheless, what information is available suggests that a large segment of the American population harbors mistaken beliefs about drugs and their effects.

For example, a 1972 poll by the National Commission on Marihuana and Drug Abuse assessed the knowledge and attitudes of American adults on drug use and users. Similar surveys were conducted in 1974 and again in 1976.[33] The responses to these surveys give some indication of the extent of the misconceptions about drugs. They also show how slowly public beliefs change: For example, in 1972 44 percent, in 1974 46 percent, and in 1976 48 percent of those surveyed agreed that "you can try marijuana once or twice with no bad effects"[34]; only 26 percent in 1972, 24 percent in 1974, and 25 percent in 1976 believed that "you can use marijuana without ever becoming addicted to it"[35]; 65 percent in 1972, 62 percent in 1974, and 60 percent in 1976 believed that marijuana makes people want to try stronger drugs, such as heroin.[36] These beliefs reinforce the idea that the use of any illicit drug will eventually lead to the use of heroin, the "worst" drug of all to most Americans.

Even the simplest pharmacological facts seem to be unknown to the public. For instance, 68 percent of the adults in the 1974 survey believed that marijuana is addictive, while only 62 percent believed methadone to be addicitve. This response changed only slightly in the 1976 survey. Such attitudes are reflected in the fact that about one-third of the American public believes that mandatory treatment is the best response to a first conviction for marijuana possession.[37]

Other studies and measures of public knowledge replicate this lack of public understanding. A 1974 television show, modeled after the National Drivers Test, asked fourteen factual questions of a Washington, D.C. viewing audience about heroin and heroin addiction treatment. According to the Bureau of Social Science Research, which analyzed the test results, the average viewer was able to answer eight of the fourteen questions correctly. Only 4 percent of the viewing audience was able to correctly answer twelve or more of the questions.[38] A similar television show on marijuana, aired in March 1976, presented thirteen questions to a Washington, D.C. viewing audience of which more than half answered six incorrectly.[39]

Improving public knowledge and changing public attitudes about drugs and their effects is, as already noted, a difficult task. The general public's first-hand experience with illicit drugs is limited inasmuch as use and possession of them are illegal. Therefore, the influence of trusted professionals who can speak authoritatively on the issues becomes stronger. Those whom the public generally regards as experts about drugs include physicians, lawyers, judges, and law enforcement authorities. In addition, the nation's news media, in conveying information from those directly involved in the drug field to the general public, strongly influence public attitudes and understanding about drugs. To find an explanation for the public's lack of appreciation of the complexities of drug issues, one must look to those on whom it depends for its information: the medical, legal, law enforcement, and communications fields.

The Medical Profession.   One source to whom the public should normally be expected to turn for information and advice about illicit drugs is the medical profession. The drug field is intricately and intimately involved with health issues, medical problems, and physician responsibilities. Yet in spite of this relationship the active involvement of the medical profession in formulating drug policies and developing treatment programs has been generally minimal.

In part, the detachment of the medical profession from illicit drug issues may be traced to the federal government's efforts, beginning with the District of Columbia Pharmacy Act of 1906, to limit the authority of the profession to employ and prescribe particular drugs in the course of medical practice.[40] Throughout much of the twentieth century the federal government's response to illicit drug use has been dominated by enforcement approaches. This perspective has enjoyed wide popular support. Treatment came to be perceived as a rather "soft-hearted" approach to an enforcement problem, and few physicians became involved in the "drug abuse" field in any active way.

Historically, the number of doctors who have treated those misusing illicit drugs has been small, basically because the facilities were so few.[41] For more than thirty years there were only two federally supported opiate treatment programs in this country—one at Lexington, Kentucky and the other in Fort Worth, Texas. These two institutions trained physicians in the complexities of opiate addiction, but the number of participating doctors was small; they developed no wide constituency within the medical community.

In recent years, with the development of methadone treatment methods and the large-scale expansion of federal support for drug treatment programs, the medical profession has gained a new foothold in the public dialogue about illicit drugs. Even so, the number of doctors involved represents only a small fraction of the three hundred thousand physicians in the country.[42] The number of medical doctors with more than a casual understanding of the pharmacological properties and effects of psychoactive drugs is still limited.[43]

For the most part, the medical profession has stuck to a rather strict definition of drug abuse.[44] Nearly all medical definitions of drug abuse use the term to apply to the use of any drug not prescribed by a physician. In effect, the acceptance of this definition would establish a medical prerogative to determine who can use which drugs and under what circumstances, and drug consumption would be limited to medical need. Any and all use of illicit drugs would constitute drug abuse.

Not all doctors have specialized knowledge about drugs. Their exposure to the latest findings about those drugs currently classified as having no legitimate medical use (such as marijuana, heroin, and cocaine) is very limited, and their formal education and training often provides only a cursory view of drug misuse problems. Moreover, since more than half of the present number of practicing physicians in this country went through medical school before the profusion of new psychoactive drugs, licit and illicit, developed, their exposure to research on these substances has been limited.[45] However, many physicians can and do take training courses periodically to update their knowledge and understanding of new developments in the drug field.

Even now only a minority of medical schools in the country offer courses in psychopharmacology, which is the basic science of how drugs affect the mind.[46] Virtually all medical schools offer courses in pharmacology—the basic science of how drugs work on the body—but these courses are a relatively small part of the physician's education. Even when they are offered, a recent survey shows they cover only the most serious and destructive symptoms resulting from the use of intoxicants.[47] Peter Dews, MD., a professor of psychiatry and psychobiology at the Harvard Medical School, has concluded that the training physicians receive regarding drugs and their actions on the human mind and body is "an overwhelming failure."[48] Other medical educators echo his sentiments.[49]

The consequences of this failure to provide physicians with an adequate understanding of drug misuse problems are many, affecting both licit and illicit drugs. For example, there is some evidence that physicians have unwittingly contributed to the widespread misuse of licit prescription drugs and thus to an improper understanding of other drugs. Approximately 275 million prescriptions for psychoactive drugs are written annually, a figure which many contend is far in excess of the actual need.[50]

Moreover, several recent studies suggest a relationship between the use of licit and illicit drugs. Blum in California, Smart in Canada, and Louria in New Jersey have shown that the use of legitimate psychoactive drugs by parents greatly increases the chances of their children using illicit drugs.[51] From his study Dr. Smart believes that "the conclusion is inescapable that the parents who are users of tranquilizers, barbiturates and stimulants are likely to have children who are users of drugs, such as marijuana, LSD, speed, as well as prescription drugs and alcohol and tobacco."[52]

The potential contribution the medical profession can make to the development of informed public attitudes about drugs is great. However, it would seem to be unwarranted at this time to hold the attitudes and opinions of the medical profession in any special status simply because of their professional background.[53] Many doctors, rather than being experts about drugs, often share the same misconceptions and biases of the public at large.

The Legal Profession.   Among the many legal doctrines that guide today's lawyers is the doctrine of *stare decisis*, the practice of standing by past legal rulings in deciding current disputes. The fact that the legal profession embraces this conservative doctrine may be a partial explanation for its continued reliance on outmoded concepts in the drug field. Although individual attorneys may be at the leading edge of drug law reform efforts, the majority of the profession echoes the more traditional views on the subject.

While it is lawyers who generally change the law through either the statute books or courtroom argument, they also uphold it through the same processes. It is difficult, therefore, to characterize the field as holding only to one view. For example, a leading textbook for trial attorneys on handling cases related to illicit drugs states,

> The addict, exposed to and in fear of withdrawal, will be driven irresistibly to any lengths to obtain a supply, and in desperation may even resort to suicide as a way out.[54]

In contrast to this traditional view of heroin overpowering the will of the user and making him uncontrollable are the views of other legal scholars, such as Professor Nicholas Kittrie at the Institute for Studies in Justice and Social Behavior at the American University and advisor to the National Commission on Marihuana and Drug Abuse. Professor Kittrie contends that illicit drugs have not been shown to be connected in any causal way with the subsequent commission of crimes. In fact, notes Kittrie, "it is the high cost of the drugs and their unavailability which often produce the reported criminal behavior."[55]

For the most part, however, drug law reform efforts sponsored by the organized bar and other traditional elements of the legal profession tend to be years behind the current state of knowledge. A good example of this time-lag process can be seen in the relatively recent boost of support for pretrial drug diversion programs: Increasingly judges, prosecutors, and defense attorneys concur that referral to treatment is the preferable course of action where the defendant has tested positive for drug use, even when the arrest had nothing to do with drugs of any kind.[56] The support for such diversion is derived from a belief in the overpowering, "irresistible" nature of certain drugs (particularly heroin), an attribute which is often viewed as inevitably involving the user in criminal activities.[57] Other traditional views figure in this formula as well: The heroin user is almost invariably seen as an addict and as unable to financially support continued use of the drug except through criminal activities. Recent information on the existence of large numbers of heroin "chippers" and other nonaddicted users and the continued failure to prove a direct heroin-crime relationship remain largely unrecognized by the legal profession.

Lawyers frequently see themselves as the executors of the law rather than its creators. Reluctant to mount frontal assaults on long-standing precedent, the legal profession favors a more gradual process of erosion, based on case-by-case factual distinctions, until the original rule collapses from an accumulation of legal undercutting. This process of change is underway in altering legal attitudes towards illicit drugs and drug users. For example, the Association of the Bar of the City of New York undertook a three-year project to analyze the effects of the 1973 "get tough" drug law in New York State. The final report issued by the Bar Association's study group challenged the efficacy of increasing drug law penalties and issued a markedly cogent series of general observations.

> First, the use of heroin and other opiates is but one element of a larger problem. The misuse of all dangerous drugs—alcohol, cocaine, opiates, and other mood-changing drugs, some prescribed and some sold over the counter—all together constitutes "the drug problem." Problems with so many components do not yield to one-dimensional solutions. As no single drug treatment method is suitable for all users, so there is not likely to be a single legal approach that is suitable for all offenders.
>
> Second, whether or not illicit drug use is for the most part a medical concern as some contend, it is incontrovertibly deeply rooted in broader social maladies. Narcotics use in particular is intimately associated with, and a part of, a wider complex of problems that includes family break-up, unemployment, poor income and education, feeble institutional structures, and loss of hope.
>
> The final observation is a corollary of the second: it is implausible that social problems as basic as these can be effectively solved by the criminal law.[58]

Bar associations and law schools are becoming more involved in sponsoring seminars to present and analyze recent research in the drug field. The Minnesota State Bar Association recently persuaded the state of Minnesota to sponsor a judicial education series providing judges, prosecutors, and defense attorneys with the latest information on the use and misuse of licit and illicit psychoactive substances as well as on the development of drug controls.[59] These educational activities by the organized bar are promising attempts to increase the profession's understanding of illicit drug issues. The influx of many younger lawyers into the bar may also have an impact on attitudes. One recent study of student attitudes in a southern law school showed a significant percentage supported liberalizing the laws relating to marijuana.[60] The personal drug experiences of so many recent law school graduates may have a profound effect on the profession's attitudes in the future.

One promising sign of the legal profession's growing awareness of the complexities of drug issues is the increasing tendency to differentiate between levels of drug use. For years, the legal approach was simply to define any use of an illicit drug as abuse, subject to penalty structures which failed to distinguish between use, misuse, or abuse. More recently, particularly with marijuana decriminalization laws, there appear to have been more concerted attempts made to separate possibly destructive drug use patterns from those which, although involving nonapproved substances, pose little apparent societal danger.

In summary, legal attitudes seem to be evolving to accommodate new knowledge and information about drug issues and problems. Nonetheless, this change is occurring very slowly, and legal precedent still supports traditional concepts even in some reform efforts. While the organized bar may play a role in educating its members, the growing number of young attorneys who have themselves had contact with illicit drugs like marijuana may have a more profound impact on the profession's attitudes in the future.

Law Enforcement Views.   Law enforcement agencies and personnel, charged with the practical administration of the law, generally view the enforcement of drug laws as an ordinary part of their overall job. However, for some the enforcement of the drug laws is of particular concern because of widely held beliefs about the close relationship between illicit drug use and criminality.[61] In addition, police and other law enforcement professionals tend to view the use of certain drugs in moral terms and see their role as protecting minimum societal standards of morality. Public pronouncements by law enforcement officials about illicit drugs often reflect rigidly moralistic stances.

In part, the views of law enforcement officials are based upon traditional understandings of the effects of drugs upon the human body. There seems to be little recognition of variance of effect from drug to drug and user to user. The tendency appears to be to assume that the "worst" case example is not only the typical but also the inevitable result of illicit drug use. For example, a leading criminology textbook makes the following statement:

> The officer sees the many ugly aspects of drug abuse such as the crime, violence, death and disorientation it causes. Sometimes he sees the more pleasant side too; for example, when he meets an individual who is no longer involved with drugs.[62]

Compounding the problem are laws that the police are charged to enforce, laws which, for example, frequently describe both marijuana and cocaine as "narcotics" when it is widely known in the scientific community that these drugs have entirely different characteristics. This misunderstanding of the basics of pharmacology helps produce the view that the use of one drug may as well be the use of another; they are all equal in the eyes of the law and thus in the eyes of the law enforcement officer.

In contrast to the more traditional enforcement views are those which, looking more pragmatically at a broad range of criminal law enforcement problems, see the enforcement of drug laws as an unwelcome burden and occasionally as counterproductive. The Knapp Commission, which investigated police corruption in New York City, found widespread problems within that police department concerning the administration of antidrug laws. The fact that most drug arrests are "spontaneous" (i.e., involving no prior investigation) suggests the haphazard way in which current laws are enforced. Maurice Cullinane, who recently retired as police chief in Washington, D.C., stated his view on marijuana law enforcement: "When you look at how you're going to utilize your manpower, going out and looking for individuals who are using marijuana just for themselves is very, very low on my priority list."[63] These kinds of observations led a Mississippi sheriffs' association to support and help pass a marijuana decriminalization bill.[64]

However, it is accurate to say that the majority of law enforcement opinion continues to be on the side of stringent antidrug laws along current lines. Drugs continue to be blamed by enforcement officials for a broad cross-section of society's ills. Writing in a professional journal, Edward Davis, then president of the International Association of Chiefs of Police, made the following statement:

> Lower penalties and decriminalization became popular political promises and narcotic use increased. Some states began issuing traffic-like citations for possessing "small amounts" of narcotics and the drug business boomed. The crime rate also increased and so did the toll of human wreckage.[65]

News Coverage of Drug Issues.   Traditionally, American newspapers have been an important, influential source of information to the public. The role and responsibilities which the free press serves are indispensable to the functioning of a democratic society. The American public has come to expect and depend upon the press to provide reliable, accurate, and unbiased news coverage; they expect the press to aggressively scrutinize government programs and policies and not just reprint press releases from official sources.

In an area such as illicit drug use where the general public lacks first-hand experience and knowledge, careful news coverage is essential. News coverage about drug use provides more than just information; since direct sources of information are so limited, the news coverage of this issue has even more influence than usual on public attitudes toward drugs.

Historical analyses of drug issues and the responses to them have not systematically examined the press's role, the sources of their reports, or their overall accuracy. The available anecdotal accounts suggest that the press has usually reflected the prohibitionary policies of the federal government without question and shared the punitive law enforcement orientation which has dominated government response.[66] However, until the current decade there have been few alternative positions for the press to report, inasmuch as nearly all established private-sector organizations have tended to reaffirm the basic philosophy of the government. On the other hand, press coverage given to some of the more sensational aspects attributed to illicit drug use may have helped to give undue credibility to the myths and exaggerations which still surround certain illicit drugs. One newspaper reporter who has written extensively about drug issues in the 1970s has observed,

> I think we in the media are to blame for compounding the drug stereotypes that have been foisted off on the public since the 1930s. We've accepted every police and law enforcement statement about drugs without question. We've failed to explore the culture of the drug user fairly, and we've failed to dispassionately explore the entire phenomenon of drug use.[67]

Just as there seemed to be little debate about drug policies within the government bureaucracy and in public forums, there also seemed to be few press challenges to the conventional wisdom about drugs.

Newspaper and television news coverage of the so-called drug abuse "crisis" of the past decade was extensive.[68] This coverage reflected the widespread public concern about "drug abuse." And although it is not possible to measure the actual impact of the news coverage given drug issues, it is reasonable to assume that it has had a strong influence on public attitudes and opinions. In at least one instance the way in which a drug story was presented in newspaper, radio, and television reports directly influenced the development of federal drug policies and programs.[69]

It was not until 1972–73 that any study of newspaper reporters was undertaken to find out how much they knew about the drug issues they were covering. Robert Bomboy, himself a journalist, interviewed nearly forty reporters, columnists, and editors from thirty newspapers and two national wire services. His observations and conclusions paint a bleak picture.[70] Among them are the following:

1. A great deal of drug reporting in major newspapers reflects ignorance, fear and false preconceptions.
2. Newspapers continue to be most strongly interested in the sensational or dramatic aspects of the drug abuse story. This has often precluded serious analysis or discussion of the problem.
3. Acting out of a lack of interest at best, class bias, racism and fear at worst, newsmen take pains to disassociate themselves from addicts.
4. Myths are reported as fact by newspapers largely because newsmen place excessive reliance on official sources of information, the local police in particular.
5. Reporters too seldom attempt to cross-check official information with sources on the street.
6. Most major newspapers do not have "drug beats." General assignment reporters often lack substantial knowledge of the drug problem and drug abuse policy, and they don't have the opportunity to develop street sources of information that would give them some perspective on the information handed out by officials.
7. Newspapers are unwilling or unable to go beyond government-provided propaganda to reach their own conclusions about the merits of one drug policy vis-à-vis another. Most newspapers simply do not have a well-formed, seriously constructed conception of the drug abuse problem.

No other studies have been undertaken on the news coverage of drug issues since Bomboy's 1973 report. Some recent developments would nonetheless suggest that the news media are now better equipped to deal with drug issues. For one, the newer and younger reporters seem to be more familiar with, and thus less afraid of, illicit drugs and their users than their counterparts from earlier years. Also, there is now a greater number of sources of information in the drug field, more readily available than in the past; today even the relatively uninformed reporter has no need to be solely dependent upon official sources of information. Finally, the tendency in the post-Watergate era is toward more aggressive reporting and more skepticism regarding the tone and substance of government reports and policies.

On the other hand, public interest in the drug issue has by now subsided and the amount of news space and time devoted to it has been substantially reduced. Thus there are fewer and less effective opportunities for the news media to convey to the general public the new insights which have developed in recent years. In addition, while there are no studies to be cited one way or the other, our impression is that newspaper editorials have generally remained wedded to old concepts and strict, punitive anti-drug stands.

Television Programming. Perhaps of even greater impact than newspaper coverage is television news coverage. Within the brief time-frame of television news reporting, the emphasis has consistently been on dramatic "scare" stories. Spreading warnings of potential disaster—no matter how disputed the evidence—usually draws accolades as being the performance of a valuable public service. On the other hand, reports of research that do *not* establish that substantial harm can result from even moderate use of illicit drugs make for rather bland news. And indicating to the public that many fears about illicit drugs may be exaggerated or that not all drug use is necessarily destructive runs the risk of being accused of softness or, worse, being implicated in causing harm. The competitive nature of the television industry, where viewer approval is so aggressively pursued, makes it unlikely that it ever can or will challenge popular public attitudes toward illicit drugs on its own accord.

Apart from newscasts, television also influences public beliefs and attitudes toward licit and illicit drugs through commercial advertising and the entertainment programs which comprise the bulk of prime-time programming. The extent of television's influence on a wide range of viewer attitudes and behavior is the subject of heated controversy. Particularly with respect to drugs is there considerable disagreement. A former commissioner of the Federal Communications Commission, for instance, has referred to television as the prime pusher of drugs in American society.[71] The research director for a marketing research company contends, on the other hand, that drug advertising is being used as a "scapegoat."[72]

Whatever the precise degree of television influence, commercial advertising of over-the-counter legal drugs is unquestionably extensive. The 1973 Report of the National Council of Churches Drug Advertising Project noted that four of the five biggest television advertisers were pharmaceutical manufacturers, and that one out of every eight television commercials advertised some type of drug.[73] One study of 126 hours of commercial television in Boston recorded 132 over-the-counter drug commercials (5.5 percent of all commercials aired).[74] Another researcher identified 465 drug commercials in a 250-hour composite week of network programming; those 465 commercials constituted 13.4 percent of all advertisements during this period.[75] A third study identified 88 over-the-counter drug commercials aired between 7:00 and 11:00 P.M. on the three major networks during a selected week in March 1973.[76] Critics of television drug advertising (including alcohol and tobacco products as well as over-the-counter non-prescription medications) have argued that these commercials contribute to patterns of drug misuse in American society.[77] The National Commission on Marihuana and Drug Abuse characterized those arguments as reasonable, but urged more effective industry self-regulation rather than government intervention, recommending further longitudinal research into the effects of various forms of communication on behavior.[78]

Particular attention has been directed towards the impact of television advertising on children, widely believed to be an audience particularly vulnerable to commercial messages. The Council on Children, Media, and Merchandising has been an especially strong critic of television advertising of potentially dangerous substances.[79] Although the television industry had issued detailed guidelines to guard against product misuse by children, these applied only to Saturday and Sunday-morning children's programs, when the advertising market consisted almost wholly of children. Critics pointed out, however, that children also watch television during prime-time hours when adults are also watching, and therefore view commercial advertisements directed towards adult audiences. In 1975, fourteen states petitioned the Federal Communications Commission to ban television advertising of OTC drugs before nine o'clock in the evening. The petition was denied, largely because of a lack of scientific research and empirical data showing a cause-and-effect relationship.[80]

Although the television industry has been criticized for airing commercial advertisements which some contend suggest and even increase the harmful use of certain licit drugs, the medium has also aired public-service advertisements warning against "drug abuse." These advertisements most often focus on the illicit drugs, although alcohol and tobacco have also been included. However, these public-service spots are shown far less often than commercial advertisments promoting various legal psychoactive substances. For example, in the March 1973 study mentioned above, only one public-service message on drug misuse was observed in those prime-time hours of programming in the week-long period when eighty-eight commercial advertisements for OTC drugs were recorded.[81] Some have criticized the television networks for airing public-service announcements during low audience-viewing periods, thereby diminishing whatever effectiveness they may have.[82]

As with the commercial advertisements for OTC drugs, the actual effect of public-service messages seems to be uncertain. Granted the extent to which they are effective, it is still difficult to overlook the conflicting messages conveyed. When, as one researcher has noted, a commercial beer advertisement urging viewers to "live life with gusto" is immediately followed by a public service announcement warning against the "dangers of drug abuse," it becomes understandably difficult to help the public grasp the subtleties and complexities of drug and drug-related problems.[83]

Even more important and less well-understood is the impact of the entertainment programs which dominate the commercial television schedule during periods of highest viewing. The use of alcohol and tobacco products in television programs is fairly common. McEwen and Hanneman report that alcohol is the most frequently depicted drug on television, and that its use is portrayed in generally positive contexts and as having "positive social (though mixed physical) consequences."[84] The authors report that tobacco products are used rather than discussed, and that possible adverse consequences of tobacco use are ignored. With respect to prescription drugs and medications, the authors note that their use in television programs is generally confined to the treatment of physical ailments, and that reference to the possible misuse of licit drugs is avoided.

The illicit drugs are handled differently in television entertainment. In general, their use—particularly that of heroin—is portrayed in negative situations. One study characterizes television's portrayal of the drug culture as "uniformly ugly."[85] Most often illicit drug use on these programs is found in the various detective and police stories. Overall, it appears that entertainment programming on television simply reflects and reinforces the stereotypes the American public has of licit and illicit drugs.

Changing Concepts in the Drug Field

The preceding sections of this chapter suggest widespread public confusion about many drug issues. The long history of misinformation which has often guided discussions of illicit drugs and drug policies cannot be easily overcome. However, the logical place to begin that process is to examine the basic terms and concepts which apply to and affect nearly every public determination about the use of psychoactive drugs.

The popular belief is that we need to prevent "drug abuse." However, the prevention of a problem requires a clear definition of it. The medical problem of an outbreak of malaria will send public health officials out searching for possible breeding grounds for mosquitos known to spread the disease; by eliminating these breeding grounds, malarial infections of humans can be prevented. Prevention with respect to drugs, however, is not so clear-cut.

What is a drug problem? Does a drug problem result from any use of a psychoactive drug? Or does it result only from the use of more than a specified amount of such a drug? Neither is a sufficient condition. Contrary to popular assumptions, problems resulting from the use of psychoactive drugs are more complex than this. In addition to the amount of a drug used, drug problems are also influenced by a variety of other factors, including the setting or circumstances in which it is used, the attitudes or expectations of the user, and the specific pharmacological effects of the drug. To complicate matters further, the problems a user may have which seem to be the result of drug use may remain, unchanged, even after drug taking ceases.

It has been common to use the term "drug abuse" to refer to the existence of a drug problem. But "drug abuse" is an ambiguous and pejorative term, one to which the American public has been conditioned to respond negatively. The fear that "drug abuse" may be spreading in our society has often been considered sufficient grounds to support harsh measures to eliminate a perceived social evil. When the term "drug abuse" is more closely examined, however, it will be seen to be imprecise, value-laden, and therefore of little utility.[86] It remains easier to urge the prevention of "drug abuse" than it has been to clearly define the term.

"Drug abuse," instead of referring to a typology of drug-using behaviors, has become a shorthand term society uses to differentiate between *licit* and *illicit* drug use.[87] Any use of an illicit drug is automatically labeled "drug abuse." The term is typically avoided when describing the excessive, indiscriminate, nonmedical use of licit drugs. Those drugs of which we as a society disapprove are classified as illegal, and any use of them becomes "drug abuse," and "drug abuse" is something we all intuitively want to prevent. The reasoning here is circular, and indicative of the problems encountered in trying to improve public knowledge and understanding of drug issues and problems. Such reasoning leads to the assumption that only illicit drugs can cause drug problems, and thus permits us to circumvent, when convenient to do so, the reality that serious drug problems can result from the misuse of legally available drugs as well.

It seems apparent therefore that the classification of drugs as licit or illicit is a root cause of public confusion. The rigidity imposed by this classification creates unnecessary difficulties in addressing contemporary drug problems. Such classification often reflects solely the question of social acceptability, and has nothing to do with potential health hazards or demonstrated risks to life or property from the drug in question. The labels "licit" and "illicit" tend to overlook such important variables as the frequency with which a drug is used, the method of administration, dosage, and the situations in which particular drugs are most commonly used. Edward Brecher, author of the reputable Consumers Union report *Licit and Illicit Drugs*, elaborated in that work on this crucial point.

A sound classification program should concern itself with modes of drug use as well as drugs themselves; it should recognize, for example, the vast difference between sniffing, smoking, or swallowing a drug and mainlining it. Society, laws and law enforcement policies already differentiate the occasional drinker of a glass of wine or beer, the social drinker, the problem drinker, and the alcoholic. Similar distinctions should be made with respect to various modes of use of marijuana, LSD, the barbiturates, and the amphetamines.[88]

The Liaison Task Panel on Psychoactive Drug Use/Misuse of the President's Commission on Mental Health recently highlighted Brecher's point, concluding, "Clearer distinctions need to be made among the variety of psychoactive drugs other than their licitness or illicitness. . . . "[89] Since the use of psychoactive drugs is endemic to American life, we need to identify where possible general principles of drug use and apply them consistently to drug-using behavior, regardless of whether the drug is alcohol, nicotine, marijuana, or cocaine. As long as arbitrary standards governing each individual drug remain, however, there will always be serious doubt expressed by some members of society whether the drug use in question has been a violation of some logical principle of pharmacology or whether it has only been a violation of social acceptability. It is, for example, an easy matter to say that no one should drive when intoxicated, no matter what the drug; such a statement applies consistently to all psychoactive drugs. Similarly, it would be just as logical to say that relaxation achieved by using a moderate amount of a drug other than alcohol in appropriate circumstances by someone over the age of consent is reasonable behavior. But there has been great resistance to this concept.

Reliance on such terms as "drug abuse" and the classification of drugs as either licit or illicit have obstructed public understanding of the need for a *consistent* approach to the use of all psychoactive substances, including alcohol and nicotine. The understanding that both licit and illicit drugs can be used or misused is a concept of paramount importance, one which could greatly influence public drug policies and programs.

There is evidence that, despite the lack of official approval, many users of illicit psychoactive drugs have developed patterns and standards of drug consumption that encourage and reinforce behavior more moderate and responsible than was previously assumed possible. For example, while all recent surveys of student drug use indicate that experimental and recreational use of a variety of drugs is extensive, none of the surveys point to an alarming number of intensive or compulsive student drug users. Millions of high school and college students have experimented with illicit drugs, but the vast majority discriminate among the different drugs available and exercise some degree of personal control and restraint in their drug-taking behavior.[90] Had this been understood earlier, it might have precluded the rush to school-based antidrug campaigns—or would at least have altered their tone and direction.

Similarly, greater public understanding of drug problems could be facilitated if public discussion were cast in terms of different types of drug-using behaviors. The National Commission on Marihuana and Drug Abuse identified five distinct categories of drug-using behaviors, each of which poses a different potential for individual dysfunction.

- *Experimental*—short-term, non-patterned trial of one or more drugs, motivated primarily by curiosity or a desire to experience an altered mood state.
- *Recreational*—occurs in social settings among friends or acquaintances who desire to share an experience which they define as both acceptable and pleasurable. Generally, recreational use is both voluntary and patterned and tends not to escalate to more frequent or intensive use patterns.
- *Circumstantial*—generally motivated by the users' perceived need or desire to achieve a new and anticipated effect in order to cope with a specific problem, situation or condition of a personal or vocational nature. This category would include the use of stimulants for work-related tasks, and the use of sedatives or stimulants to relieve tension or boredom.
- *Intensive*—drug use which occurs at least daily and is motivated by an individual's perceived need to achieve relief or maintain a level of performance.
- *Compulsive*—consists of a patterned behavior at a high frequency and high level of intensity, characterized by a high degree of dependency, such as with chronic alcoholics, heroin dependents and compulsive users of barbiturates.[91]

Others have offered somewhat different typologies by which to view different patterns of drug-taking behavior.[92] The point central to all these classification schemes, however, is that the types identified are as applicable to licit as to illicit drugs, and are intended not only to help separate use from misuse but to look at different gradations of use and misuse. Yet the concept that there are different levels of drug-using behavior has never really taken hold among the general public. The more traditional, arbitrary generalizations about "drug abuse" and licit and illicit drugs remain in vogue even though the simplicity of these categories ignores the true complexities of drug-using behavior. There is simply enormous public resistance to moving away from certainty about the evil of "drug abuse" (i.e., any use of an illicit drug) to more exacting and accurate definitions of what constitutes a drug problem on an individual, pharmacological, and situational basis.

It is this inability to develop public acceptance of the more subtle and complex perspectives which have emerged that does not bode well for the refinement of American drug policies. It is this difficulty that explains the emphasis placed on the lack of general public understanding in a chapter on drug education and prevention.

Conclusion

In considering the changing concepts in the drug field, it is clear that we need to rethink our approach to drug education and prevention. It is a mistake to think of drug education only in the narrow terms of teaching young people; all the available evidence points to the need for a much broader educational effort. American society cannot transmit to younger generations knowledge and understanding about drugs and their effects that the public at large does not yet possess.

It is also impractical to think in terms of absolute prevention of psychoactive drug use. This goal is simply impossible to achieve, as man's historical experience with an increasing variety of psychoactive substances has shown. Moreover, as our understanding of the role of drug use in American life changes, we as a society may no longer want to so avidly pursue "drug abuse prevention" as we have commonly thought of it. The price paid in terms of social dissension, confusion, and misunderstanding has been very high.

5

Marijuana and Cocaine: The Process of Change in Drug Policy

Robert R. Carr and Erik J. Meyers

MARIJUANA IS ONE OF THE FEW illicit drugs with which nearly all Americans are at least somewhat familiar. Most of us have a good idea as to how the drug is consumed, and in fact the latest surveys show that a quarter of the American adult population has used marijuana at least once—a figure that indicates that if we have not used the drug ourselves we certainly have friends, relatives, business associates, or acquaintances who have.

The continuing debate over marijuana is also a matter of great familiarity. Despite the remarkable consistency of official reports on marijuana—from the 1894 Report of the Indian Hemp Drugs Commission to the 1972 report of the National Commission on Marihuana and Drug Abuse, *Marihuana: A Signal of Misunderstanding,* and the 1977 HEW report to Congress, *Marijuana and Health*— in addressing beliefs that marijuana is addictive, leads to violent crime, and that its use results in the use of other drugs, a national debate has continued nearly unabated. Researchers have sometimes been called upon to provide evidence either of marijuana's harmfulness or of its harmlessness. Much of the public has been simply confused over the conflicting reports The factor most often lacking in this ongoing argument over public policy has been objectively derived evidence.

Given the stridence of the opponents it is remarkable that American marijuana policy has changed at all within recent years. It is instructive

The authors acknowledge with gratitude the contributions of Jared R. Tinklenberg.

to examine the process of change that has occurred. Marijuana "decriminalization" has come about within the lifetime of the readers of this report, an experience which shows that public attitudes toward a particular drug can shift significantly, leading to the abandonment of long-held beliefs and practices in favor of less socially destructive drug policies. However, the long, slow process of marijuana "decriminalization" indicates also how difficult any drug policy change is; the national experience with cocaine provides confirming evidence of this tenacity of the law enforcement approach to drug control in the United States.

We begin with a look at those who use marijuana today, at their numbers, demographic characteristics, and reasons for using the drug. Following this section, the background and process of change in the marijuana laws from harsh criminal penalties to "decriminalization" are examined. The medical and social science arguments used by both sides of the marijuana issue are reviewed in detail, and we close with an analysis of the impact of marijuana decriminalization in the state of Oregon.

The afterword on cocaine quickly reviews recent developments associated with that drug's rising popularity in the United States. Once again the medical and social science arguments are enumerated and briefly evaluated, as is the policy response to the drug. Finally, the American experiences with cocaine and marijuana are compared and contrasted, with particular attention paid to the policy impact of those differences and similarities.

Current Patterns of Use

Demographics of Use: Who Uses Marijuana Today?   The "typical" marijuana smoker today is practically indistinguishable from his nonusing peers. In the more distant past, marijuana use in this country was most commonly associated with racial and ethnic subgroups and certain occupations, such as jazz musicians. With the recent growth of use, first on college campuses and then elsewhere, marijuana in the 1970s became no longer restricted to any particular group or class within the general population. This broadening of the social base of users has undoubtedly been an important element in the move to decriminalize possession and use of marijuana.

Marijuana use cuts across all demographic lines, with age the sharpest dividing line (though the disparity of use levels between age groups masks the fact that a large number of individuals over age twenty-five have used and continue to use marijuana). Educational attainment is also highly correlated with marijuana use: Thirty percent of college graduates and those with some college experience have used marijuana, and 50 percent of present college students have at least experimented with it, while only 12 percent of those adults who are not high school graduates and 22 percent of high school graduates with no college experience have used the drug. Similarly, professional and higher-income adults rank among the highest of all occupational groups in the experimental use of marijuana.[1]

Although male users outnumber female users by two-to-one in surveys taken since 1971, recent high school student surveys indicate that this gap may be narrowing.[2] Total use within minority American population groups was estimated at 25 percent in 1976, compared with 21 percent for adult whites.[3]

Marijuana use varies significantly among cities of varying size and among regions of the country. In the largest twenty-five metropolitan areas as well as in other metropolitan areas (SMSAs) approximately one of every four adults has at least tried marijuana, whereas in nonmetropolitan or rural areas only one in eight adults has tried it.[4] Regionally, the western states have the highest percentage of use. Twenty-eight percent of western adults say they have used marijuana, while in the northeastern states 24 percent report use as do 19 percent in the north central states. The southern states, which have traditionally shown the least use, still trail other regions among adults, but use has more than tripled since 1971, from 5 to 17 percent.[5]

Prevalence and Incidence of Marijuana Use. The use of marijuana, both experimental and current,* has increased significantly since 1971, although regular use seems to be leveling off. In the 1976 national survey commissioned by the National Institute on Drug Abuse (NIDA), adults and youth showed similar experiences with marijuana: 21.3 percent of the adults (age eighteen and over) and 22.4 percent of young people (ages twelve to seventeen) reported having used marijuana.[6] Three earlier national surveys documented the upward trend in cannabis use; comparable figures for youth in both 1971 and 1972 were 14 percent, which rose to 23 percent in 1974. For adults, use went from 15 percent in 1971 to 16 percent in 1972 to 19 percent in 1974.[7]

Current marijuana use (reported use in the past month) doubled for youth between 1971 and 1974—from 6 to 12 percent—but had increased only slightly by 1976 to 12.3 percent.[8] Though experimentation among adults is as high as among youth, there are fewer current users in the adult group; this figure has remained at about 8 percent since 1972.

Marijuana experience is still predominantly associated with youth and young adults. The eighteen to twenty-five-year-old segment of the adult population has had the greatest experience with the drug, with 53 percent having used it, of whom 25 percent practice current use. The fig-

---

*The term "experimental use" generally refers to a one-time or occasional experience with marijuana. "Current use" refers to a continuing pattern of use, even if sporadic, if the user feels he currently uses the drug and is likely to do so again. Surveys conducted by the National Institute on Drug Abuse ask whether a person has used "within the past month" as a measure of current use.

ures drop for the twenty-six to thirty-four-year-old group, to a range of 36 to 11 percent, and drop still further for the thirty-five-and-older group. Among youth, total marijuana experience varies from 6 percent between the ages of twelve and thirteen to 40 percent at ages sixteen and seventeen. (Current use is 3 and 21 percent respectively for these age groups).[9]

An annual national survey of a random sample of thirteen thousand high school seniors on lifestyles and values relating to drugs shows a significant increase in marijuana smoking between 1975 and 1976 for this group: 47 percent in the class of '75 had used marijuana while 53 percent in the class of '76 had done so. Those who had used marijuana within the preceding month (current users) increased from 27 percent to 32 percent.[10]

Drug use surveys among male high school students in San Mateo County, California, have been conducted since 1968.[11] These surveys provide particularly good indications of drug use trends among school-age youth. The use of marijuana in this particular area may have reached a plateau, while the use of some other drugs seems to be diminishing; marijuana use rose from a 50 percent level in 1969 to stabilize at about 61 percent in 1972, where it has been ever since. A report of the Department of Health, Education, and Welfare notes that, now that California has decriminalized the personal possession of small quantities of marijuana (1975), the results from this annual survey may serve as one measure of the impact of decriminalization on adolescent use.[12]

The first marijuana experience for a large number of users now occurs between the ages of fourteen and twenty-one. For example, in the period 1975 to 1976, 9 percent of youths age fourteen and fifteen had tried marijuana for the first time in the previous twelve months; the corresponding figure for those sixteen and seventeen was 13 percent and for those eighteen to twenty-one, 11 percent. At present, relatively few individuals begin use after age twenty-five; incidence of first use within the past year for those age twenty-six to thirty-four is only 4 percent, and for those past thirty-five, less than .5 percent.[13]

Causes of the Increase in Use.   There are probably as many reasons for using a particular drug as there are people who use it. Obviously there must be something perceived as enjoyable in the drug's effect for beginning or continuing use to occur. However, the history of marijuana use is involved with and complicated by the political and social upheavals occurring in the 1960s and early 1970s, the time of the drug's growing popularity. For many, smoking marijuana was a symbol of protest against the Vietnam War and the "establishment" in general. These were largely concerns of college and draft-age youth, but they were echoed by others both younger and older. As use became more endemic, the teenager or young adult who had never tried marijuana was quite often in the minority within his or her subgroup; peer pressure may have played a part in getting many to experiment with the drug.

Unquestionably, during the rapid increase in use in the late 1960s the drug was seen as a political and generational symbol. Its use became a symbolic gesture of belonging to a particular political and social viewpoint and was interpreted as such by those with opposing views. Marijuana's involvement with the deep social issues of the day made it difficult for many to change their attitudes toward the drug and those who either used it or opposed it.

Another factor in continued marijuana use is that many who are not seeking to make a social or political statement simply find the drug's effects enjoyable. Marijuana use in the late 1970s has become characterized by a quiet expansion of experimental and regular use. While many of the so-called "radicals" of the sixties have been absorbed into society in a variety of mainstream pursuits, the legacy of that turbulent decade continues to influence attitudes toward marijuana. However, the sheer weight of the number of present users has begun to be reflected in legislative reforms and in a reduction of rhetoric from both sides of the marijuana issue. In summary, as the National Commission on Marihuana and Drug Abuse noted in its first report,

> For various reasons, marihuana use became a common form of recreation for many middle and upper class college youth. The trend spread across the country, into the colleges and high schools and into the affluent suburbs as well. Use by American servicemen in Vietnam was frequent. In recent years, use of the drug has spanned every social class and geographic region.[14]

Frequency of Use and the Future.   While more than one in five of the nation's youth and adults report use of marijuana, only one in twenty have used it more than one hundred times. By their own subjective measures of use, 3.5 percent of youth report "regular" marijuana use and 11.8 percent occasional use. Regular use among adults is only 2.1 percent, with occasional use at 7.9 percent. The overwhelming majority of individuals claim to be nonusers or non-current users (84.6 percent of youth and 89.8 percent of adults); many of these have experimented with marijuana and may have been occasional or regular users at one time.[15]

While it is impossible to accurately forecast future marijuana use, surveys have been conducted which attempt to determine future intentions. Half of present high school seniors say that they would not use marijuana even if it were legally available, yet a majority of young adults age eighteen to twenty-five have reported at least experimenting with it. But even among this latter group, 48 percent say they will definitely not use marijuana in the future.[16] Among the reasons given for nonuse or cessation of use, simple lack of interest is the overwhelmingly predominant response; fear of legal prosecution does not rank high among the reasons commonly given. Whatever the ultimate percentage of continuing use, marijuana smoking is presently a cultural norm for young American adults. Nothing in the surveys regarding future intentions would lead to the conclusion that it will disappear or decline to a marked extent in the near future.

Early Legislative Changes:
From Felony to Misdemeanor

To understand the policy dilemma of the late sixties and early seventies we need to examine the historical context of marijuana laws. Richard Bonnie and Charles Whitebread, in their history of marijuana prohibition in the United States, describe a fifty-year period extending through the mid-sixties in which there was a social consensus supporting the nation's marijuana laws.[18] They attribute this support to the generally accepted beliefs that marijuana was a "narcotic" drug indistinguishable from the opiates and cocaine, that use inevitably became abuse, that it was associated with the lowest levels of the socioeconomic structure where crime, idleness, and other antisocial behavior are common; and that it was perfectly proper to prohibit any personal behavior thought to be incompatible with society's best interests.

Punitive sanctions for marijuana use and possession were most severe in the 1950s. In 1951 Congress amended the Narcotic Drugs Import and Export Act and the Marihuana Tax Act to provide uniform penalties for drug violators.[19] This legislation treated marijuana as a narcotic drug—despite the lack of any pharmacological basis for doing so—and increased penalties for violations to ten to twenty years for third and subsequent offenses, with a $2,000 fine for all offenses; probation and parole were denied for all but first offenses. The Narcotic Control Act of 1956 added to these penalties and established separate penalty provisions for possession and sale.[20] Under this act possession of any amount of marijuana brought a minimum sentence of two years for the first offense, five years for the second, and ten years for third and subsequent offenses; the fine for all offenses was raised to $20,000. Conviction for sale of marijuana was punishable by a minimum sentence of five years for first offenses with ten years for second and subsequent offenses or any sale to a minor by an adult. Probation and parole were denied for all except first possession offenders. Every state in the union followed the federal lead at the time, and in some instances provided even harsher penalties.

These stringent penalties coincided with the height of the "Cold War" and concern over foreign, especially communist, subversion. While the primary drug concern during that period was over heroin (believed to be "pushed" by communist Chinese agents in an effort to subvert American youth), marijuana was also indicted, not particularly for its own sake, but because it was held to be a "stepping stone" to other illicit drugs such as heroin.[21] The fact that marijuana was described by statute as a "narcotic" drug reinforced the theory that its use led inevitably to other drugs. At any rate, the penalty structure established during the 1950s carried over into the 1960s—and from there ran headlong into controversy.

No one can say precisely how and why marijuana came to be associated with the social upheavals of the sixties. From the early civil rights movement in the South to the Free Speech movement in Berkeley to the later antiwar protests, social disobedience on a massive order characterized the new decade, in sharp contrast to the conformist pressures of the 1950s. The veneer of social unanimity on America's goals and values was quickly stripped away by fast-moving events, revealing deep-rooted, emotional differences. Marijuana was a convenient symbol of protest, an available ideological banner, particularly when compared to the use of alcohol by the "establishment". But as marijuana use spread rapidly among white and middle-class youth, especially on college campuses, the attitudes of preceding decades began to change in response.

Since 1965, over 2.75 million arrests for marijuana violations have been made by state and local authorities alone, despite consistent assertions by law enforcement officials that marijuana is a low priority. In 1976 there were 441,100 marijuana arrests, compared with less than 19,000 in 1965; the overwhelming majority of these were for possessing, not selling, the drug. By 1976 marijuana arrests were thirty times what they had been in 1965 and had increased as a percentage of all drug arrests from about 40 to 70 percent (Table 5.1).

TABLE 5.1   Marijuana Arrests, 1965–1975

Year	No. of Arrests
1965	18,815
1966	31,119
1967	61,843
1968	95,870
1969	118,903
1970	188,682
1971	225,828
1972	292,179
1973	420,700
1974	445,600
1975	416,000
1976	441,100

Source: Federal Bureau of Investigation, U.S. Department of Justice, *Crime in the United States* (Uniform Crime Reports) (Washington, D.C.: U.S. Government Printing Office, 1965–1976).

The rapid growth in arrests, most of which were for simple possession of a small quantity of the drug, reflected the increased involvement
of American criminal justice with marijuana. However, despite the dramatic increase in arrests, marijuana increased greatly in popularity during this period, and many of those using it were children of "respectable"
middle-class Americans. The thought that their own children were now
"criminals" in the eyes of the law slowly began to convince many parents
that these laws might be potentially more harmful than the drug itself.

Other costs began to become apparent as well. Legal scholars like
John Kaplan and Arthur Hellman expressed their concern that the enforcement of marijuana laws may have had an even more negative impact
than alcohol prohibition on the relationship between the American people
and their criminal justice and legislative officials.[22] Prohibition of use
seemed to be applied selectively, as well. Due to their unconventionality,
those with long hair ("hippies") seemed to be singled out for application
of sanctions. This perception of unequal enforcement of the law alienated
a substantial segment of the American people. These feelings of alienation
led in some cases—perhaps in many—to active rejection of other laws and
social conventions.[23] However, other, more far-reaching social issues—racial segregation and an undeclared war in Southeast Asia—also led to the
development of attitudes of alienation, and the role of marijuana law enforcement in producing deviant behavior should not be overstated. However, it is clear that the laws and the way they were enforced did contribute significantly to the disaffection of many Americans, particularly the
young, with the established order in general.[24]

Growing awareness of the heavy social costs of penalizing ever-increasing numbers of young Americans prompted widespread legislative
reassessment. At the state level, the process of reducing simple possession
of marijuana from a felony to a misdemeanor actually began in the mid-
1960s, in contrast to federal law, which took until the end of the decade to
change. In 1967, just prior to congressional deliberations on a new comprehensive drug statute, the United States became a signatory to the Single Convention on Narcotic Drugs, an international treaty obligating the
signatories to limit all traffic in marijuana and other drugs to that needed
for medical and scientific investigation.[25] This treaty obligated the United
States to restrict the cultivation and distribution of marijuana, but did not
require any specific punishment for illegal possession.

In 1969 several congressional committees scheduled hearings, not
only on marijuana use but on control of LSD, heroin, and many other
psychoactive substances. The result of these hearings and of discussions
between the administration, the Senate, and the House of Representatives
was the passage in 1970 of the Comprehensive Drug Abuse Prevention
and Control Act.[26] The part of the legislation dealing with control, the
Controlled Substances Act, provided five regulatory schedules for psycho-

active substances depending on their believed harmfulness, potential for abuse, and accepted level of medical use. Criminal penalties for sale and possession were determined by classification, with Schedule I drugs carrying the highest penalties, since they were considered the drugs with the highest abuse potential, highest dependency liability, and no currently accepted medical use. The placement of marijuana in Schedule I beside heroin and LSD was indicative of the continuing strong official attitude against the drug in spite of emerging scientific evidence showing users not to have any physiological dependency liability. In fact, marijuana was known to be less harmful than many substances regulated by lower schedules or unregulated by the act.

However, the Controlled Substances Act did reduce simple possession of small amounts of all the specified illicit drugs to a misdemeanor, and abolished mandatory minimum sentences for all convicted offenders except heavy traffickers. On the state level during the period 1969–72, nearly every jurisdiction also amended its marijuana penalties, so that by 1972 simple possession had been reduced to a misdemeanor in all but eight states. The new federal act also established a National Commission on Marihuana and Drug Abuse, which was to conduct a year-long study on marijuana and its effects and report its findings to the administration, Congress, and the public. As the following material describes, the commission's report set the stage for further legislative changes.

The Beginning of the Decriminalization Debate

The National Commission on Marihuana and Drug Abuse (the "Shafer Commission") was given broad responsibility for examining all aspects of the growth in illicit drug use, particularly of marijuana. Reflecting the highly charged, politicized nature of the drug issue at the time, the commission came under criticism from all sides before it even began its work. Among the criticisms were charges that it was "establishment," that there was only one commission member under forty, and that certain members might be subject to political pressure. On the other hand, President Nixon, who had himself appointed nine of the thirteen members, publicly proclaimed shortly after the commission began its work—amid rumors that some members already had doubts about current criminal policies—that whatever the commission might recommend, he was firmly against relaxing American marijuana laws.[27]

The Report of the National Commission. The publication in March 1972 of the first report of the National Commission on Marihuana and Drug Abuse, *Marihuana: A Signal of Misunderstanding*, provided one of the few dispassionate recent official reviews of marijuana use in American society.[28] Despite pressure from both advocates and opponents, the commission achieved a result that resisted their biases. Both the first report and the companion final report, *Drug Use in America: Problem in Perspective*,[29] are of value as enlightening sources of information and policy analysis on illicit drugs, several years after their publication.

The commission provided the first official recognition of the widespread and pervasive use of marijuana, the use of which was previously assumed to be confined to marginal social groups. It found that use occurred in all socioeconomic groups and occupations, that among adults it was by no means confined to college students, and that although it was highest in cities, towns, and suburbs, it was not uncommon in rural areas.

The commission profiled users, traced the factors involved in becoming one, detailed the effects of marijuana, and delineated the social impact of its use. It concluded that any risk of harm probably lay in the heavy, long-term use of the drug—although it lacked evidence even on this risk—and that in terms of social impact ". . . it is unlikely that marihuana will affect the future strength, stability or vitality of our social and political institutions. The fundamental principles and values upon which the society rests are far too enduring to go up in the smoke of a marihuana cigarette."[30] The commission also noted that public response to marijuana use, according to their national survey, was moving away from approval of jail sentences toward nonpunitive forms of control.[31]

In reaching its own consensus as to appropriate recommendations for social policy, the commission recognized that, on the one hand, "the use of drugs for pleasure or other non-medical purposes is not inherently irresponsible; alcohol is widely used as an acceptable part of social activities," and, on the other, that "society should not approve or encourage the recreational use of *any* drug, in public or private."[32] Recognizing that it would be impossible to eliminate marijuana use, the commission formulated the issue thus:

> The unresolved question is whether society should try to dissuade its members from using marihuana or should defer entirely to individual judgment in the matter, remaining benignly neutral. We must choose between policies of discouragement and neutrality.[33]

The commissioners chose a policy some have characterized as one of cautious restraint. While recommending that the sale and distribution of marijuana for profit remain felonies, they recommended that possession for personal use no longer be a criminal offense and that casual distribution of small amounts of marijuana for little or no remuneration not be a criminal offense.

Grass-Roots Forces.   Pressure was also building at the local level for reform of marijuana laws, especially in parts of the country where use of the drug had taken hold earliest—California, for example. There, a marijuana lobby group called AMORPHIA was organized in 1969; its membership consisted primarily of self-proclaimed marijuana smokers, and its early focus was legalization of the drug. Though AMORPHIA's position on marijuana law reform was too extreme for most California voters, it did succeed in 1972 in placing on the California ballot a legislative proposition to legalize possession and cultivation of marijuana. That 2.8 million Californians (one-third of the total vote) voted to legalize marijuana in 1972 may be an indication that many voters either were familiar with people who had used marijuana or perhaps had done so themselves.[34]

The most influential private effort in the marijuana law reform drive took shape around 1971—coincidentally, the same year that Congress established the National Commission on Marihuana and Drug Abuse. This group called itself the National Organization for the Reform of Marijuana Laws (NORML), and sought to influence federal and state legislation through traditional lobbying tactics. Wishing to broaden the base of support for marijuana law reform, NORML included politicians, physicians, attorneys, civil libertarians, and people from a wide range of other disciplines on its national advisory committee. Former Attorney General Ramsey Clark was perhaps the most prominent early supporter of NORML, and his early recruitment undoubtedly brought others into the organization. While Washington, D.C. was the natural headquarters for NORML—since drug policy was largely the creation of the federal government—it also went to work on the state level, concentrating its early efforts in a few key states.

The partial prohibition approach recommended by the National Commission was unsatisfactory to many. President Nixon saw it only as disguised legalization and reiterated his opposition to any scheme making marijuana less than totally prohibited. NORML viewed the commission's recommendations with skepticism, but accepted that decriminalization was a respectable platform to carry to the states. And there was precedent for such a policy; the Volstead Act had prohibited the manufacture and distribution of alcohol, but shied away from placing criminal penalties on private possession for personal use, as did all but five of the states.

The strength of the commission's recommendation to decriminalize marijuana was that it was a moderate response to an issue which had previously been argued emotionally from extreme positions and on the basis of inadequate information. Thus, this form of decriminalization of marijuana was quickly endorsed by many respected national groups, such as the National Council of Churches, the American Public Health Association, the American Bar Association, and the National Education Association. A loose-knit coalition of young activists, former National Commission members and staff, medical researchers, representatives of sympathetic organizations, and even a few chiefs of police and other law officers began to form under the banner of marijuana decriminalization.

Within eighteen months of the issuance of the National Commission's report, Oregon became the first state to adopt legislation decriminalizing marijuana.[35] The Oregon statute was similar to the approach recommended by the commission; it officially discouraged marijuana use by the imposition of a civil fine, but eliminated criminal penalties and arrest for possession of an ounce or less. Subsequently, decriminalization—at least in the sense of jail sentences being replaced by fines for personal possession of small amounts—has been adopted by ten other states: Ohio, Alaska, Colorado, Maine, California, Minnesota, Mississippi, North Carolina, New York, and Nebraska. The populations of these states amount to one-third of the total U.S. population; thus one of every three Americans now lives where simple possession of small amounts of marijuana no longer exposes one to criminal arrest and imprisonment.

Despite the carefully researched and cautiously worded conclusions of the reports of both the National Commission and Canada's Commission of Inquiry into the Non-Medical Use of Drugs (the "LeDain Commission")—reports which actually repudiated many of the myths and questioned other beliefs about marijuana—the debate continues. The cutting edge of the debate is still the disputed evidence on the health and social consequences of use of the drug. Although more is now known about marijuana than many other drugs, there are still wide areas of disagreement among professionals about its effects on health. This continuing disagreement is reflected by the countless articles on the subject which have appeared in both technical and popular journals. Unfortunately, many research studies seem to have been designed to produce a predetermined finding; while such findings make headlines, they do little to help the concerned and confused public. The media are also poorly equipped to distinguish between reputable research, research geared to a predetermined end, or that which is frankly inconclusive.

Nonetheless, policymakers must make decisions on the best available evidence. The following section reviews the research reports in those areas receiving the most concern and attention: such medical issues as brain damage, immune response, chromosome breakage, sexual dysfunction, lung damage, tolerance and dependence, psychomotor skills, and marijuana's therapeutic potential; and such social issues as crime and violence, an "amotivational syndrome," or use of other drugs.

Medical Issues

Some medical research about the effects of marijuana seems to have been influenced by the drug's reputation in this country. Although the

1930s film *Reefer Madness* appears ludicrous today, many of its portrayals of the stereotypical results of marijuana use—insanity, immorality, and crime—find a home in "modern," "scientific" studies of the drug. The legal classification of the drug by the Controlled Substances Act as a Schedule I controlled substance meant, according to the law, that it had no accepted medical use, a high potential for "abuse," and a high probability of dependency. If one looks at marijuana research over the past ten years, much of that effort seems to have been directed at substantiating this position. Any indication of possible harm to users has frequently been viewed by defenders of the status quo as justification for the stringent controls placed on the drug; in other words, punitive measures against users have been justified on the basis of preventing users from harming themselves. Many still believe marijuana must be proved totally harmless before any policy change can be justified.

Today it appears that marijuana use in moderate amounts over a short term poses far less of a threat to an individual's health than does indiscriminate use of alcohol and tobacco. Millions of dollars have been invested by public and private sources to determine what effects marijuana might be having on the growing number of users; since 1972 the U.S. government alone has given over $25 million in grants for research on marijuana.[36] The National Institute on Drug Abuse (NIDA), the federal watchdog agency on drug use and misuse, has issued six reports to Congress since 1971 summarizing the hundreds of research reports which have been published during that period. It is significant that research reports by NIDA have not concluded that marijuana poses a major public health hazard, though NIDA has specifically stated that it feels a duty to call public attention to certain potentially adverse consequences of its continued use. It is also significant that now NIDA is required to produce a marijuana report only every other year instead of annually, which indicates that extreme concern over marijuana use may be receding.

Marijuana research will in all probability never demonstrate harmlessness, nor could research on any psychoactive drug be expected to establish absolute harmlessness. Too little is known about neurophysiology and the central nervous system to make such expectations realistic. However, enough is now known about marijuana's effects to make a claim of harmlessness specious. Unfortunately, it is evident from the following review of the research that any evidence of physical harm from marijuana still tends to be regarded as justification for stringent measures to enforce prohibition rather than simply as a reason to discourage and try to control use.

Many of the scientific studies to date have been merely descriptive of the feelings of intoxication due to marijuana smoking. Common among users are short-term increases in heart rate, reddening of the eyes, drying of the mouth, and dose-related distortions of sensory information—touch, smell, taste, hearing, and vision may become intensified and perceived by many as pleasurable. However, novice users have sometimes experienced acute anxiety characterized by feelings of "losing control" and paranoia which are short-term and transient. Marijuana intoxication can be very subtle, as attested by novice users reporting that they could feel no effects whatsoever from first exposure to low dosages of the drug. Responses are also greatly influenced by the expectations of the user and the setting in which use takes place. The margin of safety in dosage—i.e., from demonstrable toxicity—is enormous; no overdose death has been reported in the United States.

Brain Damage.   There is undisputed evidence that cannabis use produces reversible, dose-related changes in brain waves as measured by electroencephalography. However, these changes are not markedly different from those caused by other psychoactive drugs.[37] More sensational reports have described irreversible organic brain damage, alleged to lead to certain permanent behavioral effects such as the "amotivational syndrome." While there is general agreement that marijuana does produce such symptoms as short-term memory loss and time distortion, these disappear as the drug's effects wear off, usually within hours.

Studies to date of populations which have long used cannabis preparations have found little evidence of significant harmful effects of continued, heavy use. Separate research projects in Jamaica,[38] Costa Rica,[39] and Greece[40] did not find any evidence of brain damage or impaired mental or physical functioning due to even heavy, chronic cannabis use. Similarly, two independent research teams in the United States—one at the Harvard Medical School[41] and one at the Washington University School of Medicine in St. Louis[42]—sought to replicate the findings of an earlier British study on brain damage. Both efforts employed a newly developed X-ray technique to scan sections of the human brain. All but one of the heavy marijuana users in both studies were healthy males with no current or antecedent history of neurological disorder or cognitive deficit. The subjects in both studies had also used other drugs, such as alcohol, LSD, amphetamines, and barbiturates. Neither study produced evidence that indicated a structural change in the brain or central nervous system due to heavy, long-term marijuana use; brain damage was not apparent on any of the X-ray scans.

These studies are to be contrasted with earlier reports of brain damage caused by chronic cannabis use. The first such study was reported by a highly respected British medical journal in 1971.[43] However, the claims made by that study are extremely doubtful in light of the scientific inadequacies of the research. For example, the ten chronic cannabis smokers observed in the study were described by the authors as "addicts" in terms of their marijuana use, despite the fact that all of them had used LSD at least a few times and the majority had used one or more other powerful drugs, such as amphetamines, barbiturates, mescaline, morphine, and cocaine. (Alcohol was also used, though this fact was, curiously, left out of the discussion on the effects of marijuana.) Simply on the basis of the subjects' own anecdotal reporting of high levels of use of drugs other than marijuana, the designation of cannabis as the sole causative factor in whatever brain atrophy might have been observed is highly suspect.[44] In addition, some of the patients suffered from epilepsy, mental retardation, schizophrenia, and past accidental head injuries. All had been brought to the attention of these researchers because of psychiatric difficulties; it seems therefore, as one American psychiatrist has noted, that "these patients are not ideal candidates for this kind of brain research."[45]

The British study is not the only suspect research on possible brain damage from marijuana use. The Journal of the American Medical Association (JAMA) published two articles in 1971 and 1972 by several American psychiatrists who reported their clinical impressions of patients in their psychiatric practice who used marijuana.[46] The first study described a wide range of psychopathological symptoms exhibited, including apathy, mental sluggishness, loss of interest in personal appearance, slowed time sense, difficulty with recent memory, confused verbal responses, ego decompensation, paranoia, sexual promiscuity, depression, and suicidal tendencies, ascribing these symptomatic changes in personality solely to drug use. Further, despite the lack of a systematic history of their patients' drug-using behavior, including alcohol consumption, the researchers concluded that it was unlikely that "any drug other than cannabis could have been the causative agent."[47] In those cases where the perceived "symptomatology" of cannabis use persisted after cessation of use, they suggested the "possibility of more permanent structural changes in the cerebral cortex," such as those reported in the British study.[48]

Another source of highly publicized reports on the effect of heavy marijuana use on the brain has been laboratory animal studies. One such study subjected rhesus monkeys to the equivalent of over one hundred marijuana cigarettes a day for a six-mongh period.[49] Not surprisingly, considering the very high dosage of smoked material, two of the monkeys died of lung complications from the smoke forced into them, and a few of the survivors were observed to have behavioral changes described as persistent. However, "permanent brain changes" were neither observed nor claimed by the researchers.[50]

These findings of "harm" from marijuana, although highly speculative, received wide national medial coverage. They were given even greater prominence and credibility in the hearings of the Senate's Subcommittee on Internal Security, where they seemed to be viewed as an explanation of the disaffection of many American youths, particularly students, with a variety of social institutions and traditional values.[51] Reports that questioned the scientific and methodological accuracy of the initial studies, even official ones such as the *Third Report to the United States Congress: Marihuana and Health* by NIDA[52], failed to receive similar widespread public coverage.

Although the research to date does not rule out the possibility of "cerebral atrophy" or other brain damage due to marijuana use, it does seem likely on the basis of the Harvard and Washington University studies and those in Jamaica, Greece, and Costa Rica that demonstrable brain damage is not a normal or probable result of continued cannabis use. In particular, there is at present no evidence to suggest that light or occasional use of cannabis has any permanent harmful effects on brain functioning. This conclusion was reached by NIDA in its 1976 report, *Marihuana and Health*, which stated, after reviewing overseas studies and other current research, that there is virtually "no evidence of impaired neuropsychologic test performance in humans at dose levels studied so far."[53]

Immune Response. During the same period when the "brain damage" reports were appearing came a report by four researchers at Columbia University claiming that a noticeable reduction in the immune response resulted from marijuana use.[54] This reduction was said to be comparable to that in cancer and uremia patients, and was interpreted to mean that marijuana smokers would eventually come to lack an essential means of defense against infectious diseases. However, the validity of this claim remains in doubt. The Columbia study was based on *in vitro* findings (observable in a test tube only); attempts to replicate them and explore their implications by testing for immune-response depression by other means have resulted in contradictory reports.[55] To further complicate matters, it has been found that marijuana obtained from illegal sources may figure in a reduction of the type of immune response involving "T-cell" or thymus-dependent lymphocytes. This reduction did not, however, occur in users smoking quality-controlled marijuana;[56] thus it may have been the result of some common factor of lifestyle other than marijuana.

As was the case with the brain damage reports, however, the initial "scare" report received the headlines. The results were described by the researchers in a press report as "the first direct evidence of cellular damage from marijuana in man."[57] It was immediately suggested that the findings of the National Commission on Marihuana and Drug Abuse be reappraised and that this study provided the "hard facts" desired by legislators and educators wishing to show the harmfulness of continued use of the drug.

The "hard facts" were not immediately forthcoming. The press release on the research preceded publication of the study by several months;

thus a considerable period of time passed before the scientific community could examine the research methodology and review the conclusions based upon it. Once the study was published, it prompted strong criticisms from other researchers, and subsequent studies at the Veterans Administration Hospital in Washington, D.C.[58] and at UCLA[59] failed to corroborate the Columbia study. The UCLA team noted "that chronic marijuana smoking does not produce a gross cellular immune defect. . . ."[60]

Missing in the controversy over cannabis inhibiting resistance to infectious diseases is information on whether the users themselves showed signs of increased infection and illness. One skeptic has pointed out,

> At colleges, where marijuana use has been documented to include over 50% of the population, one would surely expect the use of the health services to have shown a significant increase. No such increase has been reported. This lack of clinical evidence to support the decrease in immune capacity is particularly striking when one considers how marijuana is used. The ritual of passing a joint from mouth to mouth should be as good a way of spreading infections as anyone could devise. Were effective immune responses interfered with, clinicians should have been seeing a virtual deluge of infections, which is not so.[61]

Though some feel the issue of impaired immune response is still unresolved, the fact is that at present, according to the latest HEW report to Congress, there is "no evidence that users of marijuana are more susceptible to such diseases as viral infections and cancer which are known to be associated with lowered production of T-cells."[62]

Chromosome Alterations and Genetic Damage. A third health concern that received headline treatment was the furor in 1974 over a report that marijuana use, whether light or heavy, causes chromosome "breaks."[63] The press coverage of this research implied that marijuana smoking might cause birth defects similar to those associated with thalidomide. However, once again a further study undertaken shortly after the first was unable to confirm it; there was no discernible increase in chromosome alterations due to either marijuana or two more concentrated forms of cannabis.[64] The researchers in the second study concluded, "There does not seem to be any genetic damage produced by the use of marijuana in healthy individuals and without the use of any other drugs."[65]

This conclusion was endorsed by the National Institute on Drug Abuse, which convened two technical conferences on the issue in 1973 and 1974.[66] Studies of long-term cannabis use in foreign countries tends to support NIDA's findings.[67] Most important to understanding these studies is the fact that the relationship between chromosome alteration and genetic defects is poorly understood. Many substances are known to cause such breaks, including caffeine, aspirin, and Valium. Their effects, if any, on the human fetus are unknown. Despite the absence of positive evidence of genetic breaks due to marijuana use, use of it and most other drugs seem inadvisable during pregnancy, since the possibility of adverse reproductive consequences has not been entirely ruled out by current research.

Sexual Dysfunction.   One other possible health hazard has received substantial press coverage: sexual dysfunction. If one looks back over the years at popular myths about marijuana, one finds that marijuana has commonly been attributed with the power to *stimulate* sexual drive and lower inhibitions in users. Nothing has been uncovered in the interim which would confirm that marijuana is indeed an aphrodisiac, but it is ironic that the headlines in 1974 dealt with its role in *decreased* male sexual functioning.

A study by the Reproductive Biology Research Foundation in St. Louis, Missouri reported a significant decrease in the plasma testosterone levels of male research subjects from heavy marijuana use.[68] A second study by the same research team a year later reached the same result, yet another research effort—this one at Harvard University—failed to replicate the first study's findings.[69]

Limitations in both of the St. Louis studies have been pointed out by the researchers themselves as well as by colleagues. Such factors as the small sample tested, the fact that those tested might be using other unreported drugs, and lack of knowledge of the purity or potency of the marijuana used were indicated by the St. Louis researchers.[70] Other commentators have noted that testosterone levels normally vary considerably from day to day and even from hour to hour.[71] One scientist has pointed out that "it takes a very large decline to affect sexual performance much; even castration has very variable effects on sexual activity in monkeys."[72] Still another research team has suggested that "it is possible that a tolerance to marijuana develops that overcomes some inhibitory action of marijuana. . . ."[73] Faced with this data, NIDA's fifth annual report to Congress on marijuana and health concluded that the observed decreases in testosterone have still been within what are generally conceded to be normal limits, and that "their biological significance remains in considerable doubt."[74]

In addition to the health issues just discussed, four other less publicized issues deserve examination. These are lung damage, tolerance and dependence, psychomotor skills, and potential therapeutic uses.

Lung Damage.   There is growing evidence that smoking marijuana may have adverse effects on the human pulmonary function. Tetrahydrocannabinol (THC) and other psychoactive ingredients in marijuana smoke seem to have some of the same effects on the lungs as do tobacco and other kinds of smoke. A study of Jamaican marijuana users showed evidence of a reduction in lung capacity and other pulmonary deficiencies, but those studied were also heavy tobacco users.[75] Although tobacco use probably has more severe effects on the lungs than does marijuana, because it is more heavily consumed and does not dilate the bronchial passages as THC does, heavy marijuana smoking may cause similar deficiencies, since, for instance, marijuana smoke is held in the lungs longer to achieve the psychoactive effect.

Tolerance and Dependence.   Tolerance to a drug is said to occur when increasingly larger doses must be administered to obtain the same effects observed originally.[76] Any such tolerance to marijuana at the dose levels of recreational users is rarely reported, either anecdotally or experimentally. In fact, novice users very often have to use more of the drug to achieve the desired subjective effects than do experienced users who can better identify and are more sensitive to the desired effects. However, a sort of behavioral tolerance has been described which allows an individual to compensate for his or her intoxication and perform certain physical and mental functions which less experienced users would find more difficult or impossible.[77]

"Addiction" or "drug dependency" implies a permanent physiological change causing an individual to persistently crave the consumption of a particular substance. If it is withheld, the user suffers withdrawal symptoms, such as chills, pains, restlessness, perspiration, twitching of muscles, nausea, and diarrhea—symptoms which depend on the particular drug and ordinarily subside with time. While the meaning of cannabis dependency is somewhat vague, if defined as a physical dependency manifested by some physical symptoms following cessation of continued use, there is some evidence that it can occur after large THC doses. According to the 1975 HEW report, "It should be noted, however, that the after effects reported followed unusually high doses of orally administered THC under research ward conditions. Such changes have not commonly been observed in other studies nor has a 'withdrawal syndrome' typically been found among users here or abroad."[78] Additionally, the observation of heavy cannabis users in Jamaica[79] and Greece[80] following a period of abstention from use showed none of the typical symptoms associated with withdrawal.

Psychomotor Skills.   There are real and potentially serious risks involved in using cannabis while undertaking a variety of activities requiring exact time and spatial judgments, precise mental and muscular coordination, and constant alertness. Driving a motor vehicle or operating complicated machinery—all potentially hazardous when sober—become more so when intoxicated with marijuana. That conclusion is reached in the Canadian LeDain Commission report on marijuana[81], the report of the National Commission on Marihuana and Drug Abuse, and every HEW report to Congress since 1971.

However, it is generally acknowledged that marijuana results in a somewhat lesser impairment than alcohol of fine motor skills, such as those used in driving, because its effects appear to be more subtle and variable.[82] Despite these qualifications, impairment of such skills due to marijuana intoxification is clearly indicated by research findings.

Potential Therapeutic Uses.   The idea of marijuana's medical usefulness catches many contemporary Americans by surprise. However, references to the therapeutic use of cannabis can be found as early as the fifteenth century B.C.; it is still used as a folk medicine in many cultures. In this country it was used for a wide variety of ailments throughout the nineteenth century and was referred to in numerous medical publications. In fact, cannabis was contained in the *U.S. Pharmacopoeia* until 1941, when it was finally removed because of the difficulties in prescribing it after passage of the Marijuana Tax Act of 1937. The medicinal popularity of cannabis had already begun to decline in the early part of this century, however, due in part to new developments with other drugs. During the period of the early 1940s to the early 1970s medical professionals largely bypassed investigation of marijuana's potential medical uses; then, in the early 1970s, cannabis research, although focused primarily on the possible deleterious effects, began to reveal some possible therapeutic benefits.

For example, marijuana has recently been used to help reduce intraocular pressure in the eyes of glaucoma patients. In addition, it has been used experimentally to relieve the pain of cancer patients and reduce or eliminate loss of appetite, nausea, and vomiting following chemotherapy; to relieve asthmatic distress by temporarily dilating the bronchial passages; and to facilitate sleep as a sedative-hypnotic. Other possible uses of marijuana now being investigated are as an antidepressant and in the relief of migraine. If marijuana proves to have antiemetic properties, as investigators now seem to be finding, there may be other possible applications.[83]

However, in many instances where cannabis has been found to have therapeutic value, its side effects (e.g., increased heart rate) have contraindicated its acceptance by physicians. Though several state legislatures have legalized marijuana for limited therapeutic prescription, it remains pharmaceutically prohibited at the federal level. Synthetic cannabinoids have been developed which in preliminary research do not appear to have the disadvantages of natural THC, such as the "undesired" psychic effects and the instability and insolubility of the drug. For glaucoma sufferers, eye-drop preparations containing delta-9-THC have been developed, and are now being tested on laboratory animals, with promising initial results.[84]

The Controlled Substances Advisory Committee of the Food and Drug Administration is currently considering the merits of rescheduling marijuana to allow for limited medical application. An interagency coordinating committee has recently been established by White House directive under the aegis of the National Institute of Health to reassess the medical efficacy of all controlled substances, specifically marijuana and heroin. Whether or not marijuana or its chemically related synthetics will reach the pharmacists' shelves in the next few years can only be answered by further research and careful evaluation of findings. The Department of Health, Education, and Welfare has observed, "The hemp plant and its derivative chemicals turn out to be neither the best nor the worst of substances. Like everything else it should be used for its beneficial effects and avoided for its noxious aspects."[85]

Social Issues

Other concerns, whether real or imagined, have also influenced the marijuana debate. It is claimed, for instance, that use of marijuana leads to a loss of desire to work or engage in other meaningful activities. It has also been suggested that it can lead to crime and violence and to the use of other drugs. The following discussion examines these concerns.

"Amotivational Syndrome." For many years marijuana use, particularly heavy use, has been thought to be associated with an "amotivational syndrome." This belief that use of the drug leads to "a loss of interest in virtually all other activities other than drug use—lethargy, social deterioration and drug preoccupation that might be compared to that of the skid row alcoholic's preoccupation with drinking in the western world"[86]—draws heavily on the association of marijuana with minorities, lower economic groups, and, more recently, "hippies" and Vietnam War protesters. The public generally has perceived these groups as rejecting traditional societal values, such as the work ethic; it was, therefore, easy to make the assumption that marijuana use was connected to other "dropping out" symptoms.

The Canadian LeDain Commission and the National Commission on Marihuana and Drug Abuse both examined the evidence on the causal relationship between marijuana and loss of traditional motivation. Both found proof lacking. The LeDain Commission concluded, "The role of cannabis in this alleged syndrome is not clear, nor is the research adequate or conclusive."[87] The National Commission reached the same conclusion, adding, "The clinician sees only the troubled population of any group. In evaluating a public health concern, the essential element is the proportion of affected persons in the general group."[88]

More recent studies on the "amotivational syndrome" have failed to confirm its existence. Two separate longitudinal studies of college students on the West Coast were undertaken to determine whether representative samples of marijuana-using student populations differed significantly in performance and adjustment from their nonusing peers; neither study found any difference to exist.[89] In addition, heavily marijuana-using working-class populations have been studied in cultures where extensive cannabis use is traditional. These latter investigations in Jamaica[90] and Costa Rica,[91] financed by HEW, were designed to compare numerous psychological, social, and health indices among cannabis users and nonusers.

Not only do these studies fail to confirm "amotivational" differences between groups using cannabis and those not using the drug, at least one of the studies indicated that the use of cannabis in one culture was popularly associated with an *increase* in the aptitude of the user for work.[92] That study of Jamaican users of "ganja" (a form of cannabis) concluded,

> It would appear that the socio-economic profiles of smokers and controls generated by these data are virtually indistinguishable from each other. . . . From the self-reported but verified life histories, we are led to at least one conclusion: no negative effect on work history and, therefore, on work motivation due to chronic cannabis use is discernible in this sample.[93]

However, there are methodological limitations to this particular study. For example, while complaining about work may be less, efficiency might also be less than for a nonuser. In addition, the cross-cultural studies do not tell much about the effect of marijuana on complex work tasks, as opposed to simple manual labor. Despite these qualifications, no studies have found any marijuana-induced "amotivation."

Use of Other Drugs.   The belief that marijuana use leads to the use of other illicit drugs, such as heroin or cocaine, has its basis in the early public relations efforts of the Federal Bureau of Narcotics, beginning in the late 1930s. Marijuana, mislabeled a "narcotic" drug, was labeled a "stepping stone" to other drugs by the bureau. Belief in this claim is common even today; a national poll in May 1977 found a majority of adult Americans convinced that marijuana use leads to "hard drugs."[94]

Surveys measuring the nature and extent of American drug use do provide some statistical association between the use of marijuana and other illicit drugs. For example, a 1974–75 national survey of the licit and illicit psychoactive drug-using patterns of young American men found that most of those using cocaine, psychedelic drugs, heroin, stimulants, or sedatives also had used marijuana.[95] However, this survey found the same to be true for alcohol. In fact, drug use surveys show that the use of any specific drug can be *statistically* associated with that of any other drug. This statistical correlation is often confused with the notion that use of one drug—marijuana, for instance—induces through its pharmacological properties physical changes that impel the user to move on to other drugs. Such pharmacological cause-and-effect relationship between marijuana and other drugs has never been shown to exist. Recent research efforts on the issue of marijuana's involvement with subsequent use of other drugs concur on this point.[96] One study of heroin users found that 70 percent had their first drug experience with alcohol, and only 2 percent with marijuana.[97]

Crime and Violence.   A final issue in the current debate over marijuana's relative harmfulness relates to its role, if any, in the commission of criminal acts. The prevailing opinion in this country through the late 1960s was that marijuana is causally linked with murder, rape, and aggravated assault. Once again, this belief appears to have originated in the campaign of the old Federal Bureau of Narcotics to eliminate the drug from American society.[98] Despite a complete lack of empirical evidence to support this claim, a majority of Americans in 1971 believed that such a relationship did in fact exist; the National Commission on Marihuana and Drug Abuse found that 56 percent of adult Americans believed that "many crimes are committed by persons who are under the influence of marijuana."[99]

While widely held, these public attitudes are erroneous. Both the National Commission on Marihuana and Drug Abuse and the Canadian Le-Dain Commission have concluded that there is no evidence whatsoever, in the words of the National Commission, "to support the thesis that the use of marijuana either inevitably or generally causes, leads to or precipitates criminal, violent, aggressive or delinquent behavior of a sexual or non-sexual nature."[100]

A more recent study of violent crimes (particularly sexual assault) and the use of psychoactive substances (including both marijuana and alcohol), found alcohol the drug most likely to be associated with serious assaultive and sexual offenses.[101] Alcohol was also selected by the offenders themselves as the drug most likely to increase aggression. In contrast, marijuana was generally believed by offenders to *decrease* aggressive tendencies. The unanimous conclusion of recent examinations of the commonly presumed marijuana-crime relationship is that no such connection exists.

The Experience of Decriminalization

In spite of the continuing, sometimes acrimonious, debate over marijuana's hazards, several state and local governments have adopted significant policy changes. Eleven states have now decriminalized the possession of marijuana in small amounts (generally an ounce), thus eliminating criminal arrest and judicial proceedings for personal use of the drug. Several local governments, where permitted by state law, have enacted ordinances which similarly treat marijuana possession as a "civil" offense, even though state law does not. The procedure in these jurisdictions operates much like the citation-and-fine procedure for motor-vehicle traffic offenses, minimizing the involvement of the criminal justice system with marijuana possession offenses.

While no state has removed all penalties for personal possession or any criminal penalties for sale or distribution of marijuana, four of the states which have decriminalized some possession have also treated distribution of small amounts for no remuneration in a similar fashion.[102] Twenty states currently provide for the expungement of arrest and conviction records for certain categories of marijuana use, and discretionary conditional discharge is possible in most states.[103]

The judiciary as well as the legislature has become involved in revising marijuana laws. For example, the Alaskan Supreme Court has overturned criminal penalties for personal possession or use of marijuana in the home as a violation of a person's right to privacy.[104] The Alaskan court based this ruling on an explicit state constitutional right to privacy in addition to an implicit right to privacy under the federal constitution. While other constitutional challenges have been made to existing marijuana laws, rulings in favor of these challenges have been confined to relatively narrow points; most of the broadly based challenges have been rejected.[105]

Changing attitudes toward the use of criminal law against the marijuana user seem to have influenced local law enforcement authorities. More than half of the 414 cities responding to a 1976 survey by the National League of Cities and the U.S. Conference of Mayors reported that they were moving "toward decriminalization of marijuana or less enforcement of marijuana laws."[106] The slight decrease in arrests nationally between 1974 and 1975 may reflect a gradual shift in attitudes (see Table 5.1). Nonetheless, marijuana possession arrests are by far the most common drug arrests in the United States; annual arrests still number over the .4 million mark. Reformers point to this continuing high level as an indication that marijuana law reform is still a critical issue.

Oregon: A Case Study.   The focus of recent legislative debates over the effects of marijuana decriminalization has been the experience of the state of Oregon, now in its fifth year of decriminalization. Proponents and opponents alike have relied heavily upon the evidence of "success" or "failure" in Oregon. While proponents of decriminalization base their arguments on the necessity of reforming the penalty to fit the offense, opponents base their opposition on the grounds that it would promote new and continued use. Supporters of decriminalization have never argued that the policy would *reduce* marijuana use, but rather that it is a more reasonable way to *discourage* widespread nonmedical use of the drug. Thus, objective gauges of Oregon's "success" or "failure" have been difficult to construct.

Since one of the initial fears voiced by opponents of marijuana decriminalization has been of a precipitous increase in the number of regular and experimental users, in the amount of marijuana customarily consumed, and in outsiders moving to the state to take advantage of the new law, one measure of success is to look at these factors. Measuring the "humanitarian" aspect of the law is difficult to accomplish in a statistical fashion. Surveys of public opinion concerning approval of the law or a desire to see further legislative changes can give some indication of the law's acceptability. However, the best measure would seem to be the testimony of ordinary citizens and public officials alike on their perceptions of the appropriateness of public policy and the administration of justice regarding marijuana.

One of the tools used to evaluate the Oregon marijuana law experience has been the public opinion survey. Statewide surveys have been conducted annually from 1974 through 1977 to learn citizen attitudes toward the new law and how or if usage patterns may have changed.[107] Examination of these survey results shows that marijuana use in Oregon has remained at levels typical of other western states—(most of which have not "decriminalized" possession)—and national trends generally. Adult Oregonians (over age 18) who have used marijuana have increased from 19 percent of the state population in 1974 to 25 percent in 1977. Significantly, current use of marijuana has remained at a relatively constant level during this four-year period in which experimentation has risen. Although there is no way to validate the reliability of the responses, the majority of current users felt they either had not changed or had decreased their frequency of use, in every year the survey was taken. Another way of looking at these results is to say that 91 percent of Oregon adults did not engage in current use of marijuana in 1974 and 90 percent did not in 1977. Tables 5.2 and 5.3 illustrate the changes in use patterns among various age groupings in the Oregon adult population.

The public's acceptance of the new law can also be seen in the survey results. A majority of Oregon adults consistently favored either the present possession decriminalization or further revisions, such as legalizing sale and use of marijuana. In 1977 only 35 percent of the adults sur-

TABLE 5.2   Marijuana Use by Adult Age Groupings, Oregon, 1974–1977

By Age	HAVE USED				CURRENT USE			
	'74	'75	'76	'77	'74	'75	'76	'77
18–29	46%	51%	62%	62%	24%	24%	35%	30%
30–44	15	15	15	23	5	4	5	6
45–59	4	5	6	10	.5	2	3	2
60 & over	2	3	2	2	*	*	*	*
Total Adult	19	20	24	25	9	8	12	10

*Less than .5%

TABLE 5.3   Changes in Marijuana Use Among Current Users, Oregon, 1974–1977

	1974	1975	1976	1977
Decreased usage	40%	35%	39%	40%
Increased usage	5	9	9	14
No change	52	54	50	46
Undecided	3	2	2	0

veyed in Oregon advocated a return of stiffer penalties for possession. Although those who have used marijuana clearly are the most supportive of the legal reforms, those who have never used the drug also favor decriminalization or further revisions over a return to criminal penalties by a 51 to 41 percent margin.

Support for marijuana decriminalization has not had negative political effects for those legislators who supported it. Nor has decriminalization become a significant political issue for campaigning candidates to debate. Rather, the new Oregon law appears to enjoy widespread public support. J. Pat Horton, the district attorney from Eugene and a vocal supporter of marijuana law reform, noted the acceptance of decriminalization by Oregonians in testimony before a U.S. Senate subcommittee.

> Acceptance of the new legislation in Oregon has been overwhelmingly positive, especially among middle-aged people who have children in grade, junior high, or the high school level. An attempt by a small number of people in the state to restore criminal penalties for possession was overwhelmingly defeated. Virtually every candidate for office and every incumbent in the State of Oregon, when questioned on the new decriminalization law, has indicated publicly that he favors such legislation and would vote legislatively to continue it.[108]

The Oregon State Office of Legislative Research released an analysis of the law's effects one year after passage.[109] Legislative Research attempted to assess the attitudes of law enforcement agencies, courts, clinicians, and prosecutors toward implementation of the new law. Although the response to their mail survey was too low to give a representative reading, the cautious conclusion of the office indicated that decriminalization was having the desired effect.

> What evidence there is suggests that decriminalization of marijuana has successfully removed small users or possessors from the criminal justice machinery without relaxing the criminal penalties for pushers or sellers of the drug, and has enabled officials in law enforcement, district attorneys' offices and courts to concentrate on other matters within their jurisdiction.[110]

Among the most illuminating findings of the Oregon marijuana surveys were the reasons people gave for *not* using the drug. Although historically it has been assumed that the criminal law has a powerful deterrent effect, the survey results indicate that fear of legal prosecution played only a minor role in influencing personal decisions on whether to use marijuana. These responses of Oregon adults are similar to responses given in national surveys to the same questions.[111] Simple lack of interest was consistently given as the reason why most nonusers chose not to use the drug. However, in 1974 and 1975 "possible health dangers" was a frequently cited reason for not using marijuana; it was during this period that many of the reports of serious health hazards were widely publicized. Table 5.4 illustrates the findings.

Another factor in support of marijuana decriminalization is the potential cost saving to government. The Health and Welfare Agency of the state of California undertook a study of the effects of that state's marijuana decriminalization act on the criminal justice system.[112] It found, of course, that there had been a substantial reduction in reported marijuana possession offenses, based on comparative 1975 and 1976 arrest and citation data. Total arrests and citations for marijuana possession in the first six months of 1976 decreased 47 percent for adults and 14.8 percent for juveniles, compared to the first six months of 1975; arrests for cultivation also dropped 46.9 percent during that same period, and those for trafficking 5 percent. This decrease in marijuana-related arrests led to a corre-

TABLE 5.4 Reason for Not Currently Using Marijuana, Oregon, 1974–1977

	1974	1975	1976	1977
Not interested	53%	65%	64%	68%
Possible health dangers	23	28	7	9
Possibility of legal prosecution	4	3	4	6
Drug not available	2	1	4	0
Other reason	9	3	17	17
Undecided	4	0	9	0

sponding decrease in police agency and criminal justice costs. Total law enforcement costs for the six-month period dropped to $2.3 million, $5.3 million less than in the comparable period in 1975. Judicial system costs—including prosecution, diversion, and public defender costs—were reduced from $9.4 million in the first half of 1975 to $2 million in the first half of 1976, a difference of $7.4 million.[113]

As stated previously, ten more states have followed Oregon's lead in enacting similar legislation reducing the level of the marijuana "simple possession" offense to that of a traffic violation. More than twenty other states are actively considering marijuana decriminalization, and it has been proposed at the federal level by President Carter. The absence of unusually large increases in usage rates in Oregon and the other decriminalized states and the generally high level of public support for these changes once made are persuasive points for those seeking marijuana reforms at federal and state levels.

Yet the debate over marijuana's possible harmfulness continues to be argued as well. Marijuana policy continues to be more concerned with public attitudes and values than with objective consideration of the facts. Medical and scientific research disputes have been used to obfuscate the real issue in the marijuana debate. Far too often, marijuana policy is portrayed as an "all or nothing" choice.

The Future of Marijuana Policy

Persistent use for nearly a decade by large numbers, despite significant attempts to discourage marijuana use, suggests that cannabis use is more than a fad and may well prove to be an enduring cultural pattern in the United States.[114]

This statement by the National Institute on Drug Abuse recognizes a fact of modern American life: Marijuana is, has been, and will probably continue to be widely used despite policies designed to prohibit it. The recent trend toward decriminalization seems to reflect a growing attitude that civil fines are more appropriate penalties for marijuana use than criminal sanctions. A 1976 national survey by the National Institute on Drug Abuse indicated that 86 percent of adults were against sending marijuana smokers to jail for first conviction of possession, preferring other alternatives ranging from no penalty to probation and mandatory treatment.[115] More recently, a May 1977 Gallup poll found that a majority (53 percent) of Americans felt that possession of small amounts of marijuana should not be treated as a criminal offense, while 41 percent favored retention of criminal sanctions.[116]

Even more lenient attitudes toward marijuana laws are seen among the youth who will be reaching voting age in the next few years. A University of Michigan study of the lifestyles and values of youth began monitoring high school seniors in 125 high schools around the country, beginning with the class of 1975.[117] Three-fifths of the class of 1976 believed that marijuana should either be legalized or treated as a minor civil offense like a parking violation—"decriminalized". This 61.7 percent was an increase of 9 percent over the class of 1975, where only 52.9 percent approved.

If America's youth and young adults maintain the attitudes they now have, and if marijuana usage remains at its present level or increases in subsequent young adult groups, we can expect to find an increasing acceptance of marijuana in the years ahead. While acceptance of marijuana does not necessarily imply increasing pressure for the removal of all criminal sanctions, that would be a distinct possibility. A national survey in 1974 revealed a sharp division between those who have used marijuana and those who have never tried it in their attitudes toward marijuana law reform.[118] Eight of every ten adults who have used the drug favored reducing or eliminating criminal penalties, compared with only three in ten of those who have never used it.

Some observers have suggested further changes in the laws, such as the elimination of penalties for the cultivation of a few cannabis plants for personal consumption.[119] These suggestions appear less radical as time passes and public opinion surveys record increasing support for the legalization of marijuana. A 1977 Gallup poll showed that support for full-scale legalization had nearly doubled in the period 1972–77; at that it was still favored by only 28 percent of adults nationally.[120] Thus while the public remains divided on what would be the proper legal response to marijuana use, it seems to be moving toward more lenient approaches. Considerations of tax revenues to be realized from the legitimate sale of marijuana, as with tobacco products, may also fuel future legislative initiatives on marijuana legalization in a time when many levels of government are financially pressed.

Changes in attitudes and laws concerning illicit drugs have come about only after a long, tumultuous process. Debates over the proper legal mechanism for controlling the use of particular drugs are still heavily laden with values and preconceived notions of right and wrong. While the roots in racism and other prejudices of the original prohibitory laws against marijuana, cocaine, heroin, and other drugs have been largely forgotten, the "evil" label remains. The widespread use of marijuana, especially among highly visible "normal" populations of white, middle-class students and young adults, has caused significant attitudinal change. However, the legacy of the fear of marijuana lingers, and policy changes have not come about easily. Objective analysis can still be effectively countered with emotional appeals intended to protect traditional American values and institutions. The marijuana decriminalization process has pointed out the tenacity of the belief that certain drugs are inherently evil and can be controlled only by criminal law. This point is substantiated as well by the recent response to rising cocaine use in the United States.

Cocaine: A "New" Drug and Old Issues

Cocaine is a new drug to most Americans, who have only recently become aware of its use in the United States from media accounts and official warnings of a new outbreak of "drug abuse." However, upon closer examination we can see many of the same arguments and issues which have held center stage in the marijuana debate. Despite the lack of evidence of significant health risks associated with moderate use of the drug, federal drug policymakers have continued to warn of its dangers and the threat it poses to American society. In short, public discussion of cocaine policy in the late 1970s bears a remarkable resemblance to that of marijuana in the late 1960s and early 1970s.

The stimulus for the newfound governmental and public concern over cocaine is the reported increase in use, particularly among younger adults. The Office of Drug Abuse Policy estimated that approximately four million Americans used cocaine in 1976.[121] Among the eighteen- to twenty-five-year-old bracket, use has been reported by one in eight.[122] Among high school seniors, one in ten (9.8 percent) of the class of 1976 reported having tried cocaine at least once.[123] These numbers have raised sufficient concern among legislators and drug policymakers to trigger public statements calling for renewed efforts to eliminate cocaine use. However, as with marijuana, the use of cocaine by a substantial number of young adults—many of them in responsible careers and professions—has initiated a public debate which challenges the assumptions upon which current restrictive policies are based.

Medical experts generally agree that cocaine produces few observable adverse health consequences in its users. Cocaine, despite its gradually increasing use over the past ten years, is rarely mentioned in reports of drug-related deaths or hospital emergency-room entries. The *White Paper on Drug Abuse*, prepared by President Ford's Domestic Council Drug Abuse Task Force in 1975, ranked various psychoactive drugs according to the dependence liability they possessed, the severity of individual and personal consequences, and the size of the core problem. Cocaine ranked low in three of the four categories. It was ranked as "medium" with respect to social consequences—even though the *White Paper* said that, as presently used, cocaine "does not result in serious social consequences such as crime, hospital emergency room admissions or death."[124] Recently, Carter administration drug abuse officials have acknowledged that cocaine produces "few observable health consequences," but warn that it has the "potential" for serious harm if patterns of present use should alter.[125]

The following discussion briefly examines cocaine as used in America, the arguments advanced for strong prohibition against its use, and the implications of the present debate for future policy.

The Drug. Cocaine is one of several alkaloics found in the leaves of the coca plant (erythroxylon coca), which is native to the eastern watershed of the Andes Mountains in Peru, Colombia, and Bolivia. South American Indians have chewed coca-leaf preparations for centuries in order to relieve fatigue, hunger, and cold. Even today it is estimated that 90 percent of the male and 20 percent of the female population living in these areas chew the leaves daily.[126] To obtain cocaine the coca leaves are refined first into a crude paste and then into a crystalline or powder form. Cocaine generally arrives in this country in this highly refined stage.

Just what is meant by American "use" of cocaine and in what amounts and by what methods of ingestion is it taken, are questions with imprecise answers, which have plagued researchers attempting to assess the drug's effects in social and recreational settings. The Drug Enforcement Administration has estimated that the street-level purity of cocaine is only 13 percent by the time it had been cut and recut. It is usually sold in small quantities (a gram or less) and is most often cut with relatively harmless substances such as lactose, glucose, and mannitol (crystalline alcohol); occasionally with synthetic local anesthetics such as lidocaine or procaine, which have their own toxic effects; or at times with other stimulants such as caffeine or amphetamines. Except at the very highest levels of sale, no one seems to know what they are getting The unreliable quality of illicit cocaine makes it all but impossible to accurately assess what typically happens to users as a result of intermittent or prolonged ingestion. To say, for example, that an individual uses one gram per day of street cocaine could mean that he consumes an amount anywhere between zero and .9 gram, with the remainder consisting of indeterminate adulterants or impurities. Although the effects of cocaine vary enormously, depending on whether it is intravenously injected or—as is the case with the overwhelming number of American users—sniffed or "snorted," the medical literature on the drug does not consistently discern between different dosage levels or method of administration.

Cocaine use was associated with Sigmund Freud, who used it frequently at one time and recorded his experiences with it, and with Coca-Cola, which contained the drug as a standard ingredient into the early 1900s.[127] It was listed in the U.S. Pharmacopoeia and used extensively through the late nineteenth and early twentieth centuries as an anesthetic. In addition, millions of American consumers used cocaine in diluted form—as contained in wines, tonics, and soft drinks—well into the early 1900s.

This atmosphere of widespread acceptance, however, rapidly gave way to the conviction that cocaine was an evil drug that could lead to addiction, crime, and licentious behavior. As the image of evil was becoming established, racism also became an element, in that critics of cocaine use tended to cite its potential effects on feared minority populations as an additional justification for prohibition. At any rate, by the time Congress passed the Harrison Narcotic Act in 1914 and ratified the Hague Opium Convention the following year, cocaine's image as an addictive drug causing crime, violence, and sexual debauchery was becoming firmly implanted. The medical use of cocaine was severely restricted and its use for pleasure banned. To date, the federal and the state governments have continued to pursue this policy of cocaine suppression with legislation providing severe criminal penalties for sale or possession.[128]

Health Issues. As indicated above, much of the past and current justification for cocaine prohibition relies upon arguments that it is potentially lethal, is addictive, leads to psychosis, arouses sexual instincts and aggressiveness, leads to use of other drugs, and when sniffed regularly can perforate the nasal wall. The scientific literature on cocaine is surprisingly sparse, however. Investigators often must rely upon half-century–old anecdotal and literary descriptions of its effects. Much of the existing information has been compiled in a publication of the National Institute on Drug Abuse, *Cocaine: 1977*, the result of four years of work, four million dollars spent, and forty research projects.[129] An examination of that document reveals that very little is known about cocaine's effects on man. It is worthwhile to note that this lack of knowledge, as with marijuana, has been advanced as a justification for present policies criminally penalizing use of the drug.

Overdose Deaths. The lethal dose of cocaine is uncertain and variable. Almost all of the reported cardiac arrests and respiratory failures resulting from large doses of cocaine occurred during the first fifty years of its use in surgical settings as a topical anesthetic. Cocaine *can* be fatal when administered in large dosages or ingested by a small percentage of persons peculiarly susceptible to its effects. However, the scientific literature reveals at most a few hundred deaths directly attributable to cocaine throughout the history of its use in all parts of the world. The available evidence indicates that cocaine, as commonly used in the United States— i.e., nasally insufflated in small amounts—has figured in very few, if any, deaths.

Research conducted for the NIDA-produced *Cocaine: 1977*, examined the 111 cocaine deaths reported to the federal Drug Abuse Warning Network (DAWN) system between 1971 and 1976.[130] Cocaine was involved in these reported deaths only insofar as its presence was detected post-mortem. Eighty-six of the 111 deaths were said to be caused by cocaine, but morphine was detected in one-third of these and other drugs in a smaller percentage of cases. The route of cocaine administration was undetermined in sixty cases, intravenous in thirty-five, nasal in eight, oral in seven, and rectal in one.

While it is beyond dispute that cocaine has the inherent capacity to cause death when used in large quantities or by those abnormally sensitive to it, it also seems, on the basis of the best available evidence. that nasal inhalation of small amounts of the drug rarely if ever results in death. This can be compared with the likelihood of overdose with alcohol consumption.

Dependence and Tolerance. The term "physiological dependence" implies that sudden abstinence from chronic drug use would result in physical symptoms of withdrawal. "Tolerance" refers to the process of acclimation to a particular drug so that subsequent dosages of the same strength as the first would fail to elicit the desire effect, thus requiring increasing dosages over time. These pharmacological attributes are most commonly associated with heavy, long-term use of barbiturates, alcohol, and opiates.

While anecdotal accounts—e.g., that of Conan Doyle's literary character Sherlock Holmes, said to be "addicted" to cocaine—suggest the existence of cocaine "addiction," there is little scientific evidence on which to base this belief. Recent American psychiatric[131] and sociological[132] studies have failed to substantiate the view that repeated cocaine use leads to physiological dependence or tolerance. In addition, as at least one researcher has indicated, hundreds of thousands of Andean Indians who regularly used coca in the highlands have moved to the low-lying towns and urban areas, yet no withdrawal problems have ever been described. Should chronic ingestion of the cocaine alkaloid be addictive[133] it seems likely that these former coca users would experience some withdrawal symptoms.

To the extent that the observations and reports of cocaine users can be taken as an index of the drug's pharmacological properties, physical dependence does not seem to apply to nasal use, for withdrawal symptoms are not evident among users who administer cocaine in this way. No doubt severe aberrational symptomalogy can be induced in laboratory animals by introducing exorbitantly high intravenous dosages of cocaine, but the current patterns of human use of cocaine do not substantiate the popular belief of cocaine "addiction."[134] Imprecise use of medical terminology, however, can create the impression that cocaine borders on the fringe of addictive substances.

Toxic Psychosis. A "toxic psychosis" is a condition that can be caused in the user by almost any intoxicant drug. Characteristic symptoms are confusion, disorientation, and hallucinations.[135] While it appears that extended cocaine use may produce one or more of these reactions, they subside when the body eliminates the drug. This usually occurs within a matter of a few hours.[136] Investigators believe that most experienced users are able to regulate their dose levels to avoid such adverse reactions.[137] In fact, one researcher believes that in most cases toxic psychosis results from deliberate attempts to see how large a dose the user can ingest, rather than from any normal reaction to amounts of the drug ordinarily used.[138]

The relationship of cocaine to violence again derives more from fears and the longstanding bias against the drug than from any empirical data. It is significant that the comprehensive review of cocaine undertaken by the National Institute on Drug Abuse in 1977 fails to mention any violent or criminal activity associated with cocaine use.[139] Yet the drug is still widely associated in the public mind with violent behavior, an attitude stemming in part from the imaginative and inflammatory testimony in early legislative hearings of those who wished to see the drug banned.

Because cocaine is a central-nervous-system stimulant, similar in many ways to amphetamines—which *can* lead to aggressive behavior—some observers have expressed concern that cocaine may provoke similar tendencies. But, though hyperexcitability and irritability have been reported from extended use of cocaine, its effects are less intense and shorter acting than those of amphetamines. A recent comprehensive review of cocaine's evolution as a popular illicit drug and of the attendant social issues concludes that it is less likely than amphetamines, barbiturates, or alcohol to lead to violent behavior.[140]

Sexual Stimulant.   Researchers and users alike agree that cocaine does increase sexual desire or potency in some individuals. However, it is not an aphrodisiac, and may in fact produce transient impotence in some users when taken in high dosages. Both the anecdotal accounts of users and the observations of researchers, however, confirm cocaine's role in enhancing sexual activity for some users.[141] This may be the result of a combination of factors other than the drug itself; the setting in which a drug is taken and the expectations of the user are important determinants of its subjective effects.

Cocaine's early reputation as an aphrodisiac developed when its use was generally confined to those with a reputation for high sexual activity—a few entertainment-world sex symbols, pimps, and prostitutes. No doubt this early reputation influenced the expectations of other users and became self-fulfilling. But it is also true that "any drug, from amphetamine to barbiturate, that removes inhibitions may heighten erotic desires and fantasies."[142]

Nasal Damage.   The most common health complaint of users who generally administer the drug by nasal inhalation is a runny nose. Less frequent are reports of inflammation of the nasal mucous membrane, with consequent sores and bleeding. More dramatic are accounts—more common in reports prior to 1925 than recent ones—of perforated septa due to chronic cocaine use, a condition where part of the tissue wall between the nostrils has been eroded away.

While there seems to be little doubt that permanent lesions and perforations can occur from extended cocaine use, their reported occurrence in the United States is extremely rare.[143] Experienced users try to avoid problems by rinsing with water or nasal sprays and by thoroughly pulverizing the cocaine to be inhaled so that it will be quickly absorbed by the mucous membranes. As is the case with most illicit drugs, there appears to be an informal process of "drug education" of newer users by more experienced ones in the ways to avoid such undesirable effects as these.

Use of Other Drugs.   A frequent argument advanced for the continued prohibition of some drugs is that while they may not be particularly harmful in themselves they lead to the use of other drugs. As we pointed out in the earlier discussion of the marijuana policy debate, the use of almost any substance can be shown to have some statistical relationship to the use of another. What is quite difficult to establish is the *causal* relationship between the use of one drug and another. This is true with marijuana, and it is true with cocaine.

American cocaine users clearly tend to be multiple drug users in the sense that they use a variety of other psychoactive substances.[144] They also tend to be polydrug users in the sense that they use other drugs— particularly alcohol and marijuana—in combination with cocaine.[145] Cocaine is regarded by most users as a luxury drug to be enjoyed on special occasions rather than on a daily basis.[146] In this respect American cocaine use appears to resemble a common pattern in alcohol use in which fine wines or liquors are reserved for other than ordinary consumption.

Policy Implications.   While the numbers of cocaine users are much fewer than those for marijuana, the drug has commanded both public and official attention in recent years. The result of this attention is predictable: First, reports of increasing use are interpreted as evidence of a "drug problem"; second, there is much casting about for evidence of personal and social harm as a result of use, and then, sounding the alarm, there is a call for increased law enforcement efforts and legislative enactments of harsh penalties to fight this perceived threat. Policy critics tend to advise means other than the criminal law to discourage misuse of the drug; the defenders of the status quo rely upon a line of reasoning remarkably similar to that used in debates over marijuana policy.

Simply stated, that line of reasoning is as follows: While the use of cocaine presently does not appear to pose a significant public health problem, it will become a problem if official prohibition is relaxed in any way, because more people will then use the drug more often and in greater amounts. The result, so this reasoning goes, would be severe personal and social damage. In this regard, proof of cocaine's harmlessness would be necessary for any policy change to be considered; some believe that, even if there is a lack of damning medical evidence of harm, later findings will surely prove otherwise. Thus, arguments for policy reforms, however minor, are met with this circular reasoning which ends where it began, putting forth the indispensability of the prohibition approach.

The changes that are occurring in American marijuana policy may be coming about only because of the crush of numbers. When the use of a particular substance becomes sufficiently widespread, it can no longer be stigmatized as the aberrant taste of a social minority. The costs of criminalizing and alienating a substantial segment of the American people for no other reason than their use of marijuana has played a critical role in the decriminalization debate. Cocaine users, while increasing in number, are still perceived as exotic persons, and the drug still carries connotations of addiction, violence, and personal ruin from the past. While the federal government has not used rising cocaine use as an excuse to mount another all-out "war on drug abuse," neither has it indicated any desire to change the policy outlawing cocaine use.

Dr. Robert Dupont as director of the National Institute of Drug Abuse noted,

> While the evidence accumulated thus far does not justify the claim that the American public is now suffering greatly as a consequence of cocaine use, it is evident that much more needs to be known before any actions are taken that might result in wider availability at a lower cost.[147]

Robert Peterson, editor-in-chief in the division of research at NIDA, notes,

> Unfortunately, a lack of adequate information is sometimes interpreted as indicating that a drug is "safe" when it would be more accurate to admit that our knowledge is simply inadequate to specify the parameters of risk. Moreover, a substance which when used under conditions of relatively infrequent, low dosage may pose few hazards, may present quite a different picture when widely available and regularly used in larger amounts.[148]

The law has classified cocaine as a serious "drug of abuse"; yet, despite substantial efforts by some researchers to prove this contention, its moderate use does not appear to result in significant personal or social harm other than that of the effect of the criminal process on detected users. Arguments supporting the continuation of present policy are based on evidence, however unsubstantiated or unusual, of extreme harm. This is tantamount to basing alcohol control policies on the theory that the dependent alcoholic represents inevitably the typical drinker. The result is to severely damage the credibility of government in its efforts to lessen the adverse individual and social effects of drug misuse. Enforcing the law by means of the criminal justice system is as cumbersome and inefficient in reducing genuine misuse as it is in reducing any use of the drug. And the habit of using the drug control issue as a political football compounds the problems of achieving a reasonable response.

Our experience with marijuana has pointed out the need to separate rhetoric from reason. Our emerging response to rising cocaine use demonstrates that the lessons of marijuana have been imperfectly learned.

History shows that man has come to know and use an ever- increasing number of psychoactive substances. This trend shows no signs of reversal, and may in fact have accelerated during the past century or two. To lessen the costs to individuals and to society we need to pursue policies that attempt to discourage and correct the misuse of these substances in a manner that does not create greater harm than does the drug itself. A society that puts such great emphasis on due process of law ought to be prepared to modify that law in response to the weight of evidence, putting aside irrational fears and emotions.

6 American Heroin Policy: Some Alternatives

Erik J. Meyers

THOUGHTFUL OBSERVERS OF the American drug situation have frequently stated the belief that our problems may be caused more by our policies than by the drugs they seek to regulate. As one writer has commented, the United States may have "created a monster out of what was initially a gnat" in moving from a nineteenth-century laissez-faire approach to drugs to a twentieth-century preoccupation with eliminating use of certain drugs.[1] If we look at present studies on the "social costs" of drug use, we see that they examine more the costs of present drug policies to American society than the intrinsic social costs of drug use itself. Nowhere is this dilemma over drug policy more clearly shown than in our national response to heroin use.

The discussion of alternative heroin policies that follows is meant to stimulate and focus public discussion of drug policy. We hope to promote reasoned, nonrhetorical consideration of the nature of the problems and the most appropriate means of minimizing social disruption and harm to individuals. While no policy will eliminate all problems, our analysis shows that some policy responses are more likely than others to minimize detrimental effects. This discussion begins with a look at the full spectrum

The author gratefully acknowledges the contributions of the following individuals in preparing background materials for this chapter (However, the opinions expressed are those of the author and do not necessarily reflect the views of these contributors): Leon G. Hunt, Troy Duster, Jane McGrew, Charles Morgan, Jr., Hope Eastman, Norman Siegel, and Gerald F. Uelman.

of policy choices available and at specific policy models along that spectrum. Following that, we will examine the key issues heroin policy must deal with, in terms of four selected policy choices.

Our list of potential policy choices ought not be viewed as a serial progression, nor does this identification of separate, individual options necessarily preclude the adoption of more than one at a time. Implementation of one option may preclude others or instead stimulate consideration of others. The policy choices examined in the following discussion are merely illustrative of the existing possibilities; they are not intended as a complete and final list nor as a timetable for change.

The Choices

The range of possible heroin policy options is wide, extending from efforts to prohibit and eliminate all types of heroin use to official promotion of nonmedical heroin use by means of a government monopoly. The shades of difference within this spectrum of policies are nearly infinite. For example, a heroin policy could be fashioned to subject illicit sellers and distributors to criminal penalties while levying only small civil fines on those possessing small amounts of heroin for their own use. Another approach would be to subject all convicted users to long, mandatory jail terms, with lifetime parole. Both of these approaches are consistent with a policy seeking to deter use and ultimately eliminate consumption, in spite of their obvious differences in the means employed to achieve these goals. Other possible heroin policy choices falling between the poles of stringent prohibition and totally unregulated sale and consumption are: experimental use of heroin in medical and drug treatment research, development of government-sponsored heroin treatment clinics, removal of criminal penalties for personal possession, prescription of heroin by private physicians, regulation of heroin as an over-the-counter drug; and development of a "pure food and drug" model for distribution of the drug.

Complete Prohibition.   This is current American policy, in which laws provide criminal penalties for the possession, use, sale, and distribution of heroin. Federal law and a few state laws treat possession as a misdemeanor (maximum penalty: one year in jail), while other jurisdictions treat it as a felony. All jurisdictions treat sale and distribution as felonies (more than one year in jail), though penalty provisions as to fines and terms of imprisonment vary widely.

Many jurisdictions provide for the diversion of certain classes of heroin offenders into treatment programs. Successful completion of a treatment regimen may result in the dropping of pending criminal charges or may be considered evidence of rehabilitation at sentencing. Failure in treatment returns the offender to the normal criminal justice process for trial and sentencing if found guilty.

In practice, many urban criminal justice agencies do not attempt to fully enforce laws against personal use or possession of heroin. For these jurisdictions, "total prohibition" means that occasional "sweeps" may be made in areas where use levels are high or that the laws may be used selectively to punish some users while others are ignored. Conversely, many jurisdictions do not have a great many heroin users, and are inclined to arrest and fully charge every heroin offender who is apprehended.

Medical and Drug Treatment Research with Heroin.   Current federal law does not permit heroin to be prescribed for legitimate medical purposes or for "maintenance" treatment of compulsive users. The only permissible use is for certain highly restricted research projects. For example, heroin was used several years ago to test the effectiveness of narcotic-drug antagonists. However, recent interest from the medical community and segments of the general public in using heroin to alleviate the pain associated with certain types of cancer could play a role in ending official reluctance to permit research into therapeutic applications for the drug.[2] Still, despite interest in the scientific and medical communities to test the efficacy of heroin as an analgesic, an antitussive, or as a tool in opiate addiction treatment, the Food and Drug Administration (FDA) and Drug Enforcement Administration (DEA)—the agencies whose administrative approval is required—have discouraged heroin research. It is because these agencies have been so reluctant to allow research with heroin that we have identified medical and drug treatment research as an independent policy option.

Our further discussion of this option below pertains to experimental research into drug abuse treatment applications for heroin, rather than to investigation into other medical uses for the drug. The decision to confine our discussion to drug treatment research reflects the primary concern of this chapter—control of the nonmedical use of heroin. However, it should be noted that research indicating useful therapeutic applications of heroin would probably have a spillover effect on general public attitudes toward the drug.

Government-sponsored Heroin Treatment Clinics.   The "heroin treatment" envisioned by this policy could take many forms. One form would be a proposed heroin "induction" or "lure" model using heroin or injectable morphine to entice otherwise reluctant heroin users voluntarily into treatment, essentially a short-term detoxification program using heroin in the initial state and methadone in the intermediate one.[3] This model, in fact, is similar to the original Dole-Nyswander research program with methadone maintenance; in that study, morphine was administered to patients who at admission showed signs of withdrawal. Substitution of methadone (administered orally) would quickly follow that initial stage, as is generally contemplated with the "heroin-lure" model of heroin treatment. However, abstinence from all opiate use within a relatively short, one-to-two-year period is often stated as the goal of the "lure" or "induction" model, whereas the Dole-Nyswander approach contemplated indefinite maintenance on oral methadone.

Another possible form for American heroin treatment is provided by the British. The current American approach to heroin treatment differs significantly from prevailing British drug treatment practice, which allows indefinite opiate maintenance—intravenous heroin, intravenous methadone, oral methadone, or any combination of methods—for opiate drug dependents.[4] In the United States, while the new proposed federal regulations on oral methadone treatment do not *require* programs to drop patients within any definite period of time, they do, however, continue to emphasize strongly the patients' withdrawal from methadone and achievement of a completely drug-free state.[5] In England the choice of both the opiate and the method of administration is left to the discretion of the clinic physician; although abstinence is stated to be desirable, the British consider stabilization and normalization of an addict's life and keeping track of as many addicts as possible to be equally desirable goals. Therefore, if stabilization or continued treatment-involvement can be attained only by the continuing prescription of an opiate at stable dosage levels, then such maintenance meets the social policy objectives of British treatment.

A wide degree of flexibility marks the British response to the treatment of heroin dependency. In discussing the potential effects of a heroin treatment clinic policy in the United States, we include this characteristic in our policy model. Rather than one specific type of treatment model, the clinic policy examined could encompass a variety, whether "lure," induction, true maintenance, or other types. Attention will be called to potential differences among various models in the following discussion of the issues affecting heroin policy.

Prescription of Heroin by Private Physician. This option is still further removed from total prohibition and total government control of heroin. Practicing physicians—rather than special-purpose, government-sponsored clinics—would be the primary dispensers of licit heroin. However, this could still permit tight controls over heroin's legal availability, in that both recipient and prescribing physician would be subject to registration, reporting requirements, and official surveillance. The strictness of these controls could vary. Prescription could be limited either to legally or medically defined addicts or to those with a legitimate medical need for heroin other than for drug abuse, such as for relief of the severe pain associated with certain cancer conditions. Distribution and administration could be handled either directly in the prescribing doctor's office or by the

British practice of filling the prescription through general pharmaceutical outlets and self-administration of the drug.

For this to take effect, heroin would have to be rescheduled from Schedule I to a lower control schedule of the federal Controlled Substances Act and to lower state schedules as well (for those states that have adopted a form of the Uniform Controlled Substances Act). This rescheduling process would also have to occur in order to implement medical and treatment research and the over-the-counter drug and pure food and drug models which are discussed below.

A variant "option within an option" would be to allow physicians to exercise professional discretion in determining whom to treat with heroin, how long treatment should be continued, and what amounts of heroin are required. Such a model is analogous to the British pre-maintenance clinic "system" (i.e., pre-1968 practices) and is subject to the same risks namely, the abuse of discretion or outright drug-prescription profiteering by a few physicians. (The British experience with heroin regulation is discussed in greater detail on pages 216–219.) Government supervision would be minimal, similar to present FDA and DEA monitoring of Schedule III prescription drugs, where some reporting and recordkeeping is required and prescription refills are limited.

Removal of Criminal Penalties for Personal Possession.

This policy model could be referred to as heroin "decriminalization" or "legalization." However, those terms are at best ambiguous and imprecise. The heroin treatment clinic policy previously described is, of course, a form of heroin decriminalization, since it would permit heroin to be used and possessed legally under certain circumstances. The fact that such different schemes could be termed heroin "decriminalization" is reason enough to avoid use of that term.

The marijuana decriminalization legislation of recent years has largely consisted in the removal of the possibility of a jail sentence for first-time possession of a small amount of marijuana, generally an ounce or less. In most states adopting such legislation, the offense is a civil rather than criminal one, and the offender pays a fine (generally in the $20–200 range) as if for a traffic violation. This policy model anticipates a similar, though not necessarily identical, legislative scheme for heroin. Our discussion of this option will be predicated on a policy which eliminates all criminal penalties for possession of a small amount of heroin for personal use. It, like the new policy for marijuana, does *not* contemplate a legal, regulated source of supply, but merely changes the penalty for illicit possession.

Removal of criminal penalties for heroin possession could be implemented at various jurisdictional levels. For example, Congress has not changed the federal law pertaining to simple possession of marijuana;

possession continues to be a federal criminal offense punishable by a prison term of up to one year. However, since 1973 several states have enacted legislation making marijuana possession a civil offense—the equivalent of a traffic violation—within their borders. Although the marijuana user remains subject to both federal and state laws, since little federal enforcement effort is directed against simple possession offenses the state law has a greater impact on users. Similarly, in states that permit "local option" ordinances, some cities have formally adopted a civil-fine procedure for marijuana offenses that differs from the otherwise applicable state law. The same pattern of piecemeal implementation of the removal of possession penalties could occur with this heroin policy model.

Over-the-Counter Drug Regulation. Dispensing heroin without a prescription would require changes in both the federal Food and Drug Act and the Controlled Substances Act. States could not implement this policy on their own in the face of a continuing federal prohibition of heroin. Currently, the only controlled substances afforded over-the-counter regulation are those listed in Schedule V of the Controlled Substances Act. It is likely that the recipient of heroin regulated according to this policy would have to meet a minimum age requirement, offer some form of identification, and have his name entered on a record kept by the pharmacist.

In addition to the registration and minimum-age requirements, heroin sold in this manner would have to be subject to standards of purity, safety, and effectiveness set by the Food and Drug Administration. (This, however, would also be true of heroin dispensed in treatment clinics, by a physician's prescription, or in the pure food and drug model discussed below.) The Federal Trade Commission could set rules on labeling requirements and warnings as well as establish any advertising restrictions desired. Basically, this model places the decision to use heroin directly with the consumer and regulates closely only those who manufacture or distribute the drug.

Pure Food and Drug Model. This model would allow heroin to be marketed and consumed in the United States rather as caffeine presently is in coffee, tea, soft drinks, and candy. Obviously, significant statutory changes would be required at all levels of government to change heroin from a contraband substance to a legitimate product. Formal government involvement would be limited to the regulation of the quality and purity of the heroin offered for sale. Any retail establishment permitted to sell food, drugs, or other consumables would be able to market heroin. Advertising might be limited, however, in ways similar to present restrictions on the advertisement of alcoholic beverages and tobacco products in certain media.

This policy model could also be varied so that either the federal government or the states could be in direct control of manufacture and distribution. As with state lotteries, a governmental agency could have monopolistic control over the production and sale of heroin; in that case revenues realized from sales would devolve directly to the government producer. Alternatively, private production might be allowed but with sale to consumers done only by "state stores," as is currently required for alcoholic beverages in several states.

The policy models discussed above provide an idea of the variety of ways in which we control certain psychoactive substances in the United States, ways in which heroin could also be controlled. Of these policy options four have been selected for a detailed examination of their probable effects. These four—medical and treatment research, government-sponsored heroin clinics, removal of criminal penalties, and over-the-counter drug regulation—represent a diverse yet feasible sampling of points along the overall spectrum of policy choices. Research with heroin in treatment and "heroin maintenance" clinics frequently crops up as a topic in public discussions of drug abuse. Likewise, the removal of criminal possession penalties is frequently mentioned as a possible solution to present illicit drug control problems. All of these options, however, are important only insofar as they provide an analytical framework for dealing with specific concerns regarding heroin and appropriate public policy. The following discussion deals with the major issues influencing heroin policy.

The Issues

The importance ascribed to a particular issue will vary from person to person. It will also vary according to specific policy attributes. The aim of this chapter is to provide a basis for comparing the effects of different policy variables on several major areas of concern. In this way we can begin to identify those policy variables which hold special promise. An outline chart has been included (Table 6.8, pp. 244–246) to permit a summary overview of the four policy options and their predicted impact. In addition, other tables (6.1–6.7) summarize the anticipated impact of the four policy options on each specific issue.

The section below entitled "Patterns of Use" reviews the historical experiences with the fluctuating availability of other psychoactive substances as well as recent research into the extent and type of heroin use in the United States. Compulsive or dependent heroin use is a matter of particular concern in this discussion.

"Crime and the Fear of Crime" as related to heroin use is a frequently discussed topic, yet surprisingly little factual information is available on the true nature or extent of the heroin-crime link. Public attitudes and perceptions of this issue have had and will have great influence on the selection of any policy response; they are given special attention in this section.

"Community Impact" takes into account the differing impact that heroin has within the various regions, communities, and ethnic populations of the United States. Minority populations and inner-city neighborhoods are disproportionately affected by heroin at present, and are therefore emphasized in this discussion.

"Impact on Existing Drug Treatment and Prevention Efforts" and "Effects on the Criminal Justice System" deal with the impact of alternative heroin policies on these institutions, an impact depending primarily on their goals and practices. Specific policy issues such as the effect of criminal justice referrals on treatment are equally important in alternative, as well as present, policy responses.

The remaining sections deal with civil liberties, health, worker-productivity, and welfare issues. While civil liberties and health issues are matters of concern under current policy, the effect of alternatives can by no means be expected to be uniform: One policy option may create new problems to replace present ones, and another may eliminate some concerns but not others. In short, the following discussion points to no policy panacea. However, as the previous chapters herein indicate, present heroin policy is fraught with substantial shortcomings, questionable assumptions, and few identifiable benefits. The task of the policymaker is to begin to identify issues of real—as opposed to imagined—significance and reduce the costs of American heroin policy.

Patterns of Use.   The general assumption about heroin use has been that criminal penalties for possession, use, and trafficking activities deter many would-be users and keep supply at the lowest possible level by maintaining legal pressure on traffickers and consumers. Thus the conventional wisdom on proposed changes in heroin policy has been that any reduction in this pressure would result in a substantial increase in total use—and consequently in dependent use. Despite the general acceptance of these conventional theories, they have not been proven. In fact, substantial data exist on both heroin and other psychoactive substances that lead to far different conclusions.

When exploring the relationship of heroin's availability to its use, it is important to realize that there are wide variations in use patterns among those who use the drug.[6] The National Commission on Marihuana and Drug Abuse identified five primary patterns of use: experimental, recreational, circumstantial, intensified, and compulsive.[7] The latter two types of using-behavior constitute patterns most commonly considered misuse of drugs. The greatest policy concern, therefore, ought to be to minimize these intensified or compulsive use patterns.

In order to determine whether compulsive heroin use is likely to increase as a result of any specific policy decision we will need information on several other related issues. We need to ask whether a given policy change would increase the drug's availability; we need to know whether increased availability is likely to lead to increased use of all types; and we need to know about the relationship of compulsive use to total use. To help answer these questions we must look to data on the spread of use of both heroin and other psychoactive substances.

One potential source of data is the American experience with alcohol prohibition from 1917 to 1933, which provides some information on the effects of varying control measures on excessive consumption. However, these data are not uniform. For instance, while an old Bureau of Prohibition study showed a decrease in per capita alcohol consumption, the Department of Commerce found the opposite to be true.[8] Other indicators of excessive alcohol use during the period—alcoholism deaths, alcoholic psychosis incidents, arrests for public intoxication—are equally inconclusive.[9]

Another possible source of information is the "gin mania," a dramatic shift from beer drinking to gin consumption that the English experienced during the period 1700–50. While the figures on taxed gin consumption suggest a tenfold increase in per capita alcohol consumption, very little is known about the causes of the "mania" or its effect, other than to say that heavy use (drunkenness) did increase as the more potent gin gained popularity relative to beer.[10]

The more recent use of cigarettes in the United States provides another example of how compulsive use of a psychoactive drug (nicotine) can develop after use is already widespread. Although tobacco had been used in various forms in the United States since 1613, its use did not really expand until the invention of the automatic cigarette-making machine in the late nineteenth century. However, the most significant factor in the growth of cigarette use in this country appears to have been not this new invention but rather the relentless, competitive advertising among manufacturers during the period 1918–50.[11] Heavy advertising by commercial interests now seems to be a key factor in the rapidly escalating cigarette consumption in "third-world" nations.[12] The American experience with cigarette use also indicates that a particular form of a psychoactive drug can spread at the expense of other forms, and that increasing availability, as expressed by declining price, is *not* necessary for rapid growth.

These historical examples of substance control and spread provide conflicting answers on whether compulsive use is roughly constant regardless of the number of users, or whether it fluctuates in response to increased consumption.[13] The normal distribution of using behavior for most psychoactive substances (alcohol, for example) is assumed to be that represented by Figure 6.1A. According to conventional views, heroin use

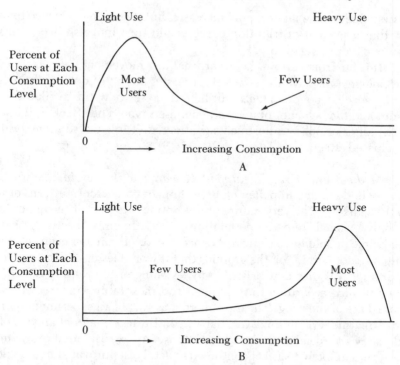

FIGURE 6-1. Two Models of Drug-Using Behavior

is distributed as shown in Figure 6.1B. However, recent studies of heroin use indicate that it is really closer to the normal curve (Figure 6.1A) than an atypical pattern of its own (Figure 6.1B). These recent studies postulate the existence of from two to four million nonaddicted users.[14] Previous information on heroin use has tended to focus on discussions of "addicts," failing to acknowledge that heroin, like other psychoactive substances, can be used in a wide variety of patterns.

    The measurement of total consumption of all types of psychotropic drugs in "normal" (i.e., non–treatment sample) populations of users shows a distribution of using behavior like that of Figure 6.1A. Since these drugs include not only heroin but also marijuana, pharmaceutical stimulants and depressants, and alcohol, it would appear that availability alone is not a controlling factor in the shape of the consumption distribution. Roughly speaking, if a drug is easy to get more people will tend to use it, but only a relatively few will be heavy consumers. If the same drug is hard to get it will tend to have fewer total users, but about the same proportion of heavy users. This argument cannot be pursued very far, of course, since we know little about the exact nature of the distributions in Figures 6.1A and B. Conceivably, the shape of the consumption- distribution curve may change somewhat as supply increases, but there is no evidence to suggest that a normal distribution curve would turn into its obverse in response to increasing supply.

It is far from certain, however, that any movement away from current policies will have the effect of increasing supply. Looking at the following specific policy models will help us to see how the availability of heroin and the behavior of users and nonusers would be affected, if at all, by the kinds of policy adjustments considered. Table 6.1 summarizes the anticipated effects.

Medical and Drug Treatment Research with Heroin. With this very limited change in policy no great impact on current patterns of use would be likely. The very nature of this option is to permit the use of heroin only by small research populations in strictly clinical settings. However, some people have expressed concern over permitting even this very limited use of heroin, on the grounds that it would lessen the strong societal disapproval that now exists.[15] Any lessening of the rigidity of official policy would, according to this view, lead inexorably to increased nonmedical use of the drug. The use of heroin as part of an experimental drug abuse treatment plan, however, hardly constitutes a major change in official policies or social attitudes toward its use. An experimental program of any type is unlikely to affect continued societal disapproval of nonmedical heroin use—unless opponents of such a change convince the public otherwise.

Government-Sponsored Heroin Treatment Clinics. Critics opposed to the experimental use of heroin would probably be equally opposed to the broad implementation of a program of treatment clinics using heroin. Objections would almost certainly be raised, in spite of the fact that abstinence would be the most likely treatment goal of heroin treatment clinics in an American context.

Once again, however, it is doubtful that a symbolic message that heroin can be used legitimately in the context of addiction treatment would have much of an effect on general use. Permitting heroin to be given to addicted users in abstinence-oriented treatment would be unlikely to reduce the revulsion commonly felt for drug addiction by the mainstream of American society. It is likely that those inclined to use heroin—recent estimates say from 2 to 4 million persons use it in a variety of using styles—already do so in the face of strong antiheroin symbolism and actions. The symbolism of this new policy message is unlikely to affect either the numbers of users or the patterns of use any more effectively than do current efforts.

More serious are the objections to heroin treatment clinics based on potential problems of diversion and nonaddicted users, or even nonusers,

TABLE 6.1   Anticipated Effects of Four Policy Models on Patterns of Use

MEDICAL AND DRUG TREATMENT RESEARCH	GOVERNMENT-SPONSORED HEROIN TREATMENT CLINICS	REMOVAL OF CRIMINAL POSSESSION PENALTIES	OVER-THE-COUNTER DRUG REGULATION
No change. (Symbolic effect doubtful).	Despite concern over diversion and non-addicted use, little change predicted. Magnitude of participation in clinics governs impact. Some symbolic effect but would not signal that heroin is socially approved.	Effect of criminal law on decision to use seems slight. Little impact predicted.	Overall use would probably increase but compulsive use may either increase or decline depending upon growth of social controls over time.

being mistakenly admitted to the clinics.[16] The evidence from both American and British opiate maintenance programs indicate that these problems are manageable. In the rapid expansion of American methadone treatment capacity in the early 1970s, some law enforcement officials noted appreciable illicit diversion.[17] However, it is now generally true that methadone diversion is relatively insignificant—few if any persons have become addicted to the drug who were not already addicted to heroin.[18] Assuming that the security systems adopted in an American heroin treatment clinic would be at least as stringent as those in present methadone programs, it is unlikely that heroin diverted from licit supplies would be a significant problem. Likewise, admission of nonusers does seem not to be an insurmountable problem.

Additional insight into these issues can be gained from the United States' brief experience with morphine and heroin maintenance clinics.[19] Opened around 1918 but closed by federal government action by 1922, the clinics—forty-four total around the country—provide valuable if disputed information on the efficacy of opiate maintenance[20] Although some problems definitely did occur and, in the case of the New York City clinic, were heavily reported in the popular press, most of the clinics appear to have been operated efficiently and effectively.[21] The closings were motivated more by a desire to see a reduction in the number of opiate addicts than by any proved failure of the clinics to contain the level of addictive drug use or aid in the social stabilization of clinic patients. Diversion of clinically supplied drugs and the administration of drugs to nonaddicted clientele do not, according to historical studies, appear to have been significant problems in practice. With illicit opiates still widely available on the street, there seemed to be little pressure to divert legal drugs.

A review of the British experience with clinic dispensation of heroin also gives credence to the view that drug diversion is not likely to be overly significant, nor is the possibility of nonaddicted users being drawn into the clinic. Factors other than the clinics themselves figure into the British heroin situation, but it appears that the clinics have contributed to a low-keyed societal response which has helped keep the heroin dependency at a fairly low level. The prevailing British view of their clinic system is one of "containment," rather than "maintenance," of opiate addiction.[22] In fact, very little heroin is currently dispensed, although clinic physicians have the discretion to prescribe it for treatment clients. The clinic system has received steady support in its effort to limit nonmedical opiate use to those already addicted and avoid creating an environment for the growth of a large, entrenched illicit heroin distribution system. Despite the presence of illicit heroin in England, the "black market" appears not to be currently large, nor is it predicted likely to grow.[23]

Adolescent heroin use is also a matter for concern. The clinic option would not necessarily exclude nor include adolescent users from treatment. The legitimate receipt of heroin by youthful clinic patients would predictably be even more explosive politically than the admission of youthful users into traditional methadone programs. Whether the perceived advantages of providing treatment attractive to the youthful user outweigh the perceived disadvantages is a matter requiring more detailed examination and the exercise of careful judgment.

Removal of Criminal Penalties for Personal Possession.   Implementation of this option would lead many to expect a dramatic increase in heroin use, an attitude that stems largely from our traditional reliance on law enforcement measures to control it. Many people believe that the only way to regulate drugs is to prohibit their use, enforcing that prohibition with criminal sanctions. However, drug policy seems to have less influence than is commonly presumed on personal decisions whether to use particular drugs. For example, an exhaustive study of the effects of the 1973 "get-tough" drug law in New York State showed that this strict law, even in areas where it was fully implemented by the court system and backed by law enforcement agencies, failed to demonstrate a discernible influence on the level of heroin use.[24] Similarly, annual surveys conducted in the state of Oregon reveal that use patterns have changed little following the substitution of civil for criminal penalties for simple possession of small amounts of marijuana.[25]

The other chapters of this report have emphasized that the decades of efforts to apprehend, jail, or treat heroin users and interdict and destroy supplies of the drug appear to have had little more than transient effects on use patterns. The criminal law seems particularly ineffective in influencing the behavior of the compulsive heroin user, who is not as prone to consider the risks involved in continued use as those less involved with drug consumption. Thus, merely changing the criminal penalty structure for personal possession seems unlikely to in itself affect personal decisions whether to use heroin.

Over-the-Counter Drug Regulation.   This option would make heroin far more accessible to far greater numbers than would any other. Yet one cannot conclude with any certainty that compulsive use would necessarily increase, even though it seems reasonable to predict that both general use and dependent (compulsive and intensified) use *would* increase to some extent. We do not know if destructive behavior would continue at the present or an increased rate; perhaps changes would also have to occur in institutional structures to promote more controlled using behavior in place of destructive patterns.

However, even though in all likelihood availability would increase, that does not seem to be the only important factor in the normal distribution curve for psychoactive drug using behavior. (See Figure 6.1 and discussion, pp. 198–200. For example, the previous discussion pointed out the role of advertising in increasing heavy, compulsive use of cigarettes in the United States and elsewhere. Heroin, contrary to sixty-year-old beliefs, appears to have developed, or is developing, a normal distribution curve similar to alcohol and marijuana use patterns.

If this is correct, one would anticipate compulsive use to continue to represent a small fraction of overall use. Nonetheless, that compulsive use would probably remain relatively small in comparison to overall use does not diminish our concern over the possibility of a net increase in compulsive or adolescent heroin use. Additionally, in light of the present widespread anxiety over any type of heroin use, any increase in general use would be of concern to most Americans. Still, current patterns of enforcement seem to be a key factor in inhibiting the development of more widely followed controlled using behavior.[26] While there is evidence of a substantial number of controlled users of heroin,[27] social controls on heroin use are probably not sufficiently advanced to prevent some increase in dysfunctional use were OTC regulation to be substituted for the current prohibition approach without other intermediate policy steps.

Crime and the Fear of Crime.   Crime is perhaps the single most important consideration in both past and present heroin policy. Were it not for the assumed close connection between heroin and crime, new use—even compulsive use—would not be as great a public concern. Yet there is remarkably little information on the relationship of heroin to crime; however, that lack of knowledge has not undercut the widespread belief that there is a proved link between heroin use and consequent criminality.[28] Heroin addicts are still presumed to support at least 60 percent of their heroin purchases through theft and robbery, for an estimated $695 million annual bill.[29] The prediction of this annual loss is given as justification for continued, even increased, law enforcement spending on programs aimed at eliminating heroin use.

The American attitude towards heroin is deeply rooted in the history of our drug laws.[30] Suppression of "narcotics"—an early catch-all word which encompassed opium, heroin, morphine, cocaine, and marijuana—proved to be popular politically. Fears of minority and immigrant groups went hand-in-hand with the fear that revolutionaries were seeking to undermine American society through drugs. For example, the Mayor of New York City established a Committee on Public Safety in 1919 to investigate "the heroin epidemic among youth and the bombings by revolutionaries."[31] Such fears repeatedly surface in the development of American drug control laws;[32] they were joined in the late 1960s by the idea that heroin was largely responsible for the rapidly rising rates of street crime.[33]

The proposition that heroin and crime are interrelated can be broken down into three more manageable concepts. The first is the "pharmacological theory," which holds that the pharmacological properties of the drug cause users to commit a variety of criminal acts, including both violent and property crimes. This view is similar to the prevailing legal view of insanity that a person can be compelled by an "irresistible impulse" to do wrong. Although this relationship is frequently assumed to exist, exhaustive studies of heroin and its pharmacological effects have not shown it.[34]

The second is the "social theory," which holds that because the law defines heroin use as illegal, the user will tend to be a criminal. By definition, possession or use of heroin constitutes a crime; therefore, by definition the user is a criminal. Similarly, heroin distribution activities are criminal because the law so states. The point that it is the law which ordains who is a criminal is often overlooked in discussions on drug policy. Because the heroin user is a "criminal," it is easier for the public to assume that he or she will commit other, unspecified criminal acts.

The third is the "price theory," which holds that users commit crimes such as theft, robbery, or property crimes to support their habits. The concern over acquisitive crimes purportedly committed to support use is at the heart of recent government and public concern with increasing heroin use.

The commonly held views of heroin use and crime contribute to the general belief that property crime is a necessary concomitant of use. Thus, the ordinary citizen is led to believe that the drug itself overbears the will of the user—by definition already a criminal—and causes him to commit crimes of theft or violence in order to obtain his drug. It is on this theory of a heroin-crime relationship that our discussion will focus.

There is no doubt that some, perhaps many, heroin users commit property crimes. Undoubtedly, heroin is an expensive drug which for many can only be obtained by additional, often illegal, income. However, compulsive heroin users often have a criminal history predating their heroin use,[35] and it is possible that "persons who are very successful in income-generating crime may spend a sizeable portion of their income on a luxury good—heroin."[36]

Recent evaluations of treatment programs for heroin users show only marginal effects on reducing crime rates for enrolled patients.[37] This finding supports the view that heroin use—even compulsive, daily use—is frequently an *aggravating factor* in property crime but is often *not* the *primary cause*. However, the conventional response is that for the criminal who uses heroin the primary cause of crime is the heroin; cessation of use is commonly equated with the "solution" of the crime problem.

Similarly, a study on the relationship between heroin price and non–drug crime rates in a large urban area (Detroit, Michigan) indicated that temporary reductions in heroin availability led to marginally higher crime rates (higher in poorer neighborhoods than in wealthier sections).[38]

While these studies do have many limitations, they do seem to indicate that, to the extent that a relationship between heroin use and property crime exists, it exists because of the high cost of heroin. Thus, to the extent that drug policies increase the cost of heroin, property crimes can be expected to increase in areas where compulsive use is high and income levels low. If it is true that an increase in heroin price may lead to increased crime, it is probably also correct to predict that lower heroin prices may lead to some decline in crime rates.

It is difficult, however, to say much at all about crime rates. Reported crimes are but a fraction of actual crime, and crimes resulting in an investigation or arrest are an even smaller fraction. Increases or declines in the number of those arrested for non–drug offenses who are also heroin users mean little if their relationship to total crime is unknown. For example, the recent report on the effects of New York's so-called "Rockefeller drug law" found that in New York City during a period of rapidly increasing crime the percentage of narcotics users among those arrested for non–drug felonies declined (from 52 percent in 1971 to 28 percent in 1975).[39] Data such as these still give an incomplete picture, since we do not know the relative proportion of reported crime to actual crime or, in fact, of heroin users to nonusers for either reported or actual crime.

While the true nature of the heroin and crime relationship may eventually be better understood, at the moment how the public perceives that link is of paramount importance. The development of our antinarcotics laws reflects a history of shifting fears about certain proscribed drugs and their users. Apart from whatever the danger actually was, these fears motivated public support and prompted policymakers' support of stringent law enforcement policies. Fear of crime, much more than actual crime, underlies our current response to heroin.

Table 6.2 summarizes the anticipated effects of the four selected policy models—research, clinics, removal of penalties, and over-the-counter drug regulation—on non–drug crime and public perceptions of the victimization risk.

Medical and Drug Treatment Research with Heroin.   Implementation of this policy option would offer the possibility of developing substantial empirical data on the pharmacological effects of heroin on compulsive users. Such information might help to put to rest the notion that the effects of the drug cause users to commit crimes.

Permitting scientific research with heroin in a treatment setting would not in itself alter our current prohibition on the use of the drug outside of that small experiment. Greater public understanding about heroin and its effects would affect public attitudes toward those using the drug. For example, wide public recognition that the high cost of heroin, rather than its pharmacological properties, leads to the revenue-producing

TABLE 6.2   Anticipated Effects of Four Policy Models on Crime and the Fear of Crime

MEDICAL AND DRUG TREATMENT RESEARCH	GOVERNMENT-SPONSORED HEROIN TREATMENT CLINICS	REMOVAL OF CRIMINAL POSSESSION PENALTIES	OVER-THE-COUNTER DRUG REGULATION
No change. Possible indirect effect on public attitudes toward heroin and crime. Policy would provide data on "pharmacological theory."	Potential impact depends upon extent to which users attracted to treatment and existing magnitude of non-drug crime occasioned by need for income for heroin. Policy would provide some data on the "price theory" of heroin-crime link.	No impact on non-drug crime predicted.	Effective elimination of heroin "black market" and crime committed to pay for heroin.

crimes some users commit would have important public-policy ramifications.

It is also possible, however, that the experimental programs may indirectly harden public attitudes toward heroin and crime. For instance, any incident involving a participant of an experimental program in a criminal act may be viewed as substantiating a firm heroin-crime link. We are all familiar with news reports headlining a person's past involvement with a mental health institution, no matter how incidental that contact is in relation to other aspects of the person's life or the incident being reported. Likewise, the tenacity of the myths and misconceptions about heroin cannot be overestimated.

Government-sponsored Heroin Treatment Clinics. For heroin treatment clinics of any type to become a reality, there must almost certainly be a strong belief in their crime-reduction potential. Substantial doubts about clinics' ability to reduce crime would leave humanitarian concern for the addicted heroin user as the chief reason for the approach, and such concern for the user's welfare really has not been a primary element in past heroin control policies; it seems unlikely to emerge as a critical consideration at this juncture. Even given an initial atmosphere of support, the public mood could shift rapidly if there were adverse publicity of clinic problems (such as occurred with morphine and heroin maintenance clinics in the period 1918–22[40]) or a lack of noticeable results in crime reduction (especially if there were a "hard-sell" public relations campaign on that issue). Because public fears about crime are based so much on perceptions, rather than actual levels of crime, the effect of heroin clinics would depend upon these intangibles and could only be assessed accurately in retrospect.

Nonetheless, studies of drug treatment reveal that criminal activity generally declines to some undetermined degree (although not completely) while a person is enrolled in treatment.[141] The real difficulty is in determining the magnitude of this reduction and which influences are responsible for it. If the addition of heroin to a treatment program—whether it be "maintenance," "lure," or some other concept—would attract a substantial portion of the large population of compulsive users who have never been in treatment, it may be possible for these clinics to have a measurable impact on non–drug crime. Even if they did not attract significant numbers of clients, they might, as current programs do, help reduce the total amount of crime. To the extent that crimes are committed to secure funds to pay for high-priced illicit heroin, enrolled clinic patients would have one less need for income.

Removal of Criminal Penalties for Personal Possession. This option would lead us to expect no change in the market prices of heroin; the mere removal of penalties for possession of small amounts would not create a legal supply of heroin nor would it effectively reduce the profitability of illicit heroin sales. Thus, one could expect whatever crime is being committed to pay the street price of heroin to continue whether possession were punishable or not.

Over-the-Counter Drug Regulation.   More than the other three options, this policy could only come about after significant changes in public attitudes toward heroin and crime had occurred, rather than be a factor in changing those attitudes. Putting aside the question whether this option would have a realistic chance of being implemented, the potential impact of over-the-counter regulation on non–drug crime would be enormous. As noted previously, heroin's high street price is undeniably a factor in the resorting to theft and other illegal sources of income by some users. Should heroin become as cheap as aspirin or Valium, it seems logical that the need to resort to theft to pay for even a heavy heroin habit would be effectively eliminated.[42]

Community Impact.   It is clear that the effects of heroin policy are felt most acutely at the local community, neighborhood level. Some neighborhoods are much more affected than others by heroin users and governmental heroin policy. There is therefore an obvious danger in talking about the effects of alternative policies on the "community" as if there were a common reference point. Certain aspects of heroin policies will have disproportionate effects on specific communities within larger metropolitan areas.

Compulsive heroin use tends to cut the user off from the society of nonusers and enmesh him deeply in that of other deviants. This "disenfranchising" effect is the most notable community impact of heroin use at present. Laws making use a criminal act stigmatize the user, as does the association of revenue-raising crimes with heroin use.

The communities most affected by heroin are those most affected by a deeply rooted set of social maladies—poverty, unemployment, racial prejudice, inadequate housing and transportation, poor education, and poor vocational training opportunities. These communities experience heroin dependence and trafficking as additional hardships.

Permitting a degree of "local option" among policy alternatives may help to minimize potential negative consequences and increase the opportunities for community improvement. Many localities—entire states, even—today have little problem with heroin use and associated social problems; for these areas it may be logical to continue a prohibitionary approach. For other areas, where the use of illicit drugs is high despite efforts to prevent it, it might be more appropriate to allow greater local discretion in the formulation of drug policies and programs. To some extent, local option occurs even under present policies; for example, some metropolitan police departments choose to ignore heroin possession offenses, and some courts establish informal penalty structures for them.

There are many precedents for "local option" in the regulation of substances or activities. Alcohol consumption regulation, for example, has been left largely to the individual states. The federal government regulates only international aspects, production, interstate transportation, and unfair practices regarding alcohol.[43] States have come up with a considerable variety of regulatory control schemes; the majority of them also provide some form of "local option" for municipalities, counties, or other organs of local government.

Other examples exist as well. Gambling is now primarily a subject for state or local, rather than federal, control.[44] Laetrile, a compound derived from apricots and claimed by some to be a cancer cure, is at present only regulated by the states (though the federal government may intervene in the future). Likewise, as discussed previously, some degree of "local option" has emerged with marijuana regulation; differences among the states and the federal government on marijuana, however, have been confined to the severity of the penalty for possession. Table 6.3 summarizes the predicted impact of particular heroin policy options at the neighborhood level and indicates where "local option" may be feasible.

Medical and Drug Treatment Research with Heroin.   Implicit in this option is a very limited scale of closely monitored experiments. Experimental research with heroin under these circumstances would not be likely to have much immediate impact on the community, local or otherwise. For example, the use of heroin as an analgesic for cancer patients would occur within established hospitals; no new facilities would have to be created nor additional patients sought. Similarly, the use of heroin in experimental drug treatment therapy would most likely be undertaken in existing medical research centers, hospitals, or drug treatment programs, carefully selected for program quality and security.

There is, however, great concern expressed by some community spokesmen that experimental heroin treatment research would lead to the rapid expansion and permanent establishment of "heroin maintenance" clinics. Those in minority communities often suspect that their desires and needs on the local level will be ignored by federal policy makers, and, just as the initial success of Drs. Vincent Dole and Marie Nyswander with methadone maintenance led to large-scale federal support for methadone clinics, so the fear is that, regardless of community feelings, experiments with heroin in drug treatment will inevitably lead to a national heroin clinic system with most centers located in inner-city areas.

Although this apprehension persists, many local leaders seem convinced of the need for heroin treatment research. The National League of

TABLE 6.3 Anticipated Community Impact of Four Policy Models

MEDICAL AND DRUG TREATMENT RESEARCH	GOVERNMENT-SPONSORED HEROIN TREATMENT CLINICS	REMOVAL OF CRIMINAL POSSESSION PENALTIES	OVER-THE-COUNTER DRUG REGULATION
Resistance to implementation possible, especially in minority neighborhoods.	Resistance possible if community not consulted beforehand. Predicted concern over presence of large numbers of social deviants in community may be either alleviated or aggravated by actual experience. (Local option possible.)	Predicted concern in some inner-city areas that this would be "giving up" on heroin, but little new use expected. (Local option possible.)	New use is likely, and more compulsive use possible. Policy effect on education efforts may encourage responsible using behavior, thus lessening present social costs to community.

Cities (NLC), as part of its 1977 National Municipal Policy Statement, passed a resolution which supported further study of heroin maintenance, including specific research studies with heroin. Reaffirmed in 1978, this action by the NLC is an indication that experimental research may indeed be not just possible but actually welcome in certain communities. Local officials and their constituents express concern over the continuing high social costs of compulsive heroin use under present policies, and seem more willing now to consider and examine alternatives previously regarded as too radical or controversial.

Medical heroin research could have a widespread educational effect, and could help break down many of the present misconceptions about the drug. Public acknowledgment that heroin is a drug with a capacity for both beneficial and adverse effects, depending upon the circumstances of its use, would be a significant advance in public understanding regarding the drug. Research studies may help to produce this public understanding.

Government-sponsored Heroin Treatment Clinics. Resistance to the location of drug treatment facilities in residential neighborhoods has frustrated the desire of many drug treatment programs to be close to the population to be served. While in the abstract everyone is eager to have community-based drug treatment, a caveat is that the proposed facility should be on someone else's block, near someone else's home, family, and neighbors. Heroin treatment clinics would face even greater hurdles of public resistance than other, existing forms of drug abuse treatment in the United States. The treatment in using heroin to stem compulsive use will have to be fully and carefully explained. In spite of explanations of the treatment process, there may still be objections to the clinics because of the fear of new crime they may engender.

To the extent that clinically supplied heroin would reduce a user's need for illegal income to pay for street heroin, the community would be better off. However, users who support their use through crime tend to rely on criminal activities to satisfy their other income needs as well. Despite the provision of clinic heroin, crimes by some program clientele *can* be expected, since such behavior already occurs in existing treatment situations. However, it would be unfortunate and inaccurate for the local community to point to such crimes as evidence of the failure of the treatment programs.

Regardless of the crimes actually committed, the presence of a group of social deviants—often criminal—within a residential area is a frightening prospect to those who see themselves or their children as likely victims. If experimental treatment programs using heroin precede the institution of heroin clinics, community perceptions of the risk involved may change. A successfully run experimental research program may help ease fears of heightened criminal activity in the neighborhood of the program. Attitudes may evolve sufficiently to permit clinics to be established within neighborhoods where the problems of compulsive heroin use are most severe. However, the potential for reversal is also great, since highly publicized, negative incidents involving a program or one of its clients could conceivably affect acceptance of all such programs and lead to demands for their abolition. This scenario occurred during the early 1900s with American morphine and heroin maintenance clinics,[45] and to a lesser degree with the more recent methadone clinics.

Removal of Criminal Penalties for Personal Possession.   To the extent that crimes are committed to pay for heroin, this policy change would not alter the present situation. While this change would eliminate the social deviance labeling of heroin use which may contribute to users' criminal behavior, it is unlikely to alter significantly present patterns of criminal behavior.

In some black and Hispanic communities, spokesmen have charged drug law enforcement authorities with an abdication to lawlessness by failing to strictly enforce penalties against heroin use and possession. This tension between the community and the authorities is heightened by both real and perceived differences in police effort between poor and wealthier sections of our cities. A policy mandating the uniform application of decriminalization of heroin possession may help end such discriminatory law enforcement practices, or may instead stimulate renewed charges of an official surrender to widespread drug use.

The policy is also unlikely to satisfy concern over new use, especially use by the young, school-age segment of the population. While white, black, and Hispanic neighborhoods are equally concerned with spreading heroin use, it is unlikely that new use would be evenly split between predominantly white suburban areas and predominantly black or Hispanic inner-city areas. At least one study suggests that inner-city neighborhoods are already nearly saturated with heroin in that it seems to be readily available.[46] However, the notion persists that removing criminal penalties would further increase availability in these inner-city neighborhoods and result in higher rates of use.[47] To the contrary, easier availability would seem to have the greatest potential impact in those neighborhoods where heroin is now typically more difficult to obtain, for example, in largely white, middle-class suburban areas.

Even in these areas new use may not automatically result from mere removal of criminal penalties for possession. Studies of drug use over a ten-year period among the school population of a suburban California school district suggest that in many communities heroin is seldom used even when available.[48] However, other recent studies suggest that the use of heroin is more prevalent than is commonly believed.[49] Regardless, the rates in inner-city areas are conceded by all to be the highest, and are thus the least likely to be greatly affected by this policy option.

If criminal penalties for possession of heroin were to be removed, there is some evidence to support the view that many people would come to eventually favor the policy. During the four years following the decriminalization of marijuana in Oregon, surveys noted increasing support for the policy, even for more liberal extensions of it.[50] However, public support of drug decriminalization does seem highly drug-specific. To suggest that such support would grow for heroin at the same rate as for marijuana would be to ignore the very real social stigma and fears in every American community surrounding heroin use, as well as the actual differences between the two drugs.

Over-the-Counter Drug Regulation. Some information on the potential impact of over-the-counter drug regulation of heroin can be obtained by examining the British experience prior to 1968. Before enacting the Dangerous Drug Act of 1967, the United Kingdom had experienced a rapid growth in the number of known heroin addicts, from 342 in 1964 to 2,240 in 1968.[51] This growth, while minimal compared to the estimated population of American addicts, alarmed the British public and their lawmakers. At the time any physician could prescribe heroin or cocaine for nearly any reason, and a very small number abused this public trust by writing prescriptions on demand to increasing numbers of users. The 1967 act and, ten years later, the 1977 Misuse of Drugs Act (which required physicians to be specially licensed), were passed in response to this problem of overprescribing.

One view of this relatively unrestricted access to heroin is that sooner or later new users will come forth, and more compulsive users will result. Doubtless this situation will be feared in nearly all communities, even though relatively little problem exists with morphine and codeine which are available now in any corner pharmacy. Some experts have postulated that for many compulsive heroin users the attraction to the needle may be as great as the attraction of the drug itself.[52] An over-the-counter policy for heroin, while unlikely at present, could conceivably become an appropriate regulatory vehicle for the control of dysfunctional heroin use at some time in the future.

Impact on Existing Drug Treatment and Prevention Efforts. The primary modes of American drug treatment for heroin addiction at present are methadone maintenance, detoxification using methadone or other pharmacological assistance, and various types of drug-abstinent programs such as "therapeutic communities." The quality and number of supportive services—which include employment, education, and psychiatric counseling—vary widely within these broad treatment categories.

The largest single mode of drug treatment in terms of numbers of heroin-using clients and official expenditures is methadone maintenance. Short-term detoxification programs generally operate within existing health facilities and are also numerous. Therapeutic communities, while fewer in number and smaller in size, provide an alternative for heroin users motivated to become totally abstinent.

As the federal effort to eliminate illicit drug use expanded rapidly in the early 1970s, court referral and diversion programs for illicit drug users emerged as an important new ingredient in the modern American heroin use treatment scheme. Clients are now referred to treatment as a condition of probation or parole or are "diverted" into it before trial. These referrals from the criminal justice system now comprise a significant portion of all treatment populations.[53] Although the selection of treatment in lieu of continued imprisonment or criminal trial proceedings is technically voluntary, the client is faced with a difficult choice between alternate forms of official supervision and control; since at least some element of coercion is involved, he or she cannot be considered an entirely "voluntary" entrant into treatment. One would therefore expect the greatest impact of alternative policies among drug treatment clientele to be felt by this group, a highly significant and numerous segment of the total heroin treatment population. Particular types of drug treatment may be disproportionately affected, depending upon the policy alternative, as is shown in Table 6.4.

In the face of rising drug use among the young in all social and economic settings, "drug abuse education" and "prevention" became national concerns by the late 1960s. The earliest school-based education programs tended to rely more on fear than fact. Later programs were geared more toward providing factual information and avoiding value judgments. However, the underlying assumption of educators seemed to be that once the pupil had the "true facts" he or she would decide not to use illicit drugs. The goal sought by all educational programs was and still is complete abstinence from illicit drugs. (In fact, in some communities the abstinence goal is so strong that undercover police activity has been termed part of those school "drug education" efforts.)[54] The reason most often given for continuing heroin prohibition is that any relaxation in official attitudes would diminish the present stigma attached to heroin use and lead to increased use.

More recently, programs have sought to reduce the use of licit psychoactive substances like alcohol and tobacco products as well as illicit drugs. However, the arbitrary and pharmacologically artificial distinctions between illicit and licit drugs place educators in a difficult position. Drug educators are caught in an inherent contradiction in telling students that licit drugs can generally be used responsibly (though they can be misused), but that illicit drugs must never be used. However, policies focused less on the drugs themselves might be better able to promote the concept of responsible use whatever the substance.[55] Policy changes which demonstrate heroin to have the capability for both harmful and beneficial applications (i.e., use as analgesic for cancer patients) might increase the understanding of the general public about drug use and misuse. Drug education of this very broad sort is the kind that seems most needed.

Table 6.4 summarizes the predicted impact on existing drug treatment and prevention efforts discussed below.

Medical and Drug Treatment Research with Heroin / Government-sponsored Heroin Treatment Clinics. The research model envisions a trial of new treatment modalities for attracting, retaining, and treating compulsive heroin users. What is curious is that many current drug treatment and drug education workers are alarmed by discussion of experimental heroin treatment research. All recent proposals to try injectable opiates as part of an experimental heroin addiction treatment program have as their ultimate goal complete abstinence,[56] as do current methadone and drug-free approaches to heroin addiction. From all appearances, the intent of proposed experimental approaches using heroin is identical that of the existing American efforts with methadone.

There are, of course, other possible program goals which do not necessarily include total abstinence from drug use. For example, a former federal drug policy spokesman has described opium maintenance in Iran, heroin maintenance in Great Britain, and methadone maintenance in the United States as identical in their predominant objectives: reduction of social costs, stabilization of the treatment patient's life, and establishment of a means of control over the patient so that a therapeutic relationship has a chance to develop between the patient and treatment personnel.[57] Heroin research and treatment programs suggested for American investigation would be unlikely to differ from these goals.

Should American researchers prove—as English clinicians have done already—that heroin can be used appropriately in a treatment setting, current American treatment and education efforts may be led to reevaluate their positions on heroin. They may consequently focus less on heroin use per se and more on making the treatment client functional in society. On the other hand, present goals expressed by treatment programs—lower social costs, stabilization, and control leading to eventual abstinence—would probably remain. The important changes would be in the general philosophical consensus on how to achieve these goals.

A fear frequently expressed when "heroin maintenance" is proposed is that new clinics would be implemented as methadone maintenance clinics were only a few short years ago, raising the public's expectation of a quick and easy solution to the social problems associated with heroin

TABLE 6.4   **Anticipated Community Impact of Four Policy Models**

MEDICAL AND DRUG TREATMENT RESEARCH	GOVERNMENT-SPONSORED HEROIN TREATMENT CLINICS	REMOVAL OF CRIMINAL POSSESSION PENALTIES	OVER-THE-COUNTER DRUG REGULATION
Little change anticipated from current American treatment goal of abstinence, despite the British experience with "stabilization" goal. Existing facilities would probably be used.	Administrative aspects could either aggravate or alleviate loss of patients from existing programs. Programs could be conducted in existing facilities. Construction of new ones would increase the impact on existing programs.	Primary impact likely to be reduced volume of criminal justice referrals. Potentially heavy impact for existing programs that now depend upon criminal justice system for clients.	Predicted elimination of criminal justice system referrals. Policy expected to accelerate development of unified health care system.

use. Leaving aside for the moment objections to using pharmacological supports in the treatment process, one can see the risks in this. Although treatment professionals can point with pride to certain benefits of methadone treatment, it has been far from the quick solution to urban crime and heroin addiction overzealous advocates promised. To make unfulfillable promises in connection with heroin clinics would tend to undermine all drug treatment, despite very real accomplishments and reasonable potential. The impact on existing treatment would largely depend upon what results are predicted from the use of heroin in treatment.

Another fear is that a large-scale program using heroin for drug treatment purposes would draw clients away from existing programs. This belief seems to be based on the assumption that heroin is so intrinsically desirable that, given the choice, people would prefer to use it over any other substance. Despite solid evidence to the contrary,[58] this belief in heroin's overwhelming attractiveness persists, convincing many that the use of heroin in treatment would virtually force other treatment modalities to cease operation.

There is another reason for believing that new-style heroin treatment clinics might draw clients from existing programs: the quality of treatment services provided. The high volume of criminal justice–referred clients in "drug-free" programs and the frequently criticized "gas station" approach of some methadone programs are just some of the problems of existing programs. These problems lend support to the view that voluntary clients would, if possible, leave present programs for the new clinics.

However, it would not be necessary for new programs to be completely independent of present treatment efforts. For example, some dependent individuals might not be ready to become abstinent or switch drugs (methadone), but they might be prepared to take an initial step toward controlling their heroin use by enrolling in a treatment program that supplied the drug; later they could be directed toward another treatment regimen. It is also possible that treatment efforts might not focus so intently upon achieving abstinence, but would tolerate or encourage controlled using behavior in return for personal and social stabilization.

Administrative regulations could either alleviate or exacerbate the potentially adverse impact on existing programs. For instance, if failure in other types of treatment were made a prerequisite for admission to the new clinics, it is possible that some would enroll in existing programs just to "fail" and be eligible to participate in a heroin clinic. Decisions on whether to allow "take home" drugs or require on-site administration would influence the relative attractiveness of the new heroin clinics over existing methadone programs. Also, having to visit a clinic for a heroin injection more than once a day, if required, might make heroin clinics relatively unattractive to those interested in stabilizing and normalizing their lives.

Some information can be obtained by looking at the English experience with heroin treatment. In what is commonly referred to in America as a "heroin maintenance system," English law and medical practice permit clinic doctors to prescribe injectable heroin to maintain addicted users, generally on a weekly basis; these prescriptions are filled through local pharmacies and reviewed frequently for dosage level—and for the question of the necessity of continuing to prescribe heroin. The ultimate decision of whether to prescribe heroin is left to the clinic physician. Actually, little heroin is currently prescribed; oral and injectable methadone are increasingly preferred by clinicians as maintenance drugs.[59] However, heroin may still be prescribed, should the clinic physician feel it to be in the best interest of the patient.

The British situation provides evidence that methadone and heroin treatment need not be incompatible. If American treatment programs would use heroin along with or in place of methadone, this addition of heroin as a support drug in the treatment process might enhance the over-all attractiveness of treatment. Drug treatment therapists stress the importance of establishing contact with the user as a first step toward controlling compulsive drug use. It is possible that heroin clinics would encourage more troubled users to seek treatment, whatever the type, rather than merely redistributing the same individuals being treated at present.

The impact of such new clinics on existing American drug treatment programs would also depend somewhat on whether new, separate facilities are required. Separate facilities for new programs would probably mean that the prospective treatment client, not the physician, would have the most control over the choice of treatment program, since current programs tend to compete for similar clientele. New facilities would require initial capital expenditures for construction, and this would either draw funds away from existing funded treatment programs or require additions to the drug abuse treatment budget. Since federal government treatment funding has been relatively stable over the last few years—reflecting both budgetary constraints and reduced interest in drugs—reallocation of existing funding is more likely than new budget additions.

However, nothing necessitates separate facilities to implement this policy. In fact, the variety of ways in which heroin could become a part of addiction treatment—e.g., use with other drugs, use only in the beginning, and so forth—suggests that its integration with existing efforts could be an eminently reasonable approach. Existing methadone programs with appropriate counseling and support services and adequate security could be adapted relatively easily to accommodate the ancillary use of heroin in treatment. And other medical delivery systems could be utilized; for example, one writer has proposed utilization of health maintenance organizations (HMOs) to provide heroin treatment.[60]

Removal of Criminal Penalties for Personal Possession.   Enactment of heroin decriminalization measures similar to current marijuana legal reforms would greatly affect the numbers of court-referred treatment clients. "Drug-free" treatment modalities would be especially affected, since most referrals at present go to them rather than to methadone programs.[61] However, should heroin decriminalization impose a requirement that the offender be referred to treatment rather than given a civil fine, more criminal justice referrals would be likely.

Aside from that possibility, indications are—despite our inability to predict precisely—that the level of treatment referrals (if treatment referrals are not mandatory) would drop. Marijuana decriminalization in California led to a dramatic drop in the number of marijuana law offenders sent to treatment or education facilities by judges who felt jail was an inappropriate or extreme punishment. Any decline in drug treatment populations is significant to the programs involved, since government funding is tied to the number of clients. If existing treatment programs were unable to enhance the quality of their present services and attract an increased number of purely voluntary entrants, treatment populations would probably decline substantially, and with that decline would come a funding reduction.

Despite removal of possession penalties for heroin, court referrals could continue to be significant to treatment programs if heroin users arrested for non–drug crimes were referred to treatment in lieu of imprisonment or trial or as a condition of probation or parole.

Implementation of decriminalization of heroin may also lead to greater acceptance of the concept of "responsible use" by drug treatment, education, and prevention professionals. No longer compelled indirectly by law to concentrate on abstinence, these professionals might begin to narrow their efforts in order to deal with truly compulsive or dysfunctional using patterns. On the other hand, the strength of the current abstinence goal of treatment programs would indicate substantial difficulty in making this conceptual change.

Over-the-Counter Drug Regulation.   Over-the-counter regulation of heroin would seem to spell an absolute end to criminal justice referrals to treatment. Whatever treatment was provided would have to be done on a purely voluntary basis, except for some minor mandatory programs similar to those for intoxicated drivers (the driving-while-intoxicated [DWI] programs) that now exist in many states.

Over-the-counter regulation of heroin would tend to accelerate the trend toward a unified health care delivery system for a variety of medical, psychiatric, and social needs. The expansion of general health services to include antiaddiction, detoxification, and similar services for those with drug problems may come through existing health maintenance organizations or similar group-care programs. Alcoholism treatment programs are presently offered by a variety of medical service systems—hospitals, HMOs, individual doctors, and private self-help organizations. Over-the-counter heroin regulation would provide an impetus for these medical care providers to expand their services to include persons with other drug problems, including heroin.

In an expansion of the traditional health care delivery system to meet the special problems of the misuse of no-longer-illicit drugs large-scale separate drug treatment programs would probably cease to exist. However, the continuation of privately funded therapeutic communities and self-help, drug-free programs would be likely; it is possible that these programs would be able to reestablish their attractiveness to voluntary clients. For example, Alcoholics Anonymous is currently a widely recognized self-help program for those with alcohol problems.

Adoption of OTC regulation for heroin would almost inevitably mean that the consensus of opinion on a relationship between heroin and crime had changed. Abandonment of the crime-control aspect of drug treatment—particularly for methadone maintenance—would also be a factor in the absorption of existing treatment into a broader health and social-service provision mechanism and the consequent disappearance of separate facilities for drug treatment.

Effects on the Criminal Justice System. The phrase "criminal justice system" refers to a varied group of institutions and individuals who together enforce and administer American criminal law. There are three major subgroups: law enforcement, the courts, and corrections. Within each of these subgroups are divisions based on a specialized function and the jurisdictional authority of the government agency in question. Federal, state, and local authorities overlap and occasionally conflict in the enforcement and administration of drug laws. In order to gain a better understanding of how alternative policies may affect particular criminal justice agencies, it is important to keep in mind the complexity of the system and its interrelationships and note that policy enacted by one level of government may conflict with that of another.

Law Enforcement. Local and state police comprise the bulk of the drug law enforcement effort. However, there are several agencies at the federal level that are significant in terms of policy leadership and as a source of law enforcement funding. These agencies—primarily the Drug Enforcement Administration, the Customs Service, and the Law Enforcement Assistance Administration—have major responsibilities and interest in American heroin law enforcement. However, their policy missions are more narrowly drawn than those of the ordinary police force.

Numerically, the most important heroin law offense involves "simple possession" of the drug. Studies of drug law arrests across the country show that, of those involving heroin, the vast majority are for "simple possession" (an amount set by each state or by federal law, corresponding to the lowest penalty for possession of heroin).[62] In about a dozen states and also under federal law, simple possession of heroin is a misdemeanor (punishable by up to one year in prison), while it remains a felony in the remaining American jurisdictions. Second in importance in terms of numbers of arrests are the "ancillary offenses," which involve such activities as being under the influence of heroin, possessing hypodermic syringes to inject the drug, or being present where drugs are sold or used. Possession with intent to distribute and sale, importation, or other heroin trafficking activities, while subject to severe criminal penalties, produce few arrests compared with possession and ancillary offenses.

However, because the practice of "overcharging"[63] is common with heroin law offenses, numbers of arrests and convictions do not tell the complete story. The vast majority (over 90 percent) of all convictions for opiate offenses are based on a guilty plea resulting from plea-bargaining between the defendant and the prosecutor. Since it is therefore likely that the initial charge will be bargained down, it is not unusual for both the arresting officer and the prosecutor to charge the defendant with the highest charge plausible (hence the term "overcharging"). Thus, neither arrest nor conviction statistics may portray the precise nature of the activity which led to the involvement of the criminal justice system.

The Judicial System.   A second major subdivision within the criminal justice system fits loosely under the label of the judicial system. Comprising this apparatus are the various courts (state and federal, trial and appellate), prosecutors, public defenders, and private attorneys. It intersects at numerous junctures with law enforcement and corrections.

Since law enforcement efforts produce primarily heroin possession arrests, it is with possession offenses that the courts most often deal. During 1976 there were an estimated 60,200 arrests in the United States for violation of drug laws involving opium or cocaine.[64] Unfortunately, the national crime statistics do not separate heroin ("opium") from cocaine, nor do they indicate the level of offense—e.g., possession, distribution, or being under the influence. However, studies have been done that give some idea of the relative importance of the various offenses within the total arrest picture. One reputable study found that heroin was involved in roughly 48 percent of all non–marijuana arrests.[65] Marijuana still produces the overwhelming number of all drug arrests—approximately 441,000 during 1976.[66] However, with all but a small fraction of heroin arrests for possession, changes in policy affecting the status of possession would have a substantial impact on court resources.

It should be noted that state courts deal with the bulk of heroin possession cases. The federal enforcement effort is aimed primarily at trafficking activities,[67] and those who find themselves in federal court are most often there on charges of selling or transporting the drug. Federal and state appellate courts also have a significant number of cases concerning constitutional challenges to drug law convictions. Many of these constitutional attacks stem from possession-related convictions or charges; a change in that aspect of heroin's legal status would affect their numbers as well.

Corrections. The most varied set of criminal justice institutions comes under the heading of "corrections". Not only jails and prisons at the local, state, and federal levels, but parole, probation, and diversion to treatment programs can be grouped together as correctional in nature.

Although drug treatment services are ordinarily considered to be apart from the correctional system, in recent years the separation of the two systems has become less distinct. Pretrial programs of diverting drug-using criminal offenders (especially heroin users) into treatment are based on the notion that the drug use is the individual's dominant problem and is largely, if not totally, responsible for his or her criminal behavior. The courts and prosecutors have increasingly utilized treatment agencies as an alternative sentencing mode, frequently requiring treatment as a condition of probation or parole. Because treatment has become so closely allied with the criminal justice system, our discussion of the effects of alternative policies on that system will include their effects on treatment referrals.

The over sixty thousand arrested in 1976 for violations of heroin and cocaine laws comprised only about .06 percent of the national total arrests of 9.6 million for all offenses.[68] Case dispositions are more difficult to determine than arrests, but 1976 FBI crime data indicate that around half of all drug offenders (including those for marijuana) were found guilty of the offense charged or a lesser one.[69] However, since the data base is small and all drugs are grouped together here, the actual conviction rate for heroin law offenses may be very different.

Aggregate studies of rates of incarceration and length of time served by heroin offenders are scarce. A study conducted by the National Commission on Marihuana and Drug Abuse reviewed arrests and disposition data for illicit drug offenses in six major metropolitan areas (Chicago, Dallas, Los Angeles, Manhattan, Miami, and Washington, D.C.)[70] The study found that where only opiates were involved, the case was least likely to be dismissed.[71] Approximately 36 percent of those charged with opiate (heroin) offenses were convicted.[72] Of those convicted, only 8 percent were found guilty by trial; the remainder used the plea bargaining process.[73] Nearly half received a sentence of incarceration.[74] Of those convicted of only one offense of possession of an opiate (generally heroin), slightly over half (53 percent) received sentences of incarceration. Sixty-eight percent of those convicted for selling an opiate were incarcerated.[75]

Thus, the study indicates that while conviction is more likely for heroin offenses than for those with other drugs, only a little more than a third of those arrested are convicted and, if their offense is possession, only half of this number go to jail. Furthermore, few of those sent to prison receive long sentences. The National Commission's study of six metropolitan areas found that of those sentenced to incarceration with no time suspended, most received a term of a year or less.[76]

Nevertheless, American jails are overcrowded, and the addition or elimination of a few thousand offenders would have a considerable impact. At present there are some 191,400 inmates in state correctional facilities,[77] 28,000 in federal penitentiaries,[78] and an estimated 136,388 adults detained in local jails and lock-ups.[79] Further increases in the nation's inmate population are predicted.[80] Expanding the housing capacity of our nation's prisons is expensive, as are the yearly costs of maintaining an inmate in an institutional setting.[81] Heroin policies that change the numbers of those sent to prisons can certainly affect the costs of our correctional system.

The most common sentencing outcome for heroin possession convictions, aside from incarceration, is probation. Roughly a third of those convicted in the study sample examined by the National Commission received a probated sentence.[82] Probation costs vary, but the nationwide average is around $2,000 a year per probation "slot."[83] Treatment is frequently required for heroin law offenders receiving a probated sentence,[84] and this increases the cost.[85] Policy changes could affect the number of those probated for heroin offenses as well as the number sent to certain types of treatment as a condition of probation.

Parole, the conditional release of an inmate, is frequently utilized for at least part of the heroin offender's sentence. These costs vary, but are roughly comparable to those for treatment required by probation or court referral. Again, changes in heroin policy may affect the numbers of those paroled for heroin offenses, the conditions of parole, and the aggregate cost to society.

Table 6.5 outlines the predicted impact on corrections and the rest of the criminal justice system of each of the four alternative models under examination.

Medical and Drug Treatment Research with Heroin.   Little effect, if any, can be expected on the criminal justice system if the medical and treatment research option is adopted.

Government-sponsored Heroin Treatment Clinics.   Law enforcement, in particular, would be concerned over the potential here for diversion of legal heroin to "street" use. This concern is often expressed over proposals to try heroin maintenance in the United States, despite the fact

TABLE 6.5 Anticipated Impact of Four Policy Models on the Criminal Justice System

MEDICAL AND DRUG TREATMENT RESEARCH	GOVERNMENT-SPONSORED HEROIN TREATMENT CLINICS	REMOVAL OF CRIMINAL POSSESSION PENALTIES	OVER-THE-COUNTER DRUG REGULATION
No change predicted.	Depending upon attractiveness of treatment design, arrests may decline or remain same. Diversion unlikely to be problem, though public-order offenses might increase near clinics. Non-drug crime may decline, but little is known on magnitude of current crime related to heroin income needs.	Possession arrests (a majority of current heroin offenses) should fall drastically. Impact on informants possible, but their current utility is questionable. May increase police morale by lessening pressure for corruption.	Nearly complete disengagement of criminal justice agencies from heroin control.

that various powerful narcotic drugs are already used by existing drug treatment programs, are allowed in "take-home" form, and are available by doctor's prescription. With none of these practices has there been a significant diversion problem. Whether heroin obtained through a legitimate clinic system would be more susceptible to diversion than methadone or morphine remains an open question. It does, however, seem possible to design dispensing arrangements that could keep diversion to a minimum.[86] The British experience with allowing treatment clinic doctors to prescribe heroin and ordinary pharmacies to fill the prescriptions without significant diversion problems may be unique to their heroin situation, population, and setting. It may also be significant that little heroin is currently prescribed there for drug treatment purposes. However, their success does provide an additional basis for believing that diversion need not be a major criminal justice problem.

If heroin clinics prove to be attractive to large numbers of compulsive users who are not at present involved in or attracted by drug treatment programs, the potential exists to reduce the amount of possession arrests and subsequent judicial and correctional involvement.[87] However, experience with existing drug treatments indicates that there are a sizable number of addicted users who do not seek treatment. The addition of heroin to the treatment pharmacopeia, especially in a strictly supervised, heavily controlled program designed to prevent diversion, may make little difference to this group. If this proves to be the case, little impact can be expected on heroin offense arrest rates.

Allowing heroin to be used in treatment would not provide legal access to the drug for "chippers" or other nonaddicted users. They can be expected in this situation to continue to deal with illegal traffickers. Even some of those involved in treatment with heroin could be expected to supplement their clinic dosages with street-obtained ones. For example, British heroin clinic patients occasionally use street drugs, and there is a continuing, albeit small, black market for heroin in that country.[88] While the provision of heroin through clinic programs could not be expected in itself to banish the enormously profitable and sizable American black market, it might significantly reduce the size and profitability of that market by drawing away the heaviest users.

Similarly, heroin treatment clinics could have an impact on non–drug crime. To the extent that the provision of heroin in a treatment setting would attract heavy users who cannot support their use solely through legitimate income, non–drug crimes committed to produce revenue would probably decline. What the public perceives to be the effect of the proposed clinics may, to an extent, prove to be self-fulfilling. It is notable that in the United Kingdom the notion that heroin users are invariably involved in other criminal activities has never surfaced as a public or governmental concern.[89]

The potential for an increase in public-order offenses like loitering, harassment and public intoxication and minor criminal offenses like shoplifting in the immediate vicinity of treatment clinics is high. Addicts' generally unsavory reputations and reports of their activities in the surrounding communities were key factors in the hurried closing of America's heroin and morphine maintenance clinics in the early 1900s.[90] However, news accounts of the time tended to sensationalize matters, emphasizing programs that were poorly administered and overlooking those that functioned smoothly, just as do modern media accounts of methadone program problems. Administrative considerations could either aggravate or virtually eliminate the problem of clinic patients' offenses in the area of the program.

Removal of Criminal Penalties for Personal Possession. Dropping criminal penalties for the "simple" possession of heroin would mean that fewer heroin law offenders would be arrested or found in court or the corrections system. Since over 80 percent of current heroin law arrests are for possession, removing that activity from the criminal law would have a major impact on the involvement of the American criminal justice community with heroin use.[91] However, a significant relationship could continue if treatment or education referrals were to be mandated in place of the former criminal penalties. Such a substitution would accelerate the absorption of drug treatment into the criminal justice system as an alternate form of supervised release.

Affected law enforcement and judicial resources could of course be reallocated to other offenses should penalties for heroin possession be dropped altogether. While most drug law arrests are "spontaneous" (no prior investigation done), the involvement of special narcotics officers, as opposed to ordinary patrolmen, is more extensive in opiate arrests than with other drugs.[92] Some savings, therefore, in the form of redirected law enforcement resources could be anticipated.

Law enforcement officials often stress the importance of penalties for relatively minor offenses like heroin possession as "leverage" on users in order to reach traffickers. The available evidence does not provide a clear answer whether informants would be harder to obtain. The National Commission has found that less than one-quarter of opiate arrests have been the subject of prior investigation,[93] and less than a quarter of these have involved an informant.[94] Yet while only 6–7 percent of all opiate arrests involve informants, these arrests could involve a high percentage of trafficking or distribution offenses (available data does not identify the type of case).

However, other data, particularly on the size of ordinary drug buys, provide some substantiation of the view that most trafficking cases involve low-level distribution offenses.[95] Most users and low-level dealers cannot lead enforcement authorities very high into the distribution system.[96] It is still possible that enforcement officials might be somewhat hampered in developing cases against major traffickers without the possession offense to hold informants, but existing data on the use of informants in major narcotics case development do little to substantiate these fears.

However, critics of the current American law enforcement approach to narcotics offenses believe that reducing the role of the informant may be a healthy development. Police corruption has been a perennial problem in drug law enforcement. For example, the involvement of police in buying and selling drugs, protecting informants, blackmailing users, taking bribes, and partaking in other related corrupt practices led to a well-publicized investigation and resultant shakeup in the New York City Police Department in the early 1970s.[97] Removing criminal penalties may lessen for enforcement officers the opportunity and pressure to participate in corrupt practices or illegal activities (illegal search and seizure, for instance).[98] However, the national experience with police corruption connected with gambling offenses suggests that the problem will not totally disappear.[99] Still, by eliminating the source of most arrests, it may be substantially reduced. Societal respect for the law and its enforcement officers, rather than lessening, may increase as a result.

The argument that heroin decriminalization would increase the difficulty of enforcing antitrafficking laws gains some support from an analogy to gambling law enforcement: The accepted general proposition with gambling is that if not all participants are subject to penalties, enforcement against the "supplier" becomes more difficult.[100] Another argument against decriminalization (frequently expressed regarding marijuana) is that such laws signal societal approval—or at least an end to strong disapproval—of that drug's use. Yet the actual effect of decriminalization on enforcement efforts is difficult to measure. Most simple possession arrests for heroin at present lead to discharge, probation, or treatment in lieu of prosecution and prison terms. In some jurisdictions, police, prosecutors, and judges are highly skeptical of the value of arrests, trials, and convictions for simple heroin possession and have instituted de facto decriminalization; arrests for possession are not vigorously pursued nor, when made, are they generally prosecuted, in these jurisdictions.[101] Formal legislative action in these areas to remove criminal penalties would seem only to assure that policies already in practice there would be applied in an even-handed fashion. It is worth noting that federal enforcement efforts are already focused upon distribution offenses and international trafficking activities.[102]

Internationally, there may be criticism and even cynicism expressed about an American heroin decriminalization policy. American officials have vigorously campaigned against illicit drugs in other countries for more than sixty years. Any retreat from our current hard-line stance on heroin may seem ironic to foreign governments long accustomed to U.S. pressure to subject their narcotics activities to stringent controls and penalties.

Over-the-Counter Drug Regulation.   With this policy option, for other than relatively minor regulatory infractions—e.g., dispensing to underage minors, possession by them, use of false identification or a false name to register for receipt of heroin, intoxication or driving while intoxicated—criminal justice agencies would probably be almost completely disengaged from their present involvement with heroin. Despite the present existence of a large, reasonably well-organized, and prosperous black-market distribution apparatus, it would seem likely that the advantages to consumers of legally obtainable, low-priced heroin would help end these illicit trafficking arrangements. An appropriate analogy is the virtual disappearance of the American bootlegging industry after the repeal of alcohol prohibition in 1933. In any case, the impact of OTC heroin regulation on criminal justice agencies of all types, at all levels, would be profound when contrasted with their present involvement.

Civil Liberties Aspects.   Critics of current American drug policies often single out the adverse consequences of present drug law and enforcement practices not only on general respect for law but on the preservation of individual rights and liberties guaranteed by the Constitution. The prohibition approach to heroin in particular has raised numerous civil liberties issues: Illegal searches and seizures, wiretapping, illegal detention, and warrantless entries into private homes have all been documented in innumerable court cases and press reports. Perhaps even more disturbing are the less visible inroads into individual rights, implemented without opposition because they are supposed to be for the public's protection—the "good of society." For example, the diversion of drug users from the ordinary criminal process into treatment, even for non-drug offenses, has been widely implemented and frequently commended; but by so doing we have allowed the blame for non-drug criminal activity to be foisted on the drug itself, and tend not to hold the defendant personally responsible. It also places the criminal justice system in the curious position of "sentencing" a defendant to receive medical and psychiatric therapy for a condition that was not even the cause of arrest, and either dropping the actual charges or considering successful completion of treatment as evidence of rehabilitation in the ultimate sentencing process.[103]

The key effects of the alternative models considered are noted in Table 6.6

TABLE 6.6   Anticipated Impact of Four Policy Models on Civil Liberties Issues

Medical and Drug Treatment Research	Government-Sponsored Heroin Treatment Clinics	Removal of Criminal Possession Penalties	Over-the-Counter Drug Regulation
Create new issues of consent to participate, anonymity, and confidentiality of records. Policy may lead to development of "right of appropriate treatment" (including heroin use).		Eliminate most current civil liberties issues due to elimination of most heroin arrests (i.e., for possession). Development of right to privacy and to appropriate treatment (including heroin use).	New issues possible—e.g., minor's access to drug—but existing issues anticipated to disappear.

Medical and Drug Treatment Research with Heroin / Government-sponsored Heroin Treatment Clinics.   A new civil liberties issue posed by the possible implementation of either of these policy options is that of the consent of research or clinic patients to participation in the proposed program. The history of medical research projects indicates that frequently those chosen as subjects are people who are the least capable of giving fully informed, voluntary consent.[104] To avoid problems, heroin treatment clinicians and researchers would need to explain to potential participants the nature of the program, the extent of supervision and monitoring required during and after the treatment of research, and the medical implications of heroin use. The extent to which the subject's anonymity would be maintained is a necessary part of the information to be given, as is acknowledgment of the patient's right to withdraw consent.[105]

Confidentiality in any drug treatment or research program is of paramount concern to both client and program because of the stigma attached to illicit drugs, especially heroin. Current federal regulations prohibit the disclosure of patient-identifying information except under certain limited circumstances.[106] However, recent proposals would allow more extensive use to be made of research subject identification for research and law enforcement purposes.[107] Regulatory interpretation of the vague statutory language concerning confidentiality changes from time to time, and usually has reflected a bias toward permitting law enforcement and "evaluation" use of identifying data. To gain and keep the full confidence of treatment clients and research subjects, the clinic must itself be relatively immune from court-ordered or enforcement-demanded disclosures of patient identity.

In the event that heroin clinics are implemented on a permanent basis, the growing judicial doctrine of a right to "appropriate" medical treatment may come to include the right to receive heroin to prevent withdrawal stress or for other legitimate reasons. For instance, the Karen Ann Quinlan case in New Jersey set forth a legal rationale for the right of the patient (or the patient's guardian) to determine appropriate treatment for herself.[108] Similarly, several courts have found a right to use laetrile as a cancer treatment, even in the face of official opposition. These recent developments suggest that it would not be unreasonable to expect a right to appropriate treatment to be applied to access to heroin in a clinical setting.[109]

Removal of Criminal Penalties for Personal Possession.   Critics of current heroin policy cite law enforcement abuses as a major reason for scrapping the prohibition approach. Warrantless seizures and searches of persons and homes and other similar violations of constitutional rights are natural outgrowths of a "war-on-drugs" philosophy where any breach of constitutionally guaranteed rights may be considered acceptable in the name of stopping the "drug traffic." The decriminalization of heroin is often posited as a potential solution to these civil liberties abuses. Certainly removing simple possession penalties for heroin would be a significant step toward ending the "war" mentality against the drug. Absent the removal of penalties for *all* present heroin offenses, however, it is likely that some civil liberties problems would continue, albeit at a lower rate than previously. Certainly the removal of criminal possession penalties would substantially lower law enforcement interest in identifying mere heroin users, except as they could assist in apprehending and prosecuting traffickers.

A right to privacy—which would encompass the right to use heroin, at least in one's home—is another factor indicating that criminal heroin possession penalties should perhaps be dropped. Many civil libertarians have long argued that individuals ought to be free to take drugs—or engage in any other personal activity—so long as no one else is hurt. A Supreme Court justice has described the notion of a constitutional right to privacy as "the right to be left alone—the most comprehensive of rights and the right most valued by civilized man."[110] Although the extent and exact nature of the consitutional right to privacy have not been fully defined, recent cases have declared it to encompass the right to possess "obscene" material in private[111], the right to possess and use contraceptives even if unmarried,[112, 113] and the right to have an abortion.[114] The Alaska Supreme Court found the use of marijuana in the home to be protected under a right to privacy provided for explicitly in the state constitution and . . . implicitly in the federal Constitution[115]; however, the same court decided against a similar privacy right to use cocaine.[116] The interpretation of this right as applying to heroin use, like the right to appropriate treatment discussed above, is a possible, but far from certain, outcome of this policy option. However, it is also possible that judicial development of these concepts may precede, and in fact lead to, policy changes.

There is some precedent for court-ordered heroin decriminalization under present law. The Supreme Court in a famous 1962 decision declared that it was "cruel and unusual punishment" to penalize the mere status of being an addict.[117] More recently, long terms of imprisonment for minor marijuana offenses have been found to violate the same constitutional prohibition.[118]

The rationale of the insanity defense has been used in the context of arrests for heroin use to assert that the defendant had an "irresistible impulse" to use the drug and therefore could not be held accountable.[119] This popular stereotype of every heroin user as controlled by the drug and unable to stop using heroin or committing other crimes is at variance with the existing and emerging data on heroin use (see pp. 197–204 above). Removing criminal possession penalties for heroin may shift public and judicial attitudes away from this criminal image toward an acceptance of the medically or mentally "sick" model. However, continued judicial acceptance of the idea of "irresistible impulse" in heroin use is certainly possible even though the concepts on which that theory is based are more folklore than scientific fact.

Over-the-Counter Regulation of Heroin. Individual rights and civil liberties would tend to suffer little with over-the-counter drug regulation, in contrast to present policy. Some problems are always possible, however. For instance, requiring the registration of heroin purchases presents the risk of unauthorized public disclosure and the possibility that some may decline to obtain needed drugs due to fear of thus being stigmatized. The U.S. Supreme Court has considered a challenge to such a filing system in New York State, and has found that it passed constitutional muster.[120]

Other issues may also appear, such as that of the right of minors to obtain and use heroin legally under an OTC system with a minimum age requirement. There are indications that some courts may rule favorably on the question of a minor's right to obtain heroin if medical necessity can be shown.[121] Enforcement response to possible diversion and fraud problems with an OTC system could perpetuate some current civil liberties issues—e.g., unreasonable search and seizure. For those disqualified from obtaining heroin legally, illicit possession would still be a punishable offense, and the current defenses of "cruel and unusual punishment" and "irresistible impulse" would probably continue to be asserted in court.

Health Issues. Present prohibitionary policies toward heroin make it necessary, of course, for users to obtain and use it illicitly in a street setting. This illicit heroin is often mixed, in order to increase the seller's profits, with a variety of substances and adulterants, some of which can lead to serious medical consequences. In contrast, heroin in a pure form, administered in a sterile manner, is relatively benign in terms of its physiological effects.[122] Thus many of the most serious health risks associated with heroin use appear to be the indirect results of the laws that ban its use. "Overdose" deaths commonly occur from the consumption of heroin in combination with certain other drugs or from adulterants contained in illicit heroin. Hepatitis and endocarditis are frequent ailments of American heroin users brought on by the failure to observe sterile conditions in intravenous self-administration of the drug. Other diseases reflect the street setting of current heroin use in different ways; for example, "The high incidence of venereal disease reflects the occupational hazard of the many females who earn their drug money through prostitution."[123]

On the other hand, other aspects of the drug indicate that there are health problems involved that cannot be eliminated by policy change. Heroin does have a strong potential for creating a physiological dependence complicated by increasing tolerance to the drug's effects. Although this potential may have been overstated in the past, its existence is beyond dispute. (The potential for dependence is also strong for other, currently legitimate drugs like alcohol and certain barbiturates.) One must also note that individuals vary widely in their response to both tolerance and toxic aspects of drug use. These factors are particularly critical for younger users.

Considerations other than their drug-taking behavior will influence the health of heroin users under any drug policy mechanism. Living in an impoverished setting, lacking adequate shelter, and having neither a balanced diet nor adequate access to medical care are as important in determining the level of individual health as heroin use itself. For all our concentration on the aspects of physical well-being that can be affected by drug policy, we sometimes overlook these external influences on health and the degree to which they affect heroin users.

Medical and Drug Treatment Research with Heroin. Implementation of this policy would offer the possibility of substantial gains in knowledge relating to heroin's usefulness in general therapeutic as well as drug treatment applications. Recently some leading public health officials have announced their backing of proposals to look into analgesic applications of heroin for those terminally ill with cancer.[124] Drug treatment research would help determine the extent to which the health of chronic, compulsive users can be improved through the provision of pure drugs in sterile settings with medical and nutritional counseling available.

Government-sponsored Heroin Treatment Clinics. To improve their health as it relates to heroin use, chronic users would have to be attracted into the treatment setting where medical services and pure drugs can be made available. As stated previously, there is a wide variety of possible program designs for use of heroin in a drug treatment setting. The specific program design and administrative aspects will determine its attractiveness to the street user, especially the compulsive one not interested in present treatment options. For clients of the new clinics, the incidence of disease from infected needles and the risk of poisoning or overdose from adulterated street heroin of uncertain potency would be lessened. The extent of the improvement would appear to depend on two major factors: the extent to which clinic patients would supplement their clinic heroin with other drugs, including street opiates, and whether the heroin is administered at the clinic or by the user himself in a "take-home" procedure. "Take-home" administration may increase the risk of hepatitis, endocarditis, and other infections from unsterile conditions. Supplements of illicit heroin would also increase the possibility of health complications. The possibility of accidental overdose would be increased by either factor.

TABLE 6.7 Anticipated Effects of Four Policy Models on Health Issues

Medical and Drug Treatment Research	Government-Sponsored Heroin Treatment Clinics	Removal of Criminal Possession Penalties	Over-the-Counter Drug Regulation
Knowledge gains possible.	Likely improvement for clinic patients, but questions of level of participation, street drug use, and self-administration make extent of improvement unpredictable.	Little change predicted. Fewer may enter treatment, since arrests likely to decline—thus, fewer treatment referrals. More might seek treatment voluntarily.	Eliminate many health complications of impure street drugs, but still are risks due to self-administration. Particular groups, (e.g., adolescents, pregnant women) continue to be vulnerable to medical complications from use.

It is undisputed that clients' use of street drugs continues in American drug treatment programs as well as in British ones. One recent study found that in England heroin maintenance patients were more likely than oral methadone maintenance patients to use street drugs of all types, and to have more frequent hospital visits for treatment of physical complications associated with illicit drug use.[125] Such evidence shows that illicit heroin and other injectable drugs may be used by a minority of clinic patients despite the provision of legally supplied heroin. This supplementing of licit heroin may be a greater problem in the United States—with its large, well-established black market—than in Great Britain, which has never had any large-scale illicit heroin trafficking.

Removal of Criminal Penalties for Personal Possession.   Implementation of this form of heroin decriminalization would probably do little to improve the health of the user. The policy would amend the criminal law by removing penalties for certain activities involving controlled substances, but would not add to existing treatment nor provide a licit, supervised, and standardized source of supply for heroin users. Present diseases associated with street heroin use can be expected to continue, as would occasional poisonings and overdoses.

If criminal justice referrals to treatment drop by reason of fewer heroin users coming into contact with enforcement authorities, this option could actually lead to a higher incidence in health problems among compulsive users. On the other hand, should the option require treatment for those cited for heroin possession, some improvement in health for compulsive users might be achieved. Removing criminal penalties may also encourage heroin users with health problems to seek medical help who would otherwise fear being reported to law enforcement authorities.

Over-the-Counter Regulation of Heroin.   Guaranteed purity levels and sterile hypodermic syringes available at local pharmacies with an over-the-counter regulatory approach would probably eliminate most black-market heroin use and resultant health complications. This policy, among all those examined, has the greatest potential to reduce the current disease complications of heroin use. A legal, readily available, reasonably priced supply of heroin would seem to virtually eliminate the competitive edge of black-market heroin.

Nonetheless, some health hazards would be expected to continue. For instance, the possibility of addicted infants as a result of maternal prenatal use is currently a problem both for heroin-using pregnant women and those on methadone. Allowing the over-the-counter purchase of heroin would not end this health problem, which is likely to be present under any policy (including the current prohibition approach). The problem with individual variations as to tolerance and toxicity levels would also continue. In addition, self-administration would continue problems of the sterility of works and uncontrolled, compulsive use.

Another area of uncertainty regarding potential health hazards in this model as well as the others, is heroin use by adolescents. An OTC model would probably establish minimum-age requirements for the purchase of heroin. While adolescent and preadolescent use appears to be low at present, it is significant enough to cause concern. Continuing adolescent heroin use means a continuing risk of overdose complications, due to the lower tolerance of youthful users to heroin toxicity. It may also provide another outlet for black-market sales, which would be expected to decline appreciably among adult users.

Adverse effects from the use of heroin in conjunction with other drugs would also be a continuing problem, as with use of prescriptive drugs before or after alcohol use, a common present-day hazard. Mixing other legal and illegal substances with heroin—whether by design or accident—quite often leads to medical complications. Over-the-counter regulation may play a role in increasing public awareness of the risks of using heroin in conjunction with other drugs, but it is unlikely to end all accidental or intentional drug mixing.

Other Issues: Worker Productivity and Welfare.   Attempts have been made to quantify in economic terms the costs to American productivity that result from heroin addiction.[126] A recent study commissioned by the National Institute on Drug Abuse estimated the loss of productivity due to heroin "abuse" at between $4.167 and $6.644 billion.[127] The greatest single component in these calculations is the cost of unemployment.[128] However, there is considerable doubt about the extent of total unemployment that can be ascribed solely to heroin use. In fact, when data are compared for heroin users and nonusers from the same socioeconomic background, there seems to be little difference in employment rates. At the very least, studies that ascribe the total cost of unemployment and absenteeism to heroin use overstate the connection. Even if unemployment were causally related to heroin use to a significant degree, the costs are largely due to the present system of control rather than intrinsic to heroin use.

Among the various costs other than unemployment associated with loss of productivity are absenteeism, heroin-related deaths, incarceration, and those associated with medical treatment—whether emergency room visits, inpatient hospitalization, mental hospitalization, or drug treatment programs. The losses due to drug-related deaths and medical treatment time away from the job might decline under some—but not all—alternative policies. As mentioned above, unemployment and absenteeism appear to be rooted in other, deeper, socioeconomic problems and policies than heroin use. Consequently, the possibility of a heroin policy change making a great impact on them one way or the other is remote, especially since the stigma of drug use would linger and lead many employers to discriminate.[129] Costs to productivity due to incarceration would probably be affected dramatically by the removal of criminal penalties for possession of heroin, but not a great deal by the other alternatives.

Our society has provided several mechanisms by which those in need receive limited funds from the public coffers. These mechanisms include public assistance payments, disability (either Social Security or Supplemental Security Income), unemployment benefits, medicaid, housing subsidies, and food stamps. The level, duration, and eligibility requirements of such payments vary widely from state to state and also among the individual recipients within any given state.

Chronic heroin users tend to come from disadvantaged backgrounds, are often undereducated and unskilled, generally cannot find jobs, and face several levels of discrimination and frustration at every turn. To identify heroin use as the sole reason for welfare payments to a person facing these handicaps is to seek a scapegoat for society's ills. Although heroin use may play a role in the equation, to design policies as if it were the only or the most important factor would be to miss the mark. The numerous attempts to make educated guesses at the amount of welfare assistance that results from heroin use remain, at best, guesses.

The effect of policy changes on these and other costs would depend upon the type and extent of heroin use developing after the particular policy change. For example, if over-the-counter regulation of heroin were adopted and compulsive use levels were to rise sharply among the present low-level or nonusing population, one would expect welfare costs to rise as well. On the other hand, if in this situation controlled use grew but the chronically using population remained about the same, one would expect little change in welfare costs. Other outcomes would also be possible, though, depending on the real relationship between heroin use and worker productivity; even with all types of use increasing under a given policy we might experience a dramatic drop in welfare costs if, simultaneously, more jobs were available in those inner-city areas with the highest incidence of compulsive heroin use.

Changing the Law: Legal Aspects of Alternative Policies.   More often than not, official obstacles to innovative heroin control measures are rooted in the attitudes of the bureaucratic agencies charged with implementing and administering the law rather than in any rigidity of the law itself. What commonly passes for "law" is frequently only the prevailing view; in practice, statutes are susceptible to a considerable range of interpretation. Present American domestic law—federal and state—permits a fairly extensive range of control policies, as do our international treaty obligations.

In the international sphere, heroin is subject primarily to the controls of the 1961 Single Convention on Narcotic Drugs as modified by the Protocol of 1972,[130] where it is listed as a Schedule I drug along with such other drugs as morphine, cannabis, and methadone. The Single Convention requires party nations, of which the United States is one, to limit opiate use and production to "medical and scientific purposes."[131] The purpose of the Single Convention is twofold: to limit the quantity of world narcotics to that needed for medical and scientific purposes, and to regulate the manufacture and use of scheduled drugs to ensure that they are used only for those approved purposes. The treaty also demands that party nations prohibit the possession of any Schedule I drug, such as heroin, "except under legal authority."[132]

"Legal authority" in the United States is supplied by the Controlled Substances Act,[133] a portion of the Comprehensive Drug Abuse Control and Prevention Act of 1970.[134] The Controlled Substances Act, like the Single Convention, arranges drugs according to schedules, but its classifications have a different meaning than do the Convention's: By definition, a Schedule I substance in the act *cannot* have an "accepted medical use in treatment in the United States."[135] Heroin, then, has no currently approved medical use in the United States, although related opiate drugs such as morphine are listed under Schedule II of the act as having legitimate medical usefulness. This distinction between the two drugs results from domestic policy, not international law.

The Food, Drug and Cosmetic Act also applies to narcotics controls.[136] This act requires FDA approval of any new drug prior to its marketing or general medical use. Thus, FDA approval may be required for heroin policy to change.

The last layer of control and regulation consists of state and local laws. Federal law preempts conflicting state rules in the areas of manufacture and medical dispensation; however, the states are deeply involved in criminal heroin law enforcement. Many—in fact, most— states have adopted the Uniform Controlled Substances Act, but there is considerable variation in their penalties and other criminal provisions. Penalties for possession, for example, range from conditional discharge to life in prison. Since the federal laws relating to possession are largely unenforced, state laws have great practical significance in this area.

Medical and Drug Treatment Research with Heroin. Existing law does permit tightly controlled, experimental medical research with any Schedule I drug, including heroin. Federal administrative action is required for this, but U.S. manufacturers can be registered to produce the heroin needed for research purposes, and practitioners registered to employ heroin in a research project.[137] Both the Drug Enforcement Administration (DEA) of the Department of Justice and the Food and Drug Administration of the Department of Health, Education, and Welfare must approve the application of a person wishing to conduct such research. Once the FDA (acting for the Secretary of Health, Education and Welfare) approves the research application, DEA (acting for the Attorney General) can reject it only on very limited grounds, such as fraud.[138] Recently, upon solicitation from the National Institute on Drug Abuse (NIDA), the Sloan-Kettering Institute for Cancer Research has received approval and funding for a five-year study evaluating heroin in relation to other narcotic analgesics in cancer therapy.[139]

The Single Convention—the international law controlling American regulation of heroin—similarly permits heroin research to be conducted at the discretion of signatory nations. The official commentary on this treaty indicates that heroin maintenance treatment of addicts was contemplated by its drafters to be within the "medical purposes" restriction.[140]

Since federal law preempts conflicting state law in the regulation of heroin, heroin research, once approved by the appropriate federal agencies, could not be prohibited by state action. Federal law would preclude any state action to stop the work of a federally-approved heroin researcher from going forward.[141]

Government-sponsored Heroin Treatment Clinics.   Using heroin in the addiction treatment process comports with international law in that both the Single Convention and the 1972 Protocol make clear that the use of heroin to maintain or otherwise treat addicts was contemplated by the treaties' drafters.[142] The United Kingdom has utilized this section of the treaty to authorize heroin maintenance programs on its home soil.

To permit treatment clinics to use heroin in their programs on a nonexperimental basis, however, heroin would have to be transferred from Schedule I to Schedule II of the Controlled Substances Act.[143] Such a scheduling transfer is accomplished by administrative action involving three federal agencies: the Department of Health, Education, and Welfare, the Drug Enforcement Administration of the Department of Justice, and the Food and Drug Administration of HEW. The rescheduling move could come about by one of three means: initiation by the Attorney General, by the Secretary of HEW, or by petition.[144] The Attorney General cannot control a drug HEW says should not be controlled, but he has the ultimate authority to decide appropriate scheduling once HEW agrees that a drug ought to be controlled. However, HEW findings on scientific and medical matters are binding.

The Attorney General is also responsible for registering practitioners who dispense narcotic drugs for use in treatment—not only methadone, but heroin as well.[145] Once a practitioner is found qualified by the Attorney General, he must approve the registration, unless he finds that the practitioner will not comply with controls against diversion. The Comprehensive Drug Abuse Control and Prevention Act of 1970 authorizes the Secretary of HEW to determine "appropriate methods of professional practice in the medical treatment of narcotic addiction of various classes of narcotics addicts."[146] If the Secretary found heroin appropriate in a treatment setting, a clinic could be established in the hospitals and other health care institutions under HEW control.

The FDA as well would be involved in a decision to permit heroin to be used as a treatment drug. Generally FDA approval is required for all "new drugs" prior to marketing.[147] If heroin is recognized as "safe and effective" for treatment use, and if it has been found to have been used to a "material extent or for a material time,"[148] it will not be required to go through "new-drug" application procedures. Since some forty-four American heroin and morphine clinics existed during the period 1918–22,[149] it is possible that the prior use requirement may in this way be met for "new-drug" purposes. Heroin might also be exempt from "new-drug" requirements through operation of the "grandfather clause" of the Food and Drug Act of 1938, which recognized prescribed drugs permitted under the earlier 1906 act.[150]

Further action would be required in order to secure an adequate supply of heroin for the clinics. Opium is currently prohibited from import for the purpose of manufacturing heroin,[151] and none is grown domestically. However, DEA might make its heroin seizures available for either research projects or established heroin clinics. Another possibility is to manufacture heroin from the concentrate of poppy straw that is now imported to manufacture codeine.[152] A more permanent source of supply—legal importation of raw opium or refined heroin or domestic cultivation—would require statutory amendment of federal law.

Without the federal administrative action above described, states cannot implement heroin clinics of their own. Conversely, they could not enforce state criminal laws against clinic patients or clinicians for heroin possession or distribution offenses if the federal government were to sponsor heroin treatment clinics. State law on controlled substances—whose regulation is a legitimate national concern having interstate commerce implications—must give way to federal law if it *directly* conflicts.[153] Whenever the two laws can coexist, the courts will generally let both stand. For instance, amendments to federal law could permit states to allow treatment programs using heroin without requiring all states to adopt such programs. In order to achieve more state initiative, however, it may be necessary to have an explicit federal statutory expression setting out a policy permitting states to determine appropriate treatment policies, including the use of heroin within their borders.[154]

Removal of Criminal Penalties for Personal Possession. This policy could be achieved without altering present international agreements by amending either federal or state law or both. Nothing in the 1961 Single Convention prevents the United States from lifting criminal penalties for the possession of heroin. The convention merely requires that possession not be allowed "except under legal authority,"[155] and permits (but does not require) signatory nations to prohibit the manufacture or use of the drug.[156] If a control measure other than prohibition seems to be the "most appropriate means of protecting the public health and welfare," that measure may be adopted.[157]

However, complete removal of criminal heroin possession penalties at the federal level would require statutory amendment of the 1970 Comprehensive Act. Rescheduling heroin to Schedule II would result in decriminalization only for those receiving clinic heroin. Such partial decriminalization of heroin possession could occur also as a result of a clearly enunciated policy position of the Department of Justice through DEA.[158] In fact, DEA has already declared its policy is to concentrate on traffickers, rather than on "the ultimate user of drugs."[159] However, a policy of nonenforcement would simply be de facto decriminalization, which could be revoked without notice or disregarded selectively for certain offenders.

States could remove criminal possession penalties from their statute books even in the face of continued federal prohibition. Such an action is not inconsistent with "supremacy requirements," since federal enforcement agents could still enforce federal law even in a heroin- decriminalized state. Only where a positive and irreconcilable conflict between federal and state law exists must state law give way.

Over-the-Counter Regulation of Heroin.   Once again, international law poses no obstacle to implementation of an American domestic policy allowing heroin users to obtain the drug as an over-the-counter preparation. The discussion above about the obligations of parties to the 1961 Single Convention to prevent "unauthorized" possession applies here as well.

Federal law would require statutory change in order to allow access to heroin as an OTC drug without prescription.[160] Specific aspects of an OTC heroin regulatory scheme, such as identification and registration of the buyer, would also require statutory action. Prescription sale of heroin, on the other hand, could be accomplished simply by administrative action to reschedule heroin to Schedules II or III of the Controlled Substances Act. FDA approval of heroin as a "new drug" would also be required, unless it was found to be exempt as discussed above.

Since statutory change is required at the federal level to accomplish over-the-counter regulation of heroin, legislative action at the state level alone could not effect this policy change. An independent over-the-counter state legislative scheme would almost certainly conflict with contrary federal law and be invalid. However, with appropriate enabling legislation at the federal level, individual states could promulgate various regulatory measures pertaining to the process of dispensing the drug, registering sales, and the like.

Concluding Thoughts

The alternative heroin policies discussed in this chapter are only a few of the many possible choices available to American policymakers. They are not a timetable for liberalizing present heroin policies, nor should the order in which they are discussed be regarded necessarily as a logical policy progression. Some policy changes could occur simultaneously with others; while the selection of some other policies would necessarily preclude certain others from being put into force at the same time. Any policy change will lead to more knowledge of the ways in which heroin policy affects both individuals and society in general, knowledge which is in large measure lacking at present. This new knowledge may give hints of promising new directions, or it may indicate what policy aspects may produce problems.

The use of heroin itself may increase even more, or may gradually decline over time. History provides no evidence on which to base a belief that the drug could ever be entirely eradicated, and one might well wonder why this particular drug should be the focus of so much attention when many other substances of equal or greater potential for abuse are readily available. More than six decades of effort to eliminate the drug from the United States through strong law enforcement measures have not caused the number of users to drop below levels observed at the beginning of this century. Even if there is general agreement that heroin use is not desirable, absolute prohibition is difficult, if not impossible, to achieve in the real world—particularly in a democratic, nonauthoritarian society such as ours.

As a society we ought to remember that by maintaining current heroin policies we are also making a choice. If we choose this option, we should evaluate the probable costs and benefits at least as carefully as with alternative policy proposals. The benefits and shortcomings of current policies can, perhaps, be judged by different and stricter standards, since so many years and so much effort have been put into the task of trying to make them work.

This chapter and those preceding it clearly question not only current drug policies but the premises on which those policies are based. Our analysis rejects stereotypical notions about heroin users and challenges the rationale for a continued strict prohibition approach. The discussion has focused on the issues involved, rather than on the policy models themselves. That the latter are by no means the only possible options is a state-

TABLE 6.8   Summary of Effects of Alternative Policy Models

<table>
<tr><td colspan="4" align="center">Issues</td></tr>
<tr>
<td>Policy Models</td>
<td>Patterns of Use</td>
<td>Crime and the
Fear of Crime</td>
<td>Community Impact</td>
</tr>
<tr>
<td>Medical and Drug Treatment Research with Heroin</td>
<td>No change. (Symbolic effect doubtful)</td>
<td>No change. Possible indirect effect on public attitudes toward heroin and crime. Policy would provide data on "pharmacological theory."</td>
<td>Resistance to implementation possible especially in minority neighborhoods of new programs without consultation as result of experiments. (Local option possible.)</td>
</tr>
<tr>
<td>Government-sponsored Heroin Treatment Clinics</td>
<td>Despite concern over diversion and nonaddicted use, little change predicted. Magnitude of participation in clinics governs impact. Some symbolic effect but would not signal that heroin is socially approved.</td>
<td>Potential impact depend upon extent to which users attracted to treatment and existing magnitude of non-drug crime occasioned by need for income for heroin. Policy would provide some data on the "price theory" of heroin-crime link.</td>
<td>Resistance possible i community not consulted beforehand. Predicted concern over presence of large numbers of social deviants in community may be either alleviated or aggravated by actual experience. (Local option possible.)</td>
</tr>
<tr>
<td>Removal of Criminal Penalties for Possession</td>
<td>Effect of criminal law on decision to use seems slight. Little impact predicted.</td>
<td>No impact on non-drug crime predicted.</td>
<td>Predicted concern in some inner-city area that this would be "giving up" on heroin, but little new use expected. (Local option possible.)</td>
</tr>
<tr>
<td>Over-the-Counter Drug Regulation</td>
<td>Overall use would probably increase, but compulsive use may either increase or decline depending upon growth of social controls over time.</td>
<td>Effective elimination of heroin "black market" and crime committed to pay for heroin.</td>
<td>New use is likely and more compulsive use possible. Policy effect on education efforts may encourage responsible using behavior, thus lessening present social cost to community.</td>
</tr>
</table>

	Issues	
Impact on Existing Drug Treatment and Prevention Efforts	*Effects on the Criminal Justice System*	*Civil Liberties Aspects*
Little change anticipated from current American treatment goal of abstinence, despite the British experience with "stabilization" goal. Existing facilities would be utilized.	No change predicted.	Create new issues of consent to participate and anonymity and confidentiality of records. Policy may lead to development of right of appropriate treatment including heroin.
Administrative aspects could either aggravate or reduce drain of patients from existing programs. Programs could be conducted by existing facilities; new ones would heighten impact on existing ones	Depending upon attractiveness of treatment design, arrests may decline or remain same. Diversion unlikely to be problem, though public-order offenses might increase near clinics. Non-drug crime may decline but little is known on magnitude of current crime related to heroin income needs.	SAME AS ABOVE
Primary impact likely to be reduced volume of criminal justice referrals Heavy potential impact for existing programs that now depend upon criminal justice system for clients.	Possession arrests (majority of current heroin offenses) should fall substantially. Impact on informants possible but their current utility is questionable. May increase police morale by lessening pressure for corruption.	Eliminate most current civil liberties issues due to elimination of most heroin arrests (i.e. for possession). Development of right to privacy and to appropriate treatment to include heroin use.
Predicted elimination of criminal justice system referrals. Policy expected to accelerate development of unified health care system.	Nearly complete disengagement of criminal justice agencies from heroin control.	New issues possible —e.g., minor's access to drug—but existing issues anticipated to disappear.

TABLE 6.8 *(Continued)*

	ISSUES		
Policy Models	*Health Issues*	*Other Issues*	*Changing the Law Legal Aspects*
Medical and Drug Treatment Research with Heroin	Knowledge gains possible.	Effects on productivity and welfare highly speculative since present costs and causes uncertain.	Can be done without statutory change with federal bureaucratic approval under existing law.
Government-sponsored Heroin Treatment Clinics	Likely improvement for clinic patients, but questions of level of participation, street drug use, and self-administration make extent of improvement unpredictable.	SAME AS ABOVE	Statutory change not necessary but rescheduling at federal level needed. State and local change can only follow federal.
Removal of Criminal Penalties for Possession	Little change predicted. Fewer may enter treatment, since arrests likely to decline—thus fewer treatment referrals. More might seek treatment voluntarily.	SAME AS ABOVE	Statutory change necessary at either state or federal level or possible at local if state law permits variance.
Over-the-Counter Drug Regulation	Eliminate many health complications of impure street drugs but still risks due to self-administration. Particular groups (e.g., adolescents; pregnant women) continue to be vulnerable to medical complications.	SAME AS ABOVE	Statutory change necessary at federal level. State and local change can only follow federal.

ment that bears repetition. At the same time, it is useful to sum up some conclusions based on this discussion.

First, there appears to be no good reason to continue to withhold approval of serious research proposals to investigate the utility of heroin in either general therapeutic or drug treatment applications. The potential knowledge to be gained is considerable and the risk minimal.

Second, the immediate implementation on a broad scale of treatment clinics using heroin is inadvisable. However, there does not seem to be good cause for rejecting carefully designed proposals submitted by individual states or local governments to initiate such clinics on a limited, test basis. Permitting greater flexibility and diversity in the national response to heroin problems is critical to the development of policies that match the needs and desires of the communities involved.

Third, while the removal of criminal penalties for possession of heroin would have a salutary effect on civil liberties, it would not be an effective response to the crime problems caused by heroin's high "black-market" cost. Greater consideration ought to be given to combining variants of this policy with the treatment clinic option or others (such as greater physician discretion and over-the-counter regulation for further detailed examination).

Fourth, our heroin policy need not be monolithic, at least not as monolithic as it is currently. The nature and extent of heroin problems vary widely from city to city and region to region. Requiring a uniform policy has proven to be self-defeating in the long run. The participation in the planning and implementation of heroin policies of the states and cities where heroin problems are most severe is a vital need.

Fifth and finally, we recognize that by proposing the serious consideration or adoption of alternative policies we run the risk of being branded as "pro heroin." Insistence on the single, unrealistic goal of the elimination of heroin has led many to mistakenly believe that our national choice is between control and no control, rather than among differing degrees of control. It is not a black-and-white issue; we feel it is important to take the risk of being misunderstood in the hope of achieving greater understanding and of effectively addressing the very real problems we face today.

In the absence of absolute knowledge and the power to foretell the future, we need to pursue more vigorously policies that minimize individual and social harm and abandon those that cause more harm than they relieve. An honest evaluation of the adequacy of our response to heroin and to all psychoactive drugs calls for the reasoned consideration of a full range of alternative policy choices.

Appendix: Activities of the Drug Abuse Council

Drug Abuse Council Grants, 1972–1978

The following list enumerates Drug Abuse Council grant recipients, with brief descriptions of the project objectives supported by the grant.

Youth Projects, Inc. ("free clinics" conference)

National Coordinating Council on Drug Education (review of drug abuse films)

Addiction Research Foundation (establishment of independent biomedical drug research unit)

Salk Institute (seminars on repetitive drug use)

NAACP Legal Defense and Education Fund (national conferences of minority groups involved in the drug abuse field)

National Federation of Concerned Drug Abuse Workers (development of drug abuse training program)

National High School Student Project (included grants to Frederick Douglass Community Center, Inc.; United Clubs of Broward County, Inc.; Chicanos Unidos and King Cobras; Metro High School; Wisconsin Student Union; Black Student Union of Boston, Inc.; Student Research Team of Wingate High School; Students Allied for Effective Community and Education of San Francisco; and Dayton Drug Project.)

Center for Policy Studies (conference on regulating new drugs)

Foundation for Research on Drug Legislation and Control (studies on drug policy)

Study of Life Style Changes by New Jersey Neuropsychiatric Institute (study of methadone maintenance patients)

National Institute for Workers' Rights (use and abuse of drugs at work)

Chicano Alliance of Drug Abuse Programs (development of minority group drug abuse programs)

National Drug Reporter (biweekly newsletter to drug field)

Washingtonian Center for Addictions (pilot study of occasional illicit drug users)

New York State Legislative Institute of Baruch College (seminar on drugs)

National Free Clinic Conference

Analysis of Drug Abuse Law Enforcement (Richard J. Bonnie, J.D.)

Evolution of American Narcotic Policies, 1945–1973 (Yale University, Dr. David F. Musto)

Free Clinic Study (Dr. Christian Heinic)

National Drug Abuse Conference (1973, 1974, 1975, 1976)

History of Narcotic Use in Britain (University of London, Institute of Psychiatry)

Regional Addiction Prevention, Inc. [RAP] (general support for drug treatment program)

National Center for Urban Ethnic Affairs (study of drug use in white ethnic populations)

Heroin Maintenance Study (Dan Waldorf)

Mid-Career Seminars in Drug Abuse Reporting at the Graduate School of Journalism, Columbia Univ.

North Charles Mental Health Research and Training Foundation (study of socially controlled drug use)

The Center for the Study of Non-Medical Drug Use (support for public drug education and legal referral programs)

Soul City Foundation, Inc. (establish city drug abuse planning capability)

Salk Institute for Biological Studies (seminar on Shafer Commission findings)

Female Drug Abusers Study (Soler and Fielding)

Study of Drug Advertising in the United States (Board of Church and Society of the United Methodist Church)

National Urban League (research on pretrial diversion)

New York Drug Law Evaluation Project (Association of the Bar of the City of New York)

PACT (development of employment opportunities for ex-addicts)

Youth Drug Prevention and Treatment (G. G. DeAngeles, Ph.D.)

Community Resources, Inc. (examination of drug use decision making)

National Foundation for the Improvement of Education (develop drug education project)

Project "Delphi" Study (National Coordinating Council on Drug Education)

Ethnographic Study of Cocaine Users (Dan Waldorf)

Legal Action Center of the City of New York (addiction law services project)

Status of Marijuana in the United States (National Coordinating Council on Drug Education)

East-West Gateway Coordinating Council (conference of criminal justice and drug treatment workers)

The John Marshall School of Law (comparative law symposium on the social control of drugs)

National Urban League Research Department (analysis of Washington, D.C. drug law arrest outcomes)

North American Association of Therapeutic Communities (support of drug conference)

Report on Drug and Alcohol Abuse in People's Republic of China (Joseph and Florence Ershun, Eagleville Hospital)

Addiction Research Foundation (follow-up study of methadone treatment clients)

Report on Americans Arrested Abroad for Drug Law Offenses (Candace L. Cowan, J.D.)

Handbook on Marijuana Laws (Center for the Study of Non-medical Drug Use)

Survey of Elected Public Officials on Drug Abuse (Howard University's Joint Center for Political Studies)

New York Academy of Sciences (scientific conference on chronic cannabis use)

Social Costs of Drug Law Enforcement (John R. Pekkanen)

National Association of Puerto Rican Drug Abuse Programs— General Support (Chelsea Coordinating Committee on Drug Addiction, Inc.)

Report on Mexican–United States Heroin Traffic (John R. Bartels, J.D.)

The Judge Baker Guidance Center (study of developmental antecedents of drug addiction)

Joint Center for Community Services, Inc. (conference on reducing drug abuse in minority communities)

Andromeda, Inc. (support for Hispanic Substance Abuse Conference)

U.S. Journal of Alcohol and Drug Dependence, Inc. (development and initial support for monthly professional journal of drug and alcohol abuse developments)

Report on Heroin Policy (Mark H. Moore, Ph.D.)

Seminar on Heroin Maintenance (American Institute for Municipal Research, Education & Training, Inc.)

Aspen Institute for Humanistic Studies (joint conference on drug abuse for national policymakers)

Yale University (support on review of drug use and mental health linkage)

Drug Abuse Council Internal Projects, 1972–1978

High School Student Project Conference

Joint Conference on Altered States of Consciousness (with the Smithsonian Institution)

Army Drug Abuse Program Report

Civil Liberties and Drug Treatment Project

Evaluation of New York State Criminal Penalties for Drug Usage

Columbia University School of Journalism Mid-Career Seminars in Drug Abuse

Seminar on Flow of Federal Drug Abuse Funds

Film Project on Vermont Legislature Public Drug Law Hearings
Police Executive Resident Institute Program
Conference of Puerto Rican Drug Program Coordinators
Assistance to National Free Clinic Council
Effectiveness of Single State Agencies System Study
Review of Urinalysis and Drug Treatment
DAC Cannabis Conference (1975)
Altered States of Consciousness Conference
Legal Issues in Addict Diversion Project (with the American Bar Association)
Development of NCCDE "Super Me/Super Yo" publication
Foreign Drug Officials Program (with the U.S. State Department)
Puerto Rican Drug Abuse Program Conference
Phoenix, Arizona Technical Assistance Project
Certification and Credentialing Standards for Drug Abuse Programs Study
Study of Quality Improvement and Cost-Savings Methods in Drug Treatment
Denver Criminal Justice Study
Community Resource Project for Ex-Addicts
Study of Sources of Federal, State, and Local Matching Funds
Institutional Use of Drugs on Young People (with Gould Foundation)
Study of Cost of Drug Law Enforcement (NYC)
Ten Cities Project
Drugs in the Workplace Study
Survey of Drug Abuse Services in Cities over 30,000 Population (with National League of Cities and U.S. Conference of Mayors)
Planning Project for 1977 National Drug Abuse Conference
Staff Assistance to RAP, Inc.
Staff Assistance to Minority Drug Abuse Treatment Programs and Associations
Marijuana Economic Study (with New England School of Law Work-Study Program)
Alternative Policy Approaches to Heroin
Anchorage, Alaska Technical Assistance Project
Staff Assistance to U.S. Journal of Drug and Alcohol Dependence
Seminar of City Drug Coordinators
Survey of Public Policy and Attitudes on Marijuana
Staff Presentations, Exhibits, and Technical Assistance to 1977 National Drug Abuse Conference
Conference on Drug Abuse (with Aspen Institute for Humanistic Studies)
Study of Marijuana Laws: Federal, State, and Local Penalties and Changing Legislation
Symposium on Heroin Abuse and the Law (with the Bar Association of San Francisco)
Feasibility Study of Integration of Drug Treatment Programs and General Health and Mental Health
Final Report: The Future of Drug Abuse Public Policy and Programs

Drug Abuse Council Contracts, 1972–1978

Controlled Substances, Inc. (report on international drug control mechanisms)

Powell Associates (report of occasional heroin users)

International City Management Association (survey of city, county, and state drug abuse activities, 1972)

Applied Urbanetics, Inc. (survey of local and federal drug control efforts)

Leon G. Hunt (heroin use study)

Regional Addiction Prevention, Inc. [RAP] (DAC orientation program)

Dr. Stephen Pittel (study of Haight-Ashbury clinic data)

Center for Naval Analysis (study of illegal drug prices)

Center for Community Change (administer high school student project)

American Bar Association (joint study of federal drug programs)

Kartemquin Films, Ltd. (documentary film)

Institute for Study of Drug Dependence (design information dissemination system)

Bio-Behavioral Research Group (drug education research handbook)

The Urban Institute (community planning guides for drug abuse control)

George Washington University (produce "Narcotic Antagonist Research Review")

Daniel Yankelovich, Inc. (research on student drug use)

Educational Broadcasting Corp., WNET, Channel 13 [NY] (live and taped coverage of DAC "Seminar on Drug Abuse")

Thomas D. Boyd & Associates, Inc. (conference support services)

National Federation of Concerned Drug Abuse Workers (survey of drug treatment workers)

Twin-City Area Educational Television Corp. [KCTA-TV] (videotaping public hearings on marijuana laws)

Different Trips, Inc. (organizational handbook for free clinics)

Design Etcetera, Ltd. (DAC conference exhibit)

Center for Naval Analysis [CNA] (analysis of heroin and crime relationship in Detroit)

Mary King Associates, Inc. (study of third-party financing of drug treatment)

Bardsley and Haschler, Inc. [1974, 1975, 1976, 1977] (survey of Oregon marijuana use and public attitudes)

Field Research Corp. (survey of California marijuana use and public attitudes)

Humanics, Inc. (study on third-party payments)

Opinion Research Corp. (national survey of marijuana use and public attitudes)

United States Journal of Alcohol and Drug Dependence, Inc. (subscription to newsletter journal)

Charles Morgan, Jr. and Associates, Chartered (study of changes in public perceptions of drug issues)

Drug Abuse Council Fellows, 1972–1975

The fellowship program of the Drug Abuse Council offered one-year fellowship grants to individuals from a variety of professions and backgrounds in order to engage in projects with a potential for increasing public knowledge and understanding of drug abuse topics.

1972–1973

Robert P. Bomboy, journalist
Edward J. Casavantes, Ph.D., psychologist
Harvey W. Feldman, Ph.D., sociologist
Patrick H. Hughes, M.D., psychiatrist/epidemiologist
David L. Lewis, Ph.D., historian
Jerry Mandel, Ph.D., sociologist
David F. Musto, M.D., psychiatrist/historian
Wesley A. Pomery, J.D., police administrator
Margaret H. Tripp, M.D., psychiatrist

1973–74

Carl Akins, Ph.D., political scientist
Frank Espada, social scientist
Mathea Falco, J.D., attorney
Thomas B. Kirkpatrick, J.D., LL.M., attorney
Roger Smith, D. Crim., criminologist

1974–75

Edward J. Epstein, Ph.D., journalist/political scientist
John R. Pekkanen, journalist
Lawrence Redlinger, Ph.D., social scientist
Jared R. Tinklenberg, M.D., psychiatrist
Philip G. Vargas, J.D., attorney/social scientist
Frances Verrinder, journalist/editor
Nancy Wynstra, J.D., attorney

Drug Abuse Council Publications*

Books

Dealing with Drug Abuse: A Report to the Ford Foundation (New York: Praeger Publishers, 1972)
Drugs: Administering Catastrophe (Washington, D.C.: Drug Abuse Council, 1975).

* These books are the results of work supported in whole or in part by the Drug Abuse Council.

Synthetic Substitutes for Opiate Alkaloids: A Feasibility Study (Washington, D.C.: Drug Abuse Council, 1975).

Survey of Analgesic Drug Prescribing Patterns (Washington, D.C.: Drug Abuse Council, 1975).

Altered States of Consciousness: Current Views and Research Problems (Washington, D.C.: Drug Abuse Council, 1975).

Alternate States of Consciousness: Multiple Perspectives on the Study of Consciousness (New York: Free Press, 1977)

Employment and the Rehabilitated Addict: Employment Experience and Recent Research Findings (Washington, D.C.: Drug Abuse Council, 1973).

Legal Issues in Addict Diversion: A Layman's Guide (Washington, D.C.: Drug Abuse Council and American Bar Association, 1975).

Legal Issues in Addict Diversion: A Technical Analysis (Lexington, Mass.: Lexington Books, 1976)

Marijuana and Health Hazards: Methodological Issues in Current Research (New York: Academic Press, 1975)

Drugs and Minority Oppression (New York: Seabury Press, 1975)

The Politics of Drugs (Washington, D.C.: Congressional Quarterly, 1975)

The Heroin Epidemics: A Study of Heroin Use in the United States, 1965–1975 (New York: Spectrum Publications, 1976)

Agency of Fear (New York: G. P. Putnam's Sons, 1977)

Behind the Wall of Respect: Community Experiments in Heroin Addiction Control (Chicago: University of Chicago Press, 1977)

Assessment of Local Drug Abuse (New York: Lexington Books, 1977)

Federal Drug Abuse Programs (Washington, D.C.: Drug Abuse Council, 1973).

Army Drug Abuse Program: A Future Model (Washington, D.C.: Drug Abuse Council, 1972).

The Nation's Toughest Drug Law: Evaluating the New York Experience (Final Report of the Joint Committee on New York Drug Law Evaluation) (New York: Association of the Bar of the City of New York and the Drug Abuse Council, 1977).

Handbook Series

Accountability in Drug Education: A Model for Evaluation
Responsabilidad en Educación Sobre Drogas
Drug Program Assessment: A Community Guide
Students Speak on Drugs: The High School Student Project
Reporter's Guide: Drugs, Drug Abuse Issues, Resources
Admission Records: A Tool for Treatment Program Planning

Public Policy Series

A Perspective on "Get Tough" Drug Laws
The Convention on Psychotropic Substances: An Analysis

Governmental Response to Drug Abuse: The 1976 Federal Budget and Single State Agency Analysis
Governmental Response to Drug Abuse: The 1977 Federal Budget
Governmental Response to Drugs: Fiscal and Organizational
Heroin Maintenance: The Issues
The Heroin Trade: From Poppies to Peoria
What's Happening with Heroin Maintenance

Monograph Series:

Employment and Addiction: Overview of Issues
Heroin Epidemics: A Quantitative Study of Current Empirical Data
Methadone: Benefits and Shortcomings
Methadone Maintenance: The Experience of Four Programs
Occasional Heroin Use: A Pilot Study
The Organization of the United Nations to Deal with Drug Abuse
Recent Spread of Heroin Use in the United States
The Retail Price of Heroin: Estimation and Applications
Survey of City/County Drug Abuse Activities: 1972
Survey of State Drug Abuse Activities: 1972

Special Studies:

Alcohol and Drugs at Work
Doing Coke: An Ethnography of Cocaine Users and Sellers
Drug Use, the Labor Market and Class Conflict
"High" States: A Beginning Study
Morphine Maintenance: The Shreveport Clinic, 1919–1923
Pot Luck in Texas: Changing a Marijuana Law
The Social Basis of Drug Abuse Prevention
The Staff Burnout Syndrome

Fellows Series:

Major Newspaper Coverage of Drug Issues
Methaqualone: A Study of Drug Control
Police Chiefs Discuss Drug Abuse
Prosecution Perspectives on Drugs
Street Status and the Drug Researcher: Issues in Participant Observation

Trends and Issues:

Drugs and Youth
Federal Drug Abuse Law Enforcement, Regulation, and Control
Heroin Supply and Urban Crime
Heroin Use: A New Look
Marijuana: Q & A
Trends and Issues in Federal Drug Abuse Activities: Forecast 1975
Turkish Opium in Perspective

Other Reports:

Drug Abuse Council Annual Report (1972 to 1976)
The Problem of Drug Abuse in the City of Phoenix, Arizona: A Report to the Mayor and the City Council
Aerosols: A New Drug Danger
An Analysis of the Federal Policy Requiring Drug Abuse Treatment Centers to Maximize the Capture of Third Party Payments
Credentialing Issues in Substance Abuse
Students and Drugs: A Report of the Drug Abuse Council

Notes

Final Report of the Drug Abuse Council, pp. 1–19

1. New York: Praeger Publishers, 1972.
2. For a list of Drug Abuse Council projects and publications, see pp. 248–256.
3. New York: Association of the Bar of the City of New York, 1977.

1. The Federal Government's Response to Illicit Drugs, 1969–1978, pp. 20–62

1. See, for example, National Commission on Marihuana and Drug Abuse, *Drug Use in America: Problem in Perspective*, second report (Washington, D.C.: U.S. Government Printing Office, 1973); Drug Abuse Survey Project, *Dealing with Drug Abuse: A Report to the Ford Foundation* (New York: Praeger Publishers, 1972); Task Force on Federal Heroin Addiction Programs, *Federal Drug Abuse Programs*, report prepared by the task force and submitted to the Criminal Law Section of the American Bar Association and the Drug Abuse Council (Washington, D.C.: Drug Abuse Council, 1972); Domestic Council Drug Abuse Task Force, *White Paper on Drug Abuse, A Report to the President*, September, 1975 (Washington, D.C.: U.S. Government Printing Office, 1975).
2. David F. Musto, *The American Disease: Origins of Narcotics Control* (New Haven: Yale University Press, 1973).
3. Rufus King, *The Drug Hang-up: America's Fifty-year Folly* (New York: Norton, 1972).
4. Public Law #148, passed May 7, 1906.
5. 38 Stat. 785 (December 17, 1914).
6. See, for example, Dan Waldorf, Martin Orlick, and Craig Reinarman, *Morphine Maintenance: The Shreveport Clinic, 1919–1923* (Washington, D.C.: Drug Abuse Council, 1974).

257

7. 45 Stat. 1085 (January 19, 1929).

8. See, for example, the review of several studies of patients who had been in the Lexington facility by Robert W. Rasor, in Leon Brill and Louis Lieberman, eds., *Major Modalities in the Treatment of Drug Abuse* (New York: Behavioral Publications, 1972), pp. 16–18.

9. Musto, *op.cit.*, p. 206.

10. *Ibid.*, p. 212.

11. 50 Stat. 551 (August 2, 1937).

12. Richard J. Bonnie and Charles H. Whitebread III, *The Marihuana Conviction: A History of Marihuana Prohibition in the United States* (Charlottesville: University Press of Virginia, 1974), pp. 175–86.

13. Musto, *op.cit.*, p. 231.

14. 65 Stat. 767 (November 2, 1951).

15. Narcotic Control Act of 1956, 70 Stat. 567 (July 18, 1956).

16. President's Advisory Commission on Narcotic and Drug Abuse, *Final Report* (Washington, D.C.: U.S. Government Printing Office, 1963).

17. *Ibid.*, p. 6.

18. 80 Stat. 1438 (November 8, 1966).

19. 114 *Congressional Record* H878 (H. Doc. No. 249).

20. For a good discussion of how the "law and order" issue evolved, see Edward Jay Epstein, *Agency of Fear* (New York: G.P. Putnam's Sons, 1977), pp. 57–58.

21. For example, see Leon Hunt and Norman E. Zinberg, *Heroin Use: A New Look* (Washington, D.C.: Drug Abuse Council, 1976) and Lee Robins et al., "Vietnam Veterans Three Years After Vietnam: How Our Study Changed Our View of Heroin."

22. Richard M. Nixon, Message to Congress, H.R. Document 91-138, July 14, 1969, pp. 1–2.

23. 84 Stat. 1236 (October 27, 1970); 21 USC §§801 et seq.

24. For a good discussion of the international heroin control efforts of the Nixon administration through 1971, see Task Force on Federal Heroin Addiction Programs, *op.cit.*, pp. 22–45.

25. Vincent P. Dole and Marie E. Nyswander, "Rehabilitation of Heroin Addicts after Blockade with Methadone," *New York State Journal of Medicine*, vol. 66 (1966), pp. 2011–17.

26. Epstein, *op.cit.*, p. 128. For a fascinating account of how the Nixon administration came to view methadone, see pp. 123–32.

27. The budget figures used for FY 69–71 are taken from Peter Goldberg and James V. DeLong, "Federal Expenditures on Drug Abuse Control," in *Dealing With Drug Abuse: A Report to the Ford Foundation*, pp. 300–328.

28. Patricia M. Wald and Peter Barton Hutt, "Drug Abuse Survey Project: Summary of Findings, Conclusions, and Recommendations," in *Dealing With Drug Abuse*, p. 39.

29. Unless otherwise cited the material in this section is drawn from Richard M. Nixon, Message to Congress, June 17, 1971.

30. See Epstein, *op.cit.*, pp. 128–32.

31. *Ibid.*, p. 128.

32. *Ibid.*
33. Strategy Council on Drug Abuse, *Federal Strategy for Drug Abuse and Drug Traffic Prevention, 1973*, p. 76.
34. Richard M. Nixon, Message to Congress, June 17, 1971.
35. Peter G. Bourne, *Methadone: Benefits and Shortcomings* (Washington, D.C.: Drug Abuse Council, 1975), p. 3.
36. Strategy Council on Drug Abuse, *op.cit.*, p. 76.
37. *Ibid.*, p. 82.
38. See Epstein, *op.cit.*, pp. 126–32.
39. "Methadone Regulations," *Federal Register* 37 (December 15, 1972): 16790.
40. Strategy Council on Drug Abuse, *op.cit.*, p. 83.
41. Richard M. Nixon, Message to Congress, June 17, 1971.
42. Task Force on Federal Heroin Addiction Programs, *op.cit.*, pp. 24, 32, 41.
43. *Ibid.*, p. 25. See also pp. 23–27, 28–30.
44. See Strategy Council on Drug Abuse, *op.cit.*, p. 118.
45. For a discussion of the limitations of the effort to eliminate the growth of opium poppies worldwide, see Sibyl Cline Halper, *The Heroin Trade: From Poppies to Peoria* (Washington, D.C.: Drug Abuse Council, 1977).
46. See Task Force on Heroin Programs, *op.cit.*, pp. 20–22, and Strategy Council on Drug Abuse, *Federal Strategy for Drug Abuse and Drug Traffic Prevention, 1974*, p. 66.
47. For a good discussion, see *The Convention on Psychotropic Substances: An Analysis* (Washington, D.C.: Drug Abuse Council, 1973).
48. U.S. Congress, House of Representatives, *Hearings on Appropriations*, 91st Cong., 2d sess., 1970, Justice, Pt. 1, pp. 987–88.
49. See Epstein, *op. cit.*, pp. 199–200.
50. Executive Order No. 11641, January 28, 1972, 37 F.R. 2421.
51. *Ibid.*, §(d).
52. Epstein, *op.cit.*, p. 215.
53. For a thorough discussion of the background and provisions of P.L. 92-255 as it relates to an organizational analysis of the federal response to drug abuse, see Peter Goldberg and Carl Akins, "Issues in Organizing for Drug Abuse Prevention" in *Governmental Response to Drugs: Fiscal and Organizational* (Washington, D.C.: Drug Abuse Council, 1974), pp. 22–26. Much of the material in the "Congressional Response" section of this chapter is drawn from that monograph.
54. See P.L. 92–255, §§221, 222, 223, 230.
55. See remarks of President Richard M. Nixon, March 21, 1972, in *Legislative History of the Drug Abuse Office and Treatment Act of 1972* (Washington, D.C.: U.S. Government Printing Office, 1972), p. 321.
56. Richard M. Nixon, Statement at the White House Conference on Treatment Alternatives to Street Crime, September 11, 1973.
57. See, for example, Frederick V. Malek, "One that Got Away," "op.-ed." column, *New York Times*, December 5, 1973.
58. Lee N. Robins, *A Follow-up of Vietnam Drug Users*, Special Action Office on Drug Abuse Prevention Monograph Series A, No. 1, April 1973 (Washington, D.C.: U.S. Government Printing Office, 1973).

59. See Wesley A. Pomeroy, *Police Chiefs Discuss Drug Abuse* (Washington, D.C.: Drug Abuse Council, 1974), pp. 31–34.

60. Reorganization Plan No. 2 of 1973, July 10, 1973, 38 F.R. 18357.

61. See Sibyl Cline, "The Federal Drug Abuse Budget for Fiscal Year 1975" and Peter Goldberg and Carl Akins, "Issues in Organizing for Drug Abuse Prevention" in *Governmental Response to Drugs: Fiscal and Organizational* (Washington, D.C.: Drug Abuse Council, 1975).

62. Sibyl Cline, *op.cit.*, p. 5.

63. Peter Goldberg and Carl Akins, *op.cit.*, pp. 27–29. The actual implementation order delineating the responsibilities of ADAMHA and NIDA was printed in the *Federal Register*, vol. 39, no. 8 (January 11, 1974), pp. 1654–58.

64. The results of the congressional review are best summed up in "Legislative History of the 1975 Amendments to the Drug Abuse and Treatment Act of 1972 (P.L. 94-237)," *U.S. Code Congressional and Administrative News*, vol. 2 (1976), pp. 375 ff.

65. Domestic Council Drug Abuse Task Force, *op.cit.*

66. *Ibid.*, p. 5.

67. These arguments are reviewed in *Legislative History of the 1975 Amendments to the Drug Abuse and Treatment Act of 1972.*

68. *Legislative History of the 1975 Amendments to the Drug Abuse and Treatment Act of 1972*, p. 382.

69. Domestic Council Drug Abuse Task Force, *op.cit.*, p. 93.

70. Mathea Falco, "Office of Drug Abuse Policy Reconsidered," unpublished and undated paper on file at the Drug Abuse Council.

71. See *Legislative History of the 1975 Amendments to the Drug Abuse and Treatment Act of 1972*, pp. 381–83.

72. *Ibid.*, p. 384.

73. Domestic Council Drug Abuse Task Force, *op.cit.*, p. 89.

74. *Ibid.*, pp. 89–90.

75. *Ibid.*, p. 90.

76. *Ibid.*, pp. 90–95.

77. Gerald R. Ford, Statement issued by the Office of the White House Press Secretary, March 20, 1976.

78. *Legislative History of the 1975 Amendments to the Drug Abuse and Treatment Act of 1972*, p. 384.

79. 90 Stat. 241 (March 19, 1976).

80. Gerald R. Ford, Statement, March 20, 1976.

81. Gerald R. Ford, Message to Congress, April 27, 1976.

82. Office of Drug Abuse Policy, Executive Office of the President: *Border Management and Interdiction: An Interagency Review*, September, 1977; *Drug Use Patterns, Consequences and the Federal Response: A Policy Review*, March, 1978; *International Narcotics Control Policy*, March, 1978; *Drug Abuse Assessment in the Department of Defense: A Policy Review*, November, 1977; *Supply Control: Drug Law Enforcement: An Interagency Review*, October, 1977.

83. Jimmy Carter, Message to Congress, *Congressional Record*, 123d Cong., H8354 (H. Doc. No. 95-200), August 2, 1977.

2. Drug Law Enforcement Efforts, pp. 63–94

1. David F. Musto, *The American Disease: Origins of Narcotic Control* (New Haven: Yale University Press, 1973), chapters 1–3; John Helmer, *Drugs and Minority Oppression* (New York: Seabury Press, 1975), chapters 1–4.

2. Act of December 17, 1914, 38 Stat. 785-790.

3. Joseph Gusfield, *Symbolic Crusade: Status Politics and the American Temperance Movement* (Urbana: University of Illinois Press, 1963).

4. For a history of the development of American drug laws, see Musto, *op. cit.*; and National Commission on Marihuana and Drug Abuse, *Drug Use in America: Problem in Perspective*, second report (Washington, D.C.: U.S. Government Printing Office, 1973).

5. The fear of cocaine and of its potent effect on blacks was also responsible for many southern police departments issuing .38 caliber instead of the smaller .32 caliber pistols. See Musto, *op. cit.*, p. 7.

6. See Rufus King, *The Drug Hang-Up: America's Fifty-year Folly* (New York: Norton, 1972).

7. Musto, *op. cit.*

8. Act of November 2, 1951, 65 Stat. 767.

9. Musto, *op. cit.*, p. 231.

10. Act of July 18, 1956 (Narcotic Control Act of 1956 or the Boggs–Daniel Act), 70 Stat. 567.

11. See, for example, Richard M. Nixon, remarks in H.R. Exec. Doc. No. 131, 92d Cong., 1st Sess., 1971, at p. 11.

12. Act of October 27, 1970, P.L. 91–513, 84 Stat. 1236.

13. Edward M. Brecher, *Licit and Illicit Drugs* (Boston: Little, Brown and Co., 1972), p. 62.

14. See Leon G. Hunt and Norman E. Zinberg, *Heroin Use: A New Look* (Washington, D.C.: Drug Abuse Council, 1976).

15. U.S. Department of Justice Law Enforcement Assistance Administration and U.S. Bureau of the Census, *Expenditures and Employment Data for the Criminal Justice System, 1975* (Washington, D.C.: U.S. Government Printing Office, 1977), pp. 24–25. See also Permanent Subcommittee on Investigations of the Committee on Government Operations, U.S. Senate, *Federal Drug Enforcement*, (hearings), 94th Cong., 2d Sess., Part 5, p. 1113 (testimony of Peter Bensinger, DEA Administrator).

16. See Sibyl Cline and Peter Goldberg, *Governmental Response to Drug Abuse: The 1977 Federal Budget* (Washington, D.C.: Drug Abuse Council, 1976), pp. 17–18.

17. See Weldon T. Johnson and Robert Bogomolny, "Selective Justice: Drug Law Enforcement in Six American Cities," appendix to vol. 3, *Drug Use in America: Problem in Perspective* (Washington, D.C.: U.S. Government Printing Office, 1973), pp. 498 ff.

18. *Ibid.*

19. Hon. Lawrence H. Silverman, testimony before Permanent Subcommittee on Investigations of the Committee on Government Operations, U.S. Senate, *Federal Drug Enforcement* (hearings), 94th Cong., 1st Sess., Part 3 (Washington, D.C.: U.S. Government Printing Office, 1975), p. 755.

20. Permanent Subcommittee on Investigations of the Committee on Government Operations, *Federal Drug Enforcement: Interim Report of the Committee on Government Operations, U.S. Senate*, 94th Cong., 2d Sess., Report No. 94-1039 (Washington, D.C.: U.S. Government Printing Office, 1976), p. 43.

21. For an explanation of the DEA criteria used to designate Class I–IV violators, see Permanent Subcommittee on Investigations, *Federal Drug Enforcement*, Part 5, pp. 1050–1053.

22. Select Committee on Narcotics Abuse and Control, U.S. House of Representatives, *Congressional Resource Guide to the Federal Effort on Narcotics Abuse and Control, 1969–1976*, 94th Cong., 2d Sess., Part I (Washington, D.C.: U.S. Government Printing Office, 1978), p. 283.

23. Permanent Subcommittee on Investigations, *Federal Narcotics Enforcement*, p. 44.

24. Knapp Commission, *The Knapp Commission Report on Police Corruption* (New York: G. Braziller, 1973); New York State Commission of Investigation, *Narcotics Law Enforcement in New York City: A Report by the New York State Commission of Investigation* (New York: New York State Commission of Investigation, 1972).

25. Mark H. Moore, *Buy and Bust* (Lexington, Mass.: Lexington Books, 1977), p. 141.

26. See generally, Jay R. Williams et al., *Police Narcotics Control: Patterns and Strategies*, vol. I, report to Police Division, National Institute of Law Enforcement and Criminal Justice, LEAA, Grant No. 76-NI-99-0109 (Research Triangle Park, N.C.: Research Triangle Institute, 1978).

27. Moore, *op. cit.*, p. 168.

28. Wesley A. Pomeroy, *Police Chiefs Discuss Drug Abuse* (Washington, D.C.: Drug Abuse Council, 1974), p. 33.

29. Executive Order No. 11641, January 28, 1972.

30. *Washington Post*, September 8, 1974.

31. Edward Jay Epstein, *Agency of Fear* (New York: G.P. Putnam's Sons, 1977).

32. *Ibid.*, pp. 213–215.

33. *Ibid.*, pp. 219–224, 304–305.

34. Permanent Subcommittee on Investigations, *Federal Narcotics Enforcement*, pp. 27–29.

35. Permanent Subcommittee on Investigations, *Federal Narcotics Enforcement*, pp. 26, 32–33.

36. See, for example, Jack Anderson, "U.S. Studies How to Plug Border," *Washington Post*, April 7, 1978, p. C15.

37. Sibyl Cline Halper, *The Heroin Trade: From Poppies to Peoria* (Washington, D.C.: Drug Abuse Council, 1977), p. 2.

38. Select Committee on Narcotics Abuse and Control, *op. cit.*, p. 274.

39. See, for example, "$631 Million in Drugs Seized by Customs in '76," *Washington Post*, January 2, 1977.

40. Halper, *op. cit.*, p. 29.

41. See Permanent Subcommittee on Investigations, *Federal Narcotics Enforcement*.

42. "The Drug War," *Washington Monthly* (May 1971).

43. John Bartels, Jr., "Mexico as a Source of Illicit Heroin," unpublished study for the Drug Abuse Council, Washington, D.C., 1976, p. 13.

44. Epstein, *op. cit.*, pp. 81–85.
45. *Ibid.*
46. Permanent Subcommittee on Investigations, *Federal Drug Enforcement*, Parts 1 and 2.
47. Select Committee on Narcotics Abuse and Control, *op. cit.*, p. 274. Seizures of marijuana increased from 161,909 pounds in 1970 to 1,385,859 in 1976.
48. *Science*, vol. 200 (April 1978), pp. 417–418.
49. Halper, *op. cit.*, p. 2.
50. *Ibid.*, pp. 2–3.
51. *Ibid.*, pp. 5–15.
52. Telephone interview with Mathea Falco, Senior Advisor to the Secretary of State and Coordinator for International Narcotics Matters, March 1978; Sibyl Cline, *Turkish Opium in Perspective* (Washington, D.C.: Drug Abuse Council, 1974), p. 6.
53. Telephone interview with Office of Public Affairs, Drug Enforcement Administration, March 1978; Halper, *op. cit.*, p. 19.
54. Halper, *op. cit.*, p. 3 (chart).
55. *Ibid.*, pp. 21–22.
56. *Ibid.*, p. 21.
57. See, for example, George F. Brown, Jr., and Lester R. Silverman, *The Retail Price of Heroin: Estimation and Applications* (Washington, D.C.: Drug Abuse Council, 1973).
58. Bartels, *op. cit.*, p. 9.
59. Personal communication, Office of International Narcotics Control, Department of State, March 1978.
60. *Narcotics Control Digest*, vol. 8, no. 4 (February 27, 1978); personal communication, Office of International Narcotics Control, Department of State, March 1978.
61. Subcommittee to Investigate Juvenile Delinquency, Committee of the Judiciary, U.S. Senate, *Hearings*, October 18, 1977.
62. Personal communication, Office of International Narcotics Control, Department of State, March 1978.
63. Personal communication, Office of Public Affairs, Drug Enforcement Administration, March 1978.
64. *Narcotics Control Digest*, vol. 8, no. 4 (February 22, 1978), p. 7.
65. "U.S. Found in Violation of Law," *The Leaflet*, vol. 7, no. 2 (April–June 1978), p. 3.
66. Press release, Department of Health, Education, and Welfare (March 12, 1978).
67. National Commission on Marihuana and Drug Abuse, *op. cit.*, pp. 154–155.
68. Robert Shellow, *Drug Use and Criminal Behavior* (Washington, D.C.: Research Triangle Institute and National Institute on Drug Abuse, 1976).
69. Jared Tinklenberg, "Drugs and Crime," in appendix, vol. 1, *Drug Use in America: Problem in Perspective* (Washington, D.C.: U.S. Government Printing Office, 1973), p. 242 ff.; Personal communication from Dr. Tinklenberg, May 1978.
70. Shellow, *op. cit.*
71. Paul Danaceau, *What's Happening with Heroin Maintenance* (Washington, D.C.: Drug Abuse Council, 1977), p. 8.

72. William I. Barton, "Drug Histories of Prisoners: Survey of Inmates of State Correctional Facilities," paper presented at National Drug Abuse Conference 1976, New York, N.Y. (March 25–29, 1976), p. 1.

73. Shellow, *op. cit.*

74. John A. O'Donnell et al., *Young Men and Drugs—A Nationwide Survey*, National Institute on Drug Abuse Monograph Series, No. 5 (Washington, D.C.: U.S. Government Printing Office, 1976), p. 84.

75. Nelson Rockefeller, testimony at Joint Hearing before New York State Senate and Assembly Codes Committees, Albany, New York (January 30, 1973).

76. See Max Singer, "The Vitality of Mythical Numbers" in Jackwell Susman, ed., *Drug Use and Social Policy* (New York: AMS Press, 1972).

77. Federal Bureau of Investigation, U.S. Department of Justice, *Uniform Crime Reports for the United States, 1971* (Washington, D.C.: U.S. Government Printing Office, 1971), pp. 15, 21–22, 29.

78. Singer and Newitt, *Policy Concerning Drug Abuse in New York State*, vol. 1 (New York: Hudson Institute, 1970).

79. New York City Police Department, Crime Analysis Section, *Narcotics, 1971: Statistical Report* (1971).

80. New York City Police Department, Crime Analysis Section, *Narcotics, 1974: Statistical Report* (1974).

81. Epstein, *op. cit.*, pp. 35–45.

82. "Urban Crime and the Price of Heroin," *Journal of Urban Economics*, vol. 4 (1977), p. 101; *Heroin Supply and Urban Crime* (Washington, D.C.: Drug Abuse Council, 1976).

83. *Ibid.*

84. Brown and Silverman, *op. cit.*, p. 2.

85. Brecher, *op. cit.*, pp. 183–192.

86. Leon G. Hunt and Norman E. Zinberg, *op. cit.*

87. *Ibid.*

88. "Narcotic Addiction and Drug Abuse Programs," Domestic Council Decision Paper (March 19, 1971).

89. Joint Committee on New York Drug Law Evaluation, *The Nation's Toughest Drug Law: Evaluating the New York Experience* (New York: Association of the Bar of the City of New York; Drug Abuse Council, 1977), p. 3.

90. *Ibid.*, p. 4.

91. *Ibid.*, pp. 7–8.

92. *Ibid.*, pp. 9–12.

93. *Ibid.*, pp. 18–19.

94. *Ibid.*, pp. 90–91.

95. *Ibid.*, p. 25.

96. "Marijuana Survey—State of Oregon," annual survey of the Drug Abuse Council, Washington, D.C. (1974–1977). See Staff Paper 5, "Marijuana and Cocaine: The Process of Change in Drug Policy" for a more complete discussion of this point.

97. As reported in Epstein, *op. cit.*, pp. 186, 298.

98. Epstein, *op. cit.*, p. 186.

99. E.g., Hunt and Zinberg, *op. cit.*; Lee Robins et al., "Vietnam Veterans Three

Years After Vietnam: How Our Study Changed Our View of Heroin," in *Problems of Drug Dependence* (1977).

3. Heroin Treatment:
Development, Status, Outlook, pp. 95–125

1. National Institute on Drug Abuse, *Executive Report: Data from the National Drug Abuse Treatment Utilization Survey (NDATUS)*, Statistical Series, Series F, No. 5 (April 1978), p.iv.
2. *Ibid.*, Table 3, at p.7. (35.2 percent of the total 240,019 1978 drug treatment slots were for methadone maintenance.)
3. *Ibid.*
4. Karst J. Besteman, Deputy Director, National Institute on Drug Abuse, prepared statement to Select Committee on Narcotics Abuse and Control, U.S. House of Representatives, *Drug Abuse Treatment: Part I* (hearings), 95th Cong., 2d Sess. (June 14, 15, and 22, 1978), p. 132.
5. Charles Terry and Mildred Pellens, *The Opium Problem* (Montclair, N.J.; Patterson Smith, 1928, reprinted 1970), pp. 67–70.
6. David F. Musto, *The American Disease: Origins of Narcotic Control* (New Haven,: Yale University Press, 1973)
7. Terry and Pellens, *op. cit.*, p. 76.
8. Musto, *op. cit.*, pp. 77–78.
9. C. Yorke, "A Critical Review of Psychoanalytic Literature on Drug Addiction," *British Journal of Medical Psychology*, vol. 43 (1970), pp. 141–159.
10. Musto, *op. cit.*, pp. 54–68.
11. Terry and Pellens, *op. cit.*, pp. 30–32.
12. Musto, *op. cit.*, p. 151; Dan Waldorf et al., *Morphine Maintenance: The Shreveport Clinic, 1919–1923* (Washington, D.C.: Drug Abuse Council, 1974).
13. James V. DeLong, "Treatment and Rehabilitation," in *Dealing With Drug Abuse: A Report to the Ford Foundation* (New York: Praeger Publishers, 1972), p. 177.
14. Musto, *op. cit.*, p. 285 (n.40).
15. *Ibid.*, p. 182.
16. James V. DeLong, *op. cit.*
17. *Ibid.*, p. 177; see also Musto, *op. cit.*, p. 85.
18. Richard Schroeder, *The Politics of Drugs* (Washington, D.C.: Congressional Quarterly, 1975), p. 136.
19. See Lewis Yablonsky, *The Tunnel Back: Synanon* (New York: Macmillan Co., 1965).
20. DeLong, *op. cit.*, p. 191, p. 249 (n.34).
21. See William B. O'Brien, "Therapeutic Community and Drug Free Approaches to Treatment," in David Smith, ed., *A Multi-Cultural View of Drug Abuse* (Cambridge, Mass.: Schenkman, 1978), pp. 359–368.
22. *Ibid.*, pp. 361–363.

23. See pp. 115–116.

24. DeLong, *op. cit.*, p. 183.

25. *Ibid.*, pp. 185–188.

26. James M. H. Gregg, statement before select Committee on Narcotics Abuse and Control, U.S. House of Representatives *Review of LEAA Narcotics Funding* (hearings), 95th Cong., 1st Sess. (June 8, 1977).

27. David Zimmerman, "Narcotic Maintenance Has Been Tried in the U.S.," *U.S. Journal of Drug and Alcohol Dependence*, vol. 1, no.8 (1977), p.3; and Vincent P. Dole, *Journal of the American Medical Association*, vol. 220, no.11 (1972), p. 1493.

28. R. d'Alarcon, "The Spread of Heroin Abuse in a Community," *Bulletin on Narcotics*, vol. 21 (July–September, 1969), pp. 17–22.

29. "Vietnam Servicemen: 30,000 to 40,000 Heroin Addicts", in *1971 CQ Almanac*, 27th Annual, (Washington, D.C.: Congressional Quarterly, 1972), p. 571.

30. See "The Federal Government's Response to Illicit Drugs 1969–1978", appendix A: A Budget Perspective, Chart I, at p. 77.

31. National Institute on Drug Abuse, *Executive Report: Data from the National Drug Abuse Treatment Utilization Survey (NDATUS)*, Statistical Series, Series F (1976,1977).

32. Norman E. Zinberg, "The Crisis in Methadone Maintenance," *The New England Journal of Medicine*, vol. 296, no. 17 (1977), pp. 1000–1002; Vincent P. Dole and Marie E. Nyswander, "Methadone Maintenance Treatment: A Ten-Year Perspective," *Journal of the American Medical Association*, vol. 235, no. 19 (May 10, 1976), pp. 2117–2119.

33. Lee Robins, *A Follow-up of Vietnam Drug Users*, Special Action Office on Drug Abuse Prevention Monograph Series A, No. 1, April 1973 (Washington, D.C.; U.S. Government Printing Office, 1973).

34. Eleanor Holmes Norton, *Employment and the Rehabilitated Addict: Employment Experience and Recent Research Findings* (Washington, D.C.: Drug Abuse Council, 1973), p.v (Foreword).

35. *Standards for Drug Abuse Treatment and Rehabilitation Programs* (Chicago: Joint Commission on Accreditation of Hospitals, 1975, revised 1978).

36. See Section 403(a) of the Drug Abuse Office and Treatment Act of 1972 (P.L. 92-255, 84 Stat. 65) for the provision requiring all Single State Agencies to formulate licensing or accreditation procedures.

37. See for example, W. Vazquez and I. Ford, *Credentialling: A Handbook for Substance Abuse Workers* (Washington, D.C.: Career Development Center, Center for Human Services, 1978).

38. Health Resources Administration, U.S. Department of Health, Education, and Welfare, *Drug Abuse: A Technical Assistance Manual for Health Systems Agencies* (Washington, D.C.: U.S. Government Printing Office, 1978); and P.A.C.E. Management, *Health Systems Planning and Drug Abuse Programming* (Washington, D.C.: National Institute on Drug Abuse, 1978).

39. L. S. Goodman and Alfred Gilman, *The Pharmacological Basis of Therapeutics*, 5th edition (New York: MacMillan Co., 1975), pp. 256, 269.

40. W. Ling, et al., "Methadyl Acetate and Methadone as Maintenance Treatments for Heroin Addicts: A Veteran's Administration Cooperative

Study," *Archives of General Psychiatry*, vol. 33 (1976), pp. 709–720; *Three Times a Week LAAM: Alternative to Methadone*, NIDA Monograph Series 8, J. Blaine and P. Renault, eds. (1976), p. 127.

41. J. Blaine, et al., "Chemical Use of LAAM," *Annals of the New York Academy of Science*, vol. 311 (1978), pp. 214–231.

42. Francis Gearing, "Proceedings of the Second National Methadone Maintenance Conference, New York," *International Journal of the Addictions*, vol. 5 (September 1970).

43. James Maddox and Charles Bowden, "Critique of Success with Methadone Maintenance," *American Journal of Psychiatry*, vol. 129, no. 4 (October 1972), pp.100–106.

44. Institute of Behavioral Research, Texas Christian University, "CODAP Data: Special Analysis of the 1976 File for the Drug Abuse Council," manuscript on file at the Drug Abuse Council, Washington, D.C. (1978).

45. Maddox and Bowden, *op. cit.*

46. *Drug Treatment in New York City and Washington, D.C.: Follow-up Studies* (Washington, D.C.: U.S. Public Health Service, National Institute on Drug Abuse, 1977), DHEW Publication (ADM) 77-506; and *Interdrug–Final Report: An Evaluation of Treatment Programs for Drug Abusers* (Baltimore: Johns Hopkins University School of Hygiene and Public Health, 1974).

47. B. Stimmel et al., "The Prognosis of Patients Detoxified from Methadone Maintenance: A Follow-up Study," in *Proceedings of the Fifth National Conference on Methadone Maintenance* (New York:NAPAN, 1973), pp.720–4; and J. Chappel et al., "Techniques of Withdrawal from Methadone and Their Outcomes over Six Months to Two Years," in *ibid.*, pp. 482–489.

48. Vincent P. Dole and Herman Joseph, "Methadone Maintenance: Outcome after Termination," *N.Y. State Journal of Medicine* (August 1977), pp. 1409–1412.

49. *Ibid.*, at p. 1411.

50. *Ibid.*, at pp. 1410–1411.

51. Addiction Research Foundation, "Five Year Follow-up of Santa Clara County Methadone Maintenance Patients: Final Report to the State Office of Narcotics and Drug Abuse," unpublished report to the Drug Abuse Council, Washington, D.C. (February 7, 1978).

52. *Ibid.*, Table 2a.

53. *Ibid.*, Table 2a.

54. Robert G. Newman, *Methadone Treatment in Narcotics Addiction* (New York: Academic Press, 1977) pp. 155–174.

55. *Ibid.*, p. 245.

56. *Ibid.*, p. 244.

57. E. Compo et al., "Evaluation of the 21-day Outpatient Heroin Detoxification," *International Journal of the Addictions*, vol. 12, no. 7 (1977), p. 925.

58. *Ibid.*, pp. 930–932.

59. Newman, *op. cit.*, p. 245.

60. Edward Senay et al., "Withdrawal from Methadone Maintenance," *Archives of General Psychiatry*, vol. 34, no. 3 (1977), pp. 361–367.

61. M. S. Gold, D. E. Redmond, and H. D. Kleber, "Clonidine Blocks Acute

Opiate-Withdrawal Symptoms," *The Lancet*, vol. 2, (1978), pp. 599–601.

62. *Narcotics Antagonists: Naltrexone Progress Report*, NIDA Monograph Series 9, D. Julius and P. Renault, eds. (Washington, D.C.: U.S. Government Printing Office, 1976), p. 181; National Research Council Committee, "Clinical Evaluation of Naltrexone Treatment of Opiate-Dependent Individuals," *Archives of General Psychiatry*, vol. 35 (1978), pp. 335–340.

63. P. Renault, "Treatment of Heroin-Dependent Persons with Antagonists: Current Status," *Bulletin on Narcotics*, vol. 30, no. 2 (1978), pp. 21–29; R. B. Resnick and A. M. Washton, "Clinical Outcome with Naltrexone: Prediction Variables and Follow-up Status of Detoxified Heroin Addicts," *Annals of the New York Academy of Sciences*, vol. 311 (1978), pp. 241–248; and David C. Lewis et al., "Narcotic Antagonist Treatment: Clinical Experience with Naltrexone," *International Journal of the Addictions*, vol. 13, no. 6 (1978), pp. 961–973.

64. National Drug Abuse Treatment Utilization Survey (NDATUS), April 1978.

65. Douglas K. Spiegel and Saul B. Sells, *Evaluation of Treatments for Drug Users in the DARP: 1969–1971 Admissions*, IBR Report #73-10 (Fort Worth, Texas: Texas Christian University Institute of Behavioral Research, 1973).

66. Institute of Behavioral Research, *op. cit.*

67. *Ibid.*

68. E. Slotkin, *Gateway's Success in the Rehabilitation of Drug Abusers* (Chicago: Gateway Foundation, 1973), p. 4.

69. M. Collier and Y. Hijazi, "A Follow-up Study of Former Residents of a Therapeutic Community," *International Journal of the Addictions*, vol. 9., no. 6, (1974), pp. 805–826.

70. Richard N. Bale, William W. Van Stone, John M. Kuldan, Thomas M. J. Engelsing and Vincent P. Zarcone, "Preliminary Two Year Follow-up Results from a Randomized Comparison of Methadone Maintenance and Therapeutic Communities," in David Smith, ed. *A MultiCultural View of Drug Abuse* (Cambridge, Mass.: Schenkman, 1978), p. 4.

71. Institute of Behavioral Research, *op. cit.*

72. William H. McGlothlin et al., *An Evaluation of the California Civil Addict Program*, DHEW Pub. (ADM)78-558 (Rockville, Md.: National Institute on Drug Abuse, 1977).

73. See, for example, R, Harford et al., "Effects of Legal Pressure on Prognosis for Treatment of Drug Dependence," *American Journal of Psychiatry*, vol. 133 (1976), pp. 1399–1404; and Joseph Perpich et al., "Criminal Justice and Voluntary Patients in Treatment for Heroin Addiction," paper presented at the National Issues and Strategies Symposium on the Drug Abusing Criminal Offender, Reston, Virginia (April 21–23, 1976); and Graham S. Finney, *Drugs: Administering Catastrophe* (Washington, D.C.; Drug Abuse Council, 1975), pp. 106,112.

74. Herman Joseph and Vincent P. Dole, "Methadone Patients on Probation and Parole," *Federal Probation* (June 1970), Table 4.

75. *Drug Use and Crime: Report of the Panel on Drug Use and Criminal Behavior*, (Washington, D.C.: National Institute on Drug Abuse, 1976), p. 60.

76. Dale K. Sechrest, *The Criminal Behavior of Drug Program Patients* (Cambridge, Mass.: Center for Criminal Justice, Harvard Law School, 1975).

77. Peter Stoloff, Daniel Levine, and Nancy Spruill, *Public Drug Treatment and Addict Crime*, (Arlington, Va.: Public Research Institute of the Center for Naval Analyses, 1975), p.14.

78. Dale K. Sechrest, "Methadone Programs and Crime Reduction: A Comparison of New York and California Addicts," *International Journal of the Addictions*, vol. 14, no. 3 (to be published during 1979).

79. DeLong, *op. cit.*, p.214.

80. Hugh Ward, *Employment and Addiction: Overview of the Issues* (Washington, D.C.: Drug Abuse Council, 1973), p.33.

81. National Institute on Drug Abuse, *Annual Summary Report, 1976*, Statistical Series E. No. 4 (Washington, D.C.: U.S. Government Printing Office, 1978), p.10.

82. National Institute on Drug Abuse, *Quarterly Report 1977*, Statistical Series D, No. 2 (Washington, D.C.: U.S. Government Printing Office, 1977), p. 21.

83. John Helmer, *Drugs and Minority Oppression* (New York: Seabury Press, 1975).

84. *Drug Use and Crime, op. cit.*, p. 60.

85. "Proposed Narcotic Treatment Program Standards and Methadone in Maintenance and Detoxification," *Federal Register* (October 28, 1977); and 21 C.F.R., Part 291, pp. 56896–56913.

86. Rehabilitation Act of 1973, 29 U.S.C. 701, at 504. See 42 *Federal Register* 22686 for the analysis of the act by the Department of Health, Education, and Welfare, which concluded that "drug addicts and alcoholics" are clearly included within the act's intended coverage.

87. Saul B. Sells, P. Person and G. Joe, "Comparison of Behavior Indices of Methadone Maintenance Patients Who Remain in Treatment with Those of Patients Who Drop Out Early," unpublished research report at Institute of Behavioral Research, Texas Christian University, Fort Worth, Texas (1972); George Vaillant, "A Twelve-Year Follow-Up of New York Narcotic Addicts: Some Characteristics and Determinants of Abstinence," *American Journal of Psychiatry*, vol. 123, no.5 (November 1966), pp. 573–585, at 576.

88. W. G. Double and L. Koenigsberg, "Private Employment and the Ex–Drug Abuser: A Practical Approach," *Journal of Psychedelic Drugs*, vol. 9, no. 1 (1977), pp. 51–58: and Louis Liberman, "The Receptivity of Large Corporations to Employ Ex-Addicts," *Journal of Psychedelic Drugs*, vol. 8, no. 4 (1976), pp. 285–289.

89. Vera Institute of Justice, *Another Approach to Welfare: Putting the Recipients and the Money to Work* (New York: Vera Institute of Justice, 1975), p. 8.

90. *Ibid.*, p. 8.

91. Dole and Joseph, *op. cit.*, p. 1411; Addiction Research Foundation, *op. cit.*, Table 2a.

92. Dole and Joseph, *op. cit.*, p. 1411.

93. Addiction Research Foundation, *op. cit.*, Table 2a. Note that "daily" is defined here as "one month or more of daily use during the year."

94. John O'Donnell, "The Relapse Rate in Narcotic Addiction: A Critique of Follow-up Studies," *Narcotic Addiction Control Commission Reprints*, vol. 2, no. 1 (1968).

95. *Ibid.*

96. Institute of Behavioral Research, *op. cit.*
97. George Vaillant, "A Twelve-Year Follow-up of New York Narcotic Addicts: I. The Relation of Treatment to Outcome," *American Journal of Psychiatry*, vol. 122 (1966), pp. 727–737, at p. 730.
98. *Ibid.*

4. The Influence of Public Attitudes and Understanding on Drug Prevention, pp. 126–152

1. Norman E. Zinberg and John A. Robertson, *Drugs and the Public* (New York: Simon and Schuster, 1972), pp. 29–30.
2. *Ibid.*
3. A particularly thorough and recent evaluation of drug prevention and education programs is Eric Shaps et al., "Primary Prevention Evaluation: A Review of 127 Program Evaluations," study sponsored by National Institute on Drug Abuse, Pacific Institute for Research and Evaluation (March, 1978).
4. U.S. Cabinet Committee on Drug Abuse Prevention, Treatment, and Rehabilitation, *Recommendations for Future Federal Activities in Drug Abuse Prevention*, report of the Subcommittee on Prevention (Washington, D.C.: U.S. Government Printing Office, 1977), pp. 1–2.
5. Seymour Halleck, "The Great Drug Education Hoax," *The Progressive*, vol. 34 (1970), p. 2.
6. Patricia M. Wald and Annette Abrams, "Drug Education," in *Dealing with Drug Abuse: A Report to the Ford Foundation* (New York: Praeger Publishers, 1972), p. 125.
7. *Ibid.*, pp. 125–26.
8. Nicholas Dorn and Anne Thompson, "Evaluation of Drug Education in the Longer Term is Not an Optional Extra," *Community Health*, vol. 7 (1976), p. 155.
9. *Drug Abuse Films* (Washington, D.C.: National Coordinating Council on Drug Education, 1973).
10. Michael S. Goodstadt, "Myths and Mythologies in Drug Education: A Critical Review of the Research Evidence," *Research on Methods and Programs of Drug Education* (Toronto: Addiction Research Foundation of Ontario, 1974), p. 122.
11. See, for example, Goodstadt, *op. cit.*, and James A. Kline, "Evaluation of a Multimedia Drug Education Program," *Journal of Drug Education*, vol. 2, no. 3 (1972), pp. 229–239.
12. National Commission on Marihuana and Drug Abuse, *Drug Use in America: Problem in Perspective*, Second report (Washington, D.C.: U.S. Government Printing Office, 1973), p. 357.
13. *Ibid.*
14. *Ibid.*
15. U.S. Cabinet Committee on Drug Abuse Prevention, Treatment, and Rehabilitation, *op. cit.*, p. 6.
16. *Ibid.*
17. *Ibid.*, p. 9

18. *Ibid.*
19. See, for example, the discussion of drug prevention in the "Report of the Liaison Task Panel on Psychoactive Drug Use/Misuse," appendix to *Report to the President from the President's Commission on Mental Health*, vol. IV (Washington, D.C.: U.S. Government Printing Office, 1978), pp. 2030–37.
20. See Office of Drug Abuse Policy, *Drug Use Patterns, Consequences, and the Federal Response: A Policy Review*, March 1978, p. 97.
21. *Washington Post*, March 22, 1978, p. 1 and *Washington Post* April 13, 1978, p. C3.
22. United States District Court, Eastern District of Pennsylvania, Montgomery County, Morristown: Civil Act. #72-2057, Michael Merriken et al. v. Wilmer B. Kressman et al., signed by Honorable John Morgan Davis, September 28, 1975.
23. *Survey of City/County Drug Abuse Activities: 1972* (Washington, D.C.: Drug Abuse Council, 1973), pp. 14–15.
24. *Ibid.*, p. 58.
25. Yankelovich, Skelly, and White, Inc. *Students and Drugs: A Report of the Drug Abuse Council* (Washington, D.C.: Drug Abuse Council, 1975), p. 47.
26. See, for example, Michael S. Goodstadt, *op. cit.*; John D. Swisher and Richard E. Horman, "Drug Abuse Prevention," *Journal of College Student Personnel* (September 1970), pp. 337–41.; John Swisher and Richard Horman, "Effecting Drug Attitude Change in College Students via Induced Cognitive Dissonance," Pennsylvania State University, 1972.
27. Richard H. Blum, *Drug Education: Results and Recommendations* (Lexington, Mass.: Lexington Books, 1976), pp. 53–54.
28. Goodstadt, *op. cit.*
29. *Ibid.*, p. 125; also, see R. Carney, "An Evaluation of the Effect of a Values-Oriented Drug Abuse Education Program Using the Risk of Taking Attitude Questionnaire," Coronado Unified School District, Coronado, Calif., 1972 (mimeographed).
30. Betty Swift, Nicholas Dorn, and Anne Thompson, *Evaluation of Drug Education: Findings of a National Research Study of Effects on Secondary School Students of Five Types of Lessons Given by Teachers* (London: Institute for the Study of Drug Dependence, 1974), p. 15.
31. Goodstadt, p. 142. However, a more recent NIDA-sponsored review of 127 drug prevention programs found them to be "slightly effective on the average" in influencing drug use behavior and attitudes (Eric Schaps et al., *op. cit.*).
32. National Commission on Marihuana and Drug Abuse, *op. cit.*, p. 376.
33. See *Drug Use in America: Problem in Perspective*, *op. cit.*; *Public Experience with Psychoactive Substances: A Nationwide Survey Among Adults and Youth* (Princeton, N.J.: Response Analysis Corporation, 1975), prepared for the National Institute on Drug Abuse; *Nonmedical Use of Psychoactive Substances: 1975/6 Nationwide Study Among Youth and Adults* (Princeton, N.J.: Response Analysis Corporation, 1976).
34. *Ibid.*
35. *Ibid.*
36. *Ibid.*
37. *Ibid.*

38. Bureau of Social Science Research, *The Metropolitan Washington Heroin Test Film: Its Impact on the Audience*, (Washington, D.C.: Bureau of Social Science Research, 1974), Appendix C, p. 32.

39. Drug Abuse Council, files.

40. Public Law #148, passed May 7, 1906.

41. David Musto, *The American Disease: Origins of Narcotics Control* (New Haven: Yale University Press, 1973), pp. 219–243. In particular, Musto's discussion notes only two federal drug treatment facilities and the very light emphasis historically given to treatment facilities in the federal budget.

42. Essentially, because the drug treatment facilities have historically been so few, physicians had very little access to drug treatment training.

43. John Pekkanen, "The Impact of Promotion on Physician's Prescribing Patterns," *Journal of Drug Issues*, vol. 6, no. 1 (Winter 1976). In particular, see reference to physician drug education and formal training in pharmacology and psychopharmacology.

44. See, for example, the discussion of medical definitions of abuse in Norman E. Zinberg, Wayne M. Harding, and Robert Apsler, "What is Drug Abuse?" *Journal of Drug Issues*, vol. 8, no. 1 (1978), pp. 15–17.

45. Pekkanen, *op. cit.*

46. *Ibid.*

47. Norman E. Zinberg, "Defining and Developing Substance Use Curricula," speech delivered to the National Conference on Medical Education in Alcohol and Drug Abuse, November 16, 1978 (Washington, D.C.).

48. Pekkanen, *op. cit.*

49. *Ibid.*

50. *Ibid.*

51. *Ibid.*

52. *Ibid.*

53. See "Report of the Liaison Task Panel on Psychoactive Drug Use/Misuse," pp. 2135–36.

54. 1974 Supplement to F. Lee Bailey and Henry B. Rothblatt, *Handling Narcotic and Drug Cases* (Rochester, N.Y.: The Lawyers' Cooperative Publishing Co., 1972), p. 3.

55. Nicholas N. Kittrie, "The History of Drug Control Laws: American Aspects," *John Marshall Journal of Practice and Procedure*, vol. 9, no. 1 (Fall 1975), p. 52.

56. See *Proceedings of the National Issues and Strategies Symposium on the Drug Abusing Criminal Offender* (Washington, D.C.: National Institute on Drug Abuse, 1976).

57. See the discussion of the heroin (drug)-crime relationship in Staff Paper 6, "American Heroin Policy: Some Alternatives," below.

58. Joint Committee on New York Drug Law Evaluation, *The Nation's Toughest Drug Law: Evaluating the New York Experience* (New York: Association of the Bar of the City of New York; and the Drug Abuse Council, 1977), p. 30.

59. See "Report of the Interdisciplinary Committee on Heroin and Other Controlled Substances," unpublished report, Minnesota State Bar Association (March 19, 1977).

60. Warren G. Brantley, "Attitudes Toward Marijuana Among Law Students: The South's Future Lawyers," unpublished report, Minnesota State Bar Association (March 19, 1977).

61. See Wesley A. Pomeroy, *Police Chiefs Discuss Drug Abuse* (Washington, D.C.: Drug Abuse Council, 1974).

62. Samuel F. Levine, *Narcotics and Drug Abuse*, Criminal Justice Text Series (Cincinnati: N. H. Anderson Company, 1973), p. 353.

63. *Wall Street Journal*, May 26, 1977, p. 42.

64. *Ibid.*

65. Edward M. Davis, "The Narcotics Problems," editorial, *The Police Chief* (March 1977), p. 8.

66. See Robert P. Bomboy, *Major Newspaper Coverage of Drug Issues* (Washington, D.C.: Drug Abuse Council, 1974); and Allan Parachini, *Reporter's Guide: Drugs, Drug Abuse Issues, Resources* (Washington, D.C.: Drug Abuse Council, 1976).

67. Allan Parachini as quoted in Bomboy, *op. cit.*, p. 26.

68. Zinberg and Robertson, *op. cit.*, p. 30.

69. Patricia M. Wald and Peter Barton Hutt, "The Drug Abuse Survey Project: Summary of Findings, Conclusions and Recommendations," in *Dealing with Drug Abuse: A Report to the Ford Foundation*, p. 39.

70. Bomboy, *op. cit.*, pp. 1–4.

71. See E. H. Kramer, "A Review of Literature Relating to the Impact of the Broadcast Media on Drug Use and Abuse," appendix to National Commission on Marihuana and Drug Abuse, *op. cit.*, vol. 2, pp. 586–611.

72. Donald E. Payne, "The Relationship Between Television Advertising and Drug Abuse Among Youth: Fancy and Fact," *Journal of Drug Education*, vol. 6, no. 3 (1976), p. 219.

73. Barry Peterson, Judith Kuriansky et al., "Television Advertising and Drug Use," *American Journal of Public Health*, vol. 66, no. 10 (1976), p. 975.

74. Barcus, Goldstein, and Pinto, "Drug Advertising on Television," Appendix to National Commission on Marihuana and Drug Abuse, *op. cit.*, vol. 2, pp. 623–668.

75. Richard Heffner Associates, "Over-the-Counter Drug Commercials: Network Television, Spring 1971," Appendix to *ibid.*, vol. 2, pp. 669–97.

76. William J. McEwen and Gerhard J. Hanneman, "The Depiction of Drug Use in Television Programming," *Journal of Drug Education*, vol. 4, no. 3 (1974), pp. 281–93.

77. One of the most active and forceful critics of drug advertising on television has been the Council on Children, Media, and Merchandising, 1346 Connecticut Avenue, N.W., Room 523, Washington, D.C. 20036.

78. National Commission on Marihuana and Drug Abuse, *op. cit.*, pp. 389–91.

79. See, for example, "Petition to Issue a Trade Regulation Rule Governing the Private Regulation of Children's Television Advertising," Council on Children, Media, and Merchandising, filed before the Federal Trade Commission, 1975.

80. *Federal Register*, vol. 41, no. 247 (December 22, 1976), pp. 55740–42.

81. McEwen and Hanneman, *op. cit.*, p. 285.

82. See F. Earle Barcus and Susan M. Jankowski, "Drugs and the Mass Media," *Annals of the American Academy of Political and Social Science*, vol. 417 (1975), p. 91.

83. Gerhard Hanneman, as cited in Barcus and Jankowski, *op. cit.*, p. 90.

84. McEwen and Hanneman, *op. cit.*, p. 290.

85. Charles Winnick, "A Content Analysis of Drug Related Network Entertainment Prime Time Programs, 1970–72," *Drug Use in America: Problem in Perspective*, Appendix to National Commission on Marihuana and Drug Abuse, *op. cit.*, vol. 2, pp. 698–708.

86. It is interesting to note that in its 1973 Report the National Commission on Marijuana and Drug Abuse explicitly took issue with its own name and recommended that the term "drug abuse" be "deleted from official pronouncements and public policy dialogue." The commission explained that such an amorphous concept, "with its emotional overtones, will serve only to perpetuate confused public attitudes about drug-using behavior." See Norman E. Zinberg, Wayne M. Harding, and Robert Apsler, *op. cit.*, problems with the term "drug abuse."

87. National Commission on Marihuana and Drug Abuse, *op. cit.*, p. 13.

88. Edward M. Brecher, *Licit and Illicit Drugs* (Boston: Little, Brown and Co., 1972), p. 526.

89. "Report of the Liaison Task Panel on Psychoactive Drug Use/Misuse," p. 2132.

90. See, for instance, Yankelovich, Skelly and White, Inc., *op. cit.*

91. National Commission on Marihuana and Drug Abuse, *op. cit.*, pp. 93–98.

92. See, for example Office of Drug Abuse Policy, *op. cit.*

5. Marijuana and Cocaine: The Process of Change in Drug Policy, pp. 153–189

1. National Institute on Drug Abuse, *Survey of Non-Medical Use of Psychoactive Substances* (Princeton, N.J.: Response Analysis Corporation, 1976).

2. Lloyd Johnston, Jerald Bachman, and Patrick O'Molley, "Monitoring the Future: A Continuing Study of the Lifestyles and Values of Youth," statement to the press from University of Michigan Institute for Social Research (November 23, 1976).

3. National Institute on Drug Abuse, *op. cit.*, p. 29.

4. *Ibid.*, p. 29 (Table 2.2).

5. *Ibid.*, p. 39 (Table 2.6).

6. *Ibid.*, pp. 28–29 (Tables 2.1 and 2.2).

7. *Ibid.* pp. 36–37 (Tables 2.5 and 2.6).

8. *Ibid.*, p. 36 (Table 2.5).

9. *Ibid.* pp. 36–37 (Tables 2.5 and 2.6).

10. Lloyd Johnston et al., *op. cit.*

11. L. Blackford, *Student Drug Use Survey—San Mateo County, California 1968–1976* (San Mateo, Calif. Department of Public Health and Welfare, 1976). Cited in Secretary of Health, Education, and Welfare, *Marijuana and Health: Sixth Annual Report to Congress* (Washington, D.C.: U.S. Government Printing Office, 1976), at p. 8.

12. Secretary of Health, Education, and Welfare, *op. cit.*

13. National Institute on Drug Abuse, *op. cit.*, p. 51.

14. National Commission on Marihuana and Drug Abuse, *Marihuana: A Signal of Misunderstanding*, first report (Washington, D.C.: U.S. Government Printing Office, 1972), p. 7.

15. National Institute on Drug Abuse, *op. cit.*, p. 51.

16. *Ibid.*, p. 51.

17. *Ibid.*; see also "Marijuana Survey—State of Oregon," press releases, Drug Abuse Council, Washington, D.C. (1974–1977).

18. Richard J. Bonnie and Charles H. Whitebread, *Marihuana Conviction: A History of Marihuana Prohibition in the United States* (Charlottesville: University Press of Virginia, 1974), pp. 222–223.

19. Act of November 2, 1951 (Boggs Act), 65 Stat. 767.

20. Act of July 18, 1956 (Boggs-Daniel Act), 70 Stat. 567.

21. Bonnie and Whitebread, *op. cit.*, pp. 212–215.

22. See Arthur D. Hellman, *Laws Against Marijuana: The Price We Pay* (Urbana: University of Illinois Press, 1975) and John Kaplan, *Marijuana: The New Prohibition* (World Publishing Co., 1970).

23. Hellman, *op. cit.*; Kaplan, *op. cit.*

24. See National Commission on Marihuana and Drug Abuse, *op. cit.*, pp. 91–102.

25. 18 U.S.T. 1408 (1967).

26. Act of October 27, 1970, P.L. 91-513, 84 Stat. 1236.

27. Bonnie and Whitebread, *op. cit.*, pp. 225–256.

28. National Commission on Marihuana and Drug Abuse, *op. cit.*

29. National Commission on Marihuana and Drug Abuse, *Drug Use in America: Problem in Perspective*, second report (Washington, D.C.: U.S. Government Printing Office, 1973).

30. National Commission on Marihuana and Drug Abuse, *op. cit.* (1972), p. 102.

31. *Ibid.*, p. 125.

32. *Ibid.*, p. 129.

33. *Ibid.*, p. 131.

34. Robert Carr, "The Pot Vote," *Human Behavior* (May 1976), pp. 56–60.

35. O.R.S. §§167.207 ff., as amended by House Bill No. 2936 (1973).

36. Secretary of Health, Education and Welfare, *op. cit.*, p. 20.

37. *Ibid.*

38. Vera Rubin and Lambros Comitas, *Ganja in Jamaica: A Medical Anthropological Study of Chronic Marijuana Use* (The Hague and Paris: Mouton, 1975).

39. P. Satz et al., "Neuropsychologic, Intellectual and Personality Correlates of Chronic Marijuana Use in Native Costa Ricans," in Rhea L. Dornbush, Alfred M. Freedman, and Max Fink, eds., *Chronic Cannabis Use*, Annals of the New York Academy of Sciences, vol. 282 (New York: New York Academy of Sciences, 1976), pp. 266–306.

40. Rhea L. Dornbush and Anna Kokkevi, "Acute Effects of Cannabis on Cognitive, Perceptual and Motor Performance in Chronic Hashish Users," in *ibid.*, pp. 313–322.

41. John Kuehnle et al., "Compulect Tomographic Examination of Heavy

Marijuana Smokers," *Journal of the American Medical Association*, vol. 237 (1977), pp. 1231–1232.

42. Ben T. Co, et al., "Absence of Cerebral Atrophy in Chronic Cannabis Users," *Journal of the American Medical Association*, vol. 237 (1977), pp. 1229–1230.

43. A.M.G. Campbell et al., "Cerebral Atrophy in Young Cannabis Smokers," *Lancet*, vol. 2, no. 7736 (1971), pp. 1219–1224.

44. Lester Grinspoon, "Marijuana and Brain Damage: A Criticism of the Study of A.M.G. Campbell et al.," *Contemporary Drug Problems*, vol I, no. 4 (1972), pp. 811–814, at p. 813.

45. *Ibid.*, p. 812.

46. Harold Kolansky and William T. Moore, "Toxic Effects of Chronic Marijuana Use," *Journal of the American Medical Association*, vol. 222, no. 1 (October 2, 1972); Kolansky and Moore, "Effects of Marihuana on Adolescents and Young Adults," *Journal of the American Medical Association*, vol. 216, no. 3 (April 19, 1971), pp. 486–492.

47. Kolansky and Moore, *op. cit.* (1972).

48. *Ibid.*

49. Robert G. Heath, "Marihuana: Effects on Deep and Surface Electro-encephalograms of Rhesus Monkeys," *Neuropharmacology* (1973), pp. 1–14. Also reported in Subcommittee to Investigate the Administration of the Internal Security Act and Other Internal Security Laws of the Committee on the Judiciary, U.S. Senate, *Marijuana-Hashish Epidemic and Its Impact on United States Security (hearings)*, 93d Cong., 2d Sess., May–June 1974 (Washington, D.C.: U.S. Government Printing Office, 1975), pp. 356–369.

50. Heath, *op. cit.*

51. Subcommittee to Investigate the Administration of the Internal Security Act, *op. cit.*

52. Secretary of Health, Education, and Welfare, *Marihuana and Health: Third Annual Report to Congress* (Washington, D.C.: U.S. Government Printing Office, 1973).

53. Secretary of Health, Education, and Welfare, *op. cit.*, (1976), p. 19.

54. Gabriel G. Nahas, et al., "Inhibition of Cellular Mediated Immunity in Marihuana Smokers," *Science*, vol. 183 (February 1974), pp. 419–420.

55. Secretary of Health, Education, and Welfare, *op. cit.*, (1976), p. 16

56. *Ibid.*

57. *New York Times*, Letter to the Editor, (May 31, 1973).

58. Steven G. White et al., "Nitrogen-induced Blastogenic Responses of Lymphocytes from Marihuana Smokers," *Science*, vol. 188 (1975), pp. 71–72.

59. Melvin J. Silverstein and Phyllis J. Lessin, "Normal Skin Test Responses in Chronic Marijuana Users," *Science*, vol. 186 (1974), pp. 740–741.

60. *Ibid.*

61. Norman E. Zinberg, unpublished memorandum, February 7, 1974.

62. Secretary of HEW, *op. cit.* (1976), p. 16.

63. Morton A. Stenchever et al., "Chromosome Breakage in Users of Marihuana," reprint article, *American Journal of Obstetrics and Gynecology* (January 1, 1974).

64. W. W. Nichols et al., "Cytogenic Studies on Human Subjects Receiving Marihuana and delta-9 Tetrahydrocannabinol," *Mutation Research*, vol. 26 (July 1974).
65. *Ibid.*
66. Secretary of HEW, *Marihuana and Health: Fourth Annual Report to Congress* (Washington, D.C.: U.S. Government Printing Office, 1974).
67. E.g., Rubin and Comitas, *op. cit.*
68. Robert C. Kolodny et al., "Depression of Plasma Testosterone Levels After Chronic Intensive Marijuana Use," *New England Journal of Medicine*, vol. 290 (1974), pp. 872–874.
69. Jack H. Mendelson et al., "Plasma Testosterone Levels Before, During, and After Chronic Marihuana Smoking," *New England Journal of Medicine*, vol. 291 (1974), pp. 1050–1055
70. Robert C. Kolodny, statement of May 16, 1974 before the subcommittee, in Subcommittee to Investigate the Administration of the Internal Security Act, *op. cit.*, pp. 117–126.
71. Norman E. Zinberg, "The War Over Marijuana," *Psychology Today* (December 1976), pp. 45–52, 102–106.
72. Lester Grinspoon, statement before the Select Committee on Narcotics Abuse and Control, U.S. House of Representatives (March 15, 1977).
73. W.J. Coggins et al., "Health Status of Chronic Heavy Cannabis Users," in Dornbush, Freedman, and Fink, eds., *op. cit.*, pp. 148–161.
74. Secretary of HEW, *Marihuana and Health: Fifth Annual Report to Congress* (Washington, D.C.: U.S. Government Printing Office, 1975).
75. Rubin and Comitas, *op. cit.*, p. 87.
76. Grinspoon, *op. cit.* pp. 231–233.
77. Abraham Wikler, "Aspects of Tolerance to and Dependence on Cannabis," in Dornbush, Freedman, and Fink, eds., *op. cit.*, pp. 126–147.
78. Secretary of HEW, *op. cit.* (1975), p. 6.
79. Rubin and Comitas, *op. cit.*
80. C. Stefanis et al., "Experimental Observations of A Three-Day Hashish Abstinence Period and Reintroduction of Use," in Dornbush, Freedman, and Fink, eds., *op. cit.*, pp. 113–120.
81. *Final Report of the Commission on Inquiry into the Non-Medical Use of Drugs* (Ottawa: Information Canada, 1973).
82. Joel S. Hochman and Norman Q. Brill, "Chronic Marijuana Use and Psychosocial Adaptation," *The American Journal of Psychiatry*, vol. 130 (1973), pp. 132–140.
83. See Zinberg, *op. cit.* (1976).
84. Secretary of HEW, *op. cit.* (1976).
85. Secretary of HEW, *op. cit.* (1975), p. 127.
86. Secretary of HEW, *Marihuana and Health: First Annual Report to Congress* (Washington, D.C.: U.S. Government Printing Office, 1971).
87. *Final Report of the Commission of Inquiry*, p. 307.
88. National Commission on Marihuana and Drug Abuse, *op. cit.* (1972), pp. 90–91.
89. Hochman and Brill, *op. cit.*; and Norman Q. Brill and Richard L. Christie, "Marihuana Use and Psychosocial Adaptation," *Archives of General Psychia-*

try, vol. 31 (1974), pp. 713–719; G.D. Mellinger et al., "The Amotivational Syndrome and the College Student," in Dornbush, Freedman, and Fink, *op. cit.*, pp. 37–55.

90. Rubin and Comitas, *op. cit.*

91. William E. Carter and Paul L. Doughty, "Social and Cultural Aspects of Cannabis Use in Costa Rica," in Dornbush, Freedman, and Fink, *op. cit.*, pp. 2–16.

92. Lambros Comita, "Cannabis and Work in Jamaica: A Refutation of the Amotivational Syndrome," in Dornbush, Freedman, and Fink, *op. cit.*, pp. 26–27.

93. *Ibid.*, p. 28.

94. George Gallup, Three-Part Series Analyzing Results of a Survey on Marijuana Use and Attitudes (Princeton, N.J., May 15–17, 1977).

95. John A. O'Donnell et al., *Young Men and Drugs—A Nationwide Survey*, National Institute on Drug Abuse Research Monograph Series, No. 5 (Washington, D.C.: U.S. Government Printing Office, 1976).

96. *Ibid.*

97. *Ibid.*

98. "Marihuana and Public Safety," appendix (technical papers), Vol. 1 of National Commission on Marihuana and Drig Abuse, *op. cit.* (1972), p. 426.

99. *Ibid.* p. 441.

100. *Ibid.*, p. 470.

101. Jared R. Tinklenberg and Kenneth M. Woodrow, "Drug Use Among Youthful Assaultive and Sexual Offenders," *Aggression*, vol. 52 (1974), p. 221.

102. The states are California (for up to 1 oz.), Colorado (for up to 1 oz.), Ohio (for up to 20 gms.), and Minnesota (up to 1½ ozs.).

103. *The Marijuana Laws: Federal, State, and Local Penalties and Related Materials* (Washington, D.C.: The Center for the Study of Non-Medical Drug Use, 1976, 1977 supplement), pp. 7–16.

104. *Ravin* v. *State*, 537 P.2d 494 (1975).

105. For a good review of constitutional challenges to marijuana laws, see Soler, "Of Cannabis and the Courts: A Critical Examination of Constitutional Challenges to Statutory Marijuana Prohibitions," 6 *Conn. L. Rev.* 601 (1974).

106. *Survey of Cities Over 30,000 in Population and Other Selected Cities to Determine Local Drug Abuse Needs and Priorities* (Washington, D.C.: National League of Cities and U.S. Conference of Mayors, 1976).

107. "Marijuana Survey—State of Oregon," press releases, Drug Abuse Council, Washington, D.C. (January 4, 1978, January 28, 1977, December 1, 1975, and December 15, 1974).

108. J. Pat Horton, statement of November 20, 1974 to subcommittee, in Subcommittee on Alcoholism and Narcotics of the Committee on Labor and Public Welfare, U.S. Senate, Marihuana Research and Legal Controls 1974 93d Cong., 2d Sess. (Washington, D.C.: U.S. Government Printing Office, 1974), p. 131.

109. *Effects of the Oregon Laws Decriminalizing Possession and Use of Small*

Quantities of Marijuana (Office of Legislative Research, State of Oregon, December 31, 1974).

110. *Ibid.*
111. National Institute on Drug Abuse, *op. cit.*
112. *First Report on the Impact of California's New Marijuana Law*, (SB95) (Sacramento: State Office of Narcotics and Drug Abuse, Health and Welfare Agency, 1977).
113. *Ibid.*
114. *Marijuana Research Findings: 1976*, Robert C. Petersen, ed., NIDA Research Monograph 14 (Washington, D.C.: U.S. Government Printing Office, 1977), p. 10.
115. National Institute on Drug Abuse, *op. cit.*, p. 114.
116. Gallup, *op. cit.*
117. Johnston, *op. cit.*
118. Drug Abuse Council, "National Survey of Marijuana Use and Attitudes," press release, Washington, D.C. (October 1974).
119. E.g., Robert L. DuPont, "Marihuana: Our Next Step," speech to Psychiatric Institute Foundation, Washington, D.C. (February 4, 1977); see also House Bill 2574, Oregon Legislative Assembly (1975 Regular Session).
120. Gallup, *op. cit.*
121. Lee Dogoloff and Peter G. Bourne, "Cocaine Policy: Past, Present and Future," paper presented to the American Association for the Advancement of Science, Washington, D.C. (February 1978).
122. National Institute on Drug Abuse, *op. cit.*
123. Johnston, *op. cit.*
124. Domestic Council Drug Abuse Task Force, *White Paper on Drug Abuse* (Washington, D.C.: U.S. Government Printing Office, 1975).
125. Dogoloff and Bourne, *op. cit.*
126. See R. T. Martin, "The Role of Coca in the History, Religion and Medicine of South American Indians," *Economic Botany*, vol. 24, no. 4 (1970), pp. 422–438.
127. See Lester Grinspoon and James E. Bakalar, *Cocaine: A Drug and Its Social Evolution* (New York: Basic Books, 1976), pp. 17–44.
128. *Cocaine: 1977*, Robert C. Peterson and Richard C. Stillman, eds., NIDA Research Monograph No. 13 (Washington, D.C.: U.S. Government Printing Office, 1977).
129. *Ibid.*, at pp. 153–192.
130. *Ibid.*, at pp. 97–118.
131. Dan Waldorf et al., *Doing Coke: An Ethnography of Cocaine Users* (Washington, D.C.: Drug Abuse Council, 1977).
132. Andrew T. Weil, "Coca Leaf as a Therapeutic Agent," *American Journal of Drug and Alcohol Abuse*, vol. 5, no. 1 (1978), pp. 75–86.
133. See Robert Byck and Craig Van Dyke, "What are the Effects of Cocaine in Man?" in Peterson and Stillman, eds., *op. cit.*, pp. 97–118; and Donald R. Wesson and David E. Smith, "Cocaine: Its Use for Central Nervous Systems Stimulation, Including Recreational and Medical Uses," in *ibid.*, pp. 137–152. See also Rich and Ashley, *Cocaine: Its History, Uses and Effects*

(New York: St. Martin's Press, 1975); and James Wood, "Behavioral Effects of Cocaine in Animals" in Peterson and Stillman, eds., *op. cit.*, pp. 63–95.

134. Andrew Weil, *The Natural Mind* (Boston; Houghton Mifflin, 1972).
135. Ronald K. Siegel, "Cocaine Recreational Use and Intoxication," in Peterson and Stillman, eds., *op. cit.*, at pp. 129–133.
136. *Ibid.*
137. Weil, *op. cit.*
138. Peterson and Stillman, eds., *op. cit.*: see also Domestic Council Drug Abuse Task Force, *op. cit.*
139. Grinspoon and Bakalar, *op. cit.*, pp. 222–231.
140. Siegel, *op. cit.*; and Waldorf, *op. cit.*
141. Grinspoon and Bakalar, *op. cit.*, p. 108.
142. Bryan S. Finkle and Kevin L. McCloskey, "The Forensic Toxicology of Cocaine," in Peterson and Stillman, eds., *op. cit.*, pp. 153–192; and Wesson and Smith, *op. cit.*
143. See, for example, J. A. O'Donnell, *op. cit.*
144. See, for example, Waldorf's ethnographic study of cocaine use in the San Francisco area (Waldorf, *op. cit.*).
145. *Ibid.*
146. Siegel, *op. cit.*
147. Peterson and Stillman, eds., *op. cit.*, Foreword by editors.
148. *Ibid.*, p. 10.

6. American Heroin Policy: Some Alternatives, pp. 190–247

1. Donald Phares, "Between a Rock and a Hard Place: What T' Do 'Bout Smack," *Journal of Psychedelic Drugs*, vol. 7, no. 1 (Jan.–March 1975), p. 620
2. See Constance Holden, "A New Look at Heroin Could Spur Better Medical Use of Narcotics," *Science*, vol. 198, no. 4319 (Nov. 25, 1977), pp. 807–809; Michael Satchell, "How to Enjoy Life—Up to the Last Minute," *Parade* (October 16, 1977); "Hospices: For the Dying, Relief from Pain and Fear," *Science*, vol. 193, no. 4251 (July 30, 1976), pp. 389–391. See also, "Heroin Use Considered," *National Health Lawyers Association News Report*, vol. 5, no. 10 (October 1977); Arthur C. Upton (Director, National Cancer Institute), statement for NBC's "Meet-the-Press" (October 1977); "Carter to HEW: Consider Heroin for Very Ill," *Washington Star* (November 9, 1977), p. 1; and "U.S. Health Officials to Study Heroin, Marijuana Medical Use," *Washington Post* (November 10, 1977).
3. Paul Danaceau, *What's Happening with Heroin Maintenance?* (Washington, D.C.: Drug Abuse Council, 1977), pp. 12–17.
4. Bruce D. Johnson, "How Much Heroin Maintenance (Containment) in Britain?" *International Journal of the Addictions*, vol. 12, no. 2–3 (1977), p. 361 ff.; Horace F. Judson, *Heroin Addiction in Britain* (New York: Harcourt, Brace Jovanovich, 1974); and Edgar May, "Narcotic Addiction and Control

in Great Britain," in *Dealing with Drug Abuse: A Report to the Ford Foundation* (New York: Praeger Publishers, 1972).

5. 42 *Federal Register* 56897 (October 28, 1977), at p. 56906, proposed revision of 21 *C.F.R.* 291.505(d) (10) (ii).

6. See Leon G. Hunt and Norman E. Zinberg, *Heroin Use: A New Look* (Washington, D.C.: Drug Abuse Council, 1976); the discussion of ten-year series of surveys of drug using by San Mateo County, California junior and senior high school students (grades 7–12) in Leon Hunt, "Evolution of Drug Abuse in Population of Youths," *Youthful Drug Abuse in the United States* (Washington, D.C.: Foundation for International Resources, 1975); Leon G. Hunt and Carl D. Chambers, *The Heroin Epidemic: A Study of Heroin Use in the U.S. 1965–1975* (New York: Spectrum Publications, 1976); Lee Robins et al., "Vietnam Veterans Three Years After Vietnam: How Our Study Changed Our View of Heroin," in *Problems of Drug Dependence* (Proceedings of the Committee on Problems of Drug Dependence), edited by L. Hains (Richmond, Virginia: Committee on Problems of Drug Dependence, 1977); and Peter G. Bourne et al., *A Study of Heroin Use in the State of Wyoming* (Washington, D.C.: Foundation for International Resources, 1975).

7. National Commission on Marihuana and Drug Abuse, *Drug Use in America: Problem in Perspective* (Washington, D.C.: U.S. Government Printing Office, 1973), pp. 30–32.

8. "History of Alcohol Prohibition," appendix Vol. III of National Commission on Marihuana and Drug Abuse, *op. cit.*, pp. 508–511.

9. M.H. Tillit, *The Price of Prohibition* (New York: Harcourt Brace & Co., 1932), pp. 35–36. See also, M. V. Rosenbloom, *The Liquor Industry: A Survey of Its History, Manufacture, Problems of Control and Importance* (Braddock: Ruffsdale Distilling Co., 1937), pp. 51–52.

10. See E. Burton, *The Pageant of Georgian England*, pp. 214–216; and L. Kronenberger, *The Extraordinary Mr. Wilkes* (New York: Doubleday Books, 1974), pp. 104–112.

11. R. K. Heimann, *Tobacco and Americans* (New York: McGraw-Hill, 1960), pp. 210–211; U.S. Public Health Service, *Adult Use of Tobacco* (Washington, D.C.: U.S. Government Printing Office, 1977); T. Bewley, "Smoking: The 16th and 17th Century Response," *International Journal of the Addictions*, vol. 8, no. 1 (1973).

12. *Washington Post*, February 11, 1978.

13. The idea that excessive consumption can be predicted from per capita levels of use has been a standard theory in the field for some time. This theory holds that the form of consumption distribution is stable and virtually universal for any given drinking population. Therefore, as the mean (or per capita consumption) increases, the fraction of the drinking population above some arbitrary "excessive level" would increase directly. (See S. Lederman, *Alcohol, Alcoolisme, Alcoolisation*, Cahier No. 29 [Presses Universitaires de France, 1956].) However, more recent and reliable research disputes the fundamental basis for this theory. (See N. Smith, "Research Note on the Lederman Formula and its Recent Applications," *The Drinking and Drug Practices*

Surveyor [Berkeley, Calif.: Social Research Group, 1976], No. 12, pp. 15–22.) Consumption and cirrhosis rate (related to heavy sustained drinking) are highly correlated, both within a single population over time and among different populations at the same time. (World Health Organization Expert Committee on Drug Dependence, *Twentieth Report*, Report Series, No. 551 [Geneva: World Health Organization, 1974], pp. 61–62; J. deLint and N. Schmidt, "The Epidemiology of Alcohol," in Y. Israel and J. Mardones, eds., *Biological Basis of Alcoholism*, [New York: Witey-Interscience, 1971], pp. 423–428. Cirrhosis rate matches average per capita consumption, which is, of course, fairly obvious. But per capita consumption, which is a looser measure, since it includes nondrinkers, is also correlated with cirrhosis rate. However, we cannot conclude from either of these indices that the proportion of heavy drinkers has increased with average consumption.

Per capita consumption is just the total volume of taxed alcohol divided by the size of some population. It could rise for two reasons: because more people were drinking the same average amount as before, or because the same number of people were drinking a greater average amount. Similarly, it could fall either because there were fewer drinkers or because the same drinkers were drinking less. Note that if alcoholics drank less, both per capita consumption and cirrhosis deaths would fall simultaneously, since studies have shown that abstinence enormously improves the longevity of even advanced cirrhosis cases. Conversely, if the same alcoholics drank more, both consumption and deaths would rise together. However, some researchers (e.g., Cahalan) state that heavy drinkers account for about two-thirds of all alcohol consumed, and therefore we might conclude that it is the amount of drinking alcoholics and not the size of the alcoholic population that varies when per capita consumption figures change. (D. Cahalan, "Can Alcoholism Be Defeated?" *The Sciences* [publ. New York Academy of Sciences], March /April 1977.)

14. See sources cited in note 6 above.
15. See, for example, Edward M. Davis, "The Narcotics Problem, *Police Chief* (March 1977), p. 8; and Eugene Hollingsworth, speech presented at Symposium on Heroin Abuse and the Law, San Francisco, California (May 4, 1977).
16. See Danaceau, *op. cit.*, pp. 4–5.
17. Peter G. Bourne, *Methadone: Benefits and Shortcomings* (Washington, D.C.: Drug Abuse Council, 1975), pp. 15–16.
18. *Ibid.*
19. Much of the material on American morphine and heroin clinics is drawn from an unpublished research paper written for the Drug Abuse Council by Troy Duster in November 1977, which in turn draws from research done for Dr. Duster's book, *The Legislation of Morality* (New York: Free Press, 1970).
20. For opposing viewpoints on the clinics, see *Annual Report of the Commissioner of Internal Revenue for the Fiscal Year Ended June 30, 1920* (Washington, D.C.: U.S. Government Printing Office, 1920); and Lindsmith, Alfred, *The Addict and the Law* (Bloomington: Indiana University Press, 1965).
21. Arrest statistics for narcotics law violations during the periods in which the

clinics operated and immediately following their closing lend some support—although not indisputable—to the viewpoint that the maintenance clinics helped to contain the problem at reasonably low levels, whereas the subsequent prohibitionary approach led to rapidly escalating numbers of arrests.

In 1918, the year before any clinics were opened, 888 federal arrests and 392 convictions for narcotics offenses were reported. In 1919, the year in which the New York Clinic operated and others were opened, arrests totalled 1,008 and convictions 582. In 1920, when the clinics (including the one in New York) were being closed, arrests rose to 3,477 and convictions to 908. In 1921, when the Prohibition Commissioner reported in June that all clinics were closed (with one exception), arrests had risen further to 4,014 and convictions to 1,583. The yearly rise continued to a peak in 1925—when the clinics had been closed for several years—with 10, 297 federal arrests and 5,600 convictions. (From Lindesmith, *op. cit.*, p. 143.)

22. Johnson, *op. cit.*, pp. 362–363. See also Martin Mitcheson and Richard Hartnoll, "A Controlled Comparison of Injected Heroin and Oral Methadone as Maintenance Treatment of Heroin Addiction," paper delivered at National Drug Abuse Conference 1977, San Francisco, Calif. (May 1977). "Overall, prescribing heroin can be seen as maintaining the status quo with a majority of HM (heroin maintenance) patients. ..."

23. Johnson, *op. cit.*, p. 392; H. B. Spear, "The British Experience," *John Marshall Journal of Practice and Procedure* 1 (Fall 1975), p. 93; Judson, *op. cit.*, pp. 139–140.

24. Joint Committee on New York Drug Law Evaluation, *The Nation's Toughest Drug Law: Evaluating the New York Experience* (New York: Association of the Bar of the City of New York; and the Drug Abuse Council, 1977).

25. Drug Abuse Council, "Marijuana Survey—State of Oregon," press release, (January 4, 1978).

26. See Norman E. Zinberg and Robert C. Jacobsen, *The Social Basis of Drug Abuse Prevention* (Washington, D.C.: Drug Abuse Council, 1974); and Norman E. Zinberg and Kathleen M. Fraser, "The Role of the Social Setting in the Prevention and Treatment of Alcoholism," pp. 20–21, for an examination of the alcohol prohibition period in the United States.

27. Leon G. Hunt and Carl D. Chambers, *op. cit.*; and Hunt and Zinberg, *op. cit.*

28. The bases for such beliefs, conjectures, and calculations are usually not clear or explicit and, if identifiable, are almost without exception open to debate; yet they have formed the underpinnings of many of our social policies for dealing with drug abuse." (Robert Shellow, *Drug Use and Crime Behavior* [Washington, D.C.: Research Triangle Institute; and National Institute of Drug Abuse, U.S. Department of Health, Education, and Welfare, 1976], p. 4.)

29. Brent L. Rufener et al., *Final Report: Management Effectiveness Measures for NIDA Drug Abuse Treatment Programs*, Vol. II, Costs to Society of Drug Abuse (Research Triangle Park, N.C.: Research Triangle Institute, 1976), p. A9.

30. For an excellent discussion of the development of American heroin and drug

laws, see David F. Musto, *The American Disease: Origins of Narcotic Control* (New Haven: Yale University Press, 1973).

31. *Ibid.*, p. 134.
32. See, for example, "History of Alcohol Prohibition," of National Commission on Marihuana and Drug Abuse, *op. cit.*, Appendix, vol. III, pp. 503–505; Act of November 2, 1951 (Boggs Act), 65 Stat. 767; Act of June 27, 1952 (Immigration and Nationality Act) 66 Stat 206; and Richard Nixon, Message to Congress (June 17, 1971): "This deadly poison [heroin] in the American lifestream is, in other words, a foreign import."
33. "The habit of the narcotics addict is not only a danger to himself, but a threat to the community where he lives. Narcotics have been cited as a primary cause of the enormous increase in street crime over the last decade. As the addict's tolerance for drugs increases, his demand for drugs rises, and the cost of his habit grows. It can easily reach hundreds of dollars a day. ... An addict can be forced to commit two or three burglaries a day to maintain his habit. Street robberies, prostitution, even the enticing of others into addiction to drugs—an addict will reduce himself to any offense, any degradation in order to acquire the drugs he craves." (Richard M. Nixon, "Proposal for Combating Drug Abuse," Message to the House of Representatives from the President of the United States, House Document No. 91–138 (June 14, 1969). In 1971 the estimate of the value of "addict" street crimes for the nation was $2 billion. (Richard Nixon, Message to Congress, [June 17, 1971].) By 1973 the federal government had increased the estimate to $6.7 billion. (*Connection* 1–3) Institute for Social Concerns [November–January 1974], p. 9.) State officials joined in the numbers game with New York State's Governor Nelson Rockefeller, proclaiming that in his state alone during 1973 addicts were responsible for $6.5 billion a year in thefts. (Nelson Rockefeller, testimony at joint hearing before New York State Assembly Codes Committees [Albany, New York], January 30, 1973.) These absurd mythical numbers were produced by multiplying inflated estimates of "addicts" by the highest conceivable level of heroin use and assuming that addicts' income came only from illegal sources. (Max Singer, "The Vitality of Mythical Numbers," in Jackwell Sussman, ed., *Drug Use and Social Policy*, (New York: AMS Press, 1972), p. 171 ff.)
34. Shellow, *op. cit.*: and Jared Tinklenberg, "Drugs and Crime," appendix Vol. 1 of National Commission on Marihuana and Drug Abuse (1973), *op. cit.*, p. 242 ff.
35. Stephanie Greenberg and Freda Adler, "Crime and Addiction: An Empirical Analysis of the Literature, 1920–1973," *Contemporary Drug Problems*, vol. 3 (Summer 1974).
36. Shellow, *op. cit.*, p. 22.
37. Paula H. Kleinman and Irving F. Lukoff, "The Magic Fix: A Critical Analysis of Methadone Maintenance Treatment," *Social Problems* (December 1977), pp. 208–214.
38. *Heroin Supply and Urban Crime* (Washington, D.C.: Drug Abuse Council, 1976).
39. Joint Committee on New York Drug Law Evaluation, *op. cit.*, Table 6, pp. 61–63.

40. See Dan Waldorf, *Morphine Maintenance: The Shreveport Clinic 1919–1923* (Washington, D.C.: Drug Abuse Council, 1974); and Troy Duster, *The Legislation of Morality* (New York: Free Press, 1970).

41. Kleinman and Lukoff, *op. cit.*, pp. 212–214; Francis Gearing, "Methadone Maintenance Treatment Five Years Later—Where are They Now?" *American Journal of Public Health Supplement*, no. 64 (1974), pp. 44–49.

42. The head of the federal Government's National Institute on Drug Abuse has stated, "If heroin were available over the counter, it would cost a penny a milligram compared with two dollars a milligram on the street now." ("Legalized Heroin Held 'Disastrous'," *Washington Post*, April 22, 1976).

43. This discussion is based on material contained in "History of Alcohol Prohibition," appendix Vol. 3 of National Commission on Marihuana and Drug Abuse (1973), *op. cit.*, pp. 511–512.

44. See Commission on the Review of the National Policy Toward Gambling, *Gambling in America*, final report (Washington, D.C.: U.S. Government Printing Office, 1976), especially pp. 5–9.

45. See Lindesmith, *op. cit.*; and Waldorf, *op. cit.*

46. Lee N. Robins and G. E. Murphy, "Drug Use in a Normal Population of Young Negro Men," *American Journal of Public Health*, no. 570 (1967), pp. 1580–1596.

47. Avram Goldstein, "High on Research," *U.S. Journal of Drug and Alcohol Dependence* (October 1977).

48. Leon Hunt, *op. cit.*

49. Peter G. Bourne, et al., *op. cit.*; Hunt and Zinberg, *op. cit.*

50. Drug Abuse Council, "Marijuana Survey—State of Oregon," press release, (January 4, 1978).

51. The information on the pre-1968 experiences with heroin use in the United Kingdom comes from Edgar May, *op. cit.* pp. 345–394. See also Judson, *op. cit.*, at pp. 3–62.

52. Bourne, *op. cit.*, p. 11.

53. *Statistical Series: Quarterly Report* ("Data from the Client Oriented Data Acquisition Process [CODAP]"), Series D, No. 2, January–March 1977 (Washington, D.C.: National Institute on Drug Abuse, 1977), Table 6, p. 13.

54. For example, see "Virginia Schools Using Undercover Police to Combat Drugs," *Washington Post*, March 22, 1978, p. 1.

55. This approach was recommended by the National Commission on Marihuana and Drug Abuse. See National Commission, *op. cit.*, pp. 206–207.

56. For discussion of recent heroin maintenance proposals, see Paul Danaceau, *op. cit.*

57. Peter G. Bourne, "Techniques of Drug Treatment," John W. Umstead Lecture delivered to North Carolina Department of Human Resources on February 11, 1976.

58. See, for example, Lee Robins et al., *op. cit.*, pp. 5–7.

59. Martin C. Mitcheson, "Maintenance Treatment of Heroin Addiction in Great Britain, 1977," paper presented at Symposium on Heroin Abuse and the Law (May 4, 1977), San Francisco, Calif.

60. August Bequai, "Developing a Legal Heroin Maintenance Program," *Police Law Quarterly*, vol. 7, no. 1 (1977), pp. 34–46.
61. Personal communication from Norman E. Zinberg (November 1977).
62. Weldon T. Johnson and Robert Bogomolny, "Selective Justice: Drug Law Enforcement in Six American Cities," appendix to Vol. 3 of National Commission, *op. cit.*, p. 577.
63. "Overcharging" refers to the practice of charging the person arrested with the highest possible offense. For example, a person arrested for possessing a small quantity of drugs may be charged with "possession with intent to distribute" instead of "simple" possession.
64. Federal Bureau of Investigation, U.S. Department of Justice, *Crime in the United States 1976*, Uniform Crime Reports (Washington, D.C.: U.S. Government Printing Office, 1976), Table 24, p. 173.
65. Johnson and Bogomolny, *op. cit.*, pp. 502–506.
66. FBI, *op. cit.*, p. 173.
67. Strategy Council on Drug Abuse, *Federal Strategy for Drug Abuse Traffic Prevention* (Washington, D.C.: U.S. Government Printing Office, 1976). This declared that heroin trafficking had federal drug law enforcement priority.
68. FBI, *op. cit.*, p. 173.
69. *Ibid.*, Table 54, p. 217.
70. Johnson and Bogomolny, *op. cit.*; see also Richard T. Bonnie and Weldon T. Johnson, *Selective Justice: The Production and Processing of Drug Arrests in Six American Cities*, Part 3, unpublished manuscript for Drug Abuse Council, 1975.
71. Johnson and Bogomolny, *op. cit.*, p. 548.
72. *Ibid.*, Table 17, p. 549.
73. *Ibid.*, Table 21, p. 565.
74. *Ibid*, p. 572.
75. *Ibid.*
76. *Ibid.*, p. 576.
77. William I. Barton, "Drug Histories of Prisoners: Survey of Inmates of State Correctional Facilities," paper presented at the National Drug Abuse Conference 1976, New York City (March 25–29, 1976), p. 1.
78. Peter L. Nacci *et al.*, "Probation Density and Inmate Misconduct Rates in the Federal Prison System," *Federal Probation*, vol. 41, no. 2 (June 1977), p. 26.
79. Neil M. Singer and Virginia B. Wright, *Cost Analysis of Correctional Standards: Institutional-Based Programs and Parole* (Washington, D.C.: National Institute of Law Enforcement and Criminal Justice, 1976), p. 10.
80. David L. Bazelon, "Street Crime and Correctional Paroles," *Federal Probation*, vol. 41, no. 1 (March 1977), p. 6.
81. Per bed construction cost of a high-security state prison is approximately $41,014; local jails are somewhat less costly, at an average of $27,342 per bed. Federal facilities generally cost as much or more than the average state prison to construct. An adult inmate in a state prison costs approximately $9,439 a year (in 1974 dollars), while a local jail inmate costs $7,041 per year (also 1974 dollars). (See Neil M. Singer and Virginia B. Wright, *op. cit.*)

82. Johnson and Bogomolny, *op. cit.*, Table 26, p. 573.

83. *Crime and Delinquency Literature* (publ. National Council on Crime and Delinquency, Hackensack, N.J.) vol. 8, no. 2 (June 1976), p. 176.

84. Johnson and Bogomolny, *op. cit.*, p. 576.

85. Diversion of drug treatment is more expensive than the average probation or parole supervision. One study estimates diversion costs to range between $1,331 to $4,490 per client year. (Ann M. Watkins, *Cost Analysis of Correctional Standards: Pretrial Diversion*, Vol. 1 [Washington, D.C.: National Institute of Law Enforcement and Criminal Justice, 1975], Figure 8, p. 52 and Notes, Appendix C-2.) The cost per referral ranges between an average low estimate of $665 to a high of $1,643. (*Ibid.*, Vol. 2, Figure 4, p. 33.) These costs reflect only the costs of having a referral and tracking agency in the criminal justice system to divert various drug offenders. The cost of actual treatment is in addition to these costs. Treatment cost is variable, depending upon the specific treatment modality employed. For instance, drug-free residential community treatment has been estimated to cost $6,254 per client year. Outpatient methadone, on the other hand, is estimated to cost between $1,300 and $2,100 per client year.

86. Danaceau, *op. cit.*, p. 4.

87. Hunt and Chambers, *op. cit.*, pp. 87–91. This is not to say that the *treatment* program population overlaps heroin users who appear in the criminal justice system. In fact, one study found that only 18 percent of treated users appeared in police records in Phoenix, Arizona. See *The Problem of Drug Abuse in the City of Phoenix, Arizona* (Washington, D.C.: Drug Abuse Council, 1975).

88. See Judson, *op. cit.*

89. Judson, *op. cit.*, at p. 91 quotes former British Home Secretary Roy Jenkins: "The thing that struck me first and most forcibly in the U.S., however, was the link—only too obvious a link—between addiction and crime. Such a link did not exist in this country [Britain], and to go out of the way to create such a link seemed self-evidently foolish."

90. See Lindesmith, *op. cit.*; Duster, *op. cit.*; and Waldorf, *op. cit.*

91. The National Commission on Marijuana and Drug Abuse's study found at least 50 percent of present possession arrests to be for amounts involving an eighth of an ounce (3⅓ grams) or less. Johnson and Bogomolny, *op. cit.*, pp. 527–534.

92. *Ibid.*, pp. 522–523 (see especially Table 9, p. 522).

93. *Ibid.*, p. 518.

94. *Ibid.*, p. 521.

95. Of arrests involving drug buys, 44 percent were for $100 or less; only 4 percent exceeded $1000. *Ibid.*, pp. 524–525.

96. See Edward Preble and J. H. Casey, Jr. "Taking Care of Business—The Heroin User's Life on the Street," *International Journal of the Addictions*, vol. 4, no. 1 (March 1969), pp. 1–24.

97. *The Knapp Commission Report on Policy Corruption*, (New York: G. Braziller, 1973); and *Narcotics Law Enforcement in New York City: A Report by the New York State Commission of Investigation* (New York: New York State Commission of Investigation, 1972).

98. Peter K. Manning and Lawrence T. Redlinger, "Invitational Edges of Corruption: Some Consequences of Narcotic Law Enforcement," in Paul E. Rock, ed. *Drugs and Politics* (New Brunswick, N.J.: Transaction Books, 1977) at p. 290 ff. Official documents substantiate these charges. See, for example, *The Knapp Commission Report*, pp. 91–92; *Narcotics Law Enforcement in New York City*, pp. 122–203; and President's Commission on Law Enforcement and Administration of Justice, *Task Force Report: The Police* (Washington, D.C.: U.S. Government Printing Office, 1967), pp. 208–215.

99. Commission on the Review of the National Policy Toward Gambling, *op cit.*, pp. 40–42.

100. *Ibid.*, pp. 39–40.

101. See, for example, the discussion on the attitudes of police and other criminal justice officials in New York City in Joint Committee on New York Drug Law Evaluation, *op. cit.*, pp. 116–121.

102. See Domestic Council Drug Abuse Task Force, *White Paper on Drug Abuse: A Report to the President* (Washington, D.C.: U.S. Government Printing Office, 1975), p. 39.

103. Thomas S. Szasz, "The Ethics of Addiction," in Jackwell Susman, ed., *Drug Use and Social Policy* (New York: AMS Press, 1972), at p. 594 makes the following comment: "We are exceedingly reluctant to hold people responsible for their misbehavior; this is why we prefer diminishing rights to increasing responsibilities. The former requires only the passing of laws, which can then be more or less freely violated or circumvented, whereas the latter requires prosecuting and punishing offenders, which can be accomplished only by just laws justly enforced. The upshot is that we increasingly substitute tender-hearted tyranny for tough-spirited liberty."

104. *See* George Annas, *The Rights of Hospital Patients* (1975), pp. 100–102; see also Subcommittee on Health and the Environment, Committee on Labor and Public Welfare, U.S. Senate, *Quality of Health Care—Human Experimentation 1973* (hearings), 93rd Cong., 1st Sess. (1973), pp. 843–863.

105. See 45 *C.F.R.* 46.101(c) (1977) requiring that subjects "be able to exercise free power of choice, without undue inducements or any elements of force, fraud, deceit, illness, or other form of constraint or coercion."

106. See 21 *C.F.R.* 1316.21 and 40 *F.R.* 27802 (July 1, 1978); "Confidentiality of Alcohol and Drug Abuse Patient Records").

107. 42 *F.R.* 31461-31462 (June 7, 1977).

108. *In the Matter of Karen Ann Quinlan*, 70 N.J. 10, 355 A.2d 647 (1976).

109. *Rutherford* v. *U.S.*, 399 F. Supp. 1208 (W.D. Okla. 1975); *Aff'd*, 542, F.2d 1137 (10th Cir. 1976); *Rizzo* v. *U.S*, 422 F. Supp. 356 (E.D.N.Y., 1977).

110. *Olmstead* v. *U.S.*, 277 U.S. 438, 478 (Justice Brandeis in dissent).

111. *Stanley* v. *Georgia*, 394 U.S. 557 (1969).

112. *Griswold* v. *Connecticut*, 381 U.S. 479 (1965).

113. *Eisenstadt* v. *Baird*, 405 U.S. 438 (1972).

114. *Roe* v. *Wade*, 410 U.S. 113 (1973).

115. *Ravin* v. *State*, 537 P.2d 494, 43 USLW 2502 (Alaska S. Ct., 1975; unanimous decision).

116. *State* v. *Erikson*, p.2d, 46 USLW 2409 (Alaska S. Ct., 1978). Other states have rejected the argument with regard to marijuana. See *State* v. *Kantor*,

53 Haw. 327, 493 P.2d 306 (Haw. S. Ct., 1972), *cert. den.* 409 U.S. 948 (1972); *State* v. *Murphy*, 46 USLW 2224 (Ariz. S. Ct., 1977); and U.S. Supreme Court *dictum* in 394 U.S. 557, at 568.

117. *Robinson v. California*, 370 U.S. 660, *reh. den.*, 371 U.S. 905 (1962).

118. *Davis v. Davis*, 21 Cr. L. Rep. 2157, 45 USLW 2542 (U.S.D.C., W. Va., 1977); *Downey v. Perini*, 518 F.2d 1288 (6th Cir., 1975), vacated on other grounds, 423 U.S. 933, 44 USLW 330. But cf., *People v. Broadie*, 44 USLW 2009 (N.Y. Ct. App., 1975).

119. See, for example, *United States* v. *Moore*, 486 F.2d 1139 (D.C. Cir. 1973), *cert. den.*; 414 U.S. 980 (1973).

120. *Whalen* v. *Roe*, S. Ct. 890, 45 USLW 4166 (1977).

121. E.g., *Eisenstadt v. Baird*, 405 U.S. 438 (1972). Also, a District of Columbia court recently concluded that a person using marijuana could not be convicted of the offense upon the showing of a "medical necessity" to prevent advancing blindness caused by glaucoma. See *U.S.* v. *Randall*, 20 Cr. L. Rep. 2299, 104 Daily Wash. L. Rep. 2246 (D.C. Super. Ct., 1976).

122. Edward M. Brecher and editors of Consumer Reports, *Licit and Illicit Drugs* (Boston: Little, Brown and Co., 1972), pp. 21–32. See also Jerome H. Jaffe, "Drug Addiction and Drug Abuse," in Louis S. Goodman and Alfred Gilman, eds., *The Pharmacological Basis of Therapeutics*, 4th ed., (New York: MacMillan Co., 1970), p. 286.

123. Jaffe, *op. cit.*, p. 286.

124. See note 2, p. 000.

125. Mitcheson and Hartnoll, *op. cit.*, pp. 5–7, 10.

126. See Paul U. Lemkau et al., *Social and Economic Costs of Drug Abuse* (Baltimore: Johns Hopkins University, 1975); A. D. Little Co., *Social Cost of Drug Abuse* (Cambridge, Mass.: A. D. Little Co., 1975); and Brent L. Rufener et al., *Costs to Society of Drug Abuse*, Vol. 2 (Washington, D.C.; NIDA, 1976).

127. Rufener, *op. cit.*, Table 3, p. 16.

128. The 1976 NIDA Study (Rufener et al.) puts this cost at between $1.2 and $3.7 billion for 1975.

129. A federal District Court—in a decision that was subsequently endorsed on appeal by the Second Circuit Court of Appeals—ordered a public carrier to end its policy of not hiring methadone treatment program clients. See *Beazer* v. *New York City Transit Authority*, 399 F. Supp. 1032 (S.D.N.Y. 1975).

130. 18 US.T. 1408 (1967), T.I.A.S. No. 6298 (acceded to by US. in 1967), as amended by Protocol of 1972 (coming into force August 8, 1975).

131. 18 U.S.T. 1408 (1967), Article 4(c).

132. *Ibid.*, Art. 33.

133. 21 U.S.C. §§801–904 (1970).

134. 21 U.S.C. §§801 ff. (1970), as amended.

135. 21 U.S.C. §812(b)(1) (1970).

136. 21 U.S.C. §§301 ff. (1970).

137. See 21 U.S.C. §§952, 956; and 21 U.S.C. §§823(a), (b), and (e).

138. 21 U.S.C. §824.

139. Constance Holden, "New Look at Heroin Could Spur Better Medical Use of Narcotics," *Science*, vol. 198, no. 4319 (November 25, 1977), p. 807.

140. Secretary General of the United Nations, *Commentary on the Single Convention on Narcotic Drugs, 1961*, Article 4, Commentary 11 (1973).

141. Under newly proposed regulations of the DEA, 42 F.R. 31461-62, the Attorney General "may" exempt researchers from prosecution under federal, state, or local laws. See 21 U.S.C. §956 for statutory basis of this rule-making authority.

142. See 18 U.S.T. 1408 (1967), Article 4(c); and Secretary General of the United Nations, *Commentary on the Single Convention on Narcotic Drugs, 1961*, Article 4, Commentary 11 (1973).

143. As a habit-forming drug, heroin could be dispensed only by prescription under the Food, Drug, and Cosmetic Act (21 U.S.C. §§352(d) and 353. See also U.S.C. §§827-29).

144. 21 U.S.C. at §823(g) (1975 supp.).

145. See House Committee on Interstate and Foreign Commerce, Narcotic Addict Treatment Act, H.R. Rep. No. 884, 93d Cong., 2d Sess. (1974). See also 21 U.S.C. at 823(g) (1975 supp.).

146. 42 U.S.C. §257(a) (1970).

147. See 21 U.S.C. 355 (1970). If a limited research program were anticipated, FDA procedures for "investigational new drugs" could be utilized instead. This was the course followed with respect to methadone.

148. 21 U.S.C. 321(p).

149. See Waldorf, *op. cit.*; Musto, *op. cit.*, p. 178; and Charles Terry and Mildred Pellens, *The Opium Problem* (Montclair, N.J.: Patterson Smith, 1928, reprinted 1970).

150. See 21 U.S.C. 321(p) and Food and Drug Act of 1906, ch. 3915, §8, 34 Stat. 768, 769 (1906). This section required the labeling of drugs to identify "morphine, opium, cocaine, heroin, or any derivative."

151. 21 U.S.C. 952.

152. See the emergency provisions of Section 952(a)(2)(A) in 39 Fed. Reg. 44033 (1974). Nothing in Section 952 prohibits the importation of poppy straw, which has been ruled not to be opium. (See Tariff Ruling 2:R:CZ:NC H, 042521 [October 24, 1975]). Therefore the Attorney General could specifically authorize the manufacture of heroin from poppy straw.

153. Article VI, U.S. Constitution. Since 1824, the U.S. Supreme Court has interpreted this language to invalidate state laws which "interfere with" the laws of Congress. See *Gibbons* v. *Ogden* 22 U.S. (9 Wheat.) 1 (1824); and *Perez* v. *Campbell*, 402 U.S. 637 (1971).

154. See *Gambling in America: Final Report of the Commission on the Review of the National Policy Toward Gambling* (Washington, D.C.: GPO, 1976), pp. 5-6, and Appendix 1 of this report, "Model Federal Statute," at p. 1047 "Section 2—Findings and Declaration of Purpose") for an interesting discussion of a federal gambling policy which would statutorily recognize state control over gambling policy within state boundaries and federal regulation of interstate and international aspects.

155. 18 U.S.T. 1408 (1967), Article 33; See also *Commentaries* 2–3.

156. *Ibid.*, Article 2(5).

157. Article 36 of the Convention is often cited in support of the idea that

penalties must be imposed for heroin possession. However, the commentaries make it clear that the "possession" referred to in Article 36 is possession by traffickers, not for personal use. See Commentary, *op. cit.*, Article 36, Commentary 6 *op. cit.*, and Article 4(c), Commentaries 15–23.

158. The courts have recognized this exercise of "prosecutorial discretion" by a governmental agency. See *United States v. Cox*, 342 F.2d 167 at 171 (5th Cir.), *cert. den. sub nom. Cox v. Hauberg*, 381 US. 935 (1965).

159. Mission Statement and Responsibilities of DEA, contained in memorandum from Peter B. Bensinger, Administrator (April 5, 1976).

160. As a habit-forming drug under the Food, Drug, and Cosmetic Act, heroin could only be dispensed by prescription, as the law is currently written. (21 U.S.C. §352(d) and 353; see also 21 U.S.C. §§827-29.) Unless remarkable changes in medical views of heroin's pharmacological properties as pertaining to its potential for abuse, physical dependency, and medical usefulness occur, heroin could *not* be sold without prescription (without statutory changes in both FDCA and CSA).